GUARDING LIFE'S DARK SECRETS

GUARDING LIFE'S
DARK SECRETS

Legal and Social Controls over

Reputation, Propriety, and Privacy

Lawrence M. Friedman

Stanford University Press
Stanford, California

Printed in the United States of America on acid-free, archival-quality paper

Library of Congress Cataloging-in-Publication Data

Friedman, Lawrence Meir, 1930-
  Guarding life's dark secrets : legal and social controls over reputation, propriety, and privacy / Lawrence M. Friedman.
    p. cm.
  Includes bibliographical references and index.
  ISBN 978-0-8047-5739-3 (cloth : alk. paper)
  1. Privacy, Right of—United States—History. 2. Libel and slander—United States—History. 3. Sex and law—United States—History. I. Title.

KF1262.F75 2007
342.7308'58—dc22

                    2007027940

Designed by Bruce Lundquist
Typeset at Stanford University Press in 10.5/15 Adobe Garamond

For Leah, Jane, Amy, Paul, Sarah, David, and Lucy

CONTENTS

Acknowledgments   ix

1   *The General Argument*   1

2   *Status and Mobility in the Nineteenth Century*   22

3   *Sticks and Stones: The Law of Defamation*   41

4   *The Victorian Compromise: Slippage and Control*
    in the Moral Laws   63

5   *The Anatomy of Blackmail*   81

6   *Good Women, Bad Women: Seduction, Breach of*
    Promise, and Related Matters   101

7   *Censorship: Its Rise and Fall*   140

8   *Into the Twentieth Century*   175

9   *Privacy and Reputation in the Late Twentieth Century*   213

10 *Defamation in Contemporary Times*   235

11 *A Summing Up—And a Cautious Look at the Future*   257

    Notes   273

    Index   331

ACKNOWLEDGMENTS

I WOULD LIKE TO THANK the many students and others who helped with the research on this book. They include Alex Lue, Catherine Crump, Samantha Wakefield, David Oyer, Pablo Jimenez-Zorrilla, Joseph Thompson, Laura Robbins, Barbara Merz, and Amiram Gill. I also want to thank George Fisher, David Langum, James Q. Whitman, and the anonymous reviewers of the manuscript, all of whom made valuable suggestions.

As always, I owe a tremendous debt of gratitude to the reference staff of the Stanford Law Library, who helped me find all sorts of arcane material and who helped in countless other ways—always efficiently and always cheerfully and intelligently. So, a special thanks to Paul Lomio, Erika Wayne, Kate Wilko, Sonia Moss, and George Wilson. Thanks, too, to my assistant, Mary Tye; and of course to my family.

GUARDING LIFE'S DARK SECRETS

THE GENERAL ARGUMENT

Who steals my purse steals trash; . . .
But he that filches from me my good name
Robs me of that which not enriches him
And makes me poor indeed.

William Shakespeare, Othello, *Act III, Scene 3*

S HAKESPEARE, as usual, was onto something. Reputation—a good name—is something that most people cherish. Your reputation, what people think about you, is not a simple thing. It is constructed brick by brick for each person out of the opinions of friends and neighbors, or, if the person is famous or an expert, out of the swirling mass of information and conjecture that pours out of modern media. A dense, subtle network of social norms—rules and standards of behavior, thought, action—determine what your reputation is or ought to be. Some of these rules are written down; some are implicit. A person who seems to follow the norms, who seems to behave properly, who gains the respect of his or her community—such a person has (we say) a good reputation. An obvious norm-breaker has a bad one.

The word *reputation* itself is one of those English words with two meanings of a particular type. *Reputation* refers generally to *any* reputation, good or bad. But the word can also mean a *good* reputation when it stands by itself. *Luck* is a similar word; there is good luck and bad luck; but when you say *luck* by itself, you mean good luck. In this book, generally, when I discuss reputation and how it is protected and nurtured, I refer, of course, to good reputation.

Reputation—good reputation—depends, as I said, on compliance with social norms. Or at least the *appearance* of compliance. The social norms that make up reputation, as with all social norms, are anything but static. They change with the times. For example, if a middle-class woman in nineteenth-century England had sex with a man before she was married or had sex with a man, not her husband, after she was married, she risked utterly losing her reputation as a respectable woman. This is obviously much less true in middle-class society today. Normative structures are always in the process of change.

In any complex society (and maybe in all societies) the legal system tends to embody or express the norms that define proper and improper behavior, the norms that make or break reputation. It does this in many ways; the whole system of criminal justice has this task. Criminal codes are, if nothing else, catalogs of forbidden actions. In everything the legal system does, which includes resolving conflicts and defining and upholding property rights, there are implicit assumptions about correct and incorrect ways of living and doing. The legal system also defines values and expresses values, and it acts to protect those values. Many of the values are economic. Some are not. Reputation, a good name, standing in the community—these are among the values that the legal system both defines and protects. This book is about the ways that the legal system has protected reputation. Some of these ways are quite obvious. Others are more subtle and covert.

Why should formal and informal law worry about individual reputations? Because, of course, people *value* reputation, and the institutions they create reflect their values. But the protection of reputation is also part of a larger and more general function. One key role of the legal order in society, a role backed up by force if necessary, is to keep society on an even keel, to preserve it more or less as it is, and, so far as change is concerned, to guarantee that change occurs in orderly and regular ways, in ways that society approves. In short, the legal system guards the status quo. Guarding the status quo sounds like a fairly reactionary thing to do. Many people never utter the phrase "status quo" without something of a sneer. In fact, there is nothing sinister or even reactionary about protecting the status quo. Everybody wants to protect some or all of the status quo. Even the most flaming revolutionary wants to overturn some things and not others.

Naturally, the existing order works best for the haves, the rich, the powerful, the people on top. But it can and does have some benefit for other people too—more or less, depending on the society. In any event the status quo is much more than a matter of money, power, and position. It is also a moral code and a set of norms. The status quo freezes a certain distribution of wealth and influence; it also freezes a certain distribution of standing, reputation, and social capital. The law thus can and does act to protect social capital, perhaps at times almost as vigorously as it acts to protect a person's house, money, power—and his or her rights in general.

My subject is the connection between law and reputation and between law and propriety and how these have changed over time. Specifically, I deal with social and legal culture roughly since the nineteenth century. What elements were part of the definition of propriety and good behavior—the elements that make up a good reputation—and how did the law act to protect respectable people and their reputations?

Reputation is not just a matter of feelings or of social intercourse. It has enormous economic importance. For businesses a bad reputation can be lethal. Trademark law, for example, is a branch of law that protects the name and goodwill of companies. If I make a shoddy wristwatch and pass it off as a Rolex, I am hurting the reputation *and* the business of the people who make Rolex watches. They can and do fight to protect that reputation, with the help of the law. Trademarks are enormously important in modern economies. Thousands of businesses need and demand trademark protection. Their value to a large extent depends on trademarks, logos, symbols, and the like. But in this particular book I want to focus primarily on individuals, not businesses, that is, on *personal* reputation.[1]

With regard to personal reputation, one branch of law, the law of defamation—libel and slander—has the overt and obvious function of protecting reputation.[2] Defamation is a tort—a civil wrong. The victim can sue for damages. Winning a lawsuit is also a way to vindicate oneself and to reclaim one's good name. But there are also other, less obvious ways in which law protects and guards reputation. In this book I will talk about some of these and how they have evolved over time. The starting point, roughly, is the nineteenth century; the end point, roughly, is now.

Your reputation, of course, is what other people think of you. What they think of you is, obviously, a function of what they know about you or think they know about you. Hence any study of reputation is also a study of the flow of information about other people—and the power to control that flow. Therefore *privacy* and reputation are connected. Many people earn and keep a reputation not because of what people know about them so much as because of what other people do *not* know. For people with skeletons in their closet, reputation depends on secrecy[3] and privacy. Reputation is after all a matter of surfaces. Nobody can read minds or look into a person's heart and soul. What we see of other people is the way they talk and act. A good person, a respectable person, a person with a good reputation is someone who at least outwardly conforms to dominant social norms.

In an important way, then, this book is as much about privacy as it is about reputation; but the two are, as I just said, intimately bound together. Privacy and reputation and their linkages have changed over the years. My main thrust in this book is to describe these changes and explain them.

Three general trends or stories form the heart of this book. First, I describe, chiefly for the nineteenth century, a complicated network of doctrines that seemed to be designed to protect reputation and that operated chiefly for the benefit of respectable men and women—people with reputations to protect. I call this network of doctrines the Victorian compromise. The doctrines—about sexual behavior notably—in practice seemed to lead to paradoxical results. On the one hand, there were strict and unbending rules of decency and propriety, but at the same time the rules gave space for slippage, for leeways, for second chances—for ways to protect and shield respectable men and women who deviated from the official norms. In this regard, it created for them an important zone of privacy.[4]

The second theme is the destruction of this network and the death of the Victorian compromise. The Victorian compromise was first attacked by strong moralists, who detested its tolerance of sin. Then, in the second half of the twentieth century the Victorian compromise was attacked by the agents of the permissive society. As a result, the old structure was largely dismantled.

The third theme, which is closely related to the second, examines privacy in our own times. And here too there is a paradox. We live in a permissive society. On the legal side the Supreme Court has interpreted the Constitution to include a constitutional right of privacy; and this has given ordinary people much more leeway, much more freedom, especially with regard to sex, reproduction, and choices of intimate partners. On the other hand, the elites—celebrities, public figures—have lost some of their privacy rights. They no longer have the freedom they once had to violate decency rules, with some degree of impunity, under the sheltering wing of the Victorian compromise.

At the end of the book I present a fourth theme—a theme I can only touch upon. Law and society have given ordinary people more privacy, more leeways, more choices, but technology threatens to take at least some of this away. More and more the modern world is a world of surveillance. Cameras are everywhere. Sophisticated devices can amass dossiers on everybody; our whole lives can be recorded, stored, and accessed—for what ultimate purpose, nobody knows. But only future years will tell us how this story turns out.

Of course, the subjects touched on in this book are immensely complicated. Big, complex societies never have a single code of rules that everybody subscribes to. Behavioral norms are different for men and women, for children and adults, for different classes and groups in society. In the nineteenth century men tended to be forgiven for sowing wild oats; women were not so easily forgiven. Time and place also alter the norms. Information (or gossip) that would have ruined a reputation a century ago—"living in sin," for example—hardly raises an eyebrow in most circles today. Despite all the complications, one basic principle is clear: As social norms change, laws that touch on reputation and privacy change along with them. On the whole, I treat the legal system as the dependent variable. It is not the prime mover in society. Rather, society moves it, molds it, alters it. Of course, legal facts and legal arrangements and the living law in general all have an impact on society. But it is a more modest impact: an echo rather than the thunder-in-chief. In this book I try to explain change along these general lines.

Much of the material in this book, unfortunately, is qualitative and even speculative. This is an exploration of legal culture and, indeed, in large part an exploration of *past* legal culture. By legal culture I mean the ideas, attitudes, and values that people hold with regard to the legal system.[5] We know little about legal culture in our own times. The past is largely a buried city. In principle, legal culture can be tested and measured empirically, through opinion surveys, for example. But for most issues in the nineteenth century and part of the twentieth century, no such surveys or other quantitative indicators existed. For most of the past we have to rely on other sources, none of them as clean and as rigorous as we might want.

Before we begin, we have to answer a few preliminary questions. The first, which might seem simpleminded, is, Why bother to protect reputation legally? Why not just leave it alone—leave it to the marketplace of ideas? The law does not protect *every* value. There are no laws today against lying. There are no laws in the United States explicitly against insulting people.[6] In Germany it might be a (minor) crime to call somebody a jerk, a fool, a nitwit, or to make an obscene gesture; but this is apparently not the case in the United States, at least not at present.[7] Why bother, then, with attacks on reputation? The obvious answer is this: The *social* and *economic* value of reputation is enormous and practically demands protection. If you call a shop owner a cheat and spread this around or say that a restaurant owner allows cockroaches, the customers will stay away by the hundreds. A lost reputation is more than hurt feelings and fewer invitations to parties. For this reason Robert Post argues that reputation "can be understood as a form of intangible property akin to good will."[8] It is this intangible property that the law of defamation protects.

Yet, as Post recognizes, a purely economic analysis cannot account for all the ins and outs of defamation law, nor can it give us a satisfying definition of reputation. Most people value their reputation, whether or not losing it will take a single penny out of their pockets. Reputation is also honor—and dignity, the "respect . . . that arises from full membership in society."[9] Losing a reputation, as Shakespeare put it, makes a person poor indeed. Shakespeare was not thinking of money. He was thinking of standing in the community, of a person's place in society. Human beings are social animals. They live in families, groups, communities. Their happiness or misery depends on how they fill their place in these families, groups, and communities. Some societies use ostracism or banishment as punishments for violating certain social norms. In all societies bad reputation is a source of shame and hurt.

But reputation—and this is one theme of this book—has a *social* meaning as well as an individual meaning. Damage to the reputation of a president, a judge, a community leader hurts the society as well as the individual. It can harm society to claim that a business leader or a politician is corrupt. It may be worse if the accusation is a lie, but it is also harmful, and possibly even more so, when the accusation is true. A cover-up would protect the business leader or politician, but it can be argued that it might in some cases even protect society—might keep it from rotting away under the caustic acid of critical judgments. This is one reason that society may want to shield its elites, even when they do not deserve this protection.

Reputation has different meanings in different societies and is gained and lost in different ways. Reputation poses special problems in modern societies, because these are mobile societies—societies in which people move about in physical and social space and in which people spend much of their lives and careers interacting with strangers. In a mobile society certain kinds of information are scarce and valuable. In a small, traditional community, say, a village, where everybody knows everybody else, reputation is based on personal knowledge or on local gossip, and information circulates in a face-to-face community. But in a big, heterogeneous society—the kind of society that developed in England or the United States in the nineteenth century—reputational information can be harder to come by. For the first time identity becomes an issue and at times a puzzle. This situation opened the door to various kinds of frauds, to confidence men, to bigamists, to sharp operators who made money out of fake identities and imaginary reputations.[10]

These mobile societies were also market societies. A market society floats on a sea of credit. In the nineteenth century accurate credit information was also hard to come by. Credit, then, depended heavily on general reputation. Business and financial reputation are crucial features that support and maintain a market society. Reputation is also vital in other kinds of markets. Rumors that a young middle-class woman was sleeping around could kill her chances in the marriage market. In a period when marriage and family were the chief role for a "decent" woman, losing a reputation for chastity or virtue was a severe blow indeed. This social fact, as we will see, was the basis of actions for breach of promise of marriage or for seduction.

Accusing a man of fooling around, sexually speaking, was much less damaging; the double standard was in full flower in the nineteenth century. Still, to accuse a clergyman of sleeping with a parishioner, for example, would strike at the very heart of his professional reputation. The sensation of the 1870s was the scandal and trial involving Henry Ward Beecher, one of the country's most famous clergymen. Beecher was accused of committing adultery with a married woman, Elizabeth Tilton.[11] Scandal could be as painful as a sharp and jagged knife. Similarly, consider the example of a businessman accused of cheating. A man of affairs was supposed to be honest and upright. A certain amount of shrewdness and cunning in business affairs could be tolerated—or even admired; but outright dishonesty was another story.

Everybody, of course, has a reputation of one sort or another. But the law has never concerned itself with everybody's reputation. In the nineteenth century the law was not disposed to worry, for example, about what people thought of burglars or prostitutes. Nor, for that matter, did anybody care much about the reputation of slaves or of tramps, hoboes, or the lumpenproletariat in general. Only people with a certain stake in society had a reputation, had something that was precious and worthy of legal protection (so people thought). In addition, only people with a certain stake in society were concerned with something called *honor*.

Honor is not an easy concept to define. It is obviously related to reputation, although honor is not the same as reputation. To be sure, both refer to a person's place in the hierarchy of respect.[12] Honor seems to imply some kind of behavior—action that conforms to some explicit or implicit code. In many societies almost nothing could be worse than dishonorable behavior, nothing more destructive than an act that brings dishonor to the family. The punishment for such an act might even be death. There are societies in which fathers kill their own daughters, if the daughters bring dishonor to the family, by sexual misconduct, for example.

In some societies, to call a man a liar or to insult him was to attack his honor; and honor required him to respond in a particular way. The *duel* was a more or less ritualized response to insult in such societies.[13] Where dueling cultures flourished, honor belonged exclusively to men, and it depended also on social class, just as reputation did. Honor was an attribute of men of the upper class. A ditchdigger had no honor. Obviously, ditchdiggers had their own sense of honor and their own mode of responding to insults and the like, and these responses could in fact be violent.[14] But the dueling codes were exclusively upper class. The equivalent of honor for upper-class women was virtue. A man who did not defend his own honor or the honor of his family was a coward, or worse; he suffered an irreversible loss of esteem. Honor had to be safeguarded through behavior; reputation, on the other hand, was safeguarded through character as well as behavior. (Women were expected, of course, to defend their virtue.) Honor had much more of a *subjective* element than reputation. Reputation is exclusively what other people think of you. Honor, in an important sense, flows from what you think of yourself.

Dueling was well known in the United States as well as in European aristocratic circles. The most famous instance was the duel between Aaron Burr and Alexander Hamilton; Hamilton died as a result.[15] A gentleman who was insulted was supposed to find satisfaction "on the field of honor." But a gentleman never dueled with a "person of the lower estates"; instead, such a person could be "horsewhipped or caned."[16] Dueling was, in short, a mark of status. It was not available to people whose rank was too low. Of course, in the United States, where there was no real aristocracy, dueling practices filtered much lower down in the social order than they did in Europe.

The duel between Hamilton and Burr took place in New Jersey, and Hamilton at the time was living in New York; but dueling was, in general, more closely associated with the conservative, aristocratic South.[17] Dueling fitted the ethos of the Northern states rather poorly and was never as common there as in the South. Many people strongly disapproved of dueling, North and South, and the practice gradually died out. Many states passed laws making dueling a crime. There were antidueling movements in the South as well as in the North. In Georgia an 1890 law barred duelists from holding public office. Later, it became a crime to challenge a person to a duel. After a duel in 1828 between two prominent young men—one of them died as a result—the legislature passed a law demanding that anybody who held any public position had to swear that he had not taken part in any duel after January 1, 1829.[18] As we will see, one way that some states tried to enforce laws against dueling was to open the door to libel actions that would, in theory, act as a substitute for the practice.[19]

My subject, however, is reputation, not honor; but the differences between these two are important. Honor is something a man must defend for himself. Reputation, however, is far more objective. It lends itself, then, to objective measures of protection. Hence reputation is, to a greater degree than honor, something the law has concerned itself with.

For example, some legal institutions have the obvious aim of shielding people against direct and unwarranted attacks on reputation. Libel and slander laws protect people who are victims of lies. What is even more interesting are those legal institutions that act to protect the reputation of people who are *not* innocent—people who are the victims, not of lies, but of the bitter truth. And these legal institutions are one of the main subjects of this book.

Take, for example, the crime of blackmail.[20] Suppose that I demand money from a man and threaten to reveal his guilty secret unless he pays up. This is blackmail; this is an act labeled a serious crime in many criminal codes. Yet who is the victim here? It is a man who has committed a crime or who has done some scandalous or awful act, one that would blacken his reputation if the news got out. Yet the law defines him as a victim. The blackmailer will be the one to go to jail. When society makes blackmail a crime, it does this not to protect the innocent but curiously enough to protect the guilty. (Whether the law actually has much of an impact on behavior one way or another is a different question.)

Blackmail is only one example of a more general phenomenon. Take the old law about breach of promise.[21] If a man promises to marry a woman and then backs out, she can sue him for damages. In many cases her real complaint is that she had sexual intercourse on the strength of his promise. For a respectable woman loss of virginity and, especially, birth of a bastard, could have a devastating effect on prospects of marriage and a middle-class life. Sometimes the lawsuit or the threat of a lawsuit could force the bounder to marry the woman and salvage her reputation. Yet here too the woman, like the blackmail "victim," is hardly innocent. She violated nineteenth-century norms. She was guilty of fornication, which in many states was actually a crime. But despite her sins and transgressions, the law gave her this remedy. Like the victim of blackmail, this sinner too was classified as a victim, with the right to seek recourse from the man who had victimized her.

The living law of prostitution is yet another example of protection for those who, in theory, had forfeited the right to protection. Prostitutes themselves were mostly social pariahs. No social leaders ever spoke out in favor of prostitution. Nonetheless, prostitution flourished. There were brothels and streetwalkers in every city. Once in a while the police cracked down on the trade. They swept prostitutes off the street, closed houses of prostitution, arrested whole troops of "sporting" women. Yet, curiously enough, prostitution itself for much of our history was not actually illegal. Prostitutes were jailed as vagrants, and brothel keepers could be prosecuted, but buying and selling sex itself was not clearly labeled a crime. What this meant is that *customers* of prostitutes were immune from prosecution. All the crusading zeal was directed against the women (especially streetwalkers) and against madams and landlords who ran disorderly houses. A screen of silence, and even some aspects of the formal law, shielded the men and protected their privacy and their reputations.

The protective rules were related to a larger legal phenomenon that I have called the Victorian compromise. This compromise put enormous emphasis on surface behavior. The official rules remained in place, sometimes expressed in quite general or absolute terms; meanwhile, the law in action was quite different. There is a kind of double standard. No real attempt is made to enforce the official rules with vigor.[22] They remain slogans or a kind of facade; or they are enforced selectively, according to norms and rules that are never made explicit. The legal position of prostitution is a good example. It was never exactly legal but never exactly illegal. There were thousands of women who sold their bodies for a living, and these women all had customers, men who came from every walk of life. Obviously, any man who had sex with a prostitute or visited a brothel was guilty of fornication or adultery; and these were criminal acts in many states. Yet no man was prosecuted for these crimes.

There is an old saying: If you can't be good, be careful. This could have been the motto for many laws about vice and sexual misconduct in the middle of the nineteenth century. Be discreet. If you must sin, sin quietly and privately. If you keep what you do under wraps, you can preserve your reputation, your place in respectable society. A man lost his reputation if he was a flagrant, blatant womanizer. A woman who had sex outside marriage forfeited any claims to decency. The same was true, of course, for people who lied and cheated, who staggered around the streets in a drunken fog, and so on. But men and women who were careful, whose sins were secret and well camouflaged, were able to avoid most evil consequences. For much of the nineteenth century it was not a person's "private" life as such that was decisive but rather the way he or she *managed* this private life.

The Victorian compromise should not be dismissed as mere hypocrisy. The living law had a curious double standard, but this had a purpose, at least implicitly. Again, we can take prostitution as an example. Men, people thought, had powerful sex drives. They could not satisfy these drives with respectable women. They had to find some other outlet. It was useless to try to stamp out vice.[23] What society should aim at was moderation, control, some way to keep the lid on. The laws relating to prostitution were like laws against speeding today. Nobody really thinks speed limits are totally effective. Everybody violates them from time to time. Enforcement is a sometime thing. But the laws, at existing levels of enforcement, are not useless or hypocritical. Arguably, they keep the *amount* of speeding under control. If you took off the lid entirely, who knows how fast and how recklessly some drivers might drive on the roads.

The great French sociologist, Émile Durkheim, had a stunning insight about the functions of criminal law. When a society defines some behaviors as criminal and provides that these behaviors can be punished, it is drawing a map of the moral boundaries of society. Punishing crime, therefore, is not simply a way of bringing to judgment people who do dangerous acts; it also reaffirms and supports the moral boundaries of society.[24] Public enforcement of the laws acts as a kind of didactic theater, as a school for teaching people where the boundary lines run and what lies on this side and that side of the line. Thus the penal code—and the other codes of conduct—have symbolic and educational purposes as well as instrumental purposes. In a sense, the criminal code is a kind of price list; it is a catalog of rights and wrongs, and the table of punishments tells the public which acts are worse than others and why and by how much.

But what if the list or catalog is, in a sense, misleading? What is the social function of codes that are *not* enforced—or enforced only sometimes or only against some people? This is part of the terrain that I am exploring here. The living law also has its messages and its functions. Its ambiguities and apparent hypocrisies serve certain purposes. And one purpose—the one that I stress in this book—is to protect the people who matter in society. In part, this is because these people surely want this protection and have the power to demand it. In part, though, it is because this protection, this shield of immunity, has a broader function: It protects society itself from severe structural damage.

The penal codes of the nineteenth century rather clearly expressed the official moral code—the code that, in effect, defined respectability. This moral code was also expressed in other laws and in literature, sermons, speeches, textbooks, and the press. The code supported the status hierarchy of the nineteenth century. The basic norms of the times are familiar enough—they are what are still called traditional values. Sex outside marriage was a sin. In some circumstances it was also an actual crime. Adultery and fornication were forbidden. It goes without saying that the "crime against nature" was also a crime against the state. So was bestiality.[25] Public drunkenness was against the law, and so, too, was gambling. Men were supposed to be faithful, moderate, law abiding; they were supposed to avoid all sorts of vice and debauchery. Women were supposed to be chaste before marriage and humble, faithful, and obedient afterward. There were of course dissenters from this or that aspect of the code—proponents of free love or Mormon polygamists, for example. In general, people treated these dissenters with horror or scorn or outright hostility.[26]

The criminal justice system was supposed to protect and maintain the traditional code by punishing those who violated that code. Paradoxically, however, protection of the moral code also meant something that on the surface seems totally inconsistent: protection of the very people who *violated* the code—or to be more accurate, protection for *some* of the people who violated it and for some who violated it in a particular way. This was the thrust of the Victorian compromise. In other words, the law did two things at once. First, it defined respectability, virtue, good reputation (reflecting wider social norms). But second, it engaged in a kind of cover-up. One strain or tendency in the law actually acted to make it more difficult for respectable people to lose their reputations. This subtle and implicit task worked to provide a kind of limited safety valve for those who gave in to their "animal" instincts. Some people (especially men) who transgressed in certain ways got second chances. The flesh, after all, was weak. In short, law and society protected bourgeois respectability in two quite distinct ways: first, by punishing (gross) deviations from the standards; and, second, by providing a shield or cover-up for *some* deviations from those very standards. How and why this second job was accomplished is one of the themes of this book.

To be sure, when I talk about subtle and implicit functions, I mean exactly that: subtle and implicit. There were no treatises, no pamphlets, no writings that clearly expressed these goals. Most people never really understand their own society, what makes it tick. Rarely or never do people recognize their cultural assumptions. Almost no one in a society can describe cultural assumptions in the way that a good anthropologist might, or perhaps a historian. We are blind to whatever is closest to us. This applies as well to lawyers and judges. In a legal culture, as in culture in general, only the outside observer is likely to have sharp vision. The outside observer may understand the system better than it understands itself.

All societies have institutions that concern themselves with socialization—molding the new generation in the shape of the old one. In all societies education means a lot more than teaching children to read and write and add up numbers. It means instilling norms and values in their minds, showing them what is good and bad behavior and what people have a right to expect of them. Parents and family do much of this educating; so do the schools in modern societies. But in a broader sense every important social system is concerned with education. Certainly this is true of the legal system.

Education and socialization have both a positive and a negative side. The negative or protective function is to keep harmful and corrupting influences away from young hearts and minds. Laws about pornography and obscenity, laws about sexual behavior, drug laws, and many other laws can be labeled this way. Historically, many societies also depended on censorship laws to keep evil influences away from children, and also from adults—the broad mass of the public, including millions of people who did not particularly want to be protected. Defamation laws, blackmail laws, and other laws that protected reputation were also part of the system for preventing these evil influences, which might otherwise engulf society and destroy it.

In short, underlying the Victorian compromise was a theory of society. Society was a delicate plant. It was at all times in unstable balance. Each generation had to be trained in the proper norms and values. Rules about reputation and propriety were *necessary*. Vice and debauchery, unless they were controlled, would run riot; and the whole system of order would come tumbling down. Nobody articulated this theory precisely in this way, and it was, perhaps, largely unconscious; but it was there nonetheless in society in the nineteenth century. We can see it if we read carefully between the lines, if we observe how the system behaved and how it formulated its basic principles. In later chapters I try to do this—that is, to read between the lines.

Social understandings, typically, are unstable. Modern societies in particular are societies in rapid evolution. Everything is in flux; change is the rule, not the exception. The implicit theory I have described ran into trouble in the late nineteenth century for complex reasons, which I try to explore later in Chapter 8. The protective shield around men and women of high standing began to erode. The Victorian compromise broke down at that time in the United States and also in England. Powerful elements in society launched a serious war against vice and sexual misconduct. The war was fueled by the belief that society could no longer afford to ignore sin, corruption, debauchery—could no longer afford to protect respectability at the cost of tolerating vice. Vice extracted too high a social cost.

What happened in the late nineteenth century seems to me, looking back, rather sudden and dramatic. In fact, social change is not an overnight thing. Structures smolder before they burst into flames. If we go back far enough, we find a legal system that supported a strongly hierarchical society. Elites had everything, or almost everything; they had the power and the money and the rights; the common folk had virtually nothing. In the Middle Ages those who defended the system described it as part of a natural God-given order. Of course, the reality of medieval life was much more complex, but in general the idea of a natural hierarchy was powerful and ubiquitous. Over time the system became weaker, more unstable. In one rather long view of history, the situation I described for the nineteenth century was the final act in a long, drawn-out drama—the last gasps of a structure of dominance that was doomed to disappear. It was disappearing, to be sure, more rapidly in the United States than in England and in other European countries. Some old rules of hierarchy were in the process of decay, even at the beginning of the nineteenth century. One instance, which I discuss in Chapter 3, was the reworking of the law of defamation—in particular, the rise of *truth* as a defense.

Social and technological change in the twentieth century was especially rapid and dramatic. In the early twentieth century the war against vice had reached some sort of climax. This was the period in the United States of the Mann Act, of the first significant federal drug laws, and of national Prohibition. By the middle of the twentieth century there were clear signs of another turn of the wheel. Prohibition had lasted little more than a decade. Later on, the war against vice lost a number of important battles. By 2007 many of the old norms of propriety, the old pillars on which a solid reputation rested, had been reduced to rubble. When the wheels of society turn, everything turns with them. Reputation and propriety get reshuffled as well. Censorship of offensive material is basically gone. Sin and vice have been substantially redefined—sometimes redefined out of existence. The private lives and sexual habits of consenting adults have been decriminalized in the United States and in many other countries. Of course, the thief and the check forger are still treated as despicable and are punished. The drug pusher and the pedophile are still social pariahs. But other acts, once vilified, have moved out of the shadows. Virginity is not what it used to be. In some countries and some cities chastity before marriage is an endangered species. Nobody blinks an eye at couples who live together without bothering to get married. Many couples—in some countries, *most* couples—live together before they go to the altar, if they go at all. In France, for example, 87 percent of all "cohabiting unions" in the 1990s had begun "outside marriage."[27] In a country such as France—or in much of the United States—in urban, middle-class circles a woman who has sex before marriage no longer forfeits her reputation or her chance at a decent marriage and social status.

Culture has moved from emphasis on self-discipline to an emphasis on self-actualization. Modern society exalts individual choice. A dominant ethos is what Robert Bellah and his associates have called expressive individualism. This is the notion that a person's main task in life is to develop, as much as possible, the self, the personality, in all its uniqueness.[28] Moreover, in the last half of the twentieth century in particular, legal and social culture changed dramatically. Old structures of cultural and political dominance broke down. The civil rights revolution swept away racial segregation. A powerful feminist movement achieved striking results. Women broke out of the kitchen, and some made it all the way into boardrooms, high government circles, and even the United States Supreme Court. Every suppressed and subordinate group began to demand its rights, its place in the sun: Chicanos, Native Americans, prisoners, students, gay people, aliens, Chinese Americans, deaf people, old people. The demands were insistent, persistent—and often successful.

Success—in life, politics, and so on—has become less dependent on traditional morality. Traditional morality depended heavily on a kind of *privacy*: on shielding the private life of elite and respectable people. Talk about sex and sex life was taboo. Sex was entirely private: a secret activity, behind closed doors, in dark rooms, in the dead of night. And legitimate sex took place only in the bedrooms of married people. Even there it was a secret—as Walter Houghton put it, it was "the skeleton in the parental chamber. No one mentioned it." There was a "conspiracy of silence."[29] Any deviation from the strict rules of privacy and prudery was totally excluded—except insofar as it was part of the Victorian compromise.

We often hear that the nineteenth century was the century of the individual and that our own times are much more collective. There is, of course, some truth to this statement, but in some ways the situation was actually the other way around. Governments surely did less in the nineteenth century to regulate the economy (although more than most people think).[30] But the moral code was much tighter, the laws and rules about sexual behavior, about marriage, divorce, and family life were more restrictive, the pressure to conform was much more severe, and the social punishment for deviation was more heartless and unyielding. It is the late twentieth and early twenty-first centuries that glorify the needs, wants, and desires of the individual self. Society was once more permissive toward business, less permissive toward private life. The opposite is true today. Now people feel freer to experiment with ways of life; they can try on different hats and different habits, can eat different kinds of food, can try new paths to salvation, can pursue new ways of making dreams come true. An Irish American woman might turn Buddhist, a baseball player might announce he is gay, and millions of native citizens might abandon hamburgers in favor of sushi.

Society is an organism of incredible complexity. Explaining social change is sometimes as hopeless a job as predicting the weather. But there are at least some obvious factors that lie behind the zigs and zags of social thought and social structure. One is capitalism itself, in particular, its inevitable handmaiden, advertising. These spread a religion of consumerism, a religion of self-satisfaction. Another important influence has been the regime of science and technology. These have transformed the modern world. They have bred affluence, upset old arrangements, and fostered a restless if not reckless spurt of economic growth. Modern science and technology seem both cause and effect of modern capitalism. Sour, hard-working, ambitious, disciplined men, imbued with an extreme form of the Protestant ethic, may have been the pillars of a capitalist order and hard-driven workaholics may still be the men and women who found great companies. But, ironically, the world they created or helped to create carries the seeds of its own destruction in one sense. The economies of developed countries foster and *have* to foster a different sort of individual—men and women who are born to shop. The system depends on the consumer and on consumption—buying, selling, getting and spending, using, discarding. And advertising is among the keys to consumption.

Yet buying and selling are, inherently, intensely individual processes. People buy for themselves or for their families. Advertising is a textbook of individualism. It is directed to the individual, the consumer, the man on the couch watching television, the woman sitting next to him. The modern economic system has been a roaring success for the broad middle class in North America, Western Europe, Japan, and other developed countries. It has created enormous wealth, and with wealth goes leisure. In France, Hong Kong, Sweden, or Canada, most men and women no longer slave away until they drop, earning barely enough to feed their bellies, and sometimes not even that. They have houses full of furniture; they have cars, refrigerators, television sets. They have yearly vacations. Extra time—leisure—creates an insatiable demand for pleasure, fun, entertainment. People fill their time with hobbies, activities, sports; they play cards, they go to the movies, they bowl, they take tennis lessons or classes in the arts, they go on cruises, they visit the Taj Mahal.

All these activities, again, are at their core strikingly individual. We get to choose our own clothing, and (within limits) we pick out the colors and the styles. Democratic societies do not have uniforms. What we wear is supposed to express our personalities. Only autocratic orders require uniforms—the army, certain groups of nuns, and the people who lived in Mao Tse-tung's China. A clothing company does not advertise to nuns or sergeants; what they wear is fixed and settled, prescribed for them in every detail. In the larger society suppression and repression are in bad odor. And what is true of clothing is also true of food, religion, sexuality—in short, almost everything in modern society.

Social scientists have of course noticed these massive changes in norms and in social structure. They have noticed that the nineteenth century laid heavy stress on character, whereas the late twentieth century changed the emphasis to personality. They have noticed how one period underscored order, discipline, moderation, whereas the later period put the self—the individual, idiosyncratic self—at center stage.[31] Schools in the nineteenth century were concerned with making little adults out of children, stuffing their heads with traditional habits and morals. Contemporary education is much more about creating unique *individuals*; it is centered more on the particular child, on self-realization and expressive individualism. This is the educational world of show-and-tell. This particular device dates back to around 1950. Little children are encouraged in school to "show or tell something they find interesting to the class." And if their "subject is very outstanding and unusual, they become the center of attraction for the rest of the day."[32] Modern elementary education is much more interactive than it used to be. Kids are free to wander about their classrooms; they do not sit rigidly at little desks fixed to the floor. These are not just American trends. Perhaps the United States was a pioneer in this development, perhaps it moved more rapidly than other countries, but the general lines of change are the same in all rich, developed democratic countries.

Basically, then, the nineteenth-century code, the code of traditional values, the code that defined reputation, entered a period of decay. Decay also set in with regard to notions of self-discipline and modesty. This was a ragged and complicated development. It had no clear beginning and no clear end. From 1870 to 1930 powerful attempts were made to keep the old code alive and to strengthen it, protecting it against the gigantic forces that social, scientific, and economic development let loose on the world. The Victorian compromise was discarded. New, tough rules about morality, vice, and sexuality were put in place.[33] In the United States the jewel in the crown was national Prohibition. This, as I said, now looks like a kind of last-gasp attempt to save a dying order. The collapse of Prohibition was followed in succeeding generations with startling reversals in the sexual code.

There was never, of course, a smooth, straight line of evolution. Change was always jagged and ragged. And the dying order refused to lie down and play dead; at the very least, it takes its time dying, if it is dying at all. It keeps fighting what may seem like a rearguard action, but it still has amazing tensile strength. Some changes seem irreversible. No one expects liquor prohibition to come back or censorship of books and movies. But other issues are still hotly contested. The rabid debates in the United States over abortion, gay rights, and traditional values in general; the tremendous power of orthodox religious beliefs; the hammer blows of fundamentalism all over the world—it is hard to write these off as nothing but the last twitches of a corpse. It may be premature to say goodbye to the old order and proclaim, "Mission accomplished."

Nobody can predict how the culture wars are going to end. One thing seems clear, however. There is no turning back. The past never recurs. There are no cycles in history. Movement goes in only one direction: into the future. History only *seems* to repeat itself. A religious fundamentalist of today is profoundly different from a religious fundamentalist of the nineteenth century, and light-years away from a devout soul of the Middle Ages. There are people who preach against Darwin or against the whole Western world, but they live in an age of computers and the Internet and TV; they live in an age of machine guns and homemade bombs; they spread their message with faxes and cell phones and websites. Nothing, really, ever remains static and unyielding, certainly not in the modern world.

Reputation, as I noted, was never the same as character, even in the heyday of character and discipline. Character was inside you. Reputation was what other people thought. Obviously, the two were closely related. For most people, perhaps, they were one and the same. Yet there were always people for whom they diverged. One theme of this book is how the law tried to bridge the gap between the two—what tricks and devices protected the reputation of respectable men and women and the theories of society that underlay these tricks and devices.

What about the world we live in today? Clearly, the ideology of the early twenty-first century is not the ideology of a century ago, or two centuries. The Victorian compromise depended on a particular notion of privacy. Privacy is still an important value, but its meaning has changed. There is still an important aspect of privacy that stresses the right to keep secrets, the right to hide and conceal—the right to cover one's naked body and to some extent the naked soul. But privacy is also now a value that stresses *choice* and much less a regime of silence and darkness, a regime of taboos and cover-ups. Of course, moral codes still exist. These codes are, as always, complex. And people still value, to be sure, their reputation, but its components have changed. It has always had different components for different sorts of people. What a basketball star or a rock guitarist can get away with is a long distance from what a U.S. senator can get away with or a minister of the Gospel. Even in this day and age, this freewheeling, permissive age, people have secrets, some of them highly embarrassing. Damage to reputation is still a real problem. It may be situational—if we discovered that a baseball player had a collection of whips and chains, it might not matter; if the collector was a certified public accountant, he might still be able to make a living; nursery school teachers or day care workers would be instantly fired. Millions of people still live, or aspire and expect to live, the way that their forefathers lived, morally speaking. In their circles nobody tolerates adultery, promiscuity, or gay sex. They and their friends still have every reason to hide their sins from the outside world. But even for senators, ministers, and kindergarten teachers, the menu of choices has widened. Exactly how law and society deal with reputation in the age of television and the Internet is a complex issue. I explore this issue in some detail in later chapters.

In the rest of the book I flesh out the general lines of the argument. Chapter 2 deals with the nineteenth-century background. Chapter 3 considers the law of defamation. Chapter 4 covers some aspects of criminal law that served to protect reputation. Chapter 5 is devoted to the fascinating crime of blackmail. Chapter 6 mainly concerns the protection of women's reputations, specifically, the actions of seduction, criminal conversation, and breach of promise. The later chapters examine how the twentieth century dramatically transformed the structures built up in earlier times.

CHAPTER 2

STATUS AND MOBILITY IN THE NINETEENTH CENTURY

THE NINETEENTH CENTURY in the United States (and in many European countries) was a period of rapid growth in population and in the economy. Most people in the United States were farmers or lived on the land. At the beginning of the century manufacturing played only a minor role in the economy. By the end of the century the population had exploded, and the nature of the economy had changed. Millions of people lived in big cities, and millions were landless workers in factories, mines, and railroad yards or salaried workers in stores and offices.

Throughout the nineteenth century there was, overall, a strong belief in a market system. The market "captured people's imagination, energy, and ambition to an extent and with a sustained hold unmatched by any other institution."[1] On the whole, this was a period of free enterprise, a period in which old restrictions on the economy were dismantled and the invisible hand was let loose to play a major economic role. The Industrial Revolution changed the social and economic landscape. This was a period of enormous expansion in the economy and also a period of optimism, of the "release of energy."[2] In addition, it was a period in the United States that "put a premium on improvisation and contrivance,"[3] when the leaders of society, the people that counted—and to a large extent ordinary men and women as well—believed in progress, getting ahead, opportunity, and growth.

Of course, belief in the free market system was never as powerful in practice as it was in theory. This is quite apart from the fact that almost the only truly autonomous economic actors were adult white men. Women had only a minor stake in business or in economic activity in general. Indeed, when a woman in the early nineteenth century married, her property rights passed almost entirely to her husband.[4] In the South black slaves, who had no property rights at all, made up a large part of the population. Moreover, the United States was certainly not committed to a purely libertarian philosophy or to a pure watchdog state. Everyone (or almost everyone) believed that governments had some responsibility for the economy. The state had a duty to provide a basis for the release of energy, and had a duty to provide an infrastructure.[5] The state could and should foster growth, through wise policies and by positive acts that would stimulate the economy. Government (mostly state government) supported and sometimes paid for roads, canals, bridges, ferries, and railroads. The legal system also bent and changed, doctrinally, in ways that lent support to growth, to dynamic enterprise. Public land policy was also enlisted to serve the same goals. The federal government owned an enormous stock of land—millions and millions of acres. It disposed of it, at cheap prices, in such a way as to advance what most people thought was America's destiny: a society of smallholders living on their land.[6] And the government also had positive duties that went beyond the bare bones of the caretaker state. It had the responsibility to provide for the general welfare. This was a vague term, to be sure. But it included all sorts of laws and doctrines, from standard weights and measures to quarantine regulations for ships to state control over gambling, liquor, and vice.[7]

Government, then, was far from inactive. Nonetheless, the focus was on individuals and individual enterprise. The American economy and society implied a high degree of mobility—in every sense of the word. First, there was geographic mobility. America was a country of immigrants. Millions of people came streaming into the country during the nineteenth century. In the first part of the century they came primarily from northern Europe; they were English, Scottish, German, and Scandinavian. In the 1840s there was a vast influx of Irish Catholics. At the end of the century millions poured in from eastern and southern Europe, from Italy, Russia, Hungary, Greece; between 1880 and 1920 more than 23 million immigrants entered the country.[8]

And within the United States countless men and families were rolling stones, moving from east to west, changing houses, changing towns. Historians argue about whether the frontier did or did not act as an economic and social safety valve, but clearly in the first half of the nineteenth century the "prospects for upward mobility were reasonably good" and they were perhaps "especially good on the frontier."[9] Mobility is not an easy variable to measure. It seems clear that many people did move around, in the physical sense, from town to town and from place to place. In the middle of the nineteenth century, between one census period and another, about 30 percent of the residents of any particular city apparently shifted to some other place.[10] Of course, moving from one town to another is not necessarily moving *up*. A footloose tramp has the same valence as a young man who travels west or elsewhere to seek (and maybe find) his fortune. Many men traveled long distances and, instead of finding their fortune, found profound failure and a lonely death among strangers.[11] But the figures do suggest that Americans—American men, at any rate—were restless and that they lived in a deeply restless society.

To be sure, mobility is much more than a matter of geography. Mobility is about movement in *social* space—movement up and down in terms of rank and status. Rank and status were not largely fixed at birth, as they were in older societies. Rank and status were fluid, flexible, and changeable. American society had always been quite proud of its commitment to equality. At the beginning of the Declaration of Independence stands the dramatic slogan: All men are created equal. Of course, nobody ever took this maxim literally. It certainly never applied to African Americans or for that matter women or Native Americans. This much is obvious. But even among white men, whether or not they were *created* equal, they clearly were not equal in society. The United States had its own status hierarchies. They were in some ways more subtle than the status hierarchies in Europe. There was a lot more "equality" in the United States than in England or on the continent. There was, to begin with, no king, no nobility, and no aristocracy. In England a tiny elite owned almost all the land; in the United States, particularly outside the South, millions of families owned a farm or a small lot in town. In the early Republican period many states restricted the vote to property owners, but the property qualification did not last long. By the middle of the century it was essentially gone, and just about all adult white men were eligible to vote almost everywhere—which was true in few other countries at the time and certainly not in England.[12] Social mobility was also on the rise in England in the nineteenth century, but it remained true that Victorian society was heavily structured; few people could bridge the chasm between manual laborers and white-collar workers. Still, everywhere in Europe mobility was increasing as people left their farms for the cities, and some of them at least moved into white-collar work.[13]

Equality was also a matter of culture. Visitors to the United States were often struck by American manners, which had a strong egalitarian tilt. In America there were no "servants," only "help," and the "help" refused to act as if they *were* mere servants.[14] Most of the visitors, to be sure, were people of some stature in their own society. They were impressed—and surprised—by how little deference Americans paid to their "betters." Travelers from genteel Europe also described Americans as crude and vulgar—people whose manners were far below European standards. Even people who were middle class lacked refinement. America was, for example, a nation of men who chewed tobacco and were addicted to spitting. At the theater in Washington, according to Frances Trollope, spitting was "incessant."[15] Her son Anthony, who also visited the United States, in the 1860s, essentially agreed. Americans were rude, crude, and egalitarian; they had no sense of propriety. Customary habits of respect for authority were nowhere to be found. Trollope found himself "pelted with the braggadocio of equality." A traveler, he said, would discover that the "corns of his Old-World conservatism will be trampled on hourly by the purposely vicious herd of uncouth democracy."[16] Indeed, by British upper-class standards Americans were extremely pushy and uncouth.

Equality was part of the American ethos. Of course, Americans were not so foolish as to believe that people really *were* equal—in wealth or character or ability. Equality meant equality of opportunity. It meant that there was no place for hereditary titles or powers. It meant that people (at least white men) were not frozen into particular social slots. It meant that it was possible to move up and down the social scale according to one's abilities and (of course) the luck of the draw.[17] This was a country where a man could be born in a log cabin and end up president of the United States, like Abraham Lincoln. "Any man's son," wrote Frances Trollope, "may become the equal of any other man's son." This was a "spur to exertion," which was good, but it was also, she thought, "a spur to that coarse familiarity, untempered by any shadow of respect, which is assumed by the grossest and the lowest in their intercourse with the highest and most refined."[18]

No doubt Frances Trollope exaggerated, but it *was* true that a man could be born into poverty and end up with enormous wealth. There was no small elite with centuries of land and power in their blood. It was the land of the self-made man (the self-made woman had not yet been invented). To be sure, in American life there were winners and losers and everything in between. Few men born poor died as millionaires. It was never easy to cross the lines between a low and a high station in life. But compared to traditional societies—to most contemporary European societies—the ladder of success at least seemed real enough. It was slippery, at times hard to access, but it was there. Men—and we are speaking here mostly of men—were free to move about, to climb up and down the social scale. They were free to succeed—or to fail. Not everybody climbed the ladder of success. Many lost their grip and fell back down into the mud. But the *ideology* of opportunity, of mobility, was genuine—it was a definite social fact.

Status, then, was a reality. The basis, however, was surely different from the basis in England or France. Different—and more subtle. Unlike the old country, high status was open to the masses; it was a prize to be won in the strenuous race for success. And success—entering the ranks of the American elite—was largely a matter of wealth. Wealth, obviously, was an important marker of status. Frances Trollope quoted an English visitor as saying that "he had never overheard Americans conversing without the word DOLLAR being pronounced between them." There was, she thought, a "unity of purpose" among Americans that could be found "nowhere else, except, perhaps, in an ants' nest."[19]

Status also depended on *respectability*, that is, a reputation for decency and good moral values. The way you lived and acted told the world whether you were or were not respectable. It was possible to be poor and respectable, and many people fit this description. But below a certain threshold—at a certain level of poverty and destitution—respectability vanished. Paupers living out their lives in a county poorhouse earned no respect. Men without jobs who lived on the fringes of society were vilified as tramps or hoboes.[20] They could even be treated as criminals (vagrants). And women who lacked virtue were shut out of polite society.

Because the United States had no hereditary elite, every man was supposed to build a reputation for himself—and, in a different sense, every woman. Success did not depend on birth; it depended on achievement, on merit. Money was a crucial element of merit, but reputation counted as well. The two were not unrelated. In a business or market economy, wealth, station, and power were heavily dependent on economic success—more so, perhaps, than in a society where position was inherited. The economy depended on credit. Ready money was in short supply. Credit information was also scarce. The banking system was primitive. There were insolvency laws in the various states and from time to time a national bankruptcy law, but all these laws were grossly deficient. Every generation or so a crisis, crash, or panic exploded with the force of a hurricane hitting the shore.[21] In a society of this sort good solid promises to pay—promissory notes or IOUs from people who were financially sound—were much more important than they are today.[22] Reputation fixed one's place in the system of money and credit; it also fixed one's place in the community. It defined a person as good or bad. Reputation was, in fact, a kind of social credit, a form of currency; it was an essential element of trust.[23]

Bankruptcy and insolvency laws were also, in a way, products of a mobile society—a society of risk takers. Bankruptcy and insolvency laws are safety nets. They afford people a chance to start over again. To be sure, the history of bankruptcy and insolvency laws is complex. These laws were always controversial. The federal constitution gave Congress the power to enact a uniform national bankruptcy law. But Congress failed to take up the challenge. An act was passed in 1800; it lasted only until 1803. Another act was passed in 1841; that law too lasted only a short time. A third short-lived law was enacted in 1867. Finally, Congress passed a bankruptcy law in 1898 that turned out to have real staying power. Much amended and altered, it is basically still in effect. In the nineteenth century, in the interim between bankruptcy laws, state insolvency laws more or less tried to fill the gap. The details do not concern us here. The key point is the ethos that lies behind bankruptcy and insolvency laws. It is the ethos of second chances—the right and the power to begin a new life, to wipe out the past and start over. This, as we will see, is a leitmotif that will appear again and again in this book.

The ethos of second chances was never simple and never absolute. The checkered history of bankruptcy laws was surely a sign of social ambivalence. State and regional issues complicated the struggle for a national bankruptcy law, and business failure always carried with it a certain stigma. Failure could be the result of chance, bad luck, locusts eating crops, or banks going out of business, but there were also "ideologies that fixed blame squarely on individual faults, not extenuating circumstances."[24] And, to be sure, sometimes business failure *was* the result of mistakes, poor judgment—or, at times, downright fraud. Yet a strong man, a man of character, even when defeated by circumstances, had the right and the power to try again. The need to make a fresh start, to bury the past, was also one of the ideas behind the explosive growth of divorce. Divorce, like bankruptcy, at one time carried with it the powerful stench of failure, if not immorality. It lost at least *some* of its stigma in the course of the nineteenth century, although this too is a complicated story.[25]

I have put a lot of stress on the importance of mobility—mobility as a fact and mobility as an ideology. A society that encourages and protects fresh starts is almost by definition a mobile society. In any event, social position was something to be earned—and learned. In the course of time, manners and customs changed. A kind of aristocracy developed gradually, especially in New England and of course in the slave-holding South. Men such as Jefferson and Washington were patricians, large landholders, men born into wealth and privilege. They, and the self-made men, created dynasties, families that carried over their privileges from generation to generation. By the late nineteenth century a definite upper class had emerged in America's large cities. The crude manners so offensive to Frances Trollope gradually declined. Codes of conduct, of etiquette, developed over the course of the century. But these codes were available to *all* respectable people; nobody was shut out by reason of birth. Thus gentility, as one writer put it, was "increasingly available as a social desire and a purchasable style and commodity. . . . Proper manners and social respectability could be purchased and learned."[26]

In the United States much more than in most other countries in the nineteenth century, a man could leave his old life behind and start a new life. If he moved to another community where nobody knew him, he had to build his reputation from scratch. This was a challenge, but it was also an opportunity. He could shuck an old, outworn, or unsatisfactory reputation and invent a new one for himself. A man with skeletons in his closet could close the closet door and move on. Mobility, and the blurring of class lines, opened up opportunities—dishonest as well as honest opportunities. A new life and a new town meant new chances to lie, cheat, and dissemble but also a new chance to invent yourself, to start over in a place where the ghosts of the past could no longer haunt you.

This was the other side of geographic mobility, another aspect of a society of second chances. A man who failed in business or who was guilty of some sort of fraud could always skip town. In the 1830s thousands of bankrupts headed west; so many Southern merchants in trouble went to Texas that "their decision to abscond came to be summed up in the abbreviation 'G.T.T.: 'Gone to Texas.'"[27] Mobility, in fact, produced a rich harvest of what I have called crimes of mobility.[28] One prime example was bigamy. Bigamy was a classic crime, but it became more common in the nineteenth century. It is hard, even impossible, to be a bigamist in a small town in traditional society, a place where everybody knows everybody else's business. No one could lead a double life. Circumstances in the United States were different. A stranger arrives in town. He meets and courts a woman. He tells her some kind of story about his past, his family, his background. Some of this story might be true. But he leaves out a few key facts—notably, that he left behind a wife (and maybe children), shedding them like a molted skin. He marries the new woman and takes up a new life. Trouble erupts when the truth somehow comes out.[29]

Almost all bigamists were men, because the mobility of women was much more restricted. But bigamy does in fact imply a change in the social position of women. Women who married bigamists were women who thought they could choose their own mates and marry for love; they were also women who willingly married a man who was, essentially, a stranger in town. As for the male bigamists, most of them seemed to be simply restless or dissatisfied husbands or men who were fed up with monogamy. Most had abandoned their first wife; a few tried to keep both families. John Wilgen had a wife and children in Minneapolis. He took up with Rena Mead of Bradford, Pennsylvania, in 1897. The Mead family ultimately became suspicious of his incessant business trips to Minnesota. The scheme fell apart. Some bigamists were swindlers, men such as J. Aldrich Brown, a serial husband who married at least seventeen times, mostly "sewing girls in wealthy families" whose meager savings he robbed before evaporating into the mists.[30]

J. Aldrich Brown was a bigamist whose career verges on that of another group of men who flourished in an atmosphere of mobility: confidence men. The confidence game (or con) refers to a cluster of new and inventive ways to swindle people out of their money.[31] The term and the role stem from the first half of the nineteenth century.[32] The period bristled with imposters—people pretending to be doctors, priests, brokers, moguls, rich mine owners, English lords—a whole army of sharpers with plans to squeeze money out of dupes and fools. New York, said James McCabe, was awash with such imposters. "One cannot mingle much in society here without meeting some bewhiskered, mysterious individual, who claims to be of noble birth."[33] One "Russian Count," who said he was on a "mission connected with the Russian navy," bilked New Yorkers out of $30,000, an immense sum for the day.[34] There were also bogus clergymen, not to mention collectors of money for nonexistent charities, men and women who specialized in conniving for free room and board at hotels, and, at the other end of the scale, one-armed and one-legged beggars "whose missing member, sound as your own, is strapped to their bodies."[35] The confidence man wore a false identity and invented a false reputation. The confidence game grew in the fertile soil of a mobile society; people were used to the presence of strangers, and a person's background was never easy to check. A slick line, a plausible story, and the *appearance* of respectability—these were the stock-in-trade of the confidence man. In the world of the nineteenth century, traditional norms that had governed "face-to-face conduct" in communities where "men and women came to know one another gradually over a long period of time, within a well-defined social context" no longer operated; it was in this new world that the confidence man flourished.[36]

The boundaries between classes were extremely porous. Mobility meant that ordinary people could at least daydream about getting rich. They might, after all, win the lottery, if nothing else. Traditional societies, in which social position is fixed, do not have lotteries—life, after all, was not a lottery but a game with rigid rules and positions. Mobile societies are societies that encourage striving and ambition; they also encourage, consciously or not, envy and emulation. In such societies social class and position become more difficult to read and comprehend from external signs. Society was not like an army, where rank is sharply marked, where men wear uniforms, and where stripes, badges, and insignia plainly tell people the status of the man in the uniform.

People in the United States could hope or dream or strive for a better status; and even where this was not possible, they could at least hope or dream or strive to *look* like their betters, in manners or dress.[37] The confidence man was, in a way, only a pathological version of the normal man. He was a man who took an illegitimate shortcut, pretending to be something he had no claim to be (and in the process, of course, he relieved gullible people of their hard-earned money). Money, after all, was the most reliable marker of value or success, and it could buy the clothes and the gewgaws that suggested money. This made some people easy prey for the confidence man. As the old saying goes, you can't cheat an honest man. In fact you can, but it is easiest to cheat a dishonest man or a man who is looking for easy money. Another group of vulnerable people were those who had some sort of skeleton in their closet and who were intent on starting over or on concealing their fall from grace. These were the people who were the natural victims of blackmail. Blackmail was one more example of a crime of mobility.

All or almost all of the swindles, the games that confidence men played, were against the law. Nobody likes being cheated and pillaged. But in a fiercely competitive society the line between cheating and shrewd business dealings was in fact somewhat indistinct. Charles Dickens, a perceptive observer, thought that Americans loved "smart" dealing. Their grudging admiration "gilds over many a swindle and gross breach of trust . . . and enables many a knave to hold his head up with the best, who well deserves a halter."[38] But probably "smart" behavior was more tolerated in business than in a man's personal life or his sex life; and for most women personal and sex lives were just about all there was.

The United States was in many ways a much more mobile society than England. Many of the social traits mentioned were either peculiar to the United States or more exaggerated there. This is why English visitors, such as Frances Trollope, were so struck by American manners. Yet in England, too, society was changing rapidly. People were moving from small villages to anonymous big cities. The class system was much more powerful and rigid than in the United States, but it was slowly eroding and the lines between classes were blurring at least somewhat. The economy was also changing dramatically. People with money from trade and merchandising were competing for power and prestige with the landed aristocracy. Money was coming to mean as much as rank; indeed, if an Englishman had enough money, he could buy himself rank or a country estate or both, and he could marry his children into the aristocracy. There were crimes of mobility in England too. In one dramatic and notorious trial in 1861 in Ireland, Maria Theresa Longworth accused her alleged husband, William Charles Yelverton, of bigamy.[39] Bigamy figured in a great many British novels of the late nineteenth century. The most sensational British novel of the 1860s, Mary Braddon's *Lady Audley's Secret*, hinged on a bigamous marriage.

Lady Audley, who gave her name to this huge best seller, had been a governess, a beautiful but impoverished young woman. She had charmed Sir Michael Audley, a middle-aged widower, so utterly that he married her and made her Lady Audley, mistress of his estate, Audley Court. Unknown to Sir Michael, Lady Audley had been married before—to a man who had gone off to Australia but who was very much alive.[40] When he returned, he posed a terrible danger to Lady Audley; she stood to lose everything. She was willing, therefore, to do anything or everything to keep her secret and bury the past. She even planned to murder her first husband.[41]

It is risky to attach too much meaning to a single novel, even one so popular as *Lady Audley's Secret*. The book owed its success to its sensational story and the skillful way it was told. But even the plot of a sensational novel has to have at least the germ of plausibility. Lady Audley was a woman who crossed social boundaries. She had been a servant who entered the upper class through marriage. She was also a bigamist, a woman with a guilty secret. In the novel she was also the victim of blackmail; her maid Phoebe had a loutish and drunken husband who milked Lady Audley for money as the price of keeping still about her crimes.[42] Toward the end of the novel, Sir Michael's nephew, Robert Audley, exposes Lady Audley. Confronted with overwhelming evidence of her crimes and deceptions, Lady Audley is forced to confess to her husband that the accusations against her are true. Sir Michael, his marriage and his happiness in ruins, turns Lady Audley over to his nephew, for whatever punishment or disposition Robert might make. Robert has her whisked away to a madhouse; she will stay there for the rest of her life, under the assumed name of Madame Taylor—the third name she has used in this novel.

Ironically, then, Lady Audley has one final and successful secret. She is never actually prosecuted. The world—English society—remains ignorant of her crimes. Why did Robert Audley take this step? Not for her sake but to spare the feelings of Sir Michael. Lady Audley's secret had to remain secret to preserve the honor, and social status, of Sir Michael.[43] This, then, is yet another theme of the novel: protection of the honor and status of elites.

Crimes and pathologies of mobility gave rise to the sensation literature in England, books such as *Lady Audley's Secret*. They also gave rise to a whole new literary genre: the detective story.[44] Among the earliest examples were short stories by Edgar Allan Poe, for example, "The Murders in the Rue Morgue" (1841). Another landmark was Willkie Collins's great novel, *The Moonstone*, published in 1868. In the United States Anna Catherine Green wrote *The Leavenworth Case* (1878), which became a runaway best seller. The most famous detective of them all, Sherlock Holmes, first made his appearance in 1887, with *A Study in Scarlet*. By the late nineteenth century the genre was flourishing, and countless mysteries and detective stories rolled off the presses. Literally thousands of such novels and short stories have been published; almost any and every conceivable plot device has been used; and there is not much that Poe, Arthur Conan Doyle, Mickey Spillane, Agatha Christie, and Dashiell Hammett have in common. Yet at the heart of almost every mystery there lies a guilty secret. In the classic English mystery someone is murdered; suspicion falls on one or more of a group of suspects. Some seem more likely than others, but the reader does not find out until the last chapter who it was that actually killed old Uncle Henry or some other victim. And the identity of the killer should come as a surprise—as something unexpected. If you can guess who killed Roger Ackroyd or guess the ending in a book by P. D. James or Ellery Queen, then the book is not really a success.

In other words, in the detective novel, at least one character is hiding something vital about his or her past; at least one character is definitely not what he or she seems to be. In many popular ("classic") British mysteries the players in the drama are members of the upper class, or at least the upper middle class. Yet one or more of them, like Lady Audley, harbors a secret and hidden flaw. Blackmail is often the engine that sets the drama going. The blackmailer knows this flaw, knows which skeletons are in which person's closet, and uses the information to extort money from the victim. This, however, is a dangerous game. In dozens of novels the wages of the blackmailer's sin are sudden death.

The nineteenth century was the century of the detective himself. The term, and the social role, were quite new. Detective squads were organized in Boston in 1846, in New York in 1857, and in Chicago in 1861. Police squads had been organized somewhat earlier but had a different function. The policeman wore a uniform and a badge. The policeman waded in to end urban riots; the police were open and visible, and this was how they acted to deter urban crime and unrest. The detective was the undercover man. He was sly, he wore no uniform, he operated in the shadows. He was the man who could ferret out false identities; he could unmask the secret evildoers, the confidence men, the men (and women) who pretended to a respectable but undeserved place in society. The detective, like his enemy, was a master of disguises and roles.[45]

To sum up, social norms and social institutions—including legal institutions—were recast in the nineteenth century. They reflected a mobile, rapidly changing society, a society of movement up and down social space, a society of new beginnings and cast-off pasts, a society in which reputation was complex and problematic—but vitally important. In the United States, in particular, mobility meant second chances; and, as we will see, many legal institutions *protected* the right to start over again. *Some* kinds of starting over, however, were downright criminal—for example, bigamy and the other crimes of mobility. Other kinds of starting over were fiercely protected by law. Blackmail laws, for example, labeled as criminal the man who knew the secrets—not the man who was trying to hide his guilty past. The law, in theory, could have made a different choice. It could have excused the blackmailer instead of his victim. One theme of this book is that the law in the nineteenth century did *not* make this choice; the law wove a subtle, complex web of norms that excused some sins and not others and that shielded some of the elites, protected their privacy, and allowed them at least some of their transgressions. Which ones and why are matters that I will consider in later chapters.

THE ANATOMY OF REPUTATION

Every society has its rules, norms, ideals—templates or patterns of expected behavior. How people actually behave is another question.

Societies are, of course, extremely complicated. There are official norms, and unofficial norms. There is never just one pattern or template, one model of approved behavior; rather, there is a wild, bewildering, inconsistent multiplicity, a riot of normative colors. This was certainly true of the United States and the major European countries in the nineteenth century. Some ideas and norms commanded the allegiance of *most* people. Or so it seemed. One caution is that we have little information about "most people." In the nineteenth century there were no survey data. Historians have to rely on a fairly thin record created by people who put down words on paper or left behind some tangible remains.

One written source is particularly valuable: guides to manners and morals, etiquette books, brochures and pamphlets that explain rules of behavior, how-to-behave books that tell people how to act in polite society. Medical advice books can also be quite revealing. There are also the laws themselves. Not all laws are important. Not all of them are obeyed. Some are dead letters; some are half-dead or paralyzed. But they all express some plan, ideal, or goal. New laws and changes in old laws are especially instructive. Legislatures do not pass laws without some reason. All laws are responses to some sort of demand or request. If a law is passed regulating the sale of milk or making lotteries illegal, *something* and very likely *somebody* stands behind the legislation.

The sources, then, are fairly good in telling us what people were *supposed* to do. They are of course much less reliable in telling us what they actually did in real life. Nobody is perfect, after all. All rules are sometimes broken. When a law is passed that makes some act or sin a criminal offense, clearly some people must be guilty of that act or sin. How many people violate the norm before the law, and after, is always an empirical question, and rarely do we have adequate data.

In the nineteenth century the country's presses published dozens of books and pamphlets about etiquette and manners. This was not, to be sure, an entirely new genre. Etiquette and protocol were vital aspects of courtly society. Rigid rules determined how one was supposed to behave at, say, Versailles during the reign of Louis XIV; even slight deviations from the rules of propriety could lead to scandal or even banishment from court. Lord Chesterfield's letters of advice to his son were a smash hit of the eighteenth century and went through many editions. But the etiquette books of the nineteenth century were not written by earls and were not meant for dukes and duchesses. They were aimed at an audience of ordinary, middle-class people. They were books on how to eat and dress and how to act in public or in company. Some books told people what rules to follow for sound, healthy, and moral living. Others were guides to propriety and respectability for men, women, and children. These books were not by any means a purely American phenomenon. One scholar claims that between 1870 and 1970 there were 700 or 800 etiquette books published in Germany, with such titles as *How Shall I Behave?*[46]

Good manners are an aspect of respectability. It was possible, of course, to have good manners and still lack respectability; the two overlap but are not the same. Still, the epidemic of books on manners and etiquette was a sign of how profoundly society was changing. Traditional society was slowly breaking down. Social mobility was on the rise. "Good breeding" once meant exactly that: coming from the right family. The extreme case, of course, was the nobility in England and other European countries. A "gentleman" or a "lady" was hardly something within the grasp of a peasant or a worker. In the United States titles of nobility were expressly outlawed by the Constitution. And from a relatively early time, social position was far more fluid than in Europe. Etiquette books, whatever their content, always carried an implicit message: You can *become* a person whose manners are impeccable and whose comportment commands respect. It is not a matter of breeding. It is a matter of information and training.[47]

What traits, habits, and behaviors were the key to a respectable life and a good reputation? The books, of course, did not always offer the same advice. But certain themes ran through most of them. On the whole, teachers and preachers insisted on discipline and self-control. Moderation in all things was the ideal. The man of character worked hard, went to church, was well regarded by his neighbor, avoided getting drunk, and was clean in body and mind. He learned to restrain himself, to control or curb his passions, to subject himself to strong self-discipline. He was punctual, frugal, and temperate; he avoided vices and temptations.[48] Liquor, except in moderate amounts, was a deadly enemy. Getting drunk was a sign of moral decay, and it could lead a man on the downward path to destruction of mind and body. "In every glass of liquor," wrote J. B. Ripley in 1861, "can be seen the coil of the never-dying worm" and "the pale, ghastly, death-fanged serpent, consumption."[49] Waves of religious fervor often swept over the nineteenth-century United States, and there were also strong waves of fervor for temperance. Too much sex, or the wrong kind of sex, was if anything, even worse than too much drunkenness and liquor.

A number of scholars have tried to connect nineteenth-century morality with the economic order and the ideology that underlay that order. Men who wanted to get ahead were told to be thrifty, to be diligent and productive, and to defer gratification. Good habits and hard work would lead to wealth and position in society. Success in a market society did not go to the idle and the profligate. The winners of the race were men who disciplined themselves. Consistent with this was encouragement to "submit willingly to a highly disciplined code of sexual behaviour." The sexual code, then, was congruent with the economic code. It asked men (and women) to defer gratification. It "promised the paradise of marriage as a reward for enduring the purgatory of abstinence."[50] The ideal, in every aspect of life, was self-discipline, moderation, and attention to what Max Weber called the Protestant ethic. This ideal, it was believed, was a pillar on which capitalism, the free market, and economic growth necessarily rested.

There was an ideal woman as well as an ideal man. The ideal woman was also hard-working; and she was even more virtuous than her husband. Women did not belong in the world of business and politics. They had their "separate sphere"; in that sphere they acted in some ways as the moral stewards of society.[51] A woman's most important job was motherhood. Motherhood was her destiny and her calling. Her place was in the home. She was supposed to be modest and obedient. The ideal wife was also "totally receptive and responsive to her husband's emotional needs"; she provided him with a "refuge from the harsh outside world."[52]

The United States was, by the standards of the times, a revolutionary democracy. This meant a society in which "the people" ruled; that is, ordinary commoners held political power. The whole ethos of American government and politics after the Revolution stressed popular sovereignty.[53] The "people" were in charge—but not *all* the people. Blacks, Indians, women, and children were not part of the people, but neither were criminals, tramps, hoboes, whores, and outcasts—those who were not part of respectable society. It is easy today to see the warts and blemishes of American life. To us a society with millions of African slaves, a society in which women had no vote and possessed few rights, a society in which something close to genocide was practiced against the native peoples hardly deserves to be called a democracy. But to contemporaries the United States was truly a democracy, and a rather extreme one at that. There was no aristocracy, no established church. Farmers and storekeepers voted and had a say in the government. To de Tocqueville the United States was a radical innovation, something new and different in the world.

In a democratic society of the American type certain controls over behavior are missing. The country has no natural ruling class. Deference is in short supply. People move about the country, immigrants pour in, nothing seems firm and settled, men rise and fall in the social scale. As a result, there is a tremendous felt need for *internalized* controls. Visitors to the country, as I noted, were always struck by American manners—or more accurately, a *lack* of manners. But the flood of books on manners and etiquette suggests that this crudeness was at least partly in the eye of the beholder or was, perhaps, gradually receding. America was in the process of constructing new forms of behavior. These may have been, in their own way, every bit as rigid as in the old country, but they rested on different norms and assumptions. And, of course, as the country matured—as it got older and wealthier—an indigenous upper crust developed on top of the middle-class masses.

The American government—the constitutional order—rested on the will of the people. That was the theory. Democratic government vested power in the people, gave the people the right to vote, and expressed in its formal institutions trust in the good sense of the mass of the voters. But not all voters deserved this kind of trust. For those who failed to measure up, American society could be harsh indeed. Gustave de Beaumont and Alexis de Tocqueville were two famous visitors to the United States. They came primarily to study the newfangled penitentiary system—a mode of punishment radically different from older systems—that had attracted their attention. The United States, they said, gave people "the most extended liberty" of any society. Yet its prisons offered "the spectacle of the most complete despotism. The citizens subject to the law are protected by it; they only cease to be free when they become wicked."[54] America's new penitentiaries were indeed egalitarian—but they were also extremely severe. They were huge, grim buildings surrounded by impervious walls and guarded night and day. Inside, in the individual cells, there were no distinctions of rank or privilege. Everybody ate the same crude food. Everybody wore the same uniform. Life was as regimented as in the most ascetic monasteries. Everybody got up, ate, worked, and went to bed at precisely the same hour. Penitentiaries were run on the silent system. No prisoner was allowed to talk. The outside world was almost completely shut off. The prisons were devoted to a kind of penitence; the soul of a convicted thief or rapist or forger of checks was to be redeemed by measures that would suit the soul of the most rigid monk or Puritan.[55]

These gigantic gloomy buildings were the stone embodiment of a penal theory. The causes of crime lay in society itself, in the evils and temptations of the big city; the criminal was a man (or woman) corrupted by bad companions, vice, idleness, and drink. The cure was a kind of radical surgery: Cut off every one of the criminal's ties to the corrupt and corrupting world; subject him to iron discipline. Whether the system worked is another question. But its harshness reflected the idea that democracies were fragile, that merciful treatment of criminals was a luxury these governments could not afford. The treatment of paupers was regarded in a similar way: In a land of opportunity many men had only themselves to blame for failure. Poverty for these men was not a natural condition. It was due to vice or utter incompetence. Poor laws should be as stigmatic and niggardly as possible; otherwise, dangerous idleness might be encouraged. In the early nineteenth century welfare policy shifted from "indoor" relief (in peoples' own homes) to "outdoor" relief (in poorhouses and poor farms). In these wretched institutions life was spartan, severe, and highly regimented. Indeed, the American poorhouse was not that different from the American penitentiary.[56]

Similar themes and similar worries about democratic society and its citizens also sounded in debates on the issue of lotteries. This subject was fiercely debated during the sessions of the New York constitutional convention of 1821. Quite a few delegates spoke out in favor of lotteries, which were, after all, an easy way to raise state money. The opponents argued vigorously, however, that lotteries were inherently evil. They had terrible effects on ordinary people. A lottery tended to "promote and encourage a spirit of rash and wild speculation amongst the poor and labouring classes—to fill their minds with absurd and extravagant hopes, which diverted them from the regular pursuits of industry." "Indulgence" in lotteries was a vice "destructive" of good habits. Lottery money would be drawn from "the pockets of the poor" and would "augment the poverty of those who were betrayed into vice."[57]

These worries and arguments flowed from the nature of a mobile society. In fact, the very idea of a lottery presupposed a certain amount of social mobility. It assumed some flow from the bottom of society to the middle or the top. In America the rich were at the top of society. The approved way to get rich was to work hard, start a business, and build it bigger and bigger. Winning the lottery was a shortcut. Many people considered it a bad and distasteful shortcut, an illegitimate way to end up rich. Implicit in the debate, too, was the notion that democratic society was inherently fragile. Winning a lottery was not as harmful a way to get easy money as crime, but it was bad enough and corrosive enough to constitute a danger.

In American society many young men (and perhaps a few young women) were eager, striving, and ambitious, working and scheming to get rich and bound and determined to rise on the social scale. They lived in what was supposed to be an open society, a society of broad horizons and big opportunities (at least for white men). Open opportunity did not mean that there were no natural leaders—men who formed an elite of virtue and competence. The public could choose its leaders; but in choosing, they would and should follow the lead of these elites. The governors, mayors, presidents, and other leaders should be drawn from the ranks of the honorable and successful. These men should also set the tone of society, ethically speaking; and their norms of behavior should be the norms that other people ought to follow. Underneath the surface, however, was a complex reality. The surface was the Protestant ethic and traditional morality. The surface was a rags-to-riches story and Horatio Alger[58] and the American dream. Underneath were what remained of a society where people deferred to authority and a hidden and disguised class system. Society was in fact highly stratified. People could be ranked in terms of money, honor, and respect. Underneath the surface, too, were the harsh realities of an imperfect world. Men, even prominent men, were not all free from vice and sin. Not all women were blameless and chaste.

In light of this reality, instruments of social control had two somewhat contradictory jobs. The first job was to support and enhance the official codes. This was obviously important in a fragile, experimental society. The second job was to protect and safeguard the men on whose broad backs the safety and health of society rested. Protect them, even when they did not walk the straight and narrow path (within limits). This job was also necessary, and for the same reason: because the social compact was fragile and experimental. How this protection worked and why is the theme of the following chapters.

CHAPTER 3

STICKS AND STONES

The Law of Defamation

T HE LAW OF DEFAMATION—libel and slander—has roots deep in the history of the common law. The law of defamation is a branch of the law of torts. By one conventional definition a tort is a civil (i.e., not a criminal) wrong. Defamation is most definitely a civil wrong. As the English writer Francis Holt put it in 1816, the wrong consists of impairing a person "in the enjoyment of general society" and injuring "rights of friendly intercourse and mutual benevolence, which man has with respect to man," by holding a person up to "scorn and ridicule, and, still, more, to any stronger feeling of contempt or execration."[1]

The common law made a central distinction between two kinds of defamation: slander (words) and libel (writings). Slander was not considered as reprehensible as libel. The spoken word was more or less soon gone with the wind; writings were more permanent. Mere "defamatory words," Holt said, were nothing but "transitory abuse," the product of "our natural passions," and typically lacked enough "substance and body" to affect "reputation." But the "act of writing" was in itself "an act of deliberation, and the instrument of a permanent mischief."[2] Libel referred originally to writings, in the literal sense, especially words in print; later it came to include "pictures, effigies or other visible and permanent forms."[3] Defamation in a movie also came to be defined as libel, not slander, even though the defamation consisted of *spoken* words (on screen), because movies, like newspapers and books, existed in a permanent form.[4]

It is certainly possible to sue a slanderer, but the case has to fall within a few specific categories of slander. If the case cannot be fitted into one of these boxes, then no lawsuit is possible, unless the plaintiff can prove that the slander actually caused him or her some sort of measurable damage. It was actionable slander to impute a person with "crimes" or "contagious disorders," because this would tend to "expel the victim from society" or to injure him "in his profession and calling." Falsely calling a man a horse thief or a leper, then, was "slander per se." ("Slander per se" is slander so bad that actual damages are *assumed*.) In other cases no action was possible without showing specific actual damages. There was no such restriction on libel. But because the gist of libel is injury done to reputation, the libel or slander had to be "published," that is, communicated to at least one other person.[5] So, for example, in one case the defendant sent a sealed, libelous letter through the mail. Nobody read it but the person to whom it was addressed. The plaintiff's lawsuit failed; the letter had never been "published."[6]

The phrase "natural passions" in the quote from Holt is significant. Mere harsh spoken words do not amount to defamation. The common law in this regard at least seems to differ from the law of some European countries that pay more attention to insults. Essentially, defamation in the common law is about lies, not opinions; about accusations of wrongdoing, not other kinds of words, no matter how harsh and hurtful they might be. The law gives no remedy for ordinary insults. In modern German law, apparently, it is a (minor) crime to call somebody an idiot or a fool.[7] American law has no obvious equivalent.[8]

This is said to be because modern continental European law gives greater protection to dignity and personal honor than American law does.[9] The Basic Law of the German Federal Republic (1949) states that "human dignity" is "inviolable" (Article 1). Under the Basic Law everyone has a right to the "free development of his personality" (Article 2).[10] Provisions more or less of this type are found in other European constitutions. Thus the Spanish Constitution of 1978 (Article 18) talks about a right to honor, of personal and family privacy, and to one's own image. There are no such provisions in the United States Constitution.

Indeed, children in the English-speaking world can respond to taunts by reciting the old slogan:

Sticks and stones will break my bones
But words will never hurt me.

But does anybody really believe this? Words can be incredibly harmful and painful. Some words can inflict far more damage than the average stick or stone. Defamation law recognizes this fact. Lies that injure a person's reputation, his pocketbook, his business, or his standing in the community, are and have been actionable.

Moreover, the differences between American and continental law may be more apparent than real. No doubt 99.9 percent of all insults in the Federal Republic of Germany never get into a courtroom. And it would be wrong to state flatly that the common law of defamation showed no concern for honor and dignity. Courts have often defined libel as "words published which tend to bring the plaintiff into public hatred, contempt, or ridicule."[11] An insult, after all, might turn somebody into an object of ridicule (or at least an object of malicious gossip). In defamation cases the jury gets to decide the amount of damages. The jury deliberates in secret and never gives reasons for what it decides. A jury might fix damages not only because a plaintiff lost business income but also because his feelings were terribly hurt or because he was embarrassed, insulted, or held up to ridicule.

Reputation is central to the law of defamation. It would be odd if, in practice, the law ignored injury to reputation, unless it was also injury to the pocketbook. The plain fact is that we know next to nothing about the living law of defamation, especially in the nineteenth century.[12] The truth lies buried in heaps of trial court records, scattered from county to county, rotting in courthouse basements. Nor do we have any tools to measure what happened to potential cases that were settled out of court. Some reported cases are at least suggestive. Some hint that the insult factor made a difference in cases of libel. In one Wisconsin case the *Oconomowoc Local*, a newspaper, sneered at the plaintiff, Solverson, in 1885. It called Solverson "king of the Norwegians," a throwback to the time when human progress was low and "the king of Babylon was changed into an ox and lived on grass." At present, this "great king," with the "blood of the ancient viking" in his veins, "has turned into an enormous swine, which lives on lame horses. . . . Doctors say there is no hope for his recovery, and he will probably remain a swine the rest of his days." Could a jury find these statements libelous? Yes, said the Supreme Court of Wisconsin; the right of a jury to decide that these statements tended to bring Solverson into "ridicule and contempt" was "too clear for . . . argument."[13]

A few years later, in 1893, another case involved the freewheeling and colorful style of local newspapers in Wisconsin. The *Oshkosh Times* published a bitter attack on a state senator, Buckstaff (thinly disguised as "Senator Bucksniff"). The attack on "Bucksniff," who was described as a "senatorial god," dripped with sarcasm. Buckstaff's face was partially paralyzed, and the newspaper wrote of his "mighty right eye"—a reference (according to Buckstaff) to his physical condition. The paper ended its screed by claiming that "Bucksniff" was a person who went his own way and did not follow the wishes of the people he represented.[14]

The Supreme Court of Wisconsin thought that the story was libelous. It was meant to hurt the senator "by bringing him into shame, disgrace, hatred, scorn, ridicule, and contempt." The newspaper account was full of "gibes, taunts, and contemptuous and insulting phrases."[15] Today, no doubt, this kind of bitter and sarcastic criticism would be considered fair comment and even privileged comment (Buckstaff was an elected official). But in the late nineteenth century it went beyond the invisible line that separated defamation from protected speech.

American defamation cases, such as the two just mentioned, often concerned vituperative newspapers, slinging mud at public figures and engaging in wild and fantastic insults. In an 1872 Missouri case the publisher wrote that the mayor of a town, James Price, was "an imp of the devil" and a "cowardly snail, that shrinks back into his shell at the sight of the slightest shadow."[16] Price sued for libel. The publisher, Abner Whitely, insisted that there was no damage to Price's reputation and hence no cause of action, but the court disagreed: The words implied that the "plaintiff was a bad man, ready in the mayor's chair to do the devil's work . . . and also that he was an arrant coward." This was likely to "degrade and injure him" and ruin his reputation, even though the charges were not "specific."[17]

The American press was certainly capable of nasty and irresponsible behavior. Harriet Martineau thought that the American press was the worst in the

world.[18] Charles Dickens, writing in 1842, called the American press a monster of depravity. The press "has its evil eye in every house, and its black hand
in every appointment in the state, from a president to a postman"; its "only
stock in trade" is "ribald slander," and its "evil" influence spreads throughout
the country.[19] Anthony Trollope, writing some twenty years later, was just as
critical; the things in the newspapers, he said, were "never true." The forte of
the press was "abuse of individuals," abuse "which is as violent as it is perpet-
ual. . . . All idea of truth has been thrown overboard. . . . The only object is to
produce a sensation. . . . Falsehood has become so much a matter of course with
American newspapers that it has almost ceased to be falsehood."[20] Historical
accounts of American journalism are almost universally bleak. The press was
pretty generally quite partisan and one-sided. Each party or faction had its
own newsprint organ. Mudslinging was epidemic. The American press seemed
more freewheeling and less deferential than the British press.[21] Defamation
cases came out of this background of vituperation.

The formal law seemed to assume that reputation could be treated as a
kind of commodity and that someone was guilty of a wrong only if he or she
had damaged the *value* of that commodity. Yet if a person or a newspaper went
too far in ridicule and abuse, an invisible line was crossed and immunity vanished. A modern English case illustrates this point. The plaintiff in the case,
decided in 1996,[22] was an actor, director, and writer named Steven Berkoff.
Julie Burchill, the defendant, in a scathing movie review, remarked that film
directors in general, from Alfred Hitchcock to the plaintiff, were "notoriously
hideous-looking." Nine months later, describing a monster in a horror movie,
she said that the creature was "a lot like Stephen (*sic*) Berkoff, only marginally
better-looking." Was this defamation? There was no attack on Berkoff's reputation "in the conventional sense." Still, the jury had the right to decide whether
the words had "passed beyond mere abuse and had become defamatory, exposing Mr. Berkoff to ridicule or causing him to be shunned or avoided."[23]

The Berkoff court admitted that there was precious little authority for its
holding. It did cite *Zbyszko v. New York American*, a 1930 New York case.[24] A
newspaper, in an article on evolution, said that the gorilla "is probably closer
to man, both in body and in brain, than any other species of ape." It printed a
picture of Stanislaus Zbyszko "in a wrestling pose" and with the caption, "Stanislaus Zbyszko, the Wrestler, Not Fundamentally Different from the Gorilla

in Physique." In "close proximity" was a photograph of a "hideous-looking gorilla," a "mounted specimen of the Great Kivu Gorilla in Lord Rothschild's private museum." Zbyszko claimed that he had an "international reputation for dignity . . . kindliness, intelligence and culture," that he was a "business man" of some repute; the words and pictures held him up to "public contempt, disgrace, hatred, infamy and reproach, caused him to be shunned and avoided and to be treated as an outcast by his wife, relatives, neighbors, friends and business associates." The court was sympathetic. If a publication renders a person "contemptible or ridiculous," the person is "entitled to redress."

These are isolated cases from different jurisdictions and different times. It would be wrong to make too much of them. And there is authority on the other side. A newspaper in 1979 carried a story about a football player for the University of Alabama, Darwin Holt. Sixteen years earlier, during a game, Holt had caused a player for Georgia Tech to suffer a broken nose and jaw and a concussion. Holt said it was an accident. In the story the newspaper called Holt the "animal from Alabama," a "caveman incarnate"; it called the incident the "New Darwin Theory" and said Holt's playing was "more bestial than academic." Was this defamation? Oh no, said the court; all this was "at worst hyperbolic"; it was just "figurative name-calling."[25]

What is at issue in these cases is a long-term dilemma in the formal law of defamation. The law protects reputation, but what is reputation? Defamation in theory provides no remedy for pain and suffering, hurt feelings, a wounded ego. Harm is supposed to be objective harm. If I said that your restaurant swarms with cockroaches, and the customers run away, there is an obvious and objective economic loss. But most aspects of life are not so clear. Reputation is a subtle and complex thing. At the core it is a social fact: what people think of you. It is the "estimate in which others hold a person." And, as I have pointed out, it is essentially different from *character*. Character is "not determined by the opinion of others" and is impervious to "scandal."[26] Character is what you *are*, not what people say you are. It is possible to have a good reputation and a bad character. But an attack on character is also an attack on reputation. In turn, an attack on reputation is an attack on standing in the community. And standing in the community is a social good, a value, a commodity, as it were. It also has economic value, but beyond that, it is the external definition of self. Your standing in the community classifies you, assigns you to a category;

it is a key that opens many doors; it is the set of instructions that tells other people how to put you together and behave toward you. Without it, you are like a random collection of pieces, like an unassembled jigsaw puzzle.

In order to understand the law of defamation and its social role, we would have to know a lot more about the cast of characters. Who sued whom? What role did defamation play in the protection of top people, of elites? These people have *more* reputation in a way; they have more to lose. In addition, their loss of reputation tends to ripple out farther, to have more consequences, than the loss of reputation of ordinary folks, just as the death of a Caesar has consequences that the death of a Roman plebe does not. It is this enhanced value of reputation that the law may have been striving to protect.

And where does insult come in? To say that a man is ugly, looks like an ape, has a screechy voice or bad table manners is in a way an attack on neither character nor reputation, but it is an attack on esteem. It is a violation of deference. It is a way of pulling the high and mighty down to the level of the gutter. It injures them—and their reputation—in the same way that you would injure and embarrass a senator if you showed a picture of him naked or in the act of urinating. Potentially at least, the law of defamation has a role to play in the protection of privacy, and protection of privacy is part of the protection of reputation. Insults, like violations of privacy or actual defamatory words, might be terrifically destructive—again, not just to the individual but also to society as a whole. In the nineteenth-century United States the ethos of equality made insulting or defaming powerful people less of an issue than in England, but it was an issue nonetheless.

The law of defamation was part of the common law inheritance. With much of the rest of the common law, it crossed the ocean to the colonies in the Western hemisphere. Cornelia Dayton has carefully studied slander cases in colonial Connecticut, with particular attention to the role of women as slanderers and as victims of slander.[27] The clergy and other leaders of small colonial settlements denounced scurrilous talk. Libel and slander cases were not at all rare during the colonial period. To take just one example, Hezekiah Dickenson sued Abraham Temple in a "Plea of Defamation" in western Massachusetts toward the end of the seventeenth century. Dickenson claimed that Temple called him a "Theife a lyar and whore Master."[28] The courts took such cases seriously. Slander was exceptionally threatening to individuals in small, tight communities and to the social fabric. As Norman Rosenberg points out, people "branded as adulterers, liars, or thieves could not easily move away from their reputation. . . . Colonials could not escape into . . . anonymity . . . or easily join alternative social groups." The stigma of a slander "could remain fastened to one's name for years"; a lawsuit was one way to try to cleanse a reputation.[29]

The law of defamation did change, however, as it crossed the Atlantic. American society was (or became) strikingly different from English society. Defamation actions declined in frequency in the late colonial period. One theory is that defamation had important meaning within the "communal ethos" of the seventeenth century; sinful behavior had to be revealed and punished. Later, an "ethic of privacy [developed] in which middle-class respectability was preserved by shielding the family name from public exposure."[30] But perhaps an ethic of privacy would *encourage*, not discourage, actions for libel and slander. Perhaps larger, more mobile and shifting communities were less exposed to harmful gossip—gossip presupposes a face-to-face society. If so, then only the emergence of muckraking journalists would cause defamation once again to come into its own.

Many commentators in more recent times have sensed strong differences between defamation in the United States and defamation in Great Britain—not necessarily in the rules themselves as flatly and abstractly stated but in the living law of libel and slander. Why? Zechariah Chafee Jr., writing in the 1940s, had a theory: An Englishman is "born into a definite status where he tends to stick for life." Therefore "what he *is* has at least as much importance as what he *does*." Any "slur on his reputation . . . may cause him to drop several rungs down the social ladder"; a failure to respond to a slur, might be "taken as an admission of truth." The situation in the United States, he thought, was different. Among other things, defamation "is just one more blow in the rough-and-tumble of politics or business." And if a man's reputation is lowered, "he can make a fresh start at his home or in a new region."[31]

Somewhat similarly, Robert Post has suggested that defamation law might operate one way in a "deference society" and quite another way in a "market society." In a market society reputation is a "private possession," created by "individual effort and is of importance primarily to those who have created it."[32] But in a "deference society" preservation of honor "entails more than the protection of merely individual interests." Honor is a public good. If you insult the king, you not only hurt the king's "personal interests," you also "damage . . . the social status with which society has invested the role of kingship."[33]

What is plausible about these conjectures is the notion that defamation's damage is a *social* damage—harm to the community, not just to the victim of libel or slander. But this would be equally true in a market society, although perhaps in a slightly different way. The United States in the middle of the nineteenth century may have had a more boisterous, bumptious press, and deference to authority was not a major value. Nonetheless, American society rested on pillars of reputation. The *class* to be protected was larger than in England. There was no aristocracy, no monarchy. But absence of a class system could make reputation all the more brittle, more needy of protection. Reputation was a public good, even in this market society. Perhaps it was defended in different ways and more subtly than in (say) eighteenth- and nineteenth-century England. Chafee's point about mobility also rings true. A man in disgrace in his community can slink away to a new town and begin again as a stranger. It was surely easier to start over in the United States than in Britain. It was easier to construct a fresh reputation; but a new reputation, like an old one, was still vulnerable to attack.

CHASTITY

Most defamation cases—at least the reported cases—were brought by men, who were suing other men (or, commonly, newspapers). Women litigants were a small minority in the nineteenth century, although they had played a bigger role in the colonial period.[34] Typically, women's cases were about chastity (or the lack of chastity); they sued over language that said or implied indecency, whoring, and sexual misconduct in general. Out of 130 reported defamation cases published between 1897 and 1906, only 43 were brought by women. All but one of these cases dealt with "imputations of immorality."[35] After all, virtue was the be-all and end-all of a woman's reputation.

Oddly enough, at the beginning of the nineteenth century it was not "slander per se" to say that a woman was unchaste or even that she was a whore. In the Victorian era this rule came under heavy fire. The rule seemed to make no sense in a period that stressed virtue, chastity, and sexual modesty for women. In England, Parliament ultimately changed the rule by statute.

The rule also changed in the United States, but this did not happen overnight. It *was* slander per se to accuse a person of committing a crime. In most states fornication and adultery were crimes. This gave women a strong argument in defamation cases. At first, the argument did not always work. In one old New York case (1809) the defendant said, "She is a common prostitute, and I can prove it." In New York a common prostitute could get hard labor, up to sixty days, as a "disorderly person." Was this enough to make the statement slander per se? No, said the court. The act had to be a crime with "moral turpitude" or one that would subject a person to an "infamous punishment." A disorderly person was, according to the court, just not degraded enough. Under the statute people who pretended to "have skill in physiognomy, palmistry, or pretending to tell fortunes" could also be labeled disorderly. Yet surely it could not be slander per se to accuse somebody of reading palms. Hence, without showing actual damages, the words alone would not do the trick.[36]

Even in a later New York case (1875) the court showed a certain reluctance. The slanderous words accused the plaintiff, a young woman, of "self-pollution."[37] The plaintiff made a feeble attempt to show that she had suffered real damages: She claimed that her father had promised her music lessons and a silk dress and then, when he heard the scurrilous remarks, backed off; he personally (the father said) did not believe these horrible accusations, but he wanted his daughter to clear herself. The defendant, said the court, "deserves punishment, but the action of slander will not afford a remedy."

This was already somewhat exceptional. In a case from 1872, A. M. Hudson said that Evelina J. Lewis had been seen "at the chicken coop of McAfee & Kellogg, with her clothes up" and with a man. He also claimed that someone had hired him to "buy her a magnetic conception preventive," a device "said to be used by the debauched and infamous in their guilty amours," and that Ms. Lewis "knew more about it than I. . . . The reason why . . . was, in my opinion, because she had been using it." Hudson insisted that this did not legally amount to slander per se. The trial court agreed; but the Supreme Court of Georgia emphatically did not. In Georgia, said the court, it was actionable to accuse someone of "any debasing act which may exclude him from society," and a female "guilty of the debasing act . . . at the chicken coop" was worse even than the "low and vicious. . . . Even among them there is still generally left some remains of at least the form of decency."[38]

Like Parliament, many states enacted statutes to make it crystal clear that imputing sexual misconduct to a woman was behavior with serious consequences. For example, an 1881 Indiana statute made it slander per se to falsely accuse "a female" of "incest, fornication, adultery, or whoredom."[39] Some courts did this on their own. As the Nebraska high court put it in 1906, a woman accused of illicit sex "is driven beyond the reach of every courtesy and charity of life, and sometimes even beyond the portals of humanity." It is the "deepest insult and the vilest charge" a woman could face. It denies her "the society in which she has been wont to move"; and if she wants to work, "her chance for self-support is injured beyond redress."[40] In one case, from Kansas (1909), the defendant said that the plaintiff, Cooper, was a "dirty slut" and repeated a story that Mrs. Cooper's little girl was born four or five months after she married Mr. Cooper.[41] The court, rather oddly, held that a slut was not necessarily an immoral woman; the word might just mean a lazy, careless, sloppy woman. But the other charge was more serious. It was slander per se, and the old rule (requiring the allegation of special damages) was obsolete; it tended to "thwart natural justice." Kansas was a state "where the most profound respect for the character of its womanhood is native to the people." To accuse a woman of sleeping with her husband before marriage would inflict an "incurable wound to the victim's feelings," plunge her into "contempt and disrepute," and exclude her "from the society of the pure." In an Ohio case from 1880 the defendant "in the presence and hearing of divers good people" claimed that the plaintiff, Angelina Ward, had slept with a certain John Fox. Words of this sort, said the court, "imputing to a woman a want of chastity," are actionable in themselves. They tend to "exclude her from society" and "bring her into disgrace," and this is "an injury from which damage necessarily results."[42]

In the 1890s Ida Gates sued the *New York Recorder* for libel.[43] The newspaper had described her as a "dashing blonde, twenty years old . . . said to have been a concert-hall singer and dancer at Coney Island"; it also said that she had secretly married a man who was 75 years old. In fact, Ida Gates was not a girl of 20 but a woman of 35; she was (she said) a schoolteacher from a farm family, and the marriage was no secret. But the heart of her complaint was the allegation that she had been a singer and dancer at Coney Island. She had never been on the stage anywhere, let alone Coney Island. A concert hall there, she said, was "a place of evil report and a resort for disorderly . . .

persons"; the "female singers and dancers therein are generally depraved and abandoned women" who are "shunned and avoided by orderly and respectable people." She introduced evidence about the horrors of these concert halls, where women "appeared in short skirts to dance and sing" and then sat in the audience "drinking with strange men."

The court was sympathetic. To be sure, not all the concerts at Coney Island were of this type. Some were quite high class—"singers and musicians of the highest reputation"—and some audiences were as "reputable" as those at the Metropolitan Opera House. But the general reader, said the court, would not associate her with these high-class places. When they read the newspaper, they would naturally think of the "cheap and disreputable entertainments" at the western end of Coney Island. Thus the newspaper account was libel per se. It implied unchastity and tended to "disgrace the plaintiff and hold her up to ridicule and contempt." The newspaper story was calamitous for a "lady who had just taken up her residence among strangers" and who hoped to "win her way" into a higher social position.[44]

This last point reminds us that mobility was sometimes a double-edged sword. It was easy to run away from a bad reputation. Yet once in a while mobility made a reputation more fragile than in traditional society. Ida Gates had "taken up her residence among strangers"; she was not living among people who had known her, and her reputation, all their lives. This made the libel that much more serious. Presumably people who *knew* Ida Gates would know her as a respectable woman, not somebody plucked by a sugar daddy from a low and disreputable dance hall. But the strangers among whom she now lived would be less able to sift fact from fantasy. They would read the hints and sly remarks—"innuendos" in the jargon of the law—and think the worst of Ida Gates.

Women's defamation cases were about sexual behavior; men, on the other hand, tended to complain about lies that hurt them in their business life.[45] Was it slander per se to accuse a man of unchastity? The case material is fairly scanty. In one Indiana case (1849) a woman claimed that Robert Lumpkins, a young man (under age 21 and hence a minor), had impregnated his own sister.[46] Under Indiana law only open and notorious adultery or fornication was a crime; the "getting of an unmarried woman with child" was not in itself an indictable offense. The incest qualified as slander per se, but not the rest of it. The case was dismissed, however, on a technicality.[47] In an Alabama case from 1927 the defendant supposedly said that the plaintiff had "a mighty bad name," ran around with girls, and "made indecent proposals" to a woman. A local statute made this kind of accusation a "per se" violation for women, but the court refused to extend the rule to men. The court thought that the words did not "impute to plaintiff a state of moral delinquency" or subject him to "disgrace, ridicule, odium, or contempt."[48] The double standard was in full, luxuriant bloom.

SEDITIOUS LIBEL

Historically, seditious libel was an extremely important form of defamation.[49] In eighteenth-century England it was in fact a crime to criticize the king, the government, or the political authorities. Prosecutions were pursued as late as the early nineteenth century; two men were prosecuted in 1811 for publishing a criticism of the way the British army treated its soldiers—in particular, the practice of flogging.[50] In 1823 two men were prosecuted for hinting that the king, George IV, was insane, suffering under a "malady" of "an alarming description" and of "an hereditary description."[51] Truth was not a defense to an action for seditious libel. Blackstone, writing in the middle of the eighteenth century, thought that the law of seditious libel was fitting and proper, even necessary. After all, "blasphemous, immoral, treasonable, schismatical, seditious, or scandalous libels" tended to "create animosities" and to "disturb the public peace."[52] And in one of the nineteenth-century cases mentioned, one judge made the point clear: "Whether a publication be true or false is not the subject of inquiry in the trial . . . but whether it be a mischievous or innocent paper."[53]

Blackstone's statement was not limited to political libels—that is, attacks on government. "Malicious" defamation of "of any person, and especially a magistrate . . . in order to provoke him to wrath, or expose him to public hatred, contempt, and ridicule" was a criminal offense.[54] But the point of the laws was primarily to protect the regime. Seditious statements were intolerable—even if they spoke nothing but the truth. The colonies, too, had sedition laws—for example, Pennsylvania in 1684. The famous Zenger trial in 1735 turned on the propriety of punishing "sedition."[55] In the turbulent years before the American Revolution, sedition was a significant issue—the role of the press was a particular sticking point, as the Zenger trial illustrates. Royalist officers believed that the colonial press incited disaffection and promoted discontent. Governor Sir Francis Bernard of Massachusetts lambasted the *Boston Evening Post*: The "Devil himself" could not have put together "a greater Collection of imprudent virulent and seditious lies." But it was hard to get local citizens to indict for sedition.[56]

TRUTH OR FICTION

The governor spoke of seditious lies. But truth was irrelevant, as we have seen. Even if sedition was the gospel truth, it was still a crime. Criticism of the king, his ministers, and the regime itself was always suspect. Authoritarian governments hate criticism, and if it cuts close to the bone, so much the worse. In fact, if the charges were true, in many ways the situation would be worse than if the charges were false (and could be disproved). Thus the old maxim, "The greater the truth, the greater the libel."

Truth was not a complete defense, even in ordinary defamation cases. It became an absolute defense only in more democratic times, when seditious libel and its cluster of doctrines melted away under the influence of the ideology of free speech. The point of sedition laws was to protect the status quo, the regime—and the reputation of elite people, respectable people in general. The line between defaming the king or the president and defaming the best people was an indistinct one. Even in post-Revolutionary America, there were doubts whether truth could and should be a defense, especially in actions of criminal libel. At the Litchfield Law School, Judge Tapping Reeve, who lectured there, insisted in the early nineteenth century that truth was *not* a defense in criminal cases. This rule was "not out of regard to the person libelled" but out of concern for "the public peace."[57] In an 1805 Pennsylvania case Joseph Dennie was indicted for libel.[58] Dennie had published an attack on "democracy," a form of government (he said) that in France had "terminated in despotism," a form of government "radically contemptible and vicious." The judge, Yeates, charged the jury that it was no "infraction of the law to publish temperate investigations." But there was no excuse for publications "plainly accompanied with a criminal intent, deliberately designed to unloosen the social band of union, totally to unhinge the minds of the citizens, and to produce popular discontent." The jury, however, found the defendant not guilty.

In an interesting case, *Commonwealth v. Clap*, decided in Massachusetts in 1808,[59] William Clap, the defendant, was indicted for "making and publishing" a "malicious libel" against Caleb Hayward, an auctioneer. Clap posted a sign in "several public places" in Boston that said "Caleb Hayward is a liar, a scoundrel, a cheat, and a swindler. Don't pull this down." Chief Justice Parsons defined a libel as a "malicious publication . . . tending . . . to blacken . . . the reputation of one who is alive, and expose him to public hatred, contempt, or ridicule." Such libels were offensive, because they led to unrest or "acts of revenge." Truth was irrelevant. Clap wanted to bring in evidence to show that his charges were true, but the trial judge refused to accept this evidence. Chief Justice Parsons agreed, and Clap's conviction was upheld.[60]

The issue of truth as a defense was still a matter of debate in England in the early nineteenth century. As late as 1843 a Select Committee of the House of Lords, appointed to consider the law of defamation, thought that the law was "defective" in making truth an absolute defense. Committee members considered this undesirable both in civil and in criminal proceedings. Better for truth to be a defense only if the defendant proved that "it was for the Benefit of the Community that the Words should be spoken, or the alleged Libel written and published."[61] Committee members were worried about how to protect respectable people from attacks on their reputation. The Lord Chancellor put forth the following case: Suppose that a woman in "early Life," living in Cornwall, 16 or 17 years old, should have "a Bastard Child; she then is reclaimed, and becomes a respectable Person" and moves to another part of the country. Then, when she has become "Mother of a Family," some despicable cad, whom she refused to have sex with, threatens to reveal her secret and "publish" her "Shame." In this case, truth, "so far from being a Mitigation, would be a very great Aggravation."[62]

It is an interesting example. The truth in this case was that this respectable woman, early in her life, had violated the moral code. What the Lord Chancellor was eager to protect here was mobility and second chances—and the right of people in "respectable society" to cover up certain of their sins.

Committee members also did not like the distinction between libel and slander. A person could not win a case of slander—verbal defamation—unless the words were "injurious to reputation" or applied to a "Man in his Business" or accused him of having "an infectious Disease." Why, asked the committee, should a cobbler be able to sue if somebody says that he "is not skilful in mend-ing Shoes," but a "Woman of high Station and unspotted Character" should be unable to sue a man who dared to "impute" to her a "Want of Chastity" and in the "coarsest Terms." Similarly, if one imputed a "Want of Veracity or Courage" as to a "Gentleman of undoubted Honesty and Honour."[63] The tone of this passage is significant. The law fails in its duty if it protects a mere cobbler but fails to give full protection to men and women of "high Station." The gentlemen on the committee were intensely concerned with this precise issue. In their eyes people of high station were vulnerable to people of low station, who might blackmail them or who might write for scurrilous news-papers. Thus the problem of defamation had an important *public* dimension. Calumny against people of high station was a threat to the social structure. The law of defamation, at least potentially and if properly structured, could perform a valuable protective service for pillars of the community—and thus for the community itself.

Yet in civil cases the defense of truth had a powerful pull. It seemed clearly unfair to allow, say, damages for calling a man a horse thief if he *was* in fact a horse thief. Thus it is no surprise that Parliament did not follow the commit-tee's advice so far as civil cases were concerned. On the issue of female chastity, as we have seen, the law evolved in the course of the nineteenth century. In England, Parliament eventually acted. An 1891 law "relating to the Slander of Women" provided that spoken words that "impute unchastity or adultery to any woman or girl" were "actionable" without any showing of "special dam-age."[64] The same results, as I noted, were achieved in many of the states.

Criminal libel was a different beast. Under an English statute of 1843 truth was a defense *only* if "it was for the public benefit that the said matters charged should be published."[65] In criminal cases the old attitudes lingered much longer. The law continued to refuse absolute immunity to defamers who were telling the truth. As an American treatise published in 1888 put it, "seditious libel" was a libel whose "object and effect" were to "disturb the peace of society or the existence of government." Because of this, truth could not be an absolute defense, but prosecutions for this crime, the writer said, were "extremely rare" in the United States. The exception was the overheated period of the Alien and Sedition Acts (1798–1801).[66]

These famous—or infamous—laws were passed during the administration of John Adams. Under these laws it was a crime to spread "any false, scan-dalous and malicious" statements about the United States government or the president or Congress with the intention of fomenting "hatred" on the part of "the good people of the United States."[67] The law was wildly controversial from the start. It was the brainchild of the Federalist Party, and Jefferson and his followers considered it an abomination. Jefferson's administration promptly repealed the law.

The Federalists, for their part, believed that such laws were a necessity. As James Iredell put it, in a democracy political defamation is even more danger-ous than in a monarchy. A republic is more "dependent upon the good opin-ion of the people. . . . Take away from a republic the confidence of the people, and the whole fabric crumbles to dust."[68] Hence the country had the duty to protect its leaders from defamation—and not only scandalous lies but also "malicious" utterances, wild exaggerations, and the like.

Legally, was truth a defense under the Alien and Sedition Acts? Many of those who defended the statute claimed that it was. In fact, the statute said so: The defendant could offer "the truth of the matter" in his defense. But, as Norman Rosenberg has pointed out, this was theory; the practice was quite different. At least eighteen libel prosecutions were brought between 1789 and 1800; in only one case was the defendant acquitted, and in a number of cases the court simply refused to hear evidence of truth.[69] The goal of the law—protecting elites and officeholders against slander, calumny, and overheated rhetoric—practically ensured that this would be the case.

After the fall of the Alien and Sedition Acts, seditious libel ceased to matter in American law. Yet the criminal codes of some states still contained provisions against criminal libel. Indeed, Samuel Merrill, writing in 1888, thought that most libels that were "civilly actionable" were also "indictable . . . as crimes."[70] The law in Maine, for example, made it a crime to publish a "malicious defa-mation of a living person . . . tending to provoke him to wrath, expose him to public hatred, contempt or ridicule, or to deprive him of the benefits of public confidence and social intercourse." It was even an offense to libel a "deceased person" if the libel was "designed to blacken and vilify his memory" and if it tended to "scandalize and provoke his relatives and friends." For public offi-cers or candidates for office truth was a "complete justification," but for other people truth was not a "complete justification" where it appeared that the publication "originated in corrupt and malicious motives."[71] Similar language appeared in other statutes well into the twentieth century.[72] Truth was or was not a complete defense, depending on the statute. Under New Jersey law, as of the 1930s, it was a misdemeanor to send "any libelous statement . . . concerning any person or corporation" to a newspaper or magazine. For this crime a person could get up to two years in jail at hard labor. However, the statute applied only to statements "untrue in fact" and only if the newspaper actually published it.[73] In Minnesota, on the other hand, a libelous publication was "justified" only if it was true and "was published with good motives and for justifiable ends" and if it was "honestly made, in belief of its truth, and upon reasonable grounds for such belief" and consisted of "fair comments upon the conduct of a person in respect of public affairs."[74] The 1870 Constitution of the State of Illinois, as part of the Bill of Rights, provided that "in all trials for libel, both civil and criminal, the truth, when published with good motives and for justifiable ends, shall be a sufficient defense."[75]

Zechariah Chafee Jr., writing in 1947, thought that the point of these statutes was perhaps to "deter people from raking up old scandals against men who had long led blameless lives."[76] This sounds plausible. It lines up with the general theme of protecting elites who have slipped or who have something to hide—provided of course that the something is out of the past and is at least arguably forgivable. The statutes are interesting but probably not of any particular importance. I have looked at a fair number of police department reports from various periods and have never seen any listing of an arrest for criminal libel. It is possible, of course, that there were a few cases and that they began in some other way—for example, if a citizen swore out a criminal complaint.[77] One finds a certain number of reported cases. P. T. Barnum, in his autobiography, claimed to be a victim of the laws against criminal libel. Starting in 1831, Barnum published a newspaper, *The Herald of Freedom*, in Danbury, Connecticut. According to Barnum, he was on the receiving end of civil suits for libel and of no less than three criminal actions. Barnum's paper stated that a prominent man of Bethel had "been guilty of taking *usury* of an orphan boy." Barnum claimed that the statement was true and that he proved it, but "the greater the truth, the greater the libel," and he was ordered to pay a $100 fine and serve sixty days in jail.[78] Of course, anything Barnum says has to be taken with a grain of salt.

Truth was an issue, although somewhat obliquely, in a criminal libel case from the time of the Civil War. The plaintiff, Palmer, published a newspaper in Concord. The newspaper was opposed to the war. It published strongly worded doggerel and news accounts, flaying the Lincoln government, the conduct of Northern soldiers, and so on. One article mentioned "heart-sickening accounts" in Southern newspapers of "murders and robberies which individuals in Old Abe's Mob are perpetrating." An enraged mob of soldiers destroyed the plaintiff's printing materials in 1861.[79]

The actual case was a lawsuit by the publisher against the city of Concord for damages under a statute that made towns "liable to indemnify the owner" when a mob destroyed property. However, if "illegal or improper conduct" caused the destruction, the owner could not recover. This led the court to discuss whether an action for criminal libel could have been brought against Palmer, the publisher. If the answer was yes, then his conduct would have been both illegal and improper. Was Palmer guilty of criminal libel? It all depended, said the court. If Palmer had published his material to inform the public and perhaps to induce citizens to "use their influence with government to repress abuses" or to "stop the war or conduct it in a more humane manner," then his "end or motive was justifiable." But if Palmer had "no justifiable motive, inasmuch as the natural and inevitable tendency of the publication" was to "injure and degrade," then he was "guilty of libel even though the facts . . . were true."

Thus there was a lingering trace in cases and statutes of limitations on truth as a defense in defamation cases. Truth was a defense if the libel was nonmalicious and had been published in good faith and with clean hands and proper motives. In *Commonwealth v. Bonner* (1845), a Massachusetts case,[80] Bonner published a bitter attack on Oliver Brown in a Pittsfield newspaper. Brown, he said, ran a "groggery" and sold to "drunkards," even "while a daughter lay a corpse" in his house, "a victim of God's chastening rod upon your guilty drunkard-manufacturing head." He was indicted for libel. Bonner tried to prove that Brown was in fact guilty of selling liquor without a license. The jury found Bonner guilty. The legal question in the case was this: Who has the burden of proof to show that the libel "was published with good motives, and for justifiable ends," and what was the definition of "malice" under the statute?

Chief Justice Lemuel Shaw upheld the conviction. The defendant bore the burden of proof. He had to show that the charges were true and also that the publication was "with good motives, and for justifiable ends." As for malice, the words did not mean "malice in its popular sense," that is, "hatred and ill will," but only that the act was "done wilfully, unlawfully, and in violation of the just rights of another." Shaw's opinion was brief and gnomic. It does illustrate that the blazing and overwhelming power of truth as a defense in libel cases was a gradual growth. It triumphed first in civil cases but lagged behind in criminal cases. In such cases, after all, it was the *state* that brought the lawsuit; and in theory, the crime, like all crimes, was an action that injured the community as well as the particular victim. Here we see at least the vestigial survival of an old notion: To stir up trouble with wild charges was an offense against society. That these were wild charges against upstanding, respectable people was of course at least implicit. Nobody cared about wild charges against a Bowery bum or for that matter against a cocktail waitress.[81]

Earlier I mentioned honor and the dueling code. The duel was common in early nineteenth-century America; in fact, no less a figure than Alexander Hamilton was killed in a duel.[82] As I pointed out, the duel was more of an institution in the American South than in the North. It was part of a code of conduct for upper-class men—a code not too different from the codes of conduct for young swells in Germany and elsewhere. The states, both North and South, went to some pains to try to stamp out dueling. For example, a statute in Virginia originally passed in 1810 and commonly called the Anti-Dueling Act, made "actionable" all "words" that could be reasonably "construed as insults" and that "tend[ed] to violence and breach of the peace."[83] Nothing in the statute turned on whether the insults were based on fact. Apparently, truth was *not* meant to be a defense under the statute.[84] Under this law, if you called a man a horse thief, your words were actionable whether or not he *was* a horse thief. The statute was specifically aimed at dueling; and the point was to encourage defamation cases instead of duels. The Virginia statute was not unique. A statute in Mississippi had much the same language.[85]

Only a few cases under these statutes were reported. In these cases the truth of the words was not an issue. In an 1888 case Mr. Batchelder sent a letter to Cora Rolland, a married woman. He said in the letter that he would meet her at the post office at 5 o'clock "for a short interview," or if not, in some other places where she could "come with safety." Cora Rolland was scandalized; she went to meet him but secretly brought along an "officer," who "shadowed her" and arrested Batchelder in the act of making "advances" to her.[86] The lower court thought that Cora Rolland had no case and dismissed the action, but the Supreme Court of Virginia reversed: The complaint stated a cause of action, and the case should have gone to the jury; the letter "was an insulting proposal to a married woman . . . written to a woman of unimpeached honor and virtue." In a Mississippi case the words "What in the God damn hell are these infernal lies you have been circulating on me?" were held to be "insulting, and calculated to lead to violence and breach of the peace."[87] In these cases, however, the court more or less *assumed* that the words were unjustified. Cora was described as a "woman of . . . honor," although we are not told why the court was so sure of this.

When the defense of truth did come up in cases under these statutes, the court was troubled by the issue. In 1850 the Court of Appeals of Virginia in effect read the defense of truth into the statute.[88] The court began by explaining that the common law gave no remedy for words that were "merely vituperative, or insulting." Calling a man "a villain, cheat, rascal, liar, coward or ruffian" or charging a woman with "vulgarity, obscenity or incontinence" did not give rise to a lawsuit, so long as they affected only "general standing or reputation." The court also discussed the Virginia antidueling statute. To be sure, said the court, the statute does not *say* that truth is relevant, but it also does *not* expressly rule out evidence of truth "in mitigation of damages." Otherwise, the worse the scoundrel, the "higher . . . his claim of damages," and the "best members of society will be placed at the mercy of the worst." A scoundrel, after all, has no reputation in the first place. Why should he be able to squeeze money from somebody else by claiming that that person had damaged what he never had in the first place? The jury must be able to consider the whole picture; this included evidence that the plaintiff spoke nothing but the truth.[89]

Defamation is a complex area of law, and there is no point looking for smooth, transparent consistency in the way the law developed. We can see a slow but significant shift in emphasis—from a policy of protecting *only* people of high station to a more general concern with reputation, particularly commercial reputation. There was also a shift away from seditious libel. These shifts were perhaps more pronounced in the United States than in England. Defamation had a protective function in both countries, but the two countries had huge differences in class structure. These differences left at least some marks on the way the law developed. One marked trend in both countries was the triumph of *truth* as a defense. Yet its triumph was never complete. The burden of proof was on the defendant to show truth, and, in order to win, the defendant, as an English treatise put it, had to prove the truth of "*all* the *material* statements contained in the libel."[90] Zechariah Chafee Jr., writing in the 1940s, pointed out that truth, even when an absolute defense, might not "be worth much practically." The defendant has the burden of proof, and it can be hard to "establish the correctness of every item of [the] defamatory statement."[91]

Moreover, the structure of the law tended to favor and protect people higher up on the social scale. After all, it costs money to bring a lawsuit. And the rather skimpy evidence suggests that these higher-ups were, in fact, the people who brought libel cases. One study of libel litigation in the late nineteenth century found that 22 percent of plaintiffs were elected or appointed government officials, 32 percent were "public figures," businessmen, doctors, lawyers, or members of the clergy, and 12 percent were journalists. Not many of the plaintiffs won big damages, or any damages. Settlements were frequent, along with publication of retractions or corrections. What was wanted, perhaps, was vindication more than anything else.[92]

In Chapter 5 I take a closer look at the law of blackmail. For now, however, I would like to point to one irony, or anomaly, in the law. Suppose that I expose some crime or sin in a person's past and that he or she sues me for defamation of character. I can win my case by proving that I was right; that my statements were true. But suppose instead of shouting the secret from the rooftops, I make an agreement with the person; I promise to keep quiet—in exchange, however, for a fistful of money. In this case I may be guilty of a crime, the crime of blackmail. And this is so, even though my allegations are completely true. In fact, the allegation is usually true—if it is fabricated, it is harder to make a credible threat, harder to squeeze money out of the "victim." The law of blackmail, then, seems inconsistent, or discordant, with the law of defamation. Both, however, arise out of a system of protection of elites.

CHAPTER 4

THE VICTORIAN
COMPROMISE

Slippage and Control in the Moral Laws

REPUTATION depends on behavior, on living up to social standards; it means obeying the dictates of the moral code—or at least appearing to obey. In the nineteenth century it was generally agreed that government had a right to enforce that moral code. Every state had laws against various kinds of sexual misconduct. There were also laws against gambling, drunkenness, and obscenity. The United States, of course, was hardly alone in this regard.

As I said, an ideal of moderation underlay the moral, social, and legal codes. The virtuous man, the ideal man, was the moderate man. He worked hard, followed the rules, and avoided vice and sin. He was never guilty of overindulgence—gambling his money away or getting drunk. He kept tight rein on his sexual passions. Ideally, he married as a virgin and stayed faithful to his one and only wife.

In the "pantheon of nineteenth-century American social values," moderation was "almost synonymous with morality." Overdoing even normal, healthy things, such as eating and drinking, was offensive to body and soul. Moderation was more than etiquette; it was the pillar of a healthy life. People, it was believed, had only a "limited complement of nervous energy"; too much of anything, including too much "sensual pleasure," could prove to be extremely harmful.[1] The key to the good life—morally and physically—was the "mastery of impulse." This was a "lifelong struggle"; moreover, not every man was likely to come out on top.[2]

Sexual life was a particularly dangerous area. All sorts of texts, including medical texts, warned that masturbation had fearful consequences. Personal "abuse" could cause weakness, epilepsy, insanity, and almost every known disease or malfunction. Yet a study of college and seminary students published in 1902 revealed the awful truth: Most students had indulged in this terrible practice. The students—devout Christians on the whole—were asked to identify the severest temptation they had faced. Masturbation was the clear winner—132 out of 232 replies listed it. "Sexual intercourse," the runner-up, was a distant second: 66 recorded this as their worst temptation. What is more, 131 out of the 132 had "yielded" to the dread temptation of masturbation. One of the students, who was "weakened in mental power and vigor" by his habit, reported that "Sunday is the day when the devil does his best work along the line of masturbation. Fellows get together, tell stories which awaken these passions, and then the temptation is too strong."[3] Dr. J. Richardson Parke, writing as late as 1909, reported the view of "physiologists" that the "loss of one ounce of semen equals that of forty ounces of blood." His description of what happens to a child who indulges in "artificial eroticism" is positively hair-raising: The child "loses its rosy complexion, becomes pale or leaden in countenance; the eyes are sunken and dull . . . the mind is sluggish and indolent." The victim then "becomes vicious and irritable . . . and displays a tendency to sleep late in the morning." At this point "general health" begins to disintegrate: "The appetite fails, the tongue becomes coated, there is emaciation"; the poor soul ends up with "hopeless neurasthenia, or even imbecility or lunacy."[4] Masturbation was also a threat to normal sex life for men; according to one expert, their genitals might "shrink and become withered" or even decay to the point where they "disappeared into the abdomen."[5]

Even ordinary sex between husband and wife had to be carefully controlled and contained. As one scholar put it, the Christian gentleman "was an athlete of continence, not coitus"; he was "continuously testing his manliness in the fire of self-denial."[6] Elizabeth Blackwell, a pioneering woman physician, writing in 1894, recommended for men "healthy limitation of sexual secretion" in order to set free "a vast store of nervous force for . . . intellectual and practical pursuits." The "squandering of adult energy" had to be avoided at all costs.[7] Misery awaited people who had too much sex. According to one writer, twice a week was definitely excessive "for the majority of men, and will certainly lead to earlier than normal extinction of the sexual powers."[8] Men (and women) who tried to follow medical advice had to walk a fine line. After all, in the view of some doctors it was also dangerous to do without sex at all; too little as well as too much could be harmful. Because sex was "a natural and most powerful human force, there is risk of injury in permanently stifling it."[9] Yet, on the whole, the stronger need was repression. People had a duty to conquer their "animal" natures; and civilization itself, as Sigmund Freud would later preach, rested on self-control and the sublimation of instincts.

Moderation was more than a matter of private behavior. It was also the rule for society as a whole. In theory, the laws regulating morality expressed what we would now call zero tolerance. In an ideal society there would be, of course, *no* murders or rapes. Also, in an ideal society, as the nineteenth century conceived it, only married people would have sexual relations. These would be parceled out with care and would also be only of the approved and kosher variety. This was not just a rule of morality; it was also in essence a rule of law. The penal codes—overall, with interesting exceptions—swallowed whole the rules of traditional morality. In so doing, they expressed and affirmed the prevailing ideology, and they gave a strong message about where the outer boundaries of acceptable conduct lay.

A visitor from another galaxy who could read the penal code of a typical American state in the middle of the nineteenth century would learn that people were not supposed to steal, murder, rape, or burn down buildings and that they were also not supposed to have sex outside marriage. But if the visitor looked more carefully at the texts—and at the *behavior* of the legal system, at law in action, the visitor would get a somewhat different picture. Here the real goal of the living law was not zero tolerance at all but caution, moderation, and a screen of privacy. The careful reader of text and behavior would notice that the norms in fact tolerated certain deviations within certain limits. The law was like a man who uttered stern words with his fingers crossed behind his back.

Some aspects of the penal code would surely puzzle our visitor from outer space. Yes, there were rules that set firm standards and threatened to punish people who fell short. Yet *some* passages in the code seemed, strangely enough, to *protect* certain people when they broke the rules. These were provisions that shielded the reputation of people who, arguably, did not deserve to be shielded. Blackmail, which I discuss in Chapter 5, is an excellent example. The blackmailer knows a dirty secret about someone. He knows, let us say, that this banker, this pillar of the church, this leader of the community, once, long ago and in another place, fathered a bastard child. The blackmailer threatens to tell the truth unless the banker pays. Under many penal codes this would constitute a crime. Threatening to punish the blackmailer was no doubt supposed to deter him, but by the same token it protected the banker's guilty secret. Here, the law protects a "respectable" man who has broken the rules. And the people who benefit from blackmail laws are almost exclusively successful people. There is no point trying to squeeze money out of a pauper, or out of someone with no reputation to lose.

The same aim and ideology lay behind other provisions of law. The ultimate goal was social stability. Social stability, arguably, required turning a blind eye at times to certain violations at certain times by certain people. Respect for authority is the cornerstone of a stable society. Respect for authority has to mean respect for the *people* in authority—for the people with reputations, for the people who ought to command respect.

Nobody enunciated this theory of society and of social control quite so plainly, crassly, and overtly. In the days of seditious libel it was more explicit. Attacking the reputation and good name of the king was a crime—whether or not the king deserved a good reputation. Nineteenth-century law was not so blatant and extreme. But a weakened form of the notion was implicit in both form and substance of the law—and in the behavior of the law as well. The first two-thirds or so of the nineteenth century is the heyday of what I have called the Victorian compromise.[10] This compromise comes out most clearly in laws about sex and morality. These laws lost some of their absolute all-or-nothing quality. It is as if society—or most of society, at any rate—was aware that vice, crime, and sexual misconduct were never going to go away. Vice at least was tolerable, although only in small amounts and only if discreet and under a good deal of control. Hence a kind of double standard evolved. A prime example was the so-called red-light zone or district. These zones flourished in city after city. Houses of prostitution, gambling dens, and all sorts of vice were rampant in these districts. The law—and the police—winked at them and accepted them as part of urban life. True, a good deal of this acceptance was bought and paid for. Corruption and payoffs are a large part of the story. But even honest police and honest governments tolerated the idea of vice districts—on condition that vice stayed put in these districts and never ventured out beyond the borders. This double standard was the essence of the Victorian compromise. It stands in sharp contrast to the attitude and behavior in (say) Puritan Massachusetts Bay, in the colonial period, with its policy of zero tolerance toward vice and illegal sex.[11]

It is easy—probably too easy—to label the Victorian compromise as nothing more than hypocrisy. Powerful people ran the country and made up rules for themselves. They protected themselves from scandal through a network of laws and practices. If they were careful and if their sins were discreet, they were effectively immune from prosecution. They were also immune from serious loss of reputation. Hypocrisy, however, does not quite capture the (implicit) social theory behind the Victorian compromise. As I mentioned, the Victorian compromise was a little bit like laws against speeding today. Everybody violates these laws—at least sometimes and to some extent. Are these laws useless? Are they dead letters? Not at all. The police do arrest some speeders—the most blatant violators, on the whole. And the public, I imagine, strongly approves of speed limits, even though the same people who approve violate the law themselves from time to time. Society needs speed limits. If we removed the speed limits, some people might drive at wild, dangerous speeds. The living law of speed limits in fact embodies a rather subtle theory of social control.

The Victorian compromise had another point as well. It provided cover, protection, and immunity for elites who strayed from the straight and narrow path. In this regard it had a social function similar to the function of the law of blackmail. The reputation of respectable people was important for society as a whole. Any attack on that reputation of people—the elites, holders of public office, prominent members of the clergy, and so on—was, like seditious libel in the old days, a danger to the fabric of society, to the structure on which society rested.

Laws and norms performed this function by making a sharp distinction between the surface of the law and its dark underbelly. It was important to maintain purity and high ideals in the external, visible sphere, the *public* and official sphere. What went on underneath was another story. The dark under-belly was meant to be kept invisible. Its secrets should never be leached out into daylight—and should never be granted legitimacy. Society, then, had to police its surfaces and outer appearances rigorously. The reputation of men who governed, who set the tone and the example for the rest, was the reputation of society in general. And this reputation was based on *external* appearance, on outward behavior. It was, as it were, a kind of costume or dress.

Why, one might ask, should there be a taboo against nudity? What is wrong with the naked body? Every man, woman, and child has a body. But the respectable body was not the naked body but the body with clothing on it—enough to mask any hint of sexuality. Moreover, the clothing had a style and cut that were symbols of respectable behavior. The taboos against nudity were not, of course, invented in the Victorian period; they are part of the Judeo-Christian tradition. But the Victorian period carried the taboo to much more of an extreme. It was, in general, an age of incredible prudery—at least so it appeared. Any discussion of sex in the public press, in books, in any material other than medical treatises, was unthinkable. The mere mention of sex was outlawed, except in the most bowdlerized and euphemistic form. Books and pictures that crossed the boundaries were banned from sale. Sex was strictly a private affair. Decent people never talked about it. Sex was meant for the pri-vacy of the home. The home had a monopoly over legitimate forms of sexual behavior.[12] Sex and nudity were matters for the private, family sphere.

Not everybody subscribed to taboos against nudity. Indeed, particularly in Germany, there was a naturist and nudist movement in the late nineteenth century. It glorified the body as something pure and beautiful. But even this nudist movement insisted on conventional morality. Nudity was not erotic; healthy nakedness, in open air and in sunlight, had nothing to do with pruri-ence. Indeed, some advocates of nudism insisted on this point: Nudism was the antithesis of bawdiness. Male "lustfulness" was induced not by "nude women but those who were clad." In fact, "veiling the human body was said to whet the sexual appetite."[13]

Laws about sex and sexual behavior made up only a small part of the pe-nal code, a few pages at most of the typical state statute book. The laws on the books were enforced rather feebly, at least in some states. On the whole, not many people were arrested or tried for fornication, adultery, or sodomy, at least in most states.[14] In this sense the laws were only marginally important. But they carried a crucial message. The ferocious repression of any hint of sex or sexuality in public life, in literature, in the arts, together with these laws, suggests strongly that this repression was a key element of the system of social control.

We know, of course, that the Victorian surface was simply that: a surface. There was always of course, that dark underside, even in the high Victorian era. Not all men (or even women) lived up to the stern ideals of the code. Men drank, gambled, broke the Sabbath, and consorted with prostitutes. Not all women were chaste and obedient. Some of this sinning—probably most of it—was done in secret. *Open* violation of the code could have terrible consequences, especially for women. Men, of course, benefited from the well-known double standard; young men especially were easily forgiven if they sowed a few wild oats. Men had a tremendous interest in preserving the chastity of daughters, wives, and sisters. The chastity of sons, brothers, and husbands was somewhat secondary. But even for men and boys, in the middle class and above, it was always wise to be discreet.

For example, plenty of pornography was available, and plainly it had an eager audience. For the most part, however, it stayed hidden, below the surface, wrapped, so to speak, in plain brown paper. Some men, of course, got rich off pornography. But pornographers were constantly dancing and feinting to avoid the iron jaws of the law. Crackdowns and crusades against smut occurred. Pornography always found a way to reemerge after the storm. In New York City, for example, bookstores and bookstands in Manhattan in the 1850s did a brisk business selling such books as *The Lustful Turk* or *The Confessions of a Voluptuous Young Lady of High Rank* along with "indecent" plates and woodcuts.[15]

Prudery is a social phenomenon; hence it must have a social meaning and function. Clearly, official prudery served to wall off the private sphere from public scrutiny. It exiled sexual behavior to the home and to the underground. Prudery and public taboos had a great value for elite men. An interesting—but complicated—case in point is the legal and social treatment of domestic violence.

Scholars have suggested that the nineteenth century was insensitive to violence in the home. Wife beating was not exactly legal, but it is disputed whether the authorities paid much attention to this crime.[16] Nice people liked to think that violence was something only men from the lower classes, or black men, indulged in. Wife beating was a "brutish" and "uncivilized" practice, "confined to those social ranks where men were not alert to the sensitivity of others."[17] Many men no doubt felt that wife beating was forgivable, or at least understandable; a husband had to have the right to "chastise" his wife, so long as he did not overdo it. For the respectable classes the indifference of the law was simply another curtain drawn over the private life of the genteel.[18]

In one interesting case from North Carolina (1868), A. B. Rhodes was actually indicted for assault and battery on his wife, Elizabeth.[19] He struck her "three licks, with a switch about the size of one of his fingers . . . without any provocation except some words uttered by her and not recollected by the witness." Rhodes was acquitted; the trial judge thought he had a right to treat his wife this way. The state appealed on the legal question, Was there in fact a right to beat a wife? The high court agreed that this violence "would without question have constituted a battery" if the victim was not married to Rhodes. The courts were "loath" to intervene in "trivial complaints arising out of the domestic relations." The "evil of publicity would be greater than the evil involved in the trifles complained of." This sort of matter should be left to "family government." Bad tempers, family quarrels, and the like are evils, but worse evil would come from "raising the curtain, and exposing to public curiosity and criticism, the nursery and the bed chamber." In a case "coming up to us from a hovel, where neither delicacy of sentiment nor refinement of manners is appreciated or known," the "parties themselves" would be amazed if a court intervened. In the middle class, "where modesty and purity have their abode," people are at times not immune to the "mysteries of passion," but what could be more "harassing to them, or injurious to society, than to draw a crowd around their seclusion." For a case "from the higher ranks, where education and culture have so refined nature, that a look cuts like a knife, and a word strikes like a hammer . . . indignity is disgrace and exposure is ruin."

The Rhodes court held, in short, not that a husband has a right to "whip his wife" but that the courts would not interfere in "trifling cases" and would not "inflict upon society" the evil of "raising the curtain upon domestic privacy." The result of the case was not, perhaps, typical. Quite a few judges in the nineteenth century held that husbands did *not* have a right to beat their wives.[20] In some states prosecutions for wife beating were not uncommon. For example, in Philadelphia in the first half of the nineteenth century, women frequently went to court to complain about abusive husbands.[21] Many of these were probably "serious or repeat offenses."[22] It may well be that in most places the most likely cases to get to court concerned really egregious and revolting examples—for example, a wife beaten so badly that she died.[23] Carolyn Ramsey has argued that men who actually *killed* their wives were treated harshly indeed; her study of New York and Denver in the late nineteenth and early twentieth centuries found that men who killed their women often went to the gallows or were locked up for long periods; women who killed abusive men, on the other hand, often got off scot-free.[24]

Here, as is often the case, what happened in the real world is complicated and perhaps not easy to explain. The reality was probably as the *Rhodes* court expressed it: a kind of genteel cover-up. The case expressed the temper of the times in its emphasis on the value of privacy as a *protection* for respectable people. The poor woman, the woman in the lower class, had to tolerate blows. Men and women at the bottom of society had no reputation to lose. On the other hand, a little mild chastising was tolerated among the rich and the elite for exactly the opposite reason—their reputation was so precious and important that it had to be protected, even when it was not exactly deserved. But there were limits: A man who went so far as to kill could not expect the velvet curtain to protect him.

The women's movement, to be sure, never shared the cavalier attitude of some judges toward domestic violence. In England the Matrimonial Causes Act of 1878 gave magistrates power to grant separations in cases where the husband was beating the wife. Brutal husbands had become an issue in some English cities—Liverpool, for example. One area of this city earned for itself the dubious nickname of the Kicking District.[25] And at the end of the nineteenth century there were organized campaigns against wife beating in the United States. Nevada, for one, even brought back the whipping post for any "male person" who struck or tortured a woman; Maryland and a few other states followed suit.[26] But, just as the temperance movement emphasized the sins of the working-class male, here too the main focus was on violence at the bottom of the social order, certainly not the sins of the elites. But the Victorian compromise was only a *limited* protection. A man who went too far could lose the subtle privileges of caste and class.

THE DOUBLE STANDARD

I have stressed one general theme: how law and society protected the reputation of elites—or, to be more accurate, how law and society acted to tolerate elite behavior that deviated at least *somewhat* from official standards. Of course, this was always a matter of more or less. A "respectable" man shown to be a serial killer could hardly expect much tolerance and protection—compared to, say, a "respectable" man who occasionally committed sins of the flesh. Moreover, the standards for men and women were sharply different. As we will see, there were also ways to shield respectable women who had given in to temptation—for example, the action for breach of promise of marriage. For women, though, chastity was a huge element of virtue and respectability. For men this was much less the case.

The English Matrimonial Causes Act of 1857 was an unusually blatant example of the double standard.[27] Before this law divorce was essentially unavailable in England. Only Parliament could grant a divorce. Practically, then, only the nobility and the extremely rich could even think about getting a divorce. The new law shifted divorce from Parliament to the courts. But it did not by any means get rid of unfairness and class bias. Divorce after 1857 was still extremely expensive, totally out of reach of the average family. Moreover, the only courts that could grant a divorce sat in London. These obstacles in the path of divorce were deliberate. The English upper class had no intention of making divorce accessible to ordinary people.[28]

The text of the law made the double standard explicit. If the wife committed adultery, the husband had grounds for divorce. But what about the husband's adultery? That was grounds for divorce only if it was incestuous or if it was adultery coupled with bigamy, rape, sodomy, or bestiality or adultery together with extraordinary cruelty or with desertion for more than two years.[29] As one writer put it, if a husband could "summon up sufficient self-control to resist the temptation to copulate with his sister, his other wife or his cow" or curb the urge to rape, and sodomize, or to torture his wife, then he could "fornicate at his pleasure."[30] Traces of this kind of double standard crop up here and there in American law as well. Under the Louisiana Civil Code of 1825 (Articles 136 and 137), a man could get a legal separation if his wife committed adultery; she, however, could get a legal separation only if her husband was outrageous enough to keep his "concubine" in their "common dwelling." Criminal law in some states also distinguished between his and her adultery. For example, in Minnesota a married woman who had sex with a man "other than her husband, whether married or not," had committed the crime of adultery. But a married *man* was criminally liable only if he had sex with a married woman.[31] In other words, for a man sex with a prostitute—or a single woman—was not criminal adultery at all. The effect of such laws was to excuse a man's adultery, except in certain blatant and offensive cases. Notably, these were cases where he cuckolded another married man.

For the most part the double standard was taken for granted. Virtue for respectable women was a defining, essential trait. Only a virtuous woman could compete in the marriage market, at least in the middle class. One justification for the double standard was the belief that men and women had different sexual needs. Men absolutely *had* to have sex, or, at any rate, had more trouble controlling their raging desires.[32] Women, on the other hand, were supposed to be passive and uninterested. No doubt, many men *did* control their desires; they were celibate before marriage and faithful afterward. Yet just as surely, many men did not. They found sexual outlets—with prostitutes or with women who were something less than nice. The double standard protected and excused these men by and large.

PASSING

Another way of putting the general point is that law (and society) protected two classes of people: the truly virtuous and those who *seemed* truly virtuous. The seemingly virtuous were not protected entirely, of course. But the law put a shield around them, a protective wall—through institutions of privacy, through rules against blackmail, or by virtue of the Victorian compromise. The system protected social and geographic mobility; it protected the right to a fresh start in life. It closed its eyes to at least *some* youthful indiscretions—and some not so youthful indiscretions. Moderation in behavior and outward respectability were key elements of the Victorian system. To some extent, then, the legal system and the social system threw up ramparts of protection for the benefit of men who were passing for respectable.

I use the word passing deliberately. The word also refers to a specific social phenomenon, which deserves at least a mention here.[33] In the United States, with its rigid racial hierarchy, a "Negro" was anyone who had "Negro" blood.

How much of this blood it took to turn one into a "Negro" was a question each state answered in its own way. In some states at some point in time, *any* amount of "Negro" blood, no matter how small, made you a nonwhite.[34] This meant that some "Negroes" in the United States had blond hair and blue eyes and looked for all the world as if they were white (which indeed they were, biologically). Because slave owners could and did have sex with their slaves in the days of slavery, every major plantation in the South came to have light-skinned slaves—and sometimes *very* light-skinned slaves. The plot of Mark Twain's novel *Pudd'nhead Wilson* hinges on this fact. Two babies—a slave baby and the master's baby—are born at the same time and are then secretly exchanged. The slave child is raised as a white man, the master's baby as a slave. Of course, this would make no sense unless the slave baby had been so light-skinned that it could reasonably "pass" for white.

After the end of slavery, people who looked like the slave in Twain's novel could pass much more easily. Of course, in order to do this, they had to leave their home community; at home everybody was likely to know their secret. It is impossible to tell how many "black" people did this. No doubt quite a few. One quite remarkable case concerned the Healy family. They were the children of Michael Healy, an Irish immigrant, and a slave woman (probably herself of mixed blood). The children were technically slaves when they were born. But they could and did pass for white. Indeed, the sons became prominent figures in society—they occupied roles that would have been totally out of bounds for them if the truth had been known. One son, Patrick Healy, a Jesuit priest, was named president of Georgetown University in 1873; another son was chosen Bishop of Portland, Maine; and another son rose to the rank of captain in the Coast Guard.[35]

A San Francisco lawyer, Ernest J. Torregano, was another man who successfully passed for white. The secret came out after his death in a court battle over his estate.[36] Torregano was born in New Orleans in 1882 as a "member of a fairly large Negro family." He married a black woman in 1902 or 1903 and produced a daughter. Torregano took a job as a railroad porter on a line that traveled between New Orleans and San Francisco. Later, he settled in San Francisco, studied law, and "commenced to pass for white." He had two addresses in the city—one for his white identity and one for receiving mail from his family in New Orleans. In 1915 his mother visited him and told him that his wife and daughter were dead. In fact they were very much alive. Why she did this is unclear. Probably she wanted to help her son keep his white identity without the burden of a black family. The mother went back to New Orleans and told another lie to the wife and daughter: She said that Torregano was dead. This interracial soap opera—one could imagine it as a movie—ultimately produced a battle over Ernest's estate when the daughter discovered who her father was and claimed her rights to the estate.[37]

Law and custom made it extremely important to pin the right label—white or black—on people whose racial identity was contested or confused. Ernest Torregano's career as a lawyer would have suffered greatly if his clients had realized who he was, that he was black, at least in the eyes of society. Racial identification could be quite problematic at times. A number of notable trials turned on the issue: Is she or isn't she (or he) white? Physical appearance was not a safe guide. Sometimes it was necessary to claw through the records, to see whether there was or was not some grandmother or great-grandfather with the taint of blackness. *Reputation* in the community was valuable evidence in court. Somebody who associated with white people and behaved as though white was assumed to be white. In one Louisiana case, for example, Stephen Boullemet insisted that "he had lived his life as a white man, that he had been accepted into white society, and that his mother was reputed to be, if not white, then Indian, but certainly not 'colored.'" One witness testified that Boullemet was "received in good circles of society as a white man." Other witnesses, however, gave evidence that seemed to contradict this.[38] In a Georgia case, decided in 1864, the issue (ownership of certain slaves) turned on whether or not the members of the Nunez family—father James and son Joseph—were black or white. James, according to some witnesses, was "never regarded as having negro blood"; he was "of dark complexion, with straight dark or black hair, which he wore in plaits, tied at the end with ribbons"; his "nose was not flat, or his lips thick, or hair kinky." He did not "associate with negroes," and he was a "graceful dancer, and attended the balls, dances and social gatherings from which negroes were excluded."

The other side insisted that James was "a mulatto" and was "so regarded" and that Joseph "was of mixed blood," that he "ate, associated and slept with negroes" and did not "eat at the same tables or sleep in the same beds with white folks," and that he "always deemed himself a mulatto." The judge,

Lumpkin (a colorful character in his own right) remarked that mistakes about "blood" occurred "daily in our midst. A mistress and her maid recently received Episcopal confirmation together, kneeling side by side at the same altar, boarding at the same hotel, where the latter was received and treated as a white woman by the inn-keeper and his female guests"; the woman "turned out to be a mulatto," at which point she was "promptly hurled from her position of social equality." "Which of us," Lumpkin asked, "has not narrowly escaped petting one of the pretty little mulattoes belonging to our neighbors as one of the family?"[39]

Whiteness or blackness was an issue in the famous Rhinelander case in 1925.[40] Alice Beatrice Jones, who came from a humble background, married Leonard Rhinelander in 1924. His family was extremely rich. The marriage soon went sour. Under family pressure Leonard tried to get the marriage annulled. His grounds? Alice was a black woman, he claimed; and when he married her, he had been unaware of this fact. Was Alice white or black? This was hotly contested. The dramatic trial was headline news. Alice's mother was surely white, but there was a question about her father. At one point in the trial the jury was allowed to look at Alice's body, naked from the waist up, so they could judge for themselves. In the end, Leonard did not get his annulment. Was Alice "colored"? The jury said yes. But did Leonard marry her thinking she was white? Here the answer was no, and hence Leonard lost the case.

Alice Jones Rhinelander *could* have passed; perhaps she did, perhaps she didn't. The scandal in the case was not just race but class. She was a nobody, marrying into millions—a classic form of mobility for women then and now. Such marriages were possible in the United States—more so than in less mobile, more rigid societies. Mobility also made passing possible. Society oppressed and discriminated against African Americans; they were shut out of white society almost entirely; jobs and opportunities were denied to them. Hence blacks who passed were not just pinning a different label on themselves; they were also, like Ernest Torregano, opening a door to respectable middle-class society.[41] As I have pointed out, in the nineteenth century countless people were passing in one form or another. Lady Audley was passing; the victims of blackmail were passing; confidence men were passing; churchgoers who went to a brothel when no one was looking were passing. Conditions of life in the nineteenth century created a breach in a classic wall, once tight and impregnable; and many men (and some women) dashed eagerly through. Passing, in other words, was more than a racial phenomenon. It was a phenomenon of a mobile society and a society of second chances. It was never legitimate to pass for white. There would be no mercy for a person unmasked as a "Negro." But it is interesting that the *tests* for whiteness were so often behavioral—that they so often turned on surfaces, on respectable behavior. Just as some men could be forgiven for youthful sins and protected in a new and respectable life, so too was it possible for some light-skinned men and women to slip free of the brutal and unforgiving system of race.

VICTIMLESS CRIMES

The penal codes of the nineteenth century, as I have said, reflected the dominant code of morality in its rules about sexual behavior and other "victimless" crimes. In the colonial period, particularly in the seventeenth century, the laws against victimless crimes were taken quite seriously. In fact, it is anachronistic to talk about victimless crimes in, say, Massachusetts Bay. So far as the leaders of the colony were concerned, fornication, adultery, and sodomy were not victimless at all. On the contrary; they were acts that threatened the whole community. God would judge and condemn a sinful community just as he judged Sodom and Gomorrah, the wicked cities of the plain. No crime was more commonly punished in the colonial records of Massachusetts Bay than fornication. In hundreds of cases, perhaps thousands, unmarried men and women were whipped, fined, or put in the stocks for having sex. Some were forced or persuaded to get married.[42] The authorities were even zealous in trying to ferret out whether married couples had had the audacity to have sex before marriage. For example, in Essex County, Massachusetts, in 1662, Hugh Joans and his wife "were presented for suspicion of fornication before marriage." The suspicion came about when the wife was "delivered of a perfect child," that is, a full-term child, some months after the marriage.[43]

By the nineteenth century—and perhaps even earlier—the steam had gone out of this particular engine. The evidence is patchy, to be sure; but American society had lost much of its zest for prosecuting and punishing these sexual crimes. In many states the formal law was reconstituted in an interesting way. Some states changed the legal definition of adultery. Now the crime was not simply adultery but only "open and notorious" adultery.[44] That is, secret, occasional, clandestine adultery was no longer against the law. The crime consisted not so much in breaking the rules as in doing it in such a way as to offend the community or by rubbing people's noses in the fact.

Some states also tinkered with the laws about fornication. In Florida, for example, under an 1868 law, ordinary fornicators could get a maximum of three months in jail. But the punishment for what we might call *flagrant* fornication was much more severe. If a man and woman, "not being married to each other," were so brazen as to "lewdly and lasciviously associate and cohabit together," they could receive up to two years in state prison.[45] Adultery was also a crime under Florida law, but the adultery statute was amended in 1874 to apply only to those who lived "in an open state of adultery."[46]

This theme—this distinction between secret sin and open sin—echoes in the laws of quite a few American states.[47] The case law moved in the same direction. In one Florida case, for example, a man and a woman were indicted for lewd and lascivious cohabiting. The two had rented a house together (although there were other people living there as well). But there was no proof that they lived together "as if the conjugal relation existed between them." An appeals court reversed the conviction. "The object of the statute," said the court, was to "prohibit the public scandal and disgrace," to "prevent . . . evil and indecent" behavior, with its "tendency to corrupt public morals. Proof of occasional acts of incontinency will not of themselves sustain the charge."[48]

This was no isolated holding. In an Indiana case (1840) the court held that "occasional illicit intercourse" between a man and a woman was simply not a crime under local law.[49] In a Texas case (1872) the evidence showed that the defendants "had carnal intercourse with each other as many as half a dozen times," but they "did not live together in any legal sense." The man made "occasional and stolen" visits to "his mistress." The appeals court overturned his conviction.[50] Similarly, in a Missouri case (1892) the ex-husband of one of the defendants, suspecting that she was carrying on with his own brother, "climbed up on the outside of the house, which was a log house, to the height of two or three logs from the ground, and looked through an aperture or hole in the chinking." He "saw defendants on the bed together in the act of adultery." The state statute used the words "open and notorious." Here at best there was "secret adultery," which was not against the law.[51]

Statutes and case law, then, turned the eye of the criminal justice system away from the occasional sinner. Sporadic illicit sex between social equals, even unmarried ones, was not a crime so long as the couple kept things decent and quiet. No one's reputation was at stake (legally at least) so long as they observed the proprieties. These statutes were, in a way, also privacy statutes. The Missouri case makes this quite clear. Because the law punished only "open and notorious" behavior, there was (in theory at least) less incentive to snoop, peek through keyholes, eavesdrop, and otherwise invade the privacy of sinners.

Law defines behavior as criminal because somehow the behavior seems to threaten society. When the conception of threat changes, then so does the way the crime is defined. The threat from adultery was a threat to official norms. Society in the nineteenth century seemed less worried than before about vengeance from an all-seeing God. The new norm also tended to protect the reputation of sinners, especially men sinners, who indulged in occasional and sporadic adultery or fornication. Technically, a man who went to a prostitute was committing fornication, but he was certainly not cohabiting with her in a lewd and lascivious way. In England in the nineteenth century rules about sexual behavior were framed in such a way as to protect the upper class, particularly upper-class men (the terms of the 1857 divorce law make this clear). In the United States class divisions were real but subtle, and protection extended farther down the line; it covered the ordinary bourgeoisie, the respectable middle class. There was a double standard—in fact, two double standards: One drew a line between men and women; the other drew a line between pillars of society and the rest of the population.

The laws about fornication and adultery, then, show the Victorian compromise at work. The same is true of laws relating to prostitution, whorehouses, and vice in general. Prostitution and vice were almost universally vilified, but they also thrived and were (unofficially) tolerated. I deal with this subject in more detail in Chapter 6.

In this chapter I have tried to show that laws against immoral behavior in the nineteenth century had a dual purpose. The two purposes seemed in a way contradictory. Law and custom enforced and upheld the code of traditional morality—no question. The penal codes were explicit on this score. The state thought that it had a duty to regulate on matters of sex, vice, and personal habits (getting drunk, gambling). It reinforced traditional norms of respectability and religion, for example, through Sunday laws. On the other hand, the law also quite clearly interposed itself to *protect* the reputation and station in life of at least some of the people who violated that code. The nineteenth-century laws about fornication and adultery were one particularly striking example. We will soon see others.

CHAPTER 5

THE ANATOMY
OF BLACKMAIL

B LACKMAIL IS NOT a particularly common crime, but it has piqued the interest of a number of scholars. They have produced something of a literature on the subject. *Blackmail*, as a term, has a single core meaning. It is the act of trying to extort money from a "victim" by threatening exposure. The blackmailer says he will tell the world or the police or a spouse about some embarrassing or disgraceful secret in the victim's past. Many state penal codes and the penal codes of many countries make blackmail in this sense a crime. Whether or not it is technically a crime, however, blackmail is considered by almost everybody to be a despicable act. Society condemns the blackmailer as low, loathsome, and unscrupulous.

Some scholars find this situation puzzling. Some even wonder why blackmail should be a crime at all. "No one," according to James Lindgren, has ever "figured out why it ought to be illegal."[1] Or, as another scholar asked, How is blackmail "different from an ordinary bargain?"[2] If I know something about you, something that happened long ago, and if you want me to keep quiet, why shouldn't you be able to buy that silence? Why isn't my silence a commodity you can legally buy? There are those who scratch their head and decide that there is no sensible answer. To these scholars the whole concept of blackmail makes no sense.[3] There should be no such crime on the books.

In 1997 a young woman named Autumn Jackson was accused of trying to extort money from the comedian Bill Cosby. Cosby, she claimed, was her father. She demanded payment; otherwise, she said, she would tell her story to the world. She was prosecuted for this offense. But why should this be a crime, asked Michael D. Rips in the *New York Times*? How can two "legal rights" add up to a "wrong"? She had the right to ask Cosby for money. She also had the right to sell her story to the press. In what way, then, was her demand a criminal act?[4]

Why, indeed, do we punish blackmail? One thing is clear: Laws, especially laws that are common and widespread, always make *some* sort of sense. That is, there has to be something behind them, some reason, some social pressure, some motive. Laws on the books are senseless only if measured by some outside standard—efficiency, for example, or justice or due process. The legislatures that passed these laws, though, obviously believed that there was a need for them, a justification. The courts that have construed these laws and the public at large all seem to agree that blackmail is an evil act. In fact, a powerful argument (as we will see) against other doctrines or laws—breach of promise, for example—has been that they encourage blackmail.[5] Almost nobody has a kind word for the blackmailer. If silence is a commodity, then in this case it is an unpopular one. Some people defend buying and selling drugs and buying and selling sex, but buying a blackmailer's silence has few defenders.

To be sure, blackmail is a dangerous act—dangerous to the victim but also to the blackmailer. Blackmail tempts the victim to strike back at his tormentor. Hence blackmail is a staple of countless mystery and detective novels. To take one example out of many, in Agatha Christie's *Death in the Clouds*, Madame Giselle, who makes a living through blackmail, dies mysteriously on an airplane, killed by a poison dart.[6] In mysteries hardly any motive for murder is more common than the desire to get out of the blackmailer's clutches.

Lawyers and other scholars have tried to solve the puzzle of blackmail, searching for some economic or normative rationale for blackmail laws—with more or less success.[7] James Lindgren sees the solution in the triangular nature of blackmail. Blackmail is not just a matter of a blackmailer and a victim; there is also an injured third party. The blackmailer demands money in exchange for "suppressing the actual or potential interests of others."[8] If I know that a man is having an affair and I threaten to tell his wife unless he pays me, my behavior also has an impact on the wife. Scott Altman has another take on the matter: Blackmail victims are "particularly vulnerable"; they "can be driven to irrational or criminal behavior." The blackmailer never lets go. You are helpless once he has you in his grip. The first payment is only the beginning. You will have to pay and pay and pay.[9] Silence is not something you can buy once and for all. Thus, like the drug pusher, the blackmailer can and does destroy the life of his victim. He is a cruel and pitiless criminal. He "never relents—once a victim, always a victim."[10] Blackmail can "enslave." Secrecy, as Kim Scheppele pointed out, "makes individual autonomy possible," and sharing secrets can create "bonds of solidarity." But if another person "knows one's secrets," then this may "make it near impossible to reestablish one's independence." It is under these circumstances that the "extreme case of blackmail" results in enslavement.[11] Ken Levy thinks that blackmail should be a crime for the same reason that harassment and stalking are crimes. They "involve the reasonable likelihood, and usually the intent, of putting the victim into a state of especially great fear and anxiety."[12] Ronald Coase points out that the "victim, once he succumbs to the blackmailer, remains in his grip for an indefinite period." Blackmail is "moral murder."[13] Sentencing a blackmailer in 1930, an English judge remarked that the defendant had "pleaded guilty to one of the most terrible crimes that could be committed."[14] Other quotes from other judges could make the same point. The blackmailer evokes an almost pathological horror.

The ordinary citizen, I would guess, does not see blackmail as much of a puzzle. To begin with, blackmailers are extremely unsavory people. Their behavior violates well-recognized social norms. Blackmail is both dishonorable and disreputable. Yet it is also *criminal*. Not everything that violates social norms gets the label of criminality. Snitching, which is in some ways the opposite of blackmail, is also widely condemned. Among many social groups, in fact, snitching is worse than blackmail. And it can also be lethal; a snitch inside a prison has reason to fear for his life (I return to this point at the end of this chapter). Again, although blackmail may be despicable behavior, so is stealing a person's money or picking his pocket. Yet blackmail has, at times, evoked a vehemence that the pickpocket never does.

None of the explanations of the blackmail puzzle seem completely convincing. In a society that exalts freedom of speech and freedom of contract and bargaining, even sharp and relentless bargaining, why *do* we have laws against blackmail? Why is the blackmailer treated with such hatred and disdain? And what about the discrepancy, which I noted earlier, between defamation and blackmail? By the end of the nineteenth century truth was almost always a complete defense in defamation cases. In cases of blackmail, however, truth was no defense at all. The law had abandoned the maxim "the greater the truth, the greater the libel." But the greater the truth, the more awful the blackmail.

One approach is to ask the question, What social function do blackmail laws serve, and why were they passed in the first place? The key to the puzzle of blackmail surely lies in its history and its social meaning. To these I now turn.[15]

BLACKMAIL DEFINED

But first, a matter of terminology. Blackmail is closely related to extortion, and the two crimes are often combined in a single statute. The California Penal Code, for example, does not use the word *blackmail*; what we would call blackmail is included in code provisions directed against extortion.[16] But there is an important distinction between the two forms of behavior. Extortion is a much less problematic crime. If I threaten to break a man's kneecaps unless he comes up with a wad of cash, there is no puzzle to be solved. Violence and the threat of violence are criminal acts in themselves. The word *blackmail*, in fact, originally referred to this kind of extortion. Newspapers and other sources often muddy the waters by calling shakedowns and other forms of extortion blackmail. In 1881 the *New York Times* described a "black-mailing plot" against a merchant. The blackmailer sent a letter (in German) to a merchant, which the merchant received at his place of business. The letter said that the merchant's life and the lives of his family members were in danger. The price of safety was $500. This "clumsy" plot was easily foiled.[17] The victim of another "blackmail" plot in the same year was the governor of Connecticut, Hobart Bigelow, who received a message telling him he would die if he failed to pay up.[18]

The California statute defines extortion as the "obtaining of property from another, with his consent . . . induced by a wrongful use of force and fear." This fear can be fear of force, but it is also within the statute to threaten to accuse a person or a member of his family of a crime or to "expose, or to impute to him . . . any deformity, disgrace or crime" or to "expose any secret affecting him." It is this sort of threat, of course, that we commonly call blackmail. The current statute in Oklahoma talks about accusing or threatening to accuse a person of "conduct which would tend to degrade and disgrace the person" or exposing or threatening to expose "any fact, report or information" that would subject the victim to the "ridicule or contempt of society" unless the victim disgorged some cash.[19] The Minnesota statute, as of the 1920s, made it a "gross misdemeanor" to "threaten another with the publication of a libel concerning the latter or his spouse, parent, child, or other member of his family"; also, every person who "offers to prevent the publication of a libel upon another person on condition of the payment of . . . money or other valuable consideration" is guilty of the same misdemeanor.[20]

The Oxford Dictionary does not trace the modern sense of the word back farther than the nineteenth century. The crime itself—and certainly the behavior—is a good deal older. In particular, in the eighteenth century it was widely believed in England that evil women accused men falsely of rape in order to squeeze them for money.[21] No doubt the accusation was not always false.

A few intriguing English cases from the eighteenth century involve acts that we would definitely now call blackmail, although the reports did not use that word. In these cases the blackmailer threatened to accuse a man of homosexual behavior. In a case from 1776 the defendant was a man named Thomas Jones.[22] His accuser, Mitchel Newman, a man of "extraordinary good character," had gone to "the upper gallery of Covent-garden Play-house." The place was crowded, and Newman (according to his story) inadvertently "touched the prisoner's breeches." Jones followed him out, went into a "public-house" with him, accused him of taking "liberties," and demanded money, grabbing him and asking, "What money have you?" and "How much can you give me?" In the end, Newman paid some 40 pounds. Jones was tried for "highway robbery" and convicted. Calling this behavior "highway robbery" was something of a stretch, of course. But the court was willing to make the stretch. The "money had been obtained in a fraudulent way, and under a false pretense." This "pretense" was "of a very alarming nature," and there was "sufficient force" to "constitute the offence of robbery."

The trial of Daniel Hickman, a "sentinel on guard in Saint James's Palace," was almost contemporaneous and was quite similar.[23] The prosecuting witness was a servant who had an apartment in the palace. The two men had "bread and cheese and ale" in the servant's apartment. Hickman, about two weeks later, accosted the servant and said, "I have come for satisfaction . . . you are a Sodomite"; he threatened to "fetch a serjeant and a file of men, and take you before a Justice." The sentinel gave Hickman money, "under an idea of preserving his character from reproach." Here too the blackmailer, Hickman, was convicted of robbery: "A threat to accuse a man of having committed the greatest of all crimes, is, as in the present case, a sufficient force to constitute the crime of robbery by putting in fear."

The English courts themselves were aware that these cases were, in legal terms, somewhat anomalous.[24] Threats accusing a man of "sodomitical practices" so horrified the judges that they were willing to expand the concept of robbery or highway robbery almost beyond recognition. The theme of sexual blackmail has been something of a constant in the legal history of English blackmail.[25] Sexual blackmail was the historic heart of the crime. A series of laws in the first half of the nineteenth century followed the early cases in labeling threats to accuse a man of an infamous crime as a kind of attempted robbery.[26] In the early cases the courts assumed that the accusations were groundless, or perhaps they did not care. As one writer put it, "The truth or falsity of the allegations . . . and the success or otherwise of the threats" were simply not "at issue in court."[27] The court regarded this kind of blackmail as particularly insidious and dangerous and as a threat to society.

In the United States in the nineteenth century, however, criminal law became explicit and systematic in defining the crime as we think of it today, that is, as (pure) blackmail—buying silence about some guilty secret. In 1817 Georgia enacted one of the first statutes that approaches the modern meaning. This law made it a crime to "send or deliver any letter or writing, threatening to accuse another person of a crime, with intent to extort money, goods [or] chattels."[28]

Note that this statute says nothing about whether the accusation is true or not. In any event an 1827 Illinois statute went a step further. This law made it illegal to "send or deliver any letter, or writing, threatening to accuse another of a crime or misdemeanor, or of exposing and publishing any of his or her infirmities or failings, with intent to extort" and so on.[29] An 1835 Massachusetts statute was even broader. Under this statute blackmail no longer required a "letter or writing"; verbal threats would do.

The English case law is earlier, but in the United States it appears that blackmail became a formal part of the penal code earlier than in England. In the United States about half of the states eventually made blackmail in the purest sense a crime. That is, blackmail covered not only threats to expose the victim's actual crimes but also infirmities, immoral conduct, or other matters that would lay the victim open to ridicule or disgrace in society.[30] The California statute has already been mentioned. The federal statute has a narrower scope. It punishes those who demand money "under a threat of informing, or as a consideration for not informing, against any violation of the law of the United States."[31] In English law the Theft Act of 1968 makes it a crime for a person to make "any unwarranted demand with menaces" for the purpose of gaining something for himself.[32]

Blackmail is by no means solely an Anglo-American crime. The penal codes of many countries also criminalize blackmail. The Spanish Criminal Code of 1995 makes it a crime to demand money "under the threat to reveal . . . facts about [someone's] private life or family relations that are not known publicly, and which could affect his reputation, credit, or interests."[33] The French Penal Code also punishes blackmail (*chantage*) and indeed with a heavy prison sentence.[34]

WHO ARE THE BLACKMAILERS?

Blackmail, by its very nature, tends to be cloaked in shadows. How much blackmail goes on and who the victims are, no one can really tell. Reported—published—cases are not particularly common. They provide little indication of how common the practice has been. Successful blackmail leaves no trace behind. The last thing a victim wants is publicity. Blackmail laws, if actively enforced, would paradoxically defeat the purpose of the laws, because the whole world would know the guilty secret. The theory has to be that blackmail laws have a deterrent effect. Otherwise, they would make no sense.

Scattered newspaper accounts suggest that blackmail is at least a bit more common than the small number of reported cases might suggest. It is not easy to say *who* the blackmailers are or what the typical victim is trying to hide. In England, as we saw, the earliest cases were about accusations of "sodomitical tendencies." We do not find cases of "heterosexual blackmail" in England until rather late in the nineteenth century. Angus McLaren, who carefully

explored the history of English sexual blackmail, thought that the "courts assumed that only the threat of a heinous crime such as sodomy would intimidate
the average man."[35] "Sodomitic tendencies" and behavior were, throughout
the nineteenth century and well into the twentieth century, one of the major
themes of blackmail trials and blackmail scandals. A well-founded accusation of "perversion" could, after all, wreck a man's life and career. The trial of
Oscar Wilde, of course, provides us with a striking and famous example. And
sodomy was a serious crime in its own right.

Blackmail, in general, seemed to have a strange fascination for the English
in the nineteenth century. It was a surprisingly common theme in English literature.[36] The British courts and authorities, according to McLaren's account,
were not just severe toward blackmailers; they also took great care to protect
the reputation of the victims. Most reported cases of blackmail with accusations of homosexual conduct took place across class lines. The victim was usually much richer and of a higher social class than the blackmailer. Blackmail
may have been fairly common in England in the nineteenth century, but the
"blackmailer who confronted a social superior faced the problem that a com-
bination of wealth and respectability usually guaranteed that the weight of the
law was behind gentility."[37] The press showed the same tendency to protect
the victim and his privacy. An article in the *London Times* in 1931, describing a blackmail trial, clearly named the defendants—Llewellyn Winthorpe
Kendrick, "a schoolmaster," and William Corbett Smith, "hairdresser"—but
referred to the victim only as "Mr. X." The blackmailers had possession of
certain embarrassing "photographic negatives." In 1928 Mr. X had been in a
place where "some bathing was going on"; two photographs were taken that
were "very indelicate, if not of an indecent nature."[38] The judge, summing up
the case, referred to a "universal rule of practice" for judges to suppress the
victim's name. "Otherwise, people might be afraid of publicity." The victim
was "a gentleman in society."[39] The maximum sentence, said the judge, "was
penal servitude for life, because the offence of blackmail was only next to murder in its gravity."[40] For various reasons, however, he graciously allowed a lesser
sentence: five years for one of the blackmailers, four years for the other.

We are not told what the "indelicate" photographs really showed. And
not one word of criticism was spoken against Mr. X, despite his questionable
behavior. In cases in which the victim was accused of sodomy, courts and the

press tended to assume that the threats were groundless. No doubt this was sometimes the case. Sometimes, however, the authorities did not seem to care very much whether they *were* groundless. The cases reek of class bias. The victim got as much privacy and courtesy as possible, but no mercy was shown to the blackmailer. The law was "concerned primarily with the victimization of well-off men with a reputation to worry about." McLaren tells of an "impoverished patient" who accused a surgeon of "an infamous offense." The patient was sentenced to ten years in prison. It was a horrendous crime, said the judge, to accuse a doctor "whose whole life and fortune depended on a good character, especially for morality"; such a charge "might simply blast him for life."[41] That the good doctor just might have actually committed the "infamous offense" did not seem to concern the judge. This was a persistent attitude. H. G. Cocks quotes the *Times* of London in 1825 with regard to anonymous letters and other blackmail techniques: "If there be any possible offence . . . besides murder, for which capital punishment can properly be inflicted," it was crimes of this sort.[42]

In one later case, in the 1950s, a servant of a young officer blackmailed the officer over a period of thirty years. The victim, another Mr. X, was a member of the nobility. The judge said, "Things happen in most men's lives which are mercifully covered up by the years"; the law "does not allow the past to be dug up, or the skeletons and bones of past misdeeds rattled in front of a man in order to frighten him into paying up."[43] In fact, complaints that existing laws against sodomy were an incitement to blackmail helped fuel the twentieth-century campaign to wipe these laws off the books. Of course, there were other factors behind this campaign. The blackmail aspect, however, concerned only those men who were not only in the closet but also prominent and usually rich.

In the United States, for whatever reasons, few blackmail cases concerned charges of homosexual behavior—judging, at least, by the fragmentary evidence of reported cases and newspaper articles. Heterosexual misconduct was a more common theme. The famous Mann Act, passed by Congress in 1910, made it a crime to transport a woman across state lines for prostitution or any other "immoral" purpose.[44] This law was aimed at "white slavery." The underlying image was the innocent young girl, lured, coerced, or seduced into a life of vice and sin. The Supreme Court interpreted the law quite broadly. If a man

crossed a state line together with a woman and they had sex, even though no
money changed hands and the sex was completely consensual, the court held
that the man had violated the Mann Act. Two young men from Sacramento,
California, found this out to their grief.[45] Drew Caminetti and Maury Diggs,
both married, roared off to Nevada with two women friends (not their wives).
They were arrested for violating the Mann Act. The defendants argued—unsuccessfully—that the case did not involve "white slavery" (the women were
not exactly dragged or drugged across state lines); the statute, they argued, was
aimed only at commercialized vice, at what could properly be called the white
slave trade. But Caminetti and Diggs had been "open and notorious"; they had
scandalized the community. In any event, their convictions were upheld.

Not everyone approved of the Mann Act. There was opposition, and the
main argument of the opposition was that the act opened wide a door to blackmail. This was not entirely fanciful.[46] The Caminetti case made matters worse.
Even before that decision, there had been warnings about blackmail. A *New
York Times* editorial (in 1914) called the law "an absurdity"; it does nothing to
break up the white slave problem, but it "does make the Federal Government
the accomplice and instrument of blackmailers."[47] The Mann Act, of course,
was not the only arrow in the blackmailer's quiver. Cases of breach of promise, alienation of affections, and seduction were also grist for the blackmailer's
mill, and fear of blackmail was (as we will see) one of the prime arguments
raised in campaigns to get rid of these laws.[48]

The difference between English and American cases may be another re-
flex of the difference in class structure between the two countries. The code
of morality in the United States was more democratic, if I can put it that way.
Everybody was supposed to behave. In high English society, suggesting that
an earl or a duke was having an affair or that a king had a mistress was hardly
the stuff of blackmail. The high and mighty generally did as they pleased.
Homosexual behavior, however, was much less tolerated. At least this is a
plausible hypothesis.

Accusations of "sodomitic behavior" were by no means completely absent
from the American record. A few echo the British cases. In *Williams v. Ohio*
(1929), the defendant threatened to accuse Louis Girz of "the crime of sodomy," presumably by giving the story to a newspaper.[49] In a Michigan case
from 1943 the defendant, Gilbert Parker, was charged with "maliciously threat-

ening to accuse Charles Bartlett of the crime of gross indecency" in order to extort $5,000. Bartlett had been "in the lavatory of a hotel." Another man "entered and made a criminal assault upon him as Parker was looking over the partition." An accomplice, who claimed to be a police officer, "Sergeant Malone," pretended to arrest the "assaulter"; but Parker then accused Bartlett of "gross indecency," and after much to-do with Sergeant Malone, and with the aim of posting bond and getting out of trouble, Bartlett paid the money. When Bartlett found out that Sergeant Malone was an imposter, he swore out a warrant.[50]

These cases never discuss whether the victim really did what he was accused of doing. It is, of course, legally irrelevant. Blackmail is blackmail whether or not the charge against the victim is true. A modern cynic, reading the case just discussed, might at least suspect that Bartlett was less a victim than a party to the criminal assault in the men's lavatory—how did the assaulter get inside Bartlett's stall? In any event, sexual blackmail of this kind could be extremely destructive, and the reaction to it—real or imagined—had considerable political force. In April 1953 President Eisenhower issued an order that barred gay men and women from jobs in the federal government.[51] During the McCarthy period and generally during the cold war, the United States government dismissed gay people from government service on the grounds that they were security risks. A Soviet agent could presumably blackmail them.

WOMEN WHO BLACKMAIL

Who were the nineteenth-century blackmailers? James McCabe, writing about New York City in the 1870s and 1880s, classified blackmailers as a type of professional criminal. Their goal was to "live at the expense of others . . . by extorting money . . . by threats." Most blackmailers, McCabe thought, were women. They were trying to squeeze money out of men—their favorite victims were "young men about to make rich marriages." The blackmailer finds one of these young men and "threatens to denounce him to his *fiancée* as her destroyer." The victim, although he "knows he is innocent . . . dreads the scandal, fears it will break off his marriage, and generally yields to the demands." When a woman makes an accusation, McCabe felt, people tend to believe them. The victim, knowing this and realizing that the blackmailer has the power to whip up a malodorous scandal, pays her off "in the hope of hushing the matter up." But this is a mistake; the victim will simply be trapped in the blackmailer's web. "Innocent men have been driven to despair and suicide by these wretches."[52]

McCabe also tells the story of a "minister, in charge of a prominent and wealthy city church," who suddenly and mysteriously leaves his town. It turns out that he was the "innocent victim of a female Blackmailer." She had "boldly charged him with a crime of which he was innocent" and demanded money. The minister paid—and paid and paid. Eventually, she made his life so miserable that he "abandoned his home and his prospects" and ran away "to escape her clutches." Eventually, his friends rescued him and "by securing the imposition of the police, compelled the woman to relinquish her hold upon her victim."[53]

Many of these female blackmailers were "very young, mere girls . . . modest in demeanor"; some of them were "attractive." Among them were "flower girls," who gained "admittance to the offices and counting rooms of professional men and merchants," ostensibly to sell flowers, and then threatened to scream and accuse the victim of "taking improper liberties with them" unless the victim was willing to pay.[54] McCabe writes in a fit of righteous anger; he also flatly states that these men were innocent victims of designing women. But surely not every victim was quite so innocent. After all, not all ministers of the gospel were pure as the driven snow. And surely some "professional men and merchants" were not above making a pass at a pretty, young "flower girl."[55]

Allan Pinkerton, writing in 1884, also identified beautiful young women as the most prominent blackmailers. Pinkerton, however, is less naive or defensive about the nature of their victims. He tells the story of Samuel Wilkins, "a merchant of high standing in the commercial world," a family man, who "mingled in the first circles of society" and had always avoided any "breath of scandal." Wilkins frequently came to New York on business. In New York he met a beautiful young woman, Mary Curtis, who claimed to be a music teacher. He fell madly in love with her and set her up in an apartment as his mistress. She kept demanding money, and he decided to "break off an alliance which was both dangerous to his standing in the church and society . . . and extremely costly in a financial sense." But he learned from the "trembling lips of the young lady" that she was pregnant. He came one day to her apartment and found a handsome stranger with a long, flowing mustache and a "fine careless air of bravado" who "appeared to be making himself perfectly at home." She said that the stranger was her doctor, "engaged to attend her in her approaching accouchement." Later, a baby duly appeared who seemed "remarkably robust and well-grown" for his age. Meanwhile, the so-called doctor presented a bill for $350. Wilkins was now suspicious; he consulted an attorney; the attorney hired Pinkerton, and the plot was exposed. The doctor was in fact the woman's lover, and the baby was borrowed from a "foundling asylum." The doctor and Mary Curtis threatened to expose Wilkins to his wife and family, but Pinkerton "came to the rescue in person" and threatened to expose *them* instead. They quickly backed off and left town in a hurry. Wilkins made a "frank and manly explanation to his wife," and everything in his life returned to normal.[56]

The victims of blackmail were usually pillars of the community; the working-class man and woman might have a reputation to protect but no money to protect it with.[57] In the 1840s in New York City disreputable weekly newspapers, with such names as the *Scorpion*, the *Flash*, and the *Whip*, indulged in sexual blackmail. They squeezed hush money out of private citizens by threatening to expose the secrets of their sex lives—"immoral practices" or "visiting infamous houses" or various acts of seduction or the keeping of mistresses. At the time New York did not have a law against blackmail; the actions against the weeklies were obscenity actions. Public outrage over these weeklies helped campaigns in New York to toughen the laws against obscenity.[58] They were also a spur to law against blackmail.

The honest whore is a staple of literature, but dishonest whores were far from rare. These women knew that their customers were not eager for publicity. Prostitutes frequently robbed their customers, believing that most of them did not dare complain to the police. Blackmailers played on these fears of publicity. Matthew Hale Smith, writing in 1880, tells about a naive New York minister who received a message about a woman, gravely ill, who "could not die in peace unless her babe was baptized" and who summoned the reverend to her "dying pillow." The minister went to the right address, but there he found himself "in one of the most notorious houses in New York"; he was told by the people there ("of the most abandoned and desperate class") that "his midnight visit . . . could easily be proved." They demanded money, and he was soon in the hands of the blackmailers.[59]

This minister, too, was said to be both innocent and naive. On the whole, however, Pinkerton's account rings truer than McCabe's or Smith's. Press and literature frequently mention blackmail gangs and blackmail rings. They preyed on men who had a bit of dishonorable fun on the side. All this brings us closer, I believe, to the point of the blackmail laws. In Pinkerton's account Mary Curtis and her lover are unscrupulous villains—which certainly seems true—and Wilkins is a solid citizen who loved not wisely but too well. That he was cheating on his wife, lying to his family, and leading a double life is admitted but is excused as just one of those things—a lapse, a deviation from an otherwise respectable life. Wilkins tells his wife the whole truth; she supposedly forgave him, and the story had a happy ending. The curtain of secrecy descends, protecting Wilkins' position in society and his precious reputation as a pillar of the community.

When such men as the good Mr. Wilkins were in the coils of the serpent, they usually did not resist; it took a long time and some desperation to induce them to take action. Some victims reacted more quickly. In 1897 Edward J. Russell, posing as a reporter, threatened a lawyer, Almet F. Jenks, a former New York corporation counsel. Russell wanted money; if Jenks refused to pay, Russell said he would "publish a story which . . . reflected on Mr. Jenks's personal character" (the *New York Times*, which reported the incident, never specified what the "story" was; apparently it had something to do with Jenks's marriage and divorce).[60] In general, newspaper accounts and reports of cases are often quite shy and unrevealing. Sometimes it is hard to figure out exactly what the blackmailer is threatening to do.[61] This reticence was itself a kind of protective device; it masked the charge and avoided the question of whether there was anything true about the accusations. In any event, lawyer Jenks pretended to go along with the scheme, but in fact he called in the police. Detectives hid in a room near Jenks's office, where the payoff was going to be made. Russell, a tall man "with a well-cut black beard," wearing glasses and "a silk hat and a Prince Albert coat," came to collect. According to plan, Jenks rapped his cane three times and shouted, "This is an outrage." The detectives came out of hiding and arrested Russell. It turned out that Russell was an ex-con who had already done a "jolt" in Sing Sing. He got ten more years for his pains.

In the situations I have discussed the blackmailer was undeniably vicious and evil, a man or woman who battened on the sins of wealthy men and plotted to ensnare them. Some of the reported cases fall into this category. In *People v. Williams* (1899),[62] the defendant, Elsie Williams, along with a male associate, was charged with trying to squeeze money ($2,000) from W. A. Nevilles. They threatened to accuse him, publicly, of adultery with Elsie Williams. Nevilles obviously did have sex with her. The defendants were convicted. The appeals court reversed the decision, partly because the trial court had allowed the prosecution to bring in improper evidence. The evidence may have been legally improper, but it was certainly revealing. It consisted of a statement by the (male) codefendant. He said he was building a house, where he would install Elsie and another woman. Then he would "bring business men out there, and we will get them full of wine, and afterwards blackmail them." This plan—an arrow through the very heart of the Victorian compromise—threatened the immunity of men like Nevilles. It endangered their right to go to a brothel and sin (at least occasionally), without losing their standing in society.

In *State v. Coleman* (1906), a Minnesota case, the wife of William D. Pencille was eager to divorce him.[63] Her lawyers enlisted Coleman, a private detective, to help her case by scraping up evidence against Pencille. Coleman entered into a scheme with Louise Oelkers, who was 19 years old, to "put Pencille in a compromising position . . . for the purpose of using the evidence in the divorce suit." Coleman hired Louise to do housework in his family and had her write to Pencille, arranging for a meeting in a rooming house. Pencille fell for the bait and registered with Louise in a rooming house as man and wife. Coleman knocked on the door of their room and "pretended great surprise at finding them together." They told Pencille he could buy their silence, for a price that ended up at around $700. The jury convicted Coleman under a statute that made it a crime to obtain "property from another . . . induced by a wrongful use of force and fear."

This case inevitably reminds us about the common plot used in New York in divorce cases and involving trumped-up hotel evidence.[64] The hotel scheme, which I have elsewhere called soft-core adultery, depended on the fact that adultery was the only practical grounds for divorce in New York. Couples that agreed to divorce sometimes manufactured phony evidence of adultery. The husband would check into a hotel; he would be joined in the room by a woman; they would both undress; a photographer would magically appear; pictures would be taken; the husband would pay the woman her fee, and the photographs would end up in court as evidence of adultery. This of course was far from blackmail. In the New York situation the husband was always privy to the scheme. But there is at least one common theme. The New York hotel device protected men who were committing real adultery—and also the women they were sleeping with. Who she was, and whether she existed at all, and the husband's transgressions in general were masked by the obvious fakery of soft-core adultery.

CRIMES AND MISDEMEANORS

Most blackmail cases probably relate to sins of private life, as in the case of the merchant Wilkins. To be sure, there are cases in which the blackmailer knows about some crime that his "victim" has committed.[65] Here, arguably, publicity serves a real social end. Society arguably benefits when someone exposes a criminal and denounces the criminal's crimes. If a person knows about some violation of law, she has a duty to report it to the authorities. This is better than keeping quiet in exchange for money, that is, selling one's silence to the criminal for cash. A number of reported blackmail cases fall into this category. In a California case from 1901 the state charged the defendant with threatening to expose the evil deeds of Mr. Greenwald; Greenwald had apparently violated federal law: He "sold and delivered cigars other than in a new box."[66] (The defendant, clearly small potatoes, wanted $30). Some of the case law—it is admittedly fairly skimpy—involved crimes against morality: adultery, for example.[67]

Truth, as I have said, was legally irrelevant, but in some cases the victim's guilt seems crystal clear. In a Michigan case the "sordid facts" were as follows: The victim, Ray Chappel, was a 64-year-old jeweler of Niles, Michigan, and a married man. He had a "small dark room in which to fit glasses in the rear of the store." He had, it seemed, other uses for this room as well. In it he conducted an "illicit relationship" with the defendant, Miss Watson. Watson later told him she was pregnant and needed a "criminal operation." This would cost some $500. He gave her the money, but she continued to beg him for more, which she needed (she said) because of her "necessitous, desperate and at times dangerous physical condition" after the operation. Finally, she sent him a note: "Do you want me to go to County House for . . . treatment?. . . .

I am ready to air the whole thing—as I am doing the suffering—not you. . . .
Think this over Ray bear—I am sorry—but I am sick and just can't help it."
Chappel then went to a lawyer. Watson was arrested, tried, and convicted. On
appeal the conviction was affirmed. It turned out that the whole pregnancy
and abortion story was most likely a lie.[68]

THE ANATOMY OF BLACKMAIL

By now it seems quite clear what social interest blackmail laws were meant to
advance. The last case mentioned illustrates the point. Ray Chappel was an
adulterer and a philanderer. He was also a merchant and a respectable citizen.
What is the point of protecting him? The blackmailer knows, or thinks he
knows, some dark secret from the citizen's past. He fathered a child without
bothering to get married, or he had a secret affair with some woman, or he
was seen going in and out of a brothel, or perhaps he served a term in jail for
writing a bad check. These are skeletons in the man's closet. Many of these
acts are not crimes; some never were. Or they may be crimes that were committed years before so that no prosecution is possible. Or, as in the case of Ray
Chappel, the victim is leading a double life.

Of course, blackmail was and is and always has been a dirty business. The
reported cases may not be typical, but they rarely suggest any reason to pity the
poor blackmailer. Blackmailers are bottom-feeders; they make their money by
causing misery and pain, by raking up the dead past, by threats and plots and
schemes. They are con men or worse, scoundrels, and often (but not always)
liars. They have found a rich vein of ore. They tap into the deep desire of their
victims for privacy and secrecy. How many people in this world have nothing
to be ashamed of? How many "respectable" people do not have a chapter of
their lives—or at least a page, a paragraph, a line—that they would be happy
to see gone and forgotten?

Some of these people are now pillars of society. Their secret life is under
threat. Whether the accusations are correct is beside the point. Here, perhaps,
is a reason to draw a line between defamation—where truth became nearly
a total defense—and blackmail laws. Defamation was much less likely to involve sharp differences in class and status, between plaintiff and defendant.
But such differences were the norm in blackmail cases.

Did blackmail laws actually deter? Doubtful. But the point of the laws seems reasonably clear. The blackmail laws were supposed to protect respectable people with guilty secrets. The laws were meant to keep the past safely buried. Was this good for society? Apparently yes; or at least people might think so. As I pointed out, the United States was a mobile society in every sense of the word: social, economic, geographic. Mobility meant freedom; mobility was an American value. Many men in America moved from place to place; they shed old lives like snakes molting their skin. They took on new lives and new identities. They went from rags to riches, from log cabins to the White House.[69] (They could also go from riches to rags.) American men, more than people in other cultures, were rolling stones. Most Americans, of course, were immigrants themselves or the children or grandchildren of immigrants. Thus most had little or no attachment to an ancestral place, a home, a native village. When gold was discovered in California, thousands of men dropped their plows and their account books and headed out to the gold fields. Thousands of families took the dangerous and arduous trip by wagon train across the Great American Desert to the Pacific coast. Other men and families made the long journey by sea. When new areas of the country opened up, whether Kansas or the Dakotas or Oklahoma, settlers streamed in by the thousands.

Other countries had similar experiences—no doubt—although probably on a lesser scale. In the United States, American culture and law put enormous emphasis on second chances.[70] Men were not to be locked into fixed positions in society. One could be born again, not only in the religious sense but in a secular sense: reborn in a new place with a new name and even a new life. This was of course true primarily of men. Women were much less mobile, in every sense of the word. Men were the rolling stones, the gold hunters of California, the fortune seekers in the West; sometimes they brought women along, but the initiative lay with the men.

The culture of second chances meant, ultimately, a more relaxed attitude toward divorce than in the past and a more relaxed attitude toward bankruptcy. The culture of second chances always had limits, of course. For example, a man who took the concept *too* literally and married a woman in his new hometown, without bothering to divorce the first one, was guilty of bigamy. He could go to jail if this fact came to light.[71] Bigamy was not one of the forgivable sins of a person's salad days. It was, after all, a serious fraud on the second wife. Her marriage was null and void. She had given up her virginity to a lying stranger. Bigamy was a serious threat to the life and reputation of a respectable woman.

The blackmailer struck a severe blow against the American culture of second chances. He brought up the ghosts of the past. He attacked people with money and with standing in the community. The blackmailer came, almost always, from a lower *class* than his victims. Blackmailers were either poor or were flat-out criminals. Courts—and society in general—assumed that "men would naturally wander"; yes, one could criticize their wandering, but it was wrong for these men to be "exploited."[72] The blackmail statutes were thus another example of the legal shield protecting reputation—protecting the *appearance* of bourgeois respectability. The blackmail laws, in other words, fit neatly into the pattern of rules, norms, and doctrine I have been discussing: the nineteenth-century form of adultery laws and the Victorian compromise in general. And the blackmail statutes began to appear roughly about the same time and with the same underlying ethos as the other laws that made up the Victorian compromise. The thesis, then—if I may repeat myself—is that the official code includes and presupposes a certain amount of slack or leeway; it leaves the door open for a certain amount of discreet deviation from the norms, but only on the part of respectable people, pillars of the community.

Consider, for example, the social norm against snitches and snitching. You might imagine it almost a patriotic duty to rat on somebody, but as the term *ratting* suggests, the situation is exactly the opposite. Ratting is severely condemned by people in general. The norm against snitching, like the norm against blackmail, is a form of protection for people who lead a double life or who have something to cover up. It is, however, much broader than the norms discussed here—it is particularly strong in deviant groups and among delinquents, jailbirds, and the like. In prison a snitch is likely to end up with a knife stuck in his ribs. Emphatically, though, the norm against snitching is not just a norm of criminals and other bad people; it is common among schoolchildren, university students, and other groups that are hardly deviant. There are rules to protect whistle-blowers, but the reality is that "the costs of reporting peers for rule breaking and occupational misconduct usually outweigh the benefits."[73] In a way the norm against snitching meshes with the norm against blackmail: It is wrong to ask for money in exchange for your silence; but it is also considered quite wrong, under many circumstances, to report your information even to the proper authorities. The safest course, if you know a guilty secret, is to keep it to yourself.

CHAPTER 6

GOOD WOMEN,
BAD WOMEN

Seduction, Breach of Promise, and Related Matters

SEDUCTION

In 1899 the legislature of Illinois passed a statute that made it a crime to "seduce and obtain carnal knowledge of any unmarried female under the age of eighteen years of previous chaste character." The punishment was a fine or a term in the county jail (up to one year) or both. The statute had two additional clauses. First, no defendant could be convicted "upon the testimony of the female unsupported by other evidence," and second, "the subsequent intermarriage of the parties shall be a bar to . . . prosecution."[1]

This statute was by no means unique. Other states had somewhat similar statutes.[2] A 1909 New York law applied to any person who "under promise of marriage, seduces and has sexual intercourse with an unmarried female of previously chaste character."[3] Note that this statute applied to women of *any* age, but it had the added clause, "under promise of marriage." An Alabama statute conveniently catalogued techniques of seduction: "Any man who, by means of temptation, deception, arts, flattery, or a promise of marriage, seduces any unmarried woman."[4] A Georgia statute in the late nineteenth century spoke of "persuasion and promises of marriage, or other false and fraudulent means," if used to "induce" a "virtuous unmarried female . . . to yield" to a man's "lustful embraces, and allow him to have carnal knowledge of her."[5] In state after state, criminal seduction laws more or less similar to the Illinois statute were passed in the late nineteenth century or in the early years of the twentieth century. In Canada in 1886 a law was passed, after a long struggle, that criminalized seduction, but this law applied only to the seduction of girls between 12 and 16 years old. Seduction of a woman under 18, under promise of marriage, also became a crime.[6]

All these statutes insisted that the woman had to be chaste or virtuous. She had to be, in other words, a virgin. As a New York court put it, a woman "can be seduced but once." Once a woman gives in and has sex with a man, she is no longer chaste. The statute required "absolute personal chastity. It is, therefore, impossible that the offense be twice committed against the same female."[7] This doctrine was good news to George Nelson. He was tried for seduction in 1895. He had sex with a 15-year-old girl after promising to marry her and then had sex with her quite a few times afterward. He never did marry her. The first sex act took place in March 1891. By the time he was tried, the statute of limitations had run out. Nelson had sex with the girl again (and again); but now she was, according to the court, no longer chaste. Nelson's conviction was reversed, and he went free.

The seduction statute was a *criminal* law. Much earlier, there were *civil* actions available to a woman whose boyfriend jilted her. These were actions for breach of promise of marriage. I will discuss them in due course. There was also an ancient tort action for "seduction." This gave a father the right to recover damages from a man who seduced his daughter. This was because, in theory at least, the father had lost the "services" of his daughter. Loss of services was "presumed" if the daughter lived at home and was underage. Even if she did not live at home—even if she was a servant in somebody else's house—the father was usually entitled to bring such an action, so long as he had not lost the (theoretical) right to claim these services.[8]

In the nineteenth century this particular theory came to seem quaint and obsolete. A daughter who had gone to work in a factory or a shop in the city and who was not living at home was not providing any services in the family. In an 1889 case in Manitoba, Canada, a young servant girl, Ellen Hebb, pregnant, claimed that her master had raped her. He denied it. A jury awarded Ellen's parent (a widowed mother, in this case) a sum of money, but the Manitoba Court of Appeal reversed: She was performing no services for her mother.[9] Courts in the United States also came to reject the old justification. As an Arkansas judge said in 1891, the doctrine was "little more than a legal fiction" that was "used as a peg to hang a substantial award of damages" for the "head of the family."[10] This was the father; if he was dead, the mother succeeded to his right.[11] Getting rid of the services doctrine signified a shift in the social meaning of this tort. Who was injured by the seduction? At first it was the father (and the family), but eventually, injury to the daughter herself became the central theme of the case law. It was the daughter who had been injured and disgraced.[12]

The shift was foreshadowed as early as 1844 in an interesting North Carolina case, *Briggs v. Evans*.[13] Lewis Briggs sued Evans, who had seduced his daughter; she became pregnant and had a baby. The daughter was living at home (Briggs alleged) and "performing service in the family" until, as the pregnancy advanced, she went to live with her grandmother. The daughter was 20 when she became pregnant but reached 21 a few months later. The father claimed that her health suffered and that she could do only "lighter" services, "such as knitting."

The trial court told the jury that a father could collect damages automatically for loss of the daughter's services, up to age 21; after that, he had to show that she still did service for him and that the defendant's misdeeds had impaired those services. But the jury could also "take into their consideration the anguish and disgrace brought upon the plaintiff and his family." The jury found a verdict for the father, and the defendant appealed, giving various technical reasons and insisting that the father lost his rights when the daughter came of age.

The appeals court disagreed. Loss of services was pretty much a "figment of the law," designed to "open . . . the door" to the "redress" of the father's "actual damage," which was, in fact, his "outraged feelings. He comes into the court as a master—he goes before the jury as a father." For this reason it was enough to show that the daughter performed even "trivial" services—even if the services were nothing more than "pouring out his tea." Seduction of an adult daughter could be even more serious a "degradation" than seduction of a minor daughter. It would be monstrous if the law failed the father in cases that carried "the largest portion of anguish and distress."

Cases of this sort bring us closer to the heart of the tort—to its social meaning. Suppose that the daughter was complicit in her seduction (if such a thing
is possible). This should have made no difference—in theory. The disgrace
to the father and the family was the same, or even worse. But courts began to
look more closely at the actual behavior of the daughter. In an Oregon case
from 1889,[14] the daughter, Stella, was not exactly a paragon of virtue. She "was
in the habit of meeting several young men . . . out in the streets and avenues"
of Salem, Oregon, as late as 9 or 10 o'clock. Stella had sex with the defendant
and became "afflicted with chronic gonorrhea." The Oregon statute provided
that a father "may maintain an action . . . for the seduction of a daughter,"
even though the daughter was not living at home and there was no "loss of
service." The defendant wanted the court to instruct the jury that the daughter
had to be "chaste" and "overcome" by the defendant through "some artifice or
promise." The court refused to give this instruction; a jury held for the plaintiff
and assessed the damages at $3,633. The appeals court reversed. If the woman
engaged in "lewd practices and habits" or sought "opportunities for criminal
indulgence," it was absurd to say she was "seduced." That would "break down
all distinctions between the virtuous and vicious, and . . . place the common
bawd on the same plane with the virtuous woman . . . whose confidence had
been betrayed by the heartless libertine."[15]

In some ways the flow of legal development here *seemed* to contradict
other trends in the law. In the late nineteenth century, as we will see, control
over sexual behavior became tighter, not looser, legally speaking. The criminal laws against seduction seemed to relax the standard for women. In a way
they excused her from responsibility and put the burden entirely on the man.
Seduction, after all, is not rape. Presumably, it is impossible to seduce a truly
virtuous woman; a truly virtuous woman will not give way, no matter what
a man promises, no matter what tricks and blandishments he uses. What the
seduction laws represent, then, is a (rather late) flowering of one aspect of the
Victorian compromise. They recognize that not all chaste women were immune from seduction, that some middle-class women, like some middle-class
men, were capable of sin. The seduction laws were one way to protect these
women and give them a second chance.

Of course, the laws also conform to one dominant Victorian image of
women—women as weak, innocent, trusting souls, easily victimized by lustful

men. As William Sanger put it, it was not the nature of a woman to "precipitate herself into an abyss of degradation and shame" unless some overwhelming "influence" brought this about. Women are "weak"; they have a "truly feminine dependence" on the promises of men. So, in "most cases of seduction, female virtue is trustingly surrendered to the specious arguments and false promises of dishonorable men."[16] Some men supposedly used even more dastardly methods. A Tennessee law made it a crime to have "carnal knowledge of a woman" by drugging her or by "any . . . means producing . . . stupor, imbecility of mind, or weakness of body" so as to "prevent effectual resistance."[17] In a Massachusetts case (1873), Charles Stratton and a friend went calling on two young women. Stratton offered them some figs; they ate the figs and got quite sick. Somebody had sold Charles and his friend "love powders"; they doctored the figs with these powders. The powders were supposed to be harmless but turned out otherwise. Charles was convicted of assault.[18]

It is hard to tell, at this distance in time, how much truth there was in tales of seduction, how often women were willing accomplices, how often they were forced, coerced, or cheated into sexual activity. One thing, though, is clear: The seduction laws meshed neatly with other norms and rules in that it protected "respectable" women who had a blot on their record, who lapsed from the ideals of Victorian morality. The same is true of the *tort* of seduction. It shed its archaic flavor and became another mode of protecting respectable women (and only these women) who had been seduced.

The official norms were clear—in general. Sex outside marriage was forbidden. A dense network of rules and laws defined respectability for women in society. A woman who lost her virtue was said to be "ruined." The Illinois statute emphasized a crucial element of the nineteenth-century code: Sexual intercourse was for married people only. Seduction, like adultery and fornication, was a wrong and a crime and had to be punished. But if that was all the statute was about, then the two added provisos would be unnecessary. The second proviso let a seducer off the hook if he married his victim and made her an honest woman. A ruined woman was damaged goods. Her value in the marriage market was impaired. Her seducer could salvage the situation: Marry the woman, and all would be well. These laws gave the woman a certain amount of leverage. The family could threaten to prosecute the seducer. Of course, the family gained little by sending to jail a man who sweet-talked a woman into sexual intercourse. Perhaps an official pronouncement that she had been "innocent" and "virtuous" before the seduction lessened the stain on her honor.

The other proviso in the statute is also significant: The woman's accusations have to be corroborated. This of course was a protection for the man. Otherwise, it would be easy for a woman to blackmail a respectable man and destroy his reputation.

The law extended its protection to respectable women, but only chaste women were or could be respectable. The statutes were, of course, silent about class and race, but class and race were there, in between the lines. Cases of black women invoking the law against a white seducer simply cannot be found.[19] The statute, by implication, applied only to people who could and should be eligible—legally and socially—to marry. In most states in the nineteenth century marriage between a white and a black was forbidden.[20] A white seducer could hardly promise to marry a black woman, nor would he be likely to do so. Sadly, the virtue of black women counted for almost nothing in law and society.

The seduction laws were exclusively about the deflowering of virgins. It was almost impossible, legally speaking, for a sexually active woman to be seduced.[21] The seduction laws protected middle-class women, respectable women. Men benefited too—brothers and fathers were spared shame and disgrace, at least theoretically. The law, of course, reflected the double standard. A woman had no right to demand a male virgin. But she did have a right to shield her own name from dishonor and to protect her place in the marriage market, which was crucial for a middle-class woman. A seduced or jilted woman or a victim of "criminal conversation" was at serious risk. The seducer also may have been middle class and (up to this point) respectable. Yet the law could not protect *both* partners, and what the woman lost far outweighed what he lost.

It is impossible to tell how often the seduction laws were enforced. A fair number of seduction cases pop up in the law reports. In the 1880s a man named Green Horton was arrested, charged with seduction, tried, and convicted.[22] The woman, Sarah Wilkerson, had sex with Horton when she was 28; Horton, she said, had promised to marry her. She also claimed that Horton was her one and only sex partner. Horton denied everything. Sarah had given birth to a baby. The child was "exhibited to the jury" to show its resemblance to Horton. The appeals court upheld his conviction. To be sure, the case did not give Sarah a husband or a real father for her child; but it gave her revenge, if she wanted it, and it shifted the blame for her disgrace onto Horton. He was a seducer, not a boyfriend or a sex partner.

Behind many of these cases, too, are irate fathers, brothers, and other family members, demanding satisfaction from the seducer—or if not satisfaction, marriage. These shotgun weddings did occur. In a Michigan case (1888) William Gould was on trial for "seducing and debauching" Kate Morrow, of Shiawasee County.[23] During a lunch break, a justice of the peace married Kate and William. That very evening, Gould ran away. He was caught and put on trial. But an appeals court reversed his conviction. The marriage—short and loveless though it was—made Gould immune from prosecution. In a Texas case (1892) W. C. Wright was on trial for seducing Willie Nisbett.[24] He stood up, brandishing a marriage license, and said he would marry her, live with her, and "discharge all his marital duties." Willie Nisbett was having none of this: "I would not marry any man who treated a woman as you have done me." But the offer was enough to get Wright off the hook; the "defendant had done all that the law required," said the court, and the case should have been dismissed.

UNWRITTEN LAWS

Charging a man with seduction—a criminal offense—was a path prescribed by law for redressing a woman's grievances. There were other, more direct methods. A Boston policeman, in his "recollections," described how in 1858 an "intelligent-looking young lady" came into the station house and gave herself up, confessing that she had shot a man. Her story was the "oft-repeated tale of seduction and desertion." The man was her "suitor." Under a "solemn promise of marriage," he "had accomplished her ruin" and then "abandoned her." In a "fit of desperation," she bought a "double-barrelled pistol," loaded with "powder and ball"; she intended to shoot him (which she did) and then kill herself (which she didn't). The man was wounded but not dead. The case went to the grand jury, which let her go free. She and her "offspring" were "sheltered by the roof of a kind father." The cad recovered, but the bullet could not be removed. He still (at the date of the writing) "moves in respectable society," although he would "carry that leaden memento of his perfidy with him to the grave."[25]

Note that the man, despite his perfidy, was never charged with any crime or brought to justice in any way. Both parties to this cautionary tale were members of polite society. Somehow they both escaped censure. Police and the grand jury conspired to excuse the woman for violently attacking the man who seduced her. In some ways the man's immunity was more striking. But the woman was excused, after all, for two offenses: first, that she shot a man, and second, that she consented to sexual intercourse. In this latter regard, what protected her was the official image of the woman as the innocent victim of a vile seducer, feeble in strength, and easily imposed upon.

Did a wronged woman have a right to violent revenge? In theory, no; but there are both written and unwritten laws. Young Clara Fallmer, of Oakland, California, shot and killed her lover, Charles LaDue, on August 2, 1897. She was 15 years old and pregnant. Charles, who was 21, had refused to marry her. Clara's murder trial was an absolute sensation. She was the center of attention as she sat in the courtroom, looking "frail and delicate" and clutching in her "neatly gloved hands a small bunch of violets." Her formal defense was temporary insanity; her real defense was that Charles deserved what he got. The jury acquitted her.[26] Of course, not every woman who killed a former lover escaped the rigors of the law. For men the unwritten law almost guaranteed an acquittal if the man took revenge on someone who had seduced or had sex with his wife. In one of the most notorious cases from the mid-nineteenth century, the defendant, charged with murder, was a congressman, Daniel Sickles. Sickles had a young wife, Teresa. He discovered that she was having an affair with Philip Barton Key. Sickles confronted her with the evidence; she confessed that it was all too true. Sickles then shot young Key to death, in broad daylight, on the streets of Washington, D.C. Sickles's trial for murder was the sensation of 1859 in the national capital. Sickles defended himself on the rather dubious (legal) grounds of "temporary insanity"; the jury acquitted him, almost surely because they thought Key deserved to die.[27]

Sickles had been defending his honor, and public opinion was on his side. If the ideal woman was delicate and demure, then the ideal man was vigorous and manly, quick to defend his family and his family's honor. This concept of honor lay at the base of the code that had once made dueling not only acceptable but even, at times, a necessity. Real men did not tolerate insults. Many states passed laws in an attempt to get rid of dueling, as I have mentioned. Dueling passed into history, but the basic notion of masculine honor was tougher and less amenable to legislation, and indeed it survives to this day.

Even more sensational than the Sickles trial was the trial of Harry K. Thaw in 1907. Thaw was married to a young and beautiful woman, Evelyn Nesbit Thaw, once a Floradora girl on the New York stage. Thaw shot to death the famous architect Stanford White in front of horrified onlookers at Madison Square Garden. He did it, he said, because White had "ruined" his wife when she was young and innocent (although this was years before he married her). The trial ended with a hung jury; a second jury found Thaw not guilty by reason of insanity.[28]

What unites these various cases of the unwritten law is the image of woman as victim—she might have been tricked, seduced, drugged, or forced, but her sins were never or almost never her fault. Of course, legal and social reality were at all times messy and complex, and it would be wrong to wring too much consistency out of individual cases and incidents. But there was a definite strain in the law—and in society—that excused respectable women who slipped a bit off the track, at least under some circumstances, just as there were strains in the law that excused respectable men. At times, the two strains came into conflict.

COMMON LAW MARRIAGE

A common law marriage is a marriage that consists of nothing more than a simple *agreement* between a man and a woman—a "contract" to marry each other. If a state recognizes common law marriage, that means that when a man and a woman say the right words to each other, at that very moment they become legally husband and wife. Nothing more is needed; no license, no ceremony, no witnesses, no judge or clergyman. The "marriage" can take place privately, secretly, in a house, in front of a roaring fire, or wherever the couple chooses to agree or says the magic words. In the first part of the nineteenth century, somewhat surprisingly, most states in the United States did in fact recognize common law marriage.[29] In these states, then, common law marriage was a real, complete, and perfect marriage, with all the benefits and burdens of a marriage performed by a bishop in front of dozens of witnesses.

The common law marriage, as I said, did not call for witnesses; and most of the time, when a widow (for example) claimed she was a partner in a common law marriage, there *were* in fact no witnesses. How then did she or anybody else *prove* the existence of a common law marriage? Mostly by reputation and behavior. If a man and a woman lived together, behaved as if they were married, kept house, had children, went to church, acted respectably, they were *presumed* to be married. Even if nobody could find any record of a ceremonial marriage—record keeping was, in any event, quite poor in the early nineteenth century—they might, after all, have entered into a common law marriage, and the law assumed in fact that they had.

The issue came up chiefly in disputes over inheritance. If a man and a woman had a common law marriage and he died, then she was a legitimate grieving widow and the children were genuine, legitimate children. This of course had a profound effect on their rights to his house, his farm, his money. But another point about the common law marriage is worth mentioning. If such a marriage was assumed, then their reputation and their honor were salvaged. They were a lawfully married couple, not fornicators; they were joined in holy matrimony, not deeply immersed in the blackest of sins.

This point was made by Justice Lumpkin, a colorful Georgia judge, in a case decided in 1860.[30] The case turned, procedurally, on whether James and Uriah Dupree were actually married. They thought they were. A minister of the gospel had united them in marriage. But it turned out that the man was not really a minister; he had been deposed and "excommunicated" and had no right to marry anybody at all, including James and Uriah. Lumpkin saved the day by dragging in the presumption of a common law marriage. He frankly admits that this was perhaps quite imaginary. James and Uriah likely never said the magic words to each other. But by invoking the doctrine of common law marriage, Lumpkin would save the "honor" of "the female," and saving her honor was "worth more than everything, even life itself." The doctrine spared men and women the shame and ignominy of "illicit intercourse." Of course, it did this simply by pretending that they were married. The doctrine of common law marriage converted fornication into holy marital intercourse.

James and Uriah probably, in fact, thought they were married. But surely *some* couples who lived together without ceremony were simply living in sin and fooling their neighbors. Such couples perhaps never heard of the doctrine of common law marriage. Yet the presumption saved their honor. The doctrine thus performed a social function very much like others I have discussed. It protected the reputation of respectable people, even those who arguably did not deserve this protection.

BREACH OF PROMISE

Most of the legal devices and arrangements discussed up to now have benefited elite and respectable men. Elite and respectable women had their own legal devices and arrangements. A woman's reputation depended on her chastity, her sexual virtue. Actions for seduction, already discussed, sometimes served as a remedy. There were others.

If a man had sex with a girl who was young enough, he could be prosecuted for statutory rape.[31] Any "carnal knowledge" of a female was defined legally as rape if the female was younger than the "age of consent." That she might have been eager and willing made no legal difference. Historically, the law of statutory rape was tilted heavily in favor of the man. The common law age of consent was ridiculously low—10 years of age.[32] This meant that only the grossest pedophiles were guilty of this crime. A grown man who had sex with a girl of, say, 13 was at most guilty of fornication, and in many states, not even that, unless the fornication was persistent and overt. Same result if the girl was 16 or 17. The low age of consent protected men who had sex with young shopgirls or with household servants and the like. As we will see later on, states generally raised the age of consent in the late nineteenth century and early twentieth century, sometimes rather dramatically, and this made a substantial change in the social meaning of the law.[33]

Another legal device, quite favorable for respectable women, was the right to sue for breach of promise of marriage. This right protected older, more marriageable women. An engagement was treated by law as a kind of contract. If one party to this contract broke it and called the wedding off, the other party could sue for breach of promise. In theory, the law was unisex; anybody who was jilted, man or woman, had the right to sue. But this was pure theory. As everybody knew, this was an action meant for women, not men. It was a remedy for respectable, mostly middle-class women who had been seduced and abandoned. Male plaintiffs were exceedingly rare. An English study found some scattered lawsuits brought by men; most of these were unsuccessful.[34] In Canada John Brandau, a carpenter, filed suit in 1894 against Annie Turnbull, who had broken off their engagement. People thought this was a most peculiar action, and the judge reminded the jurors that women suffered more than men from being jilted. The jury returned a verdict for Brandau, but gave him $1 in damages; and the judge ordered him to pay all the costs because it was "shameful" to drag a woman through such a proceeding.[35] This would hardly encourage other men to try.

A few cases brought by men were reported in the United States, but they seem quite eccentric. *Olson v. Saxton* (1917) was especially bizarre.[36] The plaintiff, Arthur P. Olson, a married man, began a relationship with Mollie Patton, the defendant. Olson and his wife were later divorced. Olson advanced money to Patton and built her a house. The debt, he said, was canceled when she promised to marry him. Instead, she married John Saxton. Olson then presented her with a bill for $1,700, but (he said) she talked him into lowering the claim, by deducting $5 for "each act of sexual intercourse." There must have been quite a few of these acts, because he cut his claim to $1,500. In any event, he lost his case.[37] In another instance Captain George Hildreth, head of the lifesaving service at Cape May, a "wrinkled and gray-haired" man of 50, sued Mrs. Sophia Cahill, widow of "the millionaire President of the Knickerbocker Ice Company," for breach of promise in a Philadelphia courtroom, but the case was "amicably adjusted" out of court.[38] As a judge in an early Alabama case (1846) put it, "In our own country, a just regard to public morals, has long since confined the action alone to the female sufferer."[39] He was, in fact, misstating the formal law, but he was correct in his assessment of general social norms. A gentleman presumably would not complain if a woman changed her mind. For the most part people did not believe that a man suffered any real loss, unless we count a possible broken heart.

Breach of promise, then, was for women, and only women. To begin with, a woman's feelings were supposed to be more delicate than a man's; she suffered greater emotional damage when the contract was broken. In one instance from 1884 in Milwaukee, Wisconsin, the plaintiff's aged father (we are told) "discovered his young daughter lying between life and death and her reason hanging in the balance" because her "lover, who first won and then saddened her youthful heart, deserted her in a base and unmanly manner." The jury awarded her $3,000.[40]

But emotional damage—humiliation, embarrassment—was not the main point of most of the reported cases. If a man promised to marry a woman and delayed and delayed and then backed out of the arrangement, he had damaged her greatly. He had taken her off the marriage market during what might have been crucial marriageable years. And the very fact that a woman had been courted and sweet-talked by another man (even if no sex was involved) may have acted as a deterrent to prospective suitors. A far more serious harm was loss of virginity. The woman had been ruined; she was used merchandise, and in elevated social circles this all but killed her marriage prospects. It was also extremely embarrassing to her and her family. In some cases premarital sex led to pregnancy and the birth of a bastard child. A careful study of English cases found that most plaintiffs were not elite women at all but "lower middle-class and working-class spinsters," women who were self-supporting and who had had long courtships. A "substantial minority had unplanned pregnancies."[41] It is hard to know how often this happened. There were fifty-four reported cases between 1880 and 1890 in the United States. In ten cases there was sexual intercourse and the birth of a child; in thirteen cases there was sexual intercourse without the birth of a child; in six cases there was no sexual intercourse, and in the rest—about half—the facts are not clear.[42] It seems certain that in most instances that got this far, there had been sexual relations between the couple. Of course, the reported cases are not a reliable guide to cases settled out of court or cases that ended at the trial level without an appeal.

The central image in the cases plainly was the innocent woman or girl, ruined and debauched by a bounder who had (falsely) promised to marry her. Thus breach of promise was the civil equivalent of the crime of seduction. In breach of promise cases, too, the victim was a woman who had been previously chaste. The civil code prepared for the state of New York in 1865 provided that a "promise of marriage" was subject to the "same rules as contracts in general," which meant of course that it was enforceable; but neither party to it was "bound" if the promise was "made in ignorance of the other's want of personal chastity," and any "unchaste conduct" would release the other party.[43] In theory, too, a divorced woman about to remarry or a widow or a young woman who had sex with somebody else before meeting the defendant, all had a perfect right to sue. But as far as I can tell, this simply did not happen.

In theory, the woman's case was also *weakened* if she had agreed to have sex (which was the normal situation). After all, "illicit intercourse is an act of mutual imprudence"; if both he and she consented to the sex, then "they are both in fault."[44] Theoretically, then, the woman would have no claim on the sympathy of the judge and jury. On the whole, though, the cases do not conform to this theory. Most of them hold that sex—under promise of marriage—makes the plaintiff's lawsuit stronger, not weaker. As one writer put it, "The courts are not disposed to make smooth the path of a seducer."[45] The seduction, said an Oregon court, makes matters that much worse: An ordinary breach of promise results in "mortification and pain," but when there is seduction, there is also "a loss of character, and social position, and not only deeper shame and sorrow, but a darkened future."[46]

A Michigan court agreed:[47] At times, a woman is not much worse off if her fiancé breaks the engagement. But this is emphatically not the case if she had been seduced by promise of marriage. This produces a "life-long blight." "Respectable society" punishes her for her "too confiding indiscretion." Yet, if the marriage had actually taken place, this fact would have "largely, if not wholly . . . relieved her from" the blight. In this particular Michigan case the defendant, John M. Bennett, faced with a lawsuit, offered to marry the plaintiff, Mary Beam. She refused. The court took her side: Bennett, supposed to be a "virtuous man of wealth, refinement and respectability," had gained her affections but accomplished her "ruin"; then he abandoned her and entered into "a life of open and notorious profligacy and debauchery." When he offered marriage, "any woman with even a spark of virtue or sensibility would shrink from his polluted touch." An offer of marriage from "such a skeleton" would naturally be refused, and Bennett could not use Mary's refusal as an excuse for the mitigation of damages.

Note that the woman was, implicitly at least, *defined* as a victim in so many of these cases. The courts consistently talked about seduction, although technically seduction was in no way an element in the law of breach of promise. In addition, in many of the cases where the court talked about seduction, there was nothing in the facts to suggest it. Seduction was simply assumed. Nice women did not have sex unless they were seduced. Yes, she had sex with her partner, but surely this was not her idea. She must have been talked into it. Again, we are reminded of the rationale for blackmail laws. A respectable person (in this case a woman) was shielded from the consequences of her sins and transgressions. For men the protection often consisted of rules that aimed to keep the secret hidden. For women secrecy was sometimes more difficult. If the woman became pregnant, it was downright impossible. Of course, a woman who sued for breach of promise must have been somewhat desperate. She was, after all, airing her dirty linen in public. What must have made this acceptable at times was the fact that the dirty linen was already public knowledge. But even when this was not the case, it was a kind of protection to classify her as a victim, as a dupe, as the prey of designing men. And the threat of a lawsuit must have led some men, however reluctantly, to the altar.

In theory, breach of promise, like action for seduction, was available to anybody, of any race or class. It was, in fact, used quite a bit by working-class women in England. But whatever their station in life, breach of promise was definitely only for respectable women. It was definitely not an option for women of the type we would today call sexually active. In a Pennsylvania case, for example, the court said solemnly that a man "has a right to require that his wife shall come to him with an unstained name." The law "will not enforce a contract of marriage in favor of a party to it who is not fit to be married at all." He would not be "bound" and held to his promise if "in ignorance of her true character," he became engaged to a woman who has led a "vicious or reckless life."[48]

On the evidence of the reported cases the plaintiff's situation sometimes had great appeal for nineteenth-century juries. The cases sometimes produced damage verdicts that were for the time quite extraordinary.[49] In *Garmong v. Henderson* (1915),[50] the jury verdict was for $116,000, an enormous sum—larger perhaps than the verdict in any tort case decided up to that point. Curiously, in *Garmong* the plaintiff's case was quite shaky, and the appeals court reversed the decision. Why the jury was so generous is hard to fathom. In a rather sensational case in Los Angeles in 1887, Louise C. Perkins demanded half a million dollars from E. J. Baldwin; the jury awarded $75,000.[51]

When both the woman and the man were middle-class respectable people, it was only natural that the law—and jury verdicts—would tilt strongly toward the woman's side of the case; her loss was greater than his. But what if the man had a higher position in society than the woman? This was a different story. This possibility helps explain why there was always controversy over actions for breach of promise, even in the nineteenth century. Some said that it was undignified—unladylike—to bring such an action. A letter from "Cordelia" to the *Ladies' Magazine and Literary Gazette* of Boston in 1830—part of a vigorous exchange on the subject—put it this way:

Law it is true provides against breaches of promise; but shall the shrinking delicacy of woman, lay open the inmost recesses of her heart before a court of Justice?. . . . Let the ladies of America, abhor such customs.[52]

Nineteenth-century sources, including literary sources, evidence deep suspicion of the action of breach of promise. Wasn't it an open invitation to gold diggers, to women who were indulging in something close to blackmail? A Canadian newspaper in 1868 claimed that a woman who would "permit her heart's secrets to be exposed . . . and her love passages made the feast of counsel" had proved that "she is not a woman whom any man ought to be compelled to marry."[53] Gilbert and Sullivan satirized the breach of promise lawsuit in *Trial by Jury.*[54] Dickens mocked it in his *Pickwick Papers.* It was often an object of derision.[55] In this literature of obloquy the image of the plaintiff is very different from the image in many reported cases. Here she is not a victim, seduced and abandoned; rather, she is a brazen young hussy, taking advantage of a man who is usually rich and sometimes an old fool. Or, in any event, she is trying to get hold of his money. In this kind of case the law tended to shift to shield the man rather than the woman. In one type of case *she* was a victim—seduced by a man. In the other type *he* was a victim, seduced by a designing woman.

In the nineteenth century at least and for a while in the twentieth century, breach of promise was able to repel all the attacks against it and retain its vitality. Juries gave the woman the benefit of the doubt. Courts defended the action. An appeals court even held in one case that a woman who said her prospective husband "smelled like a wet horse" and who was almost certainly marrying him for his money could nevertheless try to persuade a jury of her case. The jury, not surprisingly, thought otherwise. But the appeals court reversed.[56] When the woman was respectable and came from the same social class as her defendant, judge and jury were sympathetic. But when women who were lower in the social scale sued a wealthy or prominent man for breach of promise, the sympathy vanished. In the end, this became the prevailing image and, as we will see, it doomed breach of promise to extinction.

Breach of promise was a common law action. But chastity was a virtue among respectable elites all over the Western world. In Germany, for example, a provision of the Civil Code (section 1300) allowed *Kranzgeld*, literally wreath or garland money, to an engaged woman if she had permitted herself to have sexual intercourse (*Beiwohnung gestattet*) and had later been jilted.[57] There were functional equivalents of breach of promise in other systems as well. In Venezuela, for example, the 1873 civil code "tried to address the false promises of marriage men made to gain sexual access to women." If the woman was "virtuous," that is, virginal, the judge could in fact declare the couple married; this was the so-called *matrimonio a palos*. The law was meant, to be sure, only for women who lived up to elite standards of respectability. Lawsuits on this subject were, apparently, far from rare.[58]

CRIMINAL CONVERSATION AND ALIENATION OF AFFECTIONS

Breach of promise was part of a cluster of closely related types of lawsuit. Another action went by the curious and misleading name of criminal conversation. To begin with, criminal conversation was not a criminal action at all but a civil action for damages. And it certainly had nothing to do with conversation. The subject of the lawsuit was not words but heavy sex.

A deceived husband could bring a criminal conversation (or "crim con") lawsuit against a man who had sex with his wife. In England criminal conversation goes back at least to the seventeenth century.[59] Criminal conversation in turn was closely linked to another remedy, the lawsuit for alienation of affections. This was broader than criminal conversation; it could be brought against anybody who spoiled the relationship between husband and wife. A man, for example, could conceivably sue his mother-in-law for alienation of affections if she poisoned his wife's mind against him. In one notable case Jacob Vanderbilt married a woman named Violet Ward. Violet was not a member of the "social circles in which the Vanderbilts moved." Vanderbilt's father made a huge fuss and told young Jacob never to bring his wife to the Vanderbilt home. Later, Jacob walked out on his wife. Violet sued Captain Jacob Vanderbilt, the father, for alienating her husband's affections.[60] In another case the son of Alexander Pollock, described as "rich, educated, and well bred," married Ellen, a "poor Irish-woman, without education and even without good looks." The father "set at work at once to free his son from the obnoxious union." He succeeded, but it cost him money. Ellen Pollock filed suit against Alexander for alienation of affections in 1893; she asked for $50,000 in damages, a princely sum. Apparently, she made an excellent impression on the jury—she fainted twice in the courtroom—and in the end the jury ordered her father-in-law to pay heavy damages: $37,500."[61] In these two cases the plaintiff was a woman, suing for alienation of affections. In criminal conversation cases the plaintiffs were rarely women. These were usually cases of men suing men.

Men and women were, of course, judged by different standards. In one Maine case (1890) the plaintiff, a married woman, complained that the defendant, another woman, "debauched and carnally knew" the plaintiff's husband, "thereby alienating his affection and depriving her of his comfort, society, and support."[62] The Supreme Court of Maine was unsympathetic. True, a husband could sue "for the seduction of his wife." A wife's "infidelity," after all, could throw "suspicion upon the legitimacy of his . . . children." A man's infidelity, however, had "no such consequences." If women could bring this kind of lawsuit, they would have the power to inflict "untold misery upon others with little hope of redress for themselves."[63]

In a Wisconsin case (1890) the wife of Frank W. Duffies sued her mother-in-law for alienation of affection. The mother-in-law, she claimed, had "wrongfully induced, persuaded, and caused" her husband to "refuse further to live and cohabit with the plaintiff, and to support . . . her . . . and . . . their child, and maliciously enticed him away."[64] The Wisconsin Supreme Court refused to allow the case. A wife had no such right to sue at common law, and there was good reason for this rule. Husband and wife live under "natural and unchangeable conditions" that make their situations "radically unequal and different." She is "more domestic," and the home is her natural habitat. She is "purer and better by nature than her husband, and more governed by principle and a sense of duty and right." As for the husband, he is "engaged . . . in the business and various employments of the outside world." The "exigencies" of his business "may keep him away from . . . home for months or years. He is exposed to the temptations, enticements, and allurements of the world." Suits by women in Mrs. Duffies's position would be a "fruitful source of litigation" and would do society no good. The complaint was dismissed.

These cases reek of the double standard, of course. Men had more leeway sexually than women. Men debauched women, not vice versa. This was believed to be a fact of life. Boys will be boys, and husbands are only grown-up boys. The Maine court no doubt reflected a common social understanding. If a wife could sue her husband's mistress or sexual partner, this would strip away a valuable layer of protection for men. Wives whose husbands had affairs were expected to forgive and forget—unless his behavior was too egregious, unless he stepped over an invisible line. A man's adultery was regrettable; it was sinful; but when it was discreet and sporadic, it was basically harmless. A woman's adultery was much more serious.

Yet, as we have seen, a woman's adultery was not always fatal to her social standing or her reputation. What helped her in many situations was the assumption that she was weak and easily seduced. When a man sued another man for alienation of affections or criminal conversation, he rarely alleged that his wife had been drugged or defrauded or raped. She had consented to sex, but this was, in a way, almost irrelevant. The law presumed that she was a victim. A smooth-talking rascal had won her over, despite herself. And even if she was not *really* a victim, the focus of these cases was on the man—the defendant—who had slept with her and who by that act had caused (legal) harm to the plaintiff.

The rule that a woman was not entitled to sue for alienation of affections or criminal conversation weakened considerably in the early twentieth century and even earlier in some states. In a Connecticut case in 1889 Laura Foot, who had been living "happily" with Enos Foot "in the enjoyment of . . . conjugal affection and society," lost him to the "arts, blandishments and persuasion" of Maria Card. Enos Foot began a long period of "adulterous intercourse." The case was thrown out of court, but on appeal, the Supreme Court of Connecticut disagreed. Married people have equal rights, and "each owes to the other the fullest possible measure of conjugal affection and society."[65] In a New Jersey case from 1910, one woman sued another woman for "maliciously enticing away" her husband.[66] The court cited a statute of 1906, which gave married women the right to sue in tort, under their own name; it followed, said the court, that women had the right to sue for *this* tort too. In 1930 the *New York Times* reported that Cecilia Bairnsfather, "wife of Bruce Bairnsfather, cartoonist and playwright," was suing an actress named Constance Collier for alienation of affections; she asked for $100,000 in damages. The defendant, she alleged, "maliciously enticed" the husband and talked him into leaving her. All this imposed on her "great distress of mind and body." Bruce left his wife, moved in with Constance, and "announced his intention of terminating" his marriage.[67] The case was probably settled out of court.

Originally, actions of criminal conversation and alienation of affection had their roots in a spouse's right to "consortium." This was something similar to a property right; a husband did not exactly own his wife, but he did have the right to exclusive custody, services, and affections. The services of course included sex. A woman also had a right of consortium, but it was valued much less than the husband's right.

Criminal conversation had a long history in English law and in the English-speaking countries,[68] but, as we have seen, its social meaning changed over the years. These actions were recast in the nineteenth century to serve as ways of protecting reputation—like the action of breach of promise of marriage. Criminal conversation and alienation of affections, like breach of promise, gave off mixed messages, however. They did protect middle-class honor and respectability. They did serve as a shield for women who slipped—by promoting an image of women as chaste but weak, as easily seduced, or as cheated out of their innocence. But they also came, more and more, to look like invitations to blackmail and extortion. As we will see, the second image came to predominate in the twentieth century.

POLYGAMY

Bigamy—marrying more than one person—was a well-established and well-recognized crime. It was a crime in the colonial period, and it was a crime in England. After the American Revolution it was a standard feature of state penal codes. Bigamy, of course, was a crime that could flourish only in the dark; it needed utter secrecy. The bigamist was a man (few were women) who hid a particular guilty secret. His wives were definitely victims—especially wife number two (or three). A man had lied to her, defrauded her, cheated her. He had also compromised her respectability. He had ruined her by entering into a marriage that was legally no marriage at all, and she was therefore a woman living in sin, even if unintentionally. No wonder, then, that bigamy was severely punished. This was not one of those sins that the law tended to wink at or forgive, even if the bigamist was "respectable." It was simply too gross a violation of norms.

Bigamy, as we have seen, was a classic crime of mobility. It is hard or even impossible to pull off the crime in a small, inbred village, where everybody knows everybody else's business.[69] Bigamy also reflects a shift in the nature of marriage. Women in the nineteenth century were not rolling stones the way that some men (including bigamists) were. They were, however, somewhat liberated compared to their grandmothers. They chose their mates on an individual basis and were willing, as I noted, to marry a stranger and to marry for love.

Polygamy was another matter. The polygamist obviously violated old-fashioned, time-honored bigamy laws. But polygamy was a different and more serious issue. Polygamy, of course, was associated with the Church of the Latter Day Saints (the Mormons). Joseph Smith founded the church in the 1830s in upstate New York. In 1843 Smith received a "Revelation on Celestial Marriage." According to the revelation a Mormon man was entitled to more than one wife; indeed, it was almost a duty for good Mormons to marry and marry again. At first, the leading members of the church kept the practice secret. Only a few officials of the church and their women knew about these celestial marriages. But in 1852 in Utah, where the main body of Mormons lived, the 1843 revelation became public knowledge, and polygamy, at least for leaders of the church, became official policy.[70]

There were other reasons that the Mormons would almost inevitably cause suspicion and hatred among "gentiles." Orthodox Christians were suspicious of any group that claimed fresh revelations from God. Was the Mormon church Christian at all? Anti-Mormon writers and publicists also attacked aspects of Mormon life that seemed downright theocratic. The leaders of the church seemed to have almost dictatorial control over the members.[71] But nothing was as shocking to the country as polygamy. This was a dagger in the heart of official morality. Mormon polygamy quickly became a major political issue. Outside the heartland of the Mormons, nobody defended the practice. Lurid, sensational books flew off the presses, claiming to describe the horrors of life in polygamous households. Some of these were works of fiction; others at least claimed to be telling the truth. Mrs. T. B. H. Stenhouse, the estranged wife of a Mormon elder, called polygamy a "cruel wrong to womankind" and a "terrible wrong to innocent children," "wicked" in "every sense of the word."[72] One congressman in 1860 called polygamy a "crying evil; sapping not only the physical constitution of the people practicing it, dwarfing their physical proportions and emasculating their energies" but also "perverting the social virtues, and vitiating the morals of its victims. . . . It is a scarlet whore."[73] The Republican Party platform of 1856 called for the abolition of the "twin relics of barbarism"—slavery and polygamy.[74]

The country recoiled in horror at the idea of plural wives and its encouragement of lust. In the fantasy world of many good, honest burghers all over the United States, life in a Mormon household was an orgy of debauchery. Such a life had to lead in the end to destruction of body and soul. As one contemporary put it, the "lowest" aspect of the "sexual principle" is "mere amativeness," the "feeling which the male animal has for the female" and which is "common to man with the brutes." Mormon marriage thus catered to the "lowest, basest part" of a man's nature. It corrupted the children as well. Among poor families, for example, a husband and two wives often shared one bed, and "when we consider the scenes and conversations to which these children are witnesses," we can understand their lack of "purity." Children under these circumstances "become precociously prurient." Polygamy might possibly seem natural in "voluptuous climes where soft airs incline to sensual indulgence," but it was "tenfold more unnatural" in a place such as Utah, a "barren land" with a "harsh clime."[75] J. W. Buel, writing in 1883, echoed this horrifying picture of families "living together like hogs"; its members, crowded together in a small space, "practice such undisguised sensuality that the children are raised up utterly destitute of the smallest spark of modesty or virtue."[76]

Utah was a territory, hence under the control of the federal government. The federal government, in the hands of Lincoln's Republicans from 1860 on, mounted a strong campaign against plural marriage. In 1862 Congress passed the so-called Morrill Act, a law "to punish and prevent the Practice of Polygamy in the Territories." Polygamists could get up to five years in prison for violating the statute. The law also "disapproved and annulled" any and all laws of the Territory of Utah that might "establish, support, maintain, shield, or countenance polygamy," even when this was "evasively" called "spiritual marriage" and "however disguised by legal or ecclesiastical solemnities, sacraments, ceremonies, consecrations, or other contrivances."[77] Armed with this law, the federal government took legal action against some of the more prominent Mormon polygamists.

George Reynolds, a bookkeeper, had acted as private secretary to leaders of the church. Reynolds was a married man, but he also took a second wife, Amelia Jane Schofield. Reynolds was arrested and charged under the Morrill Act. Amelia testified at the trial and admitted she was married to Reynolds; her appearance—she was pregnant—was a sensation. Her frank testimony made it obvious that Reynolds was guilty as charged. Reynolds was convicted and appealed to the United States Supreme Court.[78] He based his defense on the First Amendment: his constitutional right to freedom of religion. But the Supreme Court decided against him, unanimously. Chief Justice Waite wrote the opinion, in which he fulminated against polygamy. He called it a "patriarchal" practice, suitable only for African and Asian people, not Americans. The Court brushed aside the argument about religious freedom. Suppose (said the Court) that your religion ordered the burning of widows; surely that would not be allowed. Reynolds had broken the law and would have to go to jail.

Nowadays, I doubt that many people would put marrying two women in the same category as burning a widow to death. The analogy, bizarre as it may seem today, reflected the horror that polygamy evoked. And the campaign against Mormon polygamy sounded themes that were common in the nineteenth century. Official norms always had a problem with the brutish instincts of the male human animal. The good man kept these instincts under control. Nice women hardly had these instincts at all. Civilization depended on moderation, as we have seen, and this meant curbing and restraining male appetites. Polygamy, on the other hand, was an open invitation to men to satisfy their lusts with a whole string of women.

In light of what we know about nineteenth-century morals and mores, it is easy to see why polygamy seemed so scandalous, why it so horrified respectable citizens. There were, naturally, men with mistresses, men who slept with other women, men who went to prostitutes. But they never claimed legitimacy. Mormon polygamy was "open and notorious"; it even masqueraded as a religious duty. Hence it was a tremendous offense against traditional norms in their most sensitive area: sexual life. Polygamy was a special crime against moderation; it put a stamp of approval on men with more than one sex partner. In fact, they could flaunt it and even call it a religious obligation. This kind of behavior—and the *openness* of it—was the worst possible attack on the normative basis of nineteenth-century morality. A man with several wives was a man with several sexual outlets, and this was a situation that could not be (openly) tolerated. The idea, too, that a woman would choose to share a man openly with another woman—that she would willingly become part of a harem—was also deeply offensive to nineteenth-century thought.

Something similar might be said about the small free love movement of the nineteenth-century. Advocates of free love were opposed to traditional marriage and male dominance; they were willing to discuss sex and sexual pleasure freely and openly. In some ways they were models of purity (the Mormons also made a claim to purity). Free love advocates despised prostitution. They had no brief for sexual promiscuity. Yet this point was lost on the general public. Free love was an abomination. It "evoked fears that uncontrolled promiscuity would undermine the moral base of the society—the family."[79] In this regard, free love was potentially as dangerous as Mormon polygamy.

The image of the lustful Mormons and the free love zealots stood in total opposition to the image of the respectable white man. The churchgoing moral citizen was a man who kept his impulses under tight control. He kept the sexual side of his life under constant restraint and surveillance; it was a captive animal, locked in its cage in the zoo, fed only when it needed to be fed, fed only the right food, and fed only under the right and proper conditions. Sometimes, to be sure, the animal slipped free. The Victorian compromise allowed for certain leeways. But, as we have seen, only up to a point and only so long as the core of the moral code was not openly flouted or attacked.

PROSTITUTION

Sexual relations between people who are not married to each other is either fornication or adultery if we take these words in their ordinary meanings. Fornication and adultery had been crimes in the colonial period, as I noted; and even in the nineteenth century they were still part of the penal code. Some states simply continued to criminalize them; in other states the crimes were punishable only if "open and notorious." Laws never bother to forbid things that nobody does or thinks of doing. Adultery and fornication were certainly not extinct in the nineteenth century. How much of this sort of thing went on is anybody's guess. Useful statistics are almost impossible to find.

One thing is perfectly clear, however: Thousands and thousands of men, married and unmarried, went to brothels, either occasionally or frequently, or otherwise consorted with prostitutes. And thousands of women earned a living by selling their bodies. Bishop Simpson, of the Methodist Episcopal Church, claimed (in 1866) that there were more prostitutes than Methodists in New York City (the Methodists numbered between 11,000 and 12,000). James McCabe, who reported the bishop's remark, thought it was somewhat exaggerated (with regard to prostitutes, not Methodists). His own estimate was 600 "houses of ill-fame" and 5,000 professional prostitutes plus a certain number of part-timers. There were of course all types and manner of "fallen women" spread across the whole social spectrum. Some were "living in luxury"; others were "poor wretches who are dying by inches in the slums."[80] A letter from the superintendent of the Metropolitan Police of New York in 1866 also quoted the figure of 600 "houses of prostitution" and, in addition, "houses of assignation, ninety-nine. Concert Saloons of ill repute, seventy-five"; the superintendent's guess was that something on the order of 3,300 prostitutes were doing business in New York City.[81] Dr. William Sanger's estimate, in the late 1850s, of the number of "known public prostitutes" in New York City was 6,000. If we added to this number "women who visit houses of assignation for sexual gratification," "women who visit houses of assignation to augment their income," and a certain proportion of "kept mistresses," we would come up with 7,860 women "lost to virtue." Sanger noted that if these women were placed "in line, side by side," the line would extend "two miles and four hundred and eight yards. Let them march up Broadway in single file" and "allow each woman thirty-six inches," and they would reach from City Hall to 40th Street. Or, if they were to ride "in the ordinary city stages, which carry twelve passengers each," one would have to hire 500 "omnibuses for their conveyance."[82]

Sanger defined houses of assignation as houses "used especially as places for the meeting of the sexes with a view to illicit intercourse." The houses fell into various categories or classes. The toniest of them were "situated in the quietest and most respectable portion of the city." The visitors to these houses were "confined to the upper walks of life"—businessmen and women from "fashionable society." Sanger naturally deplored the brothel business. He blamed the evil of prostitution on such things as theories of free love or the tastes of "fashionable novel-reading people" or "weak romantic heads made giddy by the sudden acquisition of wealth." Foreign influences were another source of pollution. Many Americans traveled to Europe, where they learned bad habits and observed loose morals. European refugees, "styling themselves *artistes*" came to the states, bringing with them "an excessive devotion to fashion" and such horrors as "the low-necked dress and lascivious waltz." Obviously, he was describing the vices of the well-to-do; ordinary Americans never traveled to Europe. There were also many less exclusive and luxurious houses of assignation. At the bottom of the scale were the "cheap and nasty" houses where the lowest class of prostitutes, the streetwalkers, took their "company."[83]

New York, of course, was not the only city with prostitutes. Every city, big and small, had its share. Dr. Sanger collected data from a number of these cities. Thus the mayor of Norfolk, Virginia (population 18,000), thought that there were about 150 "public" prostitutes and 50 "private" prostitutes and that about "six or eight" men kept mistresses in the city. Philadelphia's mayor put the number of local prostitutes at 580. Newark's mayor, however, believed that "no houses of ill fame" and "no public prostitutes" graced that city; the city was so close to New York that "as soon as a girl turns out she makes her way to it, where associations and congenial amusements make it more agreeable." On the other hand, New Orleans was described as the "greatest brothel city of all time—a veritable Mecca of whores."[84]

Prostitution is supposed to be the oldest profession. In any event, it flourished in the nineteenth century in every Western country. The estimates for London in the middle of the nineteenth century vary wildly, but some investigators put the number of prostitutes between 80,000 and 100,000 and the number of brothels between 1,000 and 6,000. Clearly, there were many, many prostitutes, and "the average Victorian citizen was aware of their existence."[85]

In literature, scholarship, and perhaps the public mind, the central image of the prostitute vacillated between two poles. She might be seen as a victim: a "preyed-upon innocent, driven by starvation's threat or by a seducer's treachery." Or she might be, quite to the contrary, a "hard, vice-ridden jade, who sold her body to satisfy a base appetite for sex or . . . liquor."[86] At various times one or the other image has been dominant. Obviously, reformers trying to redeem "fallen women" took one approach; angry citizens, disgusted by the rot and the vice in their neighborhoods, took quite another. But whatever one's opinion about the women in the trade, nobody in public life had anything kind to say for the institution itself. It was (officially at least) always treated with loathing.

Yet the *law* of prostitution is not without its puzzles and mysteries. If prostitution was so morally repulsive, then surely the law made it a crime to buy or sell sex for money. But was this actually so? This is a surprisingly difficult question to answer. Under the current California penal code, in the twenty-first century, the answer is reasonably clear. A person who "solicits or who agrees to engage in or who engages in any act of prostitution" is guilty of a crime (a misdemeanor). Prostitution is defined to include "any lewd act between persons for money or other consideration."[87] Yet this statute is not ancient and time-honored. It dates back only to 1961.

The nineteenth-century statutes were much more limited. The Illinois statutes of 1845 had a provision that made it a crime (punishable by fine or jail sentence up to six months) to "be guilty of open lewdness, or other notorious act of public indecency, tending to debauch the public morals." It was also a crime to "maintain or keep a lewd house or place for the practice of fornication" or to keep a "common ill-governed and disorderly house, to the encouragement of idleness, gaming, drinking, fornication or other misbehavior."[88] Laws of this nature were common. They certainly made it a crime to be in the brothel *business*, but what is striking about the Illinois laws and others of the period is the lack of any clear language that parallels the language of the modern California code. Nothing *explicitly* made prostitution itself a crime, and the word did not appear in the Illinois statute. Nothing in the code made it a crime to buy or sell sex.

In Massachusetts in the nineteenth century it was a crime to be a "common night walker" under a law inherited from the colonial period. Offenders could be punished by up to six months in jail.[89] But what was a common night walker? The term seems fairly vague. There are clues in some practical texts of the period, giving forms to be filled out if one wanted to make a complaint against a "common Night Walker." The language is interesting: So-and-so at such and such times "did walk and ramble in the streets and common highways" in a given town "at unseasonable hours of said nights, without having any lawful business, and . . . against good morals and good manners."[90] This was unquestionably, then, a law that could be used against streetwalkers. Three women were arrested "for being night-walkers" in 1718; they were whipped, and fined. On May 7, 1870, the Boston police "arrested 183 night-walkers, most of whom were subsequently sent to their friends out of the city."[91] In 1908 the Boston police arrested 249 women as "common night walkers"; another 119 women were "arrested in the streets" (and were presumably prostitutes) but were for some reason not classified as common night walkers.[92] Originally, night walking had no necessary connection with prostitution; it referred to any suspicious activity at night. By the late nineteenth century, however, it had come to mean street prostitution for all practical purposes.[93] Note, however, that nobody could pin the label of common night walker on a woman who worked indoors in a brothel.[94] Massachusetts law did, in fact, make it a crime to keep a house of "ill fame," but here too prostitution as such was not criminalized.

In Boston, as elsewhere, the authorities from time to time roused themselves and indulged in a crackdown or sweep of brothels. A 1908 report for Boston recorded 114 prosecutions for keeping a house of ill fame. But the same report admitted that "high-class" houses seemed beyond the reach of the law. And the punishments handed out were hardly draconian. Forty-nine of the brothel keepers paid a fine of $50; a fair number were discharged or placed on probation; only twenty-five went to jail (for terms up to one year), and only two went to prison. Seventy-eight men and 130 women who were found in the houses were arrested, either because they were "actually engaged in the commission of crime or as idle and disorderly persons." *All* the men were released on the payment of small fines. Of the women, twenty-two were sent to prison or jail.[95]

Keeping a brothel was almost universally a criminal offense.[96] Or, as in Massachusetts as of the 1870s, any building "resorted to for prostitution" or "lewdness" was declared a "common nuisance," which meant that it could be suppressed by an action at law.[97] It was also a crime to take away "an unmarried woman, of a chaste life . . . for the purpose of prostitution at a house of ill-fame, assignation, or elsewhere" if done "fraudulently and deceitfully."[98] This was a quite common type of law. Legal condemnation of prostitution seemed to become more explicit in the late nineteenth and early twentieth centuries. In New York, under the tenement house law of 1901, a woman who "knowingly resides in or commits prostitution . . . in a tenement house" was deemed a "vagrant," and another section of New York law defined a "common prostitute, who has no lawful employment," as a vagrant. This statute, after 1900, pinned the label of vagrant on any man who "lives wholly or in part on the earnings of prostitution" or who, in public, "solicits for immoral purposes."[99]

The fact that no law *explicitly* criminalized prostitution did not mean that prostitutes had nothing to fear from the law. In fact, the police regularly arrested prostitutes. But they were usually arrested as vagrants or for disorderly conduct. It is likely, too, that the police mostly arrested common night walkers, or in other words, streetwalkers, whatever the content of the legal texts. In any event there was a curious reticence at the heart of the law. Typically, no *general* statute in the nineteenth century made it a crime to buy or sell sex for money. In most states, the cities, towns, and villages had the responsibility of controlling vagrancy, gambling, and prostitution through local ordinances. They did so, but so far as I can tell, most of the action was against streetwalkers. Vagrancy was the charge of choice for prostitutes. This was the case, for example, in Oakland, California; streetwalkers were arrested and charged as vagrants. There were occasional raids on brothels, but even in these cases the women were charged with vagrancy.[100] The more genteel the clientele, the less likely that police would take action against prostitutes. In some places police were probably tougher on black prostitutes than on white prostitutes. In 1929 there were 121 arrests for soliciting prostitution in the District of Columbia; all but 24 of these were "colored"; of 167 arrests for this offense in the preceding year, only 15 had been white.[101] Note that even where the crime was defined as soliciting, it was curiously one-sided. Nobody was arrested for *responding* to solicitation.

For many women "vagrants," the legal process was a revolving door. They were arrested again and again, fined, sent to jail for a day or two, and then released. Rarely did prostitutes use a lawyer. Rarely did they appeal their convictions; hence their fate made almost no mark on official legal records or in recorded cases. An unusual exception occurred in New York state, near the end of the nineteenth century.[102] A woman named Nellie Cowie was arrested in Franklin County in September 1894; the warrant for her arrest accused her of "being a common prostitute" in that she had "unlawful sexual intercourse with one Philip Goosha" for money and with "divers and sundry persons prior and subsequent thereto, whose names are . . . unknown." She argued that it was no crime to be a "common prostitute." Under the Code of Criminal Procedure, vagrancy was a crime, and engaging in "common prostitution" was evidence of vagrancy but was not a crime in itself.

The appeals court affirmed her conviction. The court cited a law of 1881.

Under this law a woman could be sent to the "House of Refuge for Women" for the crime of being a common prostitute.[103] What is especially unusual about this case is that the charge actually named one of her customers. The case also shows that until 1881 prostitution was not recognized in and of itself as a crime in New York. Even then, it was criminalized in an oblique, sideslipping way; and in general, whatever laws that existed were enforced mostly against the lowest class of prostitutes—streetwalkers.

Dr. Willoughby Cyrus Waterman (writing in 1932) argued that prostitution was "not regarded as an offense in . . . Common Law"; it became an offense only when it was "annoying to the passerby." The offense consisted of soliciting for sex on the street or running a bawdy house that disturbed the neighborhood. Waterman thought this was because "the rank and file of society" considered prostitution "inevitable and perhaps even desirable." Cities had red-light districts where "disorderly elements of society" were "herded together." Decent people could avoid "annoyance" simply by staying away.[104]

Waterman wrote not about the segregation of sex work but about the movement to abolish it (see Chapter 8). In the early twentieth century there was a furious attack on the idea that the "social evil" was "inevitable." The law came down hard on brothels and vice districts. But in the late nineteenth century brothels flourished in every major city. They were located for the most part in specialized vice areas—the so-called red-light districts. In city after city—San Francisco, Chicago, New Orleans, New York, and many others—the districts acted, as it were, as shopping malls for sex and vice. They had brothels, gambling dens, saloons, and dance halls.[105] No bawdy house was supposed to locate itself outside the red-light district; actual practice was somewhat looser, to be sure. By and large, for obvious reasons, the red-light districts were in neighborhoods where poor people lived.[106] Often, too, they were in or near African American neighborhoods, to the dismay of many leaders of the black community.[107]

As late as the early twentieth century, the system of red-light districts was in full sway.[108] Under the prevailing system prostitution was semilegal but segregated. There were sporadic crackdowns and raids, to be sure. Normally, the police hardly bothered, but occasionally cries of indignation from the clergy or from respectable citizens forced some sort of action. In some cities there were "brothel riots," when citizens took the law into their own hands and tried to get rid of the houses.[109] Raids were also a way to squeeze more money out of the houses. The police never made a serious attempt to get rid of prostitution. The system depended, of course, at least in part, on corruption—payoffs to the police or to politicians to buy immunity.

In the early twentieth century many cities appointed vice commissions, and typically these commissions soberly investigated the situation and then issued a report on the "social evil." These reports are a valuable source of information about prostitution and red-light districts. According to the Hartford, Connecticut, Vice Commission, eleven houses of prostitution were open for business in Hartford in 1911. They were "raided occasionally"; the keepers and inmates paid a fine, and the "houses re-opened on the day the cases were disposed of in the police court."[110] In Little Rock, Arkansas, according to its *Vice Commission Report* (1913), the police allowed nineteen brothels to stay open for business. Each brothel keeper paid a fine of $25 a month, and each inmate paid a monthly fine of $5. Once the money was paid, "these people are not molested in their business."[111]

The red-light districts were themselves "open and notorious." In many cities the vice districts were bustling, busy, and even something of a tourist attraction. This was true of San Francisco's Barbary Coast, Storyville in New Orleans (called, as I noted, a "veritable Mecca of whores"),[112] and the Levee in Chicago. In the early twentieth century the Levee was twenty blocks square, with 500 saloons and 500 brothels where no less than 3,000 women worked. Two sisters who called themselves Minna and Ada Everleigh ran the fanciest house of them all, on South Dearborn Street, a "glittering palace of sin" with gold-plated spittoons, thick rugs, tapestries, solid silver dinner service, and "cages of sweetly singing canaries." Their clients were wealthy and prominent men. After the house had become firmly established, it was almost as hard to gain admittance as it was to be accepted into a fancy country club. Their business made millionaires out of the Everleigh sisters.[113]

In the big cities, at least, everyone who cared to know (including the police) could easily find the vice district and even the location of individual houses. In some cities there were even published guidebooks—the earliest example, in New York, from 1839, was piously titled *Prostitution Exposed*. What it really exposed, for those who wanted to know, were the exact addresses of the bawdy houses of New York City. This was, of course, a great boon for out-of-town customers. The writer sported the marvelous pseudonym of A. Butt Ender.[114]

Chicago in the 1880s had a *Sporting and Club House Directory*, and in New
Orleans the *Blue Books* were guides to houses and women of that city.[115]

The red-light system was in one sense an example of the "shame of the
cities" in the corrupt days of the Gilded Age. Cities were political sewers controlled by rotten and venal machines. Corruption was certainly rampant. The
Everleigh sisters paid thousands of dollars every year for "protection."[116] But
corruption was more an effect than a cause. Much of the general public—not
all, of course—simply accepted the system or even welcomed it. After all, there
was no shortage of customers. If nobody had patronized the gambling dens,
dance halls, and bawdy houses, they would have had to shut their doors. The
system worked; and it had the side effect of protecting the customers. Streetwalkers—the lowest of the prostitutes and the ones who catered to the lowest class of customers—were harassed, fined, arrested, sometimes even jailed.
Brothel owners were socially something of a pariah class; they were tolerated,
however, as a kind of necessary evil and had to pay through the nose for their
privileges. In many cities this amounted to a kind of licensing system with a
regular schedule of fines. Because in most places and for much of the nineteenth century prostitution as such was not a crime, the customer himself had
almost total immunity.[117] This was especially true for customers of the richer
and more expensive houses.

This was, in short, another example of the Victorian compromise—and it
was geared to protect the reputation of elite and middle-class men. Men, after
all, were not angels. They needed their sexual outlets. Sex was supposed to be
confined to married men, but not all men were married. And nice girls did not
sleep with unmarried men. Society needed a way to let men have sex without
losing their status and position in society. Rich men in Europe had mistresses.
Some Americans did too, but American society frowned on "open and notorious" adultery. Prostitution helped fill in the blanks. The women, of course, were
almost never the social equal of their customers. An occasional "courtesan" or
"madam" rose in the ranks of society, but this was exceptional.

Prostitution thus became a kind of regulated industry, almost but not quite
legal. So long as the women behaved, particularly the more high-class prostitutes, they were tolerated. But they had to watch their step. The mayor of
St. Paul, Edmund Rice, told the police to arrest prostitutes who wore "gaudy
or flagrantly striking apparel" in public. And under an ordinance of St. Paul,

women of "evil name or fame" were not to "ride in any buggy, carriage or
other vehicle in the city of St. Paul, or voluntarily walk or appear in company
with any person upon the streets . . . or enter into any saloon, restaurant or
eating house." Prostitution, in short, was not to "intrude" into the "respectable world."[118] In Chicago the superintendent of police issued rules in 1910
"governing the regulation of vice." For example, no young messenger or de-
livery boy was allowed to enter a brothel; "short skirts, transparent gowns or
other improper attire" were not permitted in "the parlors, or public rooms";
no woman was to enter a saloon without a male escort; and no "soliciting"
was allowed "on the streets, from doorways, from windows or in saloons."
Moreover, brothels were not to have "signs, lights, colors or devices" advertising the "character of premises occupied by a house of ill-repute"; "swinging
doors that permit of easy access or a view of the interior from the street" were
strictly verboten. Nor was any "house of ill-fame" allowed to locate outside
the red-light district or within "two blocks of any school, church, hospital or
public institution, or upon any street car line."[119]

Sometimes ordinances and police regulations established the boundaries of the red-light district. In New Orleans an ordinance of 1897 set these
boundaries; it was introduced by Alderman Sidney Story, and the red-light
district was known from then on as "Storyville."[120] Sometimes, as in Chicago,
the rules specified the way "respectable" brothels (as it were) were supposed to
operate—rules that regulated an illegal or semi-illegal business. A survey of
1910–1911 found thirty-two cities in which vice was regulated; in quite a number of cities the social evil was segregated; in some of these, there was a regular
(although never official) system of physical examination of prostitutes. In some
cities brothels simply paid monthly fines as a kind of license fee.[121] In St. Paul,
Minnesota, for example, under a plan in effect in the 1860s, madams of local
brothels came to police court once a month and paid a fine. City officials denied
that this amounted to a system of licensing, but what else was it?[122] When the
Municipal Association of Bellingham, Washington, in 1909 demanded a crackdown from the mayor and the police, the mayor, James de Mattos, agreed, but
he pointed out that the prostitution industry paid $17,000 in fines and taxes,
out of a total budget of $150,000. Shutting down the red-light district would
compel the city to forgo two fire trucks.[123] Bellingham was surely not the only
city benefiting from these ill-gotten gains.

Thousands of women worked as prostitutes and worked at their trade through the night. This meant tens of thousands—maybe millions—of customers. Some men went frequently, some sporadically. For some, sex with prostitutes might have been "open and notorious" behavior; for others it was hidden, clandestine, a secret vice. There were probably regional differences. Prostitution meant one thing in New York or Boston, quite another in some Western mining towns, where the supply of respectable women was limited and vastly outnumbered by men. But everywhere the double standard was in full operation. It was sustained by the widespread belief, already referred to, that men (unlike women) had powerful sex drives, overwhelming urges that needed some outlet, and that only the saintly could resist.

This was indeed standard doctrine. Richard von Krafft-Ebing, in his famous book on the psychology of sex, announced that "Man has beyond doubt the stronger sexual appetite," a "mighty impulse of nature." A woman, on the other hand, "if physically and mentally normal, and properly educated, has but little sensual desire. . . . Woman is wooed for her favour. She remains passive. Her sexual organisation demands it, and the dictates of good breeding come to her aid."[124] Many women apparently agreed with him. In one classic study of married women (1929), the vast majority of the women thought that their husband had "desire" more often than they did.[125] This does not mean, of course, that the women had no sensual urges. Indeed, the study was powerful evidence that woman's frigidity was a myth. But her sensuality was much weaker than her mate's. Or so it was believed.

Experts endlessly repeated the mantras about the male sex drive. Dr. G. Frank Lydston, in a sexual hygiene book published in 1912, affirmed that for men "sexuality is more imperative in its demands and less controlled than in the female."[126] Dr. William Sanger came to the same conclusion in his important, pioneering book on prostitution, published originally in the late 1850s: "Man is the *aggressive* animal, so far as sexual desire is involved." "Nature" has made him "more susceptible" to lust than woman, "with the beneficent design of repressing those evils which must result from mutual appetite equally felt by both."[127] Sanger held to this belief, even though his survey of New York's prostitutes suggested a somewhat more complicated situation. Sanger asked the women, "What was the cause of your becoming a prostitute?" Many, of course, said they did it to earn money. Many jobs for young women paid wretched salaries; prostitution promised to pay a lot more. But out of 2,000 responses to Sanger's questions, no less than 513 answered "inclination" (another 124 gave "an easy life" as the reason for becoming prostitutes). Sanger found this suggestion of "inner depravity" and "want of true womanly feeling . . . incredible." The "force of desire" was a reality. But "in the bosoms of most females that force exists in a slumbering state until aroused by some outside influences."[128]

Male sexuality, then, made prostitution (as one writer put it) a necessity. Without prostitutes, presumably men would run riot; in the worst case they would seduce, pillage, and rape. Prostitution was a little bit like sacrificing virgins to the volcano gods. Only by offering up "a certain percentage of the women of the community to a life of prostitution" could society preserve the "sexual integrity of the great majority" and protect them from "seduction, fraud or force."[129] This meant that, in a way, respectable women needed prostitutes as much as respectable men did. The men had to have a ready supply of loose women, to protect the women who were not quite so willing. In England the large, wretched army of shopgirls and domestic servants helped provide the necessary supply. Women of the lower class were seduced and often raped by men of a higher class, who saw this almost as a privilege of their rank in society. Every respectable household in England had women servants, and they were "vulnerable, permanently available and had, in a sense, already been paid for."[130]

In the United States there were fewer of these domestic servants. But there was a large army of women workers in shops and factories, miserably paid, who longed for a better, brighter life. English servant girls and American shopgirls and waitresses often became reluctant converts to a kind of semi-prostitution. In hindsight the role of low wages seems crystal clear. Many vice commission reports stressed this point. In Newark, according to the *Vice Commission Report* (1913–1914), the average weekly earning of prostitutes was $38.50. A salesgirl who made $7 a week on her job might earn $40 from selling her body.[131] No wonder, then, that thousands of women chose prostitution as a part-time or occasional business. There was a "subculture of working women"[132] who traded their "sexual favors . . . for gifts, treats, and a good time." These "charity girls" were not prostitutes, but only a "thin line" separated them from women who sold sex for a living. The charity girls went to the dance halls in droves, looking for a little excitement. According to one account, waitresses, too, often took on a "life of semi-prostitution."[133] They were on the prowl for rich husbands or for any kind of husband at all. Most of them never found what they were looking for. Many men, on the other hand, probably did find what they were looking for.

As we have seen, prostitution operated in a twilight zone, half in and half out of the dark waters of illegality. It was not explicitly criminalized in the nineteenth century. On the other hand, with rare exceptions, it was never explicitly *legalized*. From time to time various people suggested a system of regulation and control or some sort of inspection system for health reasons. This was not at all uncommon in Europe. The police commissioner of Pittsburgh, for example, proposed a system of regulation and inspection in 1903.[134] In New York City a report of the Board of Aldermen (recognizing that prostitution was here to stay) suggested "licensing and regulating" the brothels. In 1867 the New York state assembly asked the metropolitan boards of police and health to give their opinion on a scheme for regulating prostitution. In 1868, 1871, and 1875 bills were introduced to regulate prostitution, especially in the interests of public health. All these attempts ultimately failed. Minneapolis, early in the twentieth century, tried a "semi-official system of medical inspection." It lasted five months. It led to a "general protest" on the grounds that the system was "immoral, illegal . . . ineffective" and that it led to "official corruption and public demoralization." That put an end to that noble experiment.[135] Later, in 1913, San Francisco, too, had a brief fling with a sort of licensing system. The city opened a clinic for prostitutes. The women were examined by doctors. Those who passed the test were allowed to go back to work; those who did not were treated; if they refused treatment, they were charged with vagrancy. But reformers soon insisted, successfully, that the clinic had to be shut down.[136]

Perhaps the most elaborate experiment was carried out in St. Louis, Missouri. In 1865 the city had 300,000 people and an estimated 2,500 prostitutes. In 1870 the city passed an ordinance that gave police the authority to license brothels. The Board of Health had the right, too, to examine prostitutes for evidence of venereal disease.[137] The ordinance lasted only four short years. There was a firestorm of criticism. Clergymen warned of opening the "floodgates of pent-up lust" and of importing the "deplorable standards of Parisian morality." The legislature, panicked by the opposition, hastily killed the plan.

The reference to pent-up lust is, I think, significant. This was the problem that also plagued polygamy: open and notorious recognition of "immoral" behavior. The rulebook insisted that marriage was a holy state, joining together two virgins, a male and a female. The ideal husband slept only with this one wife, either before or after the honeymoon. Of course, everybody knew that this was very likely an illusion. The real world was different. But if brothels were licensed officially, then the brothel was a legitimate business. And if it was a legitimate business, then men could patronize it legitimately and the women could sell their bodies legitimately. One doctor in Minneapolis put the case this way: "There can be no medical examination without at least an implied recognition and license," and this would be both "illegal and immoral." Others pointed out that the proposals were always one-sided; nobody suggested examining and regulating customers. Regulation gave official endorsement to the view that men needed "debauchery." To vast numbers of people this kind of pact with the devil was simply wrong—a "wrong and vicious theory."[138]

Moreover, regulation could have disastrous consequences. It could lead to a carnival of vice. It could bring down the whole structure of society. It would upset a delicate balance. Charles Loring Brace, another opponent of regulation, was willing to recognize the "strength of men's passions"—as well as the "misery and degradation" of prostitutes. But he felt that the authorities should do nothing to "weaken the respect of young men for virtue." A license system would also have an impact on that "large class of poor and ignorant girls . . . who are always just on the line between virtue and vice."[139] Brace admitted that society could not stamp out prostitution. But he believed it could be contained and controlled. William McAdoo, a former police commissioner of New York, writing in 1906, thought that vice districts were a good way to localize sin. Washington, D.C., he felt, was a model in this regard. The district was "so located as not to interfere with the citizens in general"; the police could easily control it, and it keeps "professionally bad women" out of "hotels, boarding, or apartment houses."[140]

The system was the essence of the Victorian compromise. Of course, millions of solid citizens did not buy into the compromise. They wanted enforcement and abolition, not licensing and regulation. They thought it was wrong to give a license to "immorality." But for decades the system survived. Common prostitutes were arrested in droves and "shuttled in and out of court." The level of harassment was, apparently, enough to satisfy a felt need to preserve public morality and at the same time to keep the "unrespectable classes of society" under control. And of course, nobody ever suggested that the customers should also be "shuttled in and out of court."[141] That was only for the women.

Vice lived in a world whose theme was containment and control. As I noted, society also seemed to tolerate adultery, provided that there was not too much of it and that it was not open and notorious. The vice system was somewhat more complex. Vice was not acceptable, but it was tolerated in a way—so long as it stayed put, in its place, where it belonged. The Victorian compromise made sense as a practical technique for monitoring and limiting behavior. It was supposed to keep vice within tolerable limits, prevent it from spreading, and prevent it from corrupting the cities beyond a certain point. The vice laws were thus, as I have pointed out before, in function something like modern laws against speeding. The worst and most blatant offenders are caught and punished; the ordinary speeder gets away with his offense. And speeding laws surely cut down on the sheer *amount* of speeding.

This control function was certainly one point of the Victorian compromise. Some contemporaries defended the system, red-light districts and all, on this basis. General Theodore A. Bingham, a former police commissioner in New York, writing as late as 1911, made the point forcefully. The social evil was a fact. It was never going to go away. The solution to the problem was segregation. His model was Toledo, Ohio. Streetwalkers were allowed only on designated streets. Prostitution in general was limited to those streets. "They allow no pianos, no noise, no revelry. Nothing exists in Toledo's red-light district except the plain, unadorned business of prostitution." There was also no "white slavery" there—or police graft (at least according to Bingham). Cleveland was another one of these model cities.[142]

But, as I have said before, the Victorian compromise had another function as well. A law that punished only open and notorious adulterers was more than a way to impose a kind of speed limit on adultery. It was also a way to protect respectable men who occasionally and quietly wandered offtrack. The same was obviously true of johns, the men who patronized houses in the red-light district. They ran no particular risk if they kept within the rules, just as the houses themselves ran no particular risk if they kept within the rules. Prostitution—the buying and selling of sex—was in theory just as wrong for the man who bought sex as for the woman who sold sex, but law and society did not operate that way. The customers were almost never arrested. They were not tested for disease. They were not classified as vagrants. Rarely did their names appear in the newspaper.

The existing system had the rancid smell of class bias. It protected the customers but not the women. The men who patronized the better houses were often respectable men, men with reputations and positions in society.[143] A prostitute, however, had no reputation to lose. The more high class the gentleman, the more the immunity. These men went to polite, well-managed houses—the houses that paid fines and were protected by the police. A kind of gentlemen's agreement tended to shield such men from scandal. The ordinary newspapers kept discreetly quiet. Their prudery and self-censorship were an essential part of the shield.

Of course, this gentlemen's agreement broke down from time to time, and sometimes quite sensationally. Seduction cases, when they went to trial, sometimes besmirched the reputation of a person of standing. The adultery trial of the Reverend Henry Ward Beecher was a famous instance of scandal that touched a man on the top rungs of the ladder.[144] Still, in general, the gentlemen's agreement had a long run indeed. To a degree, it was still around, in modified form, in the 1960s, when the press kept a discreet silence about President Kennedy's personal life and the parade of women he went to bed with. Law and social practice tended to respect and guarantee the privacy of people who were well off or held public office. This kept their reputations and their respectability intact.

But the Victorian compromise began to unravel long before President Kennedy. It began to come apart as early as the late nineteenth century, and by the middle of the twentieth century it was all but gone. The developments were ragged and full of zigzags and detours. The chronology of change was never clean and decisive. But the trend was quite clear. At first, what destroyed the Victorian compromise was the demand for zero tolerance—for an end to the cozy arrangements that protected vice and sin. Then, even more dramatically, the wheel turned in the last half of the twentieth century, and vice and sin won a smashing victory. These stories will be told in later chapters.

CHAPTER 7

CENSORSHIP

Its Rise and Fall

THE SOCIAL INTEREST IN REPUTATION

I have looked at a number of legal institutions and arrangements that consciously or unconsciously went to some lengths to shield and coddle the reputations of the bourgeoisie. I also asked why. One rather cynical answer is that the men who ran the country and made the laws were eager to protect themselves and people like themselves. They also had a certain interest in protecting the reputations of their sisters and daughters. Moreover, high-class respectable men thought that they had more to lose than members of the lower orders. They had farther to fall if they fell from grace. Beyond this, there was a serious point (or rationalization?). Just as open and notorious adultery was a threat to society, so too was open and notorious debauchery of any sort; it weakened the faith of ordinary citizens in the folks above them. It sapped their belief in the honesty and probity of the rich, the well-born, and the dominant political classes. It was vitally important for people to believe in their moral leaders. In any event this is what the "best people" might think was the case. The problem of sin in high places could be dealt with in two ways: One way was to punish it severely; another way was to bob and weave and conceal.

Elite people, no doubt, believed in themselves—in their strength and intelligence. They had earned the right to lead. They were willing to forgive some of their own sins. But what about the sins of ordinary people? This was a different situation. For one thing the common man or woman was in a sense more fragile—more easily ruined and perverted. Vice for them was a kind of contagious disease. Democracy, after all, was a brittle structure. It gave power to masses of people, but it did so on faith: in the belief that ordinary people could be trusted, that they would act in a responsible, respectable way, that they would exercise self-control. If you believed in democracy, you believed that most people would try to live up to this standard. But surely not all of them would succeed.

Law and society had a duty to help out. Ordinary citizens were like children—prone to corruption, easily ruined by false ideas. The shepherds were supposed to show the members of the flock how to behave. They were to be role models. It was dangerous, therefore, if people went about slinging mud at the shepherds. The flock also had to be protected from the seductions that trapped even the elites from time to time. These seductions were even more likely to entrap the man on the street.

The conventional story about America is a story of steady progress to more and more democracy; democratic habits and institutions slowly expanded over time. This is certainly a plausible story. The states dropped property qualifications in the nineteenth century. A man no longer needed to own land or pay taxes to earn the right to vote. By 1850 all adult white males had the franchise.[1] After the Civil War a constitutional amendment aimed to guarantee the right of black men to vote, although the Southern states by the end of the nineteenth century had effectively suppressed this right. In the twentieth century women gained the vote. More and more people had the right to elect their leaders—including judges (after about 1850 only federal judges and judges in a mere handful of states were appointed to office).[2] America was the land of mobility and opportunity. It was also the land where ordinary people had a say in running the government.

But each step in the direction of more democracy, more power to "the people," met with resistance. Each step led to a certain amount of anxiety among older elites. At all stages in American history, important people and important segments of society harbored deep suspicion of the mass public—or at least suspicion of *some* of the mass public, maybe the bottom quarter or third. From the dawn of the republic one political faction or another accused the other side of elitism, of monarchical or aristocratic tendencies, and the like—not without at least a grain of truth. In general, American culture praised and exalted the people, but it had nothing but contempt for the mob. Officially there was great faith in the common man, but not in men who were *too* common and certainly not in the have-nots, or in tramps, hobos, confidence men, paupers, and the lumpenproletariat.

Suspicion of the masses cropped up at various points in the legal system. One notable example was the reaction against the election system for judges in the late nineteenth century and into the twentieth century. States did not eliminate elections, but they tried to render them toothless.[3] From time to time there were outbursts of elitism and xenophobia. There were discrimination and occasional riots against the swarms of Irish immigrants in the first half of the nineteenth century. Later in the century, corrupt big cities, teeming with unwashed immigrants, seemed poor advertisements for popular democracy. There was certainly no joyous welcome for the huddled masses who came by the millions in the 1890s and later. They came from weird places, babbled in weird languages, followed ignorant customs, put coal in their bathtubs and never washed, and threatened to swamp true Americans by breeding like rabbits.

Society obviously had a duty to teach, or to try to teach, good morals to the masses. Whatever might corrupt the morals of the common man was a danger to democracy and to society as a whole. The exact policies varied from period to period. During colonial days punishment was always a public event—whipping in the town square, putting men and women in the stocks. Even public hangings were a form of didactic theater.[4] The whole town turned out, including women and children. Sometimes the miserable creatures whose necks were about to be broken made speeches from the gallows. Sometimes they gave advice, telling people how to avoid their own awful fate, warning them that vice and drink led them on a downward path, that petty crimes grew into greater crimes and in the end doomed people to a painful death. One man confessed that at the age of 10 he took to "stealing small Things, such as Fruit, Knives and Spoons"; he was thus on a path that led inexorably to the gallows.[5]

Public executions ended in the nineteenth century. The colonial villages had been small, ingrown, inbred. In some colonies they were under the iron control of clergy and magistrates. After independence there were more and more large, raucous, brawling cities. Now the impact of public hanging ap-

peared to be perverse. This was no longer moral theater; it was instead a bar-
baric spectacle, which only fed the bloodlust of the mob. Executions moved
out of the public square and into the courtyard of jails and prisons; then, with
the invention of the electric chair, the death penalty was carried out as far
away as possible from the eyes of the prurient public.[6] Some states required
executions to take place in the middle of the night. A Minnesota law (of 1889)
insisted on nighttime executions and barred reporters from the scene. Newspapers were not to give any details about an execution, only the fact that it
had actually happened.[7]

CENSORSHIP

American society was acutely aware of the importance of *messages*, of the didactic, moral nature of public action. The history of the death penalty shows
this growing distrust of the mass public. Perhaps the distrust was justified
in a way. By the end of the nineteenth century the United States was a big,
sprawling, mobile, heterogeneous country, fiercely democratic in some ways
but in constant danger (some people thought) of slipping into anarchy and
mob rule. The Minnesota law just mentioned indirectly reflects this fear. It
also represents at least a mild form of censorship. Censorship, in general, arose
out of fear: How far can the people really be trusted?

Western democratic societies have had a lot of experience with censorship,
and censorship has usually sounded a single basic theme. Ordinary people—
vulnerable people—should be protected from material that might possibly
corrupt their morals. Censorship has always shown a strong class bias.

Dictatorships, of course, are not shy about censoring materials. In dictatorships the point of censorship is much broader than in democracies.
Dictatorships tend to forbid criticism of authority. Yet even in dictatorships
class bias creeps into the practice of censorship. For example, in the Soviet
Union and its satellites during the palmy days of communism, the party
rigidly controlled books, newspapers, and broadcasts. But of course scholars
and high party members could always gain access to such dangerous stuff as
the *New Yorker* or the *New York Times*.

Political censorship seems undemocratic and un-American. American censorship has been, on the whole, less about politics than about sex, violence, and
lurid descriptions of crime—but not entirely. I have mentioned the notorious

Sedition Act, passed when John Adams was president. Before the Civil War Southern states banned literature that they considered subversive—for example, books and pamphlets that attacked the institution of slavery. It was a crime to import or produce or circulate writing that, in the words of a Louisiana statute, had a "tendency" to cause "discontent" or "insubordination" among African Americans.[8] Sedition was a crime during World War I. The Sedition Act of 1918 banned "disloyal, profane, scurrilous, or abusive language" against the government. During the Red Scare after that war, there were crackdowns on subversive literature. The first important Supreme Court cases on freedom of speech came from this period and concerned subversive literature.[9] A number of states at this time passed laws against "criminal syndicalism."[10] The Supreme Court has had to wrestle with the issue of the limits of political speech many times; this was a major problem for the Court during the McCarthy era (the 1950s), when the cold war was at its hottest and anything "communistic" was suspect. A number of countries today have restrictions on "hate speech";[11] and, in an age when people are frightened to death of radical Muslim terrorists, the urge to censor or suppress dangerous writings and fiery speeches in the mosques is almost irresistible.

A pervasive and more consistent theme of censorship has been the ban on immoral books and pictures.[12] I have mentioned the concept of obscene libel.[13] It was fairly generally agreed in the nineteenth century that the state had the right—indeed the duty—to prevent people from making and selling dirty books and pictures. Moral and religious leaders consistently denounced this kind of literature. It was a clear and present danger to the health of society. Young people in particular had to avoid "evil books and evil pictures," as Henry Ward Beecher warned. A "pure heart would shrink from these abominable things as from death." The danger was real enough. Not everybody had a pure heart or shrank away from abominations. Pollution flowed in from overseas, too. The French, Beecher said, were flooding the world with "literature redolent of depravity"; modern French novels seemed at times "scooped out of the very lava of corrupt passions."[14]

Probably every state in the Union ultimately made obscenity or pornography a criminal offense. In England a strong demand for legal action surfaced as early as the end of the eighteenth century. The problem became acute when the ordinary citizen learned how to read and write.[15] In the United States the earliest case on the subject apparently was *Commonwealth v. Sharpless* (Pennsylvania, 1815).[16] Jesse Sharpless and other "evil disposed persons" were the defendants. They were indicted for exhibiting for money "a certain lewd, wicked, scandalous, infamous and obscene painting, representing a man in an obscene, impudent, and indecent posture with a woman, to the manifest corruption and subversion of youth, and other citizens." The aim of the defendants was to "debauch and corrupt" their audience and to raise in the minds of their customers "inordinate and lustful desires." Sharpless argued, however, that no law on the books covered this particular crime. The court brushed this argument aside. The courts are "guardians of the public morals"; they have the power to punish any act that tends "to the corruption of morals."

Other early cases also upheld indictments for obscenity, even in the absence of any law on the books. *Commonwealth v. Holmes* (1821), a Massachusetts case, dealt with that randy classic, *Memoirs of a Woman of Pleasure* (better known as *Fanny Hill*), a book so "lewd, wicked and obscene" that it could not (according to the indictment) be "placed upon the records" of the court.[17] This book, too, was said to corrupt the morals and evoke "inordinate and lustful desires." No statute explicitly made it a crime to tell the tale of Fanny Hill's sexual adventures, but the court sustained the indictment and conviction anyway.

These early cases sounded themes that resonate throughout the history of obscenity law: corrupting the morals, especially of young people; and evoking "lustful" desires. These early cases treated obscenity as a common law crime, that is, behavior that was criminal, even though nothing in the penal code specifically covered the subject. Courts in the early republic occasionally exercised the power to invent such crimes. The power evoked considerable opposition, however, and most states in the end took the position that you could be punished for a crime only if the penal code specifically listed that crime.[18] With regard to obscenity, this issue soon became moot. The states all passed laws aimed at obscene books and pictures. A Florida statute applied to books and prints "manifestly tending to the corruption of the morals of youth." An Indiana statute imposed a fine of up to $500 for offensive material, but it was a more serious crime to exhibit obscene material to a "female"; this could bring a jail sentence of up to three months. The Kentucky statute put a ban on newspapers or periodicals if their "chief feature" was to "record the commission of crimes" and "to display by cuts or illustrations crimes committed . . . pictures of criminals, desperadoes, fugitives from justice" and "cuts and illustrations of men and women in improper dress, lewd and unbecoming positions, or men and women influenced by liquors, drugs or stimulants."[19] A federal statute passed in 1842 made it a crime to import "indecent and obscene" pictures.[20] There were some prosecutions under this law; in the first of these, in 1843, obscene pictures were "attached to snuff boxes" imported from Europe. The goods were confiscated.[21]

Not much is known, in general, about enforcement of obscenity laws. It was surely sporadic and perhaps in many places ineffective. We do know that pornography existed and even flourished and that there was certainly a demand for it. Publishers also put out racy books, periodicals, and pictures that skirted the edges of legality. In New York City after the 1840s, there was a thriving pornography business; a number of bookstands hawked lewd books and pictures. Naturally, a movement arose to suppress these obnoxious products. Some pornographers were prosecuted; in 1846, for example, William Haines, one of the pillars of the business, was indicted in New York for selling (among other things) a book called *The Curtain Drawn Up, or the Education of Laura. Translated from the French.* Haines was convicted and spent three months in the New York jail known to all as the Tombs.[22]

As is well known, the Victorian age was an age of prudery. It was not just hard-core pornography that was under the ban. Any frank, open discussion of sex was taboo. Only doctors who wrote soberly and cautiously could discuss reproduction, sexual intercourse, venereal diseases, and the like. Such a man as Frederick Hollick, who lectured to big audiences about sex in the 1840s and who praised the "generative act" as both necessary and wonderful, was apt to land in trouble, and indeed he did. Hollick, when he lectured, displayed a large papier-mâché model of a naked woman, notable for its "completeness and accuracy." He also published a book, *The Origin of Life*, which was too much for the district attorney of Philadelphia.[23] Hollick went on trial. He had his corps of supporters, though, who admired his attempts to enlighten Americans about sex. His career reminds us that even in the depths of the Victorian era, there were countervailing points of view. On the whole, however, the moralists had the upper hand. The wonders and secrets of the "generative act" had to stay hidden, private, and under wraps.

Outright pornography on the whole was never as shrill and overt as, say,

Frederick Hollick. It was quiet and surreptitious—and almost impossible to control. For one thing it had an eager audience. The state laws against pornography and obscenity were in any event fatally flawed. Publishers and peddlers of obscene books soon learned how to evade these laws. The New York companies that specialized in smut began to sell their wares by mail, from out of state, in plain brown wrappers. New York had no power, or right, to stop this interstate traffic.[24]

This situation led to demands for national, federal legislation. Congress was happy to oblige. The law of 1842, as we have seen, made it unlawful to import "indecent and obscene" prints and pictures; in 1857 daguerreotypes and photographs were added to the list.[25] There was a feeling—not altogether wrong—that a good deal of the supply of obscene pictures came from overseas. A law of 1865, however, dealt with domestic traffic: It became a misdemeanor to "knowingly" mail any "obscene book, pamphlet, picture, print, or other publication of a vulgar and indecent character."[26] In 1873 the so-called Comstock Law ratcheted up the federal war on smut. This act made it a crime to send through the mail any "obscene lewd or lascivious book, pamphlet, picture, paper, print, or other publication of an indecent character."[27] The statute also applied to "articles or things" that were "intended or adapted for any indecent or immoral use" and to "scurrilous" postcards, and, most significantly, any "article or thing designed or intended for the prevention of conception or procuring of abortion."[28] "Comstock" of course refers to Anthony Comstock, perhaps the most famous nineteenth-century crusader against vice, prostitution, abortion, pornography, and assorted evils.[29]

Comstock himself worked tirelessly to see to it that these laws were effective. Congress made him a postal inspector, which gave him the authority to carry on his war on smut. In two years he confiscated and destroyed more than 60,000 "rubber articles."[30] But he was by no means always successful. In 1873 he had George Brinckerhoff arrested; Brinckerhoff was the owner of the Eugenic Manufacturing Company, which made "Ladies Rubber Goods." Brinckerhoff had mailed contraceptives to an undercover agent of the postal service. Brinckerhoff pleaded not guilty, and the prosecutor dropped the charges.[31] Contraceptives were in wide use and, despite their dubious legal character, were quite popular. Big companies, such as Sears, Roebuck, advertised devices for men and women, including "vaginal pessaries" and "male caps," in their catalogue.[32] Big sellers (and their customers) were hardly bothered by law enforcement officials. Some incident, story, or special motive probably lay behind each actual prosecution—or the work of a zealot like Comstock, who looked for violators behind every bush. Most of his victims were small fry.

One case, for violation of the Comstock Law, went all the way up to the United States Supreme Court (1897); it concerned John R. Dunlop and his publication, the *Chicago Dispatch*.[33] The obscenity here consisted of "advertisements by women, soliciting or offering inducements for the visits of men, usually 'refined gentlemen,' to their rooms, sometimes under the disguise of 'Baths' and 'Massage.'" Note that the language of the ads was not in itself the least bit obscene. The judge charged the jury that obscenity was a matter "of your own conscience and your own opinions." What is obscene had to be tested in terms of the "ordinary reader." Would the material tend to "deprave him, deprave his morals, or lead to impure purposes." Were the ads, then, "calculated to lower that standard which we regard as essential to civilization," or were they "calculated to excite those feelings which, in their proper field, are all right, but which, transcending the limits of that proper field, play most of the mischief in the world."[34]

The Supreme Court saw no problem with the judge's charge. Anything that tended to "deprave" by "exciting sensual desires and lascivious thoughts" could be labeled obscene. Those "sensual desires" were admittedly—as the judge had said—perfectly acceptable in their "proper field." After all, as everybody knew, the species could hardly go on if nobody ever had sensual desires and lascivious thoughts. But such thoughts and desires were a source of enormous mischief if they went beyond proper limits.

This was the Victorian compromise with a vengeance. To keep a lid on vice and impurity, vice and impurity must be outlawed—even if enforcement was a sometime thing. First, the law sends a moral and symbolic message, enforced or not. Second, and more significantly, illegality and occasional enforcement might keep the lid on—might control the amount, time, and manner of violations. The laws also expressed and (to a degree) enforced the idea of moderation and control. As I mentioned and as is well known, the nineteenth century was positively obsessed with the notion that masturbation was a dangerous act.[35] Masturbation was a prime example of a lack of self-control. It was the opposite in fact; it was self-abuse. Dirty books and pictures led to lascivious thoughts and sensual desires. Such desires and thoughts were only for respectable, married people. In other men they would lead to such evils as masturbation, which would, of course, destroy in time both body and mind. Sexuality had to be kept in its cage—hence the constant drumbeat of arguments against anything that might stimulate lascivious thoughts.

Suppression had its class elements as well. On the whole, suppression shielded the elites, the respectable upper stratum of society. The code of censorship, I have argued, protected a whole way of life. If the code were to collapse, the social structure itself would be in danger. And in the late nineteenth century the code was in serious trouble. The mass public could read and write, and a mass medium—the press—catered to the public's love for lurid and exciting and vaguely titillating material. The campaign against smut was fueled by fear of this public. Some pornography was elegant and expensive. But many wicked periodicals and pictures did not cost much. Some cheap pamphlets, newspapers, and magazines skirted the fringes of pornography. These induced a kind of moral panic among respectable members of the elite.

The mass public was vulnerable—young people the most vulnerable of all. Anthony Comstock wrote a whole book on the subject: *Traps for the Young*. There were so, so many of these traps. "Evil thoughts," he wrote, "like bees, go in swarms." "Light literature"?—a "devil-trap to captivate the child by perverting taste and fancy." He railed against the dime novels so popular in his day. As for the newspapers, they were full of "sickening details of loathsome crimes." Comstock condemned the "newspaper that gathers up the letters of the libertine, the secret doings of the rake, the minute descriptions of revolting crimes, the utterances of lips lost to all shame, the oozing of corruption from the debauched, and then weaving that into a highly sensational story, decks it with flying colors and peddles it out each day for the sake of money."[36] Worst of all, these newspapers were cheap, they were "within the reach of all classes," and "they enter the homes," where children can see them. There were also "low theaters and bawdy playhouses"—"portholes through which death-shots are hurled," the very "sinks of hell."[37]

The lower orders, like young people, also had to be protected from slime. Comstock was not the only one in the late nineteenth and early twentieth centuries who thought something should be done to curb the yellow press. Lurid accounts of crime and violence simply bred more crime and violence and corrupted the young.[38] The Pennsylvania Chautauqua Circle, in a letter sent to the editor of the *North American*, complained about the enormous coverage of "crime and immorality" in daily and Sunday papers. This kind of reporting has a "vicious and demoralizing effect upon the public in general and especially upon the minds of the young." The members of the Circle wished to "earnestly protest and remonstrate against such annals of crime and immorality being published in detail repeatedly . . . in your otherwise valuable paper."[39]

The problem got legislative attention in a number of states. I have mentioned already the Kentucky statute, aimed at criminal news, "deeds of bloodshed, lust or crime," and "men and women in improper dress, lewd or unbecoming positions, or men and women influenced by liquor, drugs, or stimulants."[40] A statute of this sort was, of course, quite general. It did not make an exception for educated people, elite people, and those whose immune systems, so to speak, protected them from "corruption." But clearly such statutes were aimed primarily at ordinary people, not elites. This was always a key theme in censorship—of books, movies, plays, and even art. Extraordinary people were, in a sense, not as easily corrupted. Still, in Comstock's view even so-called classics of literature and art had no special claim to legitimacy. Why protect, "under the name of *art*," the "filthy conceptions upon canvas" that some "foul-minded man" had placed there? If a scholar wanted to read, say, Boccaccio, let him learn Italian. But if "base men" were so degraded as to translate this man into English and "prostitute" the book to their foul designs—and especially if they let the book fall into the "ever-ready hands of the youth"—then these men "ought to be stopped by the rigid enforcement of [the] . . . laws."[41]

On the other hand, even Comstock drew a distinction between a "grand oil painting" and photographs of the same painting (of a nude, for example)— presumably, it was the distinction between the rich people who owned the art and the vulgar masses who would look at the work in cheap reproductions.[42] A sexual hygiene book for boys, published in 1912, put the matter this way: "Such books as the Decameron, Heptameron, the unexpurgated Arabian Nights, Rabelais and Zola's productions should be denied the young, given in sparing doses to the mature who have passed the danger point, and permitted chiefly to the old."[43] Presumably "the old" were no longer prone to lustful thoughts.

In 1924 Thomas Seltzer was indicted in New York for selling a "certain obscene, lewd, lascivious, indecent and disgusting book," *Casanova's Home-*

coming, by the well-known Austrian author and playwright Arthur Schnitzler.[44] Seltzer objected (in legal terms, he demurred). But the appeals court reinstated the indictment. The law, said the judge, aimed to protect not the "mature and intelligent," who had strong minds and could resist, but rather "the young and immature, the ignorant and sensually inclined." The opinion of "literary critics" did not impress the judge, nor did the fact that the book was accepted in other countries. We can "assert with pride . . . that we are essentially an idealistic and spiritual nation and exact a higher standard than some others." The nation had the right "to protect our youth against the corruption of their morals." In 1930 a jury in Boston decided that Theodore Dreiser's *American Tragedy* was obscene, and an appeals court agreed.[45] This happened despite rallies and appeals outside the courtroom for a more rational attitude, complete with reminders of how cases of this sort made Boston a laughingstock in more enlightened circles.[46]

The elitist attitude underlying these cases explains a curious aspect of publishing history in the English-speaking world: censoring books by simply refusing to translate the naughty parts. As I noted, Comstock told the potential Boccaccio lover to learn Italian.[47] It was, in fact, the practice not to translate the Italian text of the "extremely sensual tenth story of the third day" in the *Decameron*.[48] In some editions of the works of the Marquis de Sade, the ripest passages were simply left in French. Some translations of that hoary classic of antiquity, *The Satyricon of Petronius Arbiter*, left offensive passages safely hidden in the original Latin. The practice rested on the idea, no doubt, that only the well-educated elite could be safely exposed to such dangerous works. In 1922 the Society for the Suppression of Vice struggled mightily to get the *Satyricon* banned; the publisher claimed, in defense, that this was a limited edition; the Society countered by arguing that the book "was freely sold to anybody who could find the $20 to pay for it," and in fact the publisher had offered deep discounts to booksellers.[49]

In the late nineteenth century and early twentieth century, some judicial cases reached progressive results and rejected censorship, as applied to classics and serious literary works, but not by running up the flag of freedom of expression. Rather, the courts argued that only educated people read such books. In a New York case from 1894, *In re Worthington Co.*,[50] a publishing company had gone bankrupt. What was to be done with its stock of books?

Could they be sold, or were they unsellable because they were "immoral"? The books in question included an edition of the *Arabian Nights*, Fielding's *Tom Jones*, Rabelais, Ovid, and Boccaccio. The receiver naturally wanted to sell the books, but the New York Society for the Suppression of Vice appeared in opposition. The court held for the receiver. The books in question were "choice editions . . . specimens of fine-book-making." They were also great literature; they had "artistic character" and "high qualities of style." They lacked those "glaring and crude pictures, scenes and descriptions which affect the common and vulgar mind." These books, then, were not like the "gross and obscene writing" that public authorities had a duty to "suppress." These "rare and costly books" would not be "bought nor appreciated by the class of people from whom unclean publications ought to be withheld." And they would never fall into the hands of the young.

The panic over corrupting the masses lasted deep into the twentieth century and was, perhaps, more virulent in England than in the United States. D. H. Lawrence's novel *Lady Chatterley's Lover* aroused a storm from the time it was published (in Italy) in 1928. As late as 1960 the authorities tried to stop Penguin Books from bringing out an unexpurgated edition in England. Mervyn Griffith-Jones, who handled the case for the Crown, asked the jurors (nine men and three women), "Is it a book that you would have lying around your house? Is it a book that you would even wish your wife or your servants to read?" The jury was apparently not the least bit frightened; they sided with Penguin.[51]

The class distinction was not always overt, and the truest of the true believers never distinguished between rich and poor, learned and ignorant. Filth, after all, was filth. It was fit for no one. John Weld Peck, a federal judge in Ohio, fined a man in 1922 for "sending obscene and indecent literature in interstate commerce." The books were Boccaccio's *Decameron* and the works of Rabelais. In Peck's opinion, "Most of the people who buy the so-called classics buy them for the filth that is in them rather than for their literary value." If it was a question of mere literature or artistry, "an expurgated edition would do equally as well as an unexpurgated edition." Indeed, the "existence of expurgated editions" was "conclusive evidence" that parts of these books were "not fit to be read by the average person."[52] Boccaccio and Rabelais had long been in trouble; being old, famous classics did not save them from persecution.[53]

Senator Smoot of Idaho agreed with Judge Peck. It would be better, he said, "that a few classics suffer . . . the expurgating shears than that this country be flooded with the books . . . that are wholly indecent."[54]

As late as the second half of the twentieth century, most European countries had laws against obscene literature.[55] The Censorship Board of Ireland, set up in 1929, banned thousands of books. The list of the damned included many that would hardly raise an eyebrow today. As St. John-Stevas put it, "titles like *Hot Dames on Cold Slabs* . . . are found side by side with" Proust and Gide; four winners of the Nobel Prize for literature made the list, along with "nearly every Irish writer of distinction." One defender of the Board put it this way: "There are things . . . higher than art or literature . . . namely the morals, the virtues, the chastity of a nation."[56]

Looking back, we find it easy to mock the extremists, the bluenoses, the men who censored books, especially those that today we think of as totally innocuous. One reviewer of H. G. Wells's novel *Ann Veronica* (1909) called it a "book capable of poisoning the minds of those who read it," a book that aroused "loathing and . . . indignation" because it could undermine "that sense of continence and self-control in the individual which is essential to a sound and healthy state"[57]—this with regard to a book without a single "coarse word" and no real sex or violence, a book that today we would consider totally demure (and probably boring). Its sin was that Ann Veronica had an affair with a married man. Books, said another writer, that "undermine" the "moral foundations" of a "civilised Christian society" have no "valid claims to exist. . . . They should be stamped out like . . . yellow fever."[58]

But the differences between bluenoses and progressives were often a matter of degree, not kind. Probably the most famous progressive decisions of the first half of the twentieth century concerned *Ulysses*, that huge (and difficult) novel by James Joyce.[59] The federal government wanted the book condemned and destroyed; federal law outlawed importing "any obscene book." A federal judge in New York, John Woolsey, decided against the government. *Ulysses* was neither obscene nor pornographic. Despite the book's "unusual frankness," Judge Woolsey did not "detect anywhere the leer of the sensualist." An obscene book was one that tended "to stir the sex impulses or to lead to sexually impure and lustful thoughts." But *Ulysses* was not that kind of book; nowhere did it act as "an aphrodisiac."[60]

If we take Woolsey literally, then the state *could* ban books if they were meant to "stir the sex impulses." Moreover, Joyce's book had been praised by literary critics; Joyce was a famous author, and, what is perhaps more to the point, *Ulysses* is awfully tough sledding. A book so knotty that even college students majoring in English literature struggle to get through it can hardly play much of a role in corrupting the young or arousing the prurient interests of the masses in general. John and Jane Public would find the bulk of *Ulysses* rather baffling. The famous soliloquy by Molly Bloom at the end was something of an exception, but anybody who really wanted pornography could find it in a more concentrated and accessible form.

Woolsey's decision was upheld in a split decision by the Court of Appeals. Augustus Hand, who wrote the majority opinion, held that the book "as a whole" was "not pornographic," nor did it "tend to promote lust."[61] There were, to be sure, long passages that were "obscene under any fair definition of the word," but they were "relevant to the purpose of depicting the thoughts of the characters." They were not "introduced . . . to promote lust or portray filth for its own sake." Hand, too, seemed to imply that the state could ban books if, unlike *Ulysses*, they did indeed "promote lust." Martin Manton, the dissenting judge, argued that the law should not "disregard the protection of the morals of the susceptible," even to satisfy the "benefits and pleasures" of those who "pose as the more highly developed and intelligent." The point of the law was to protect "the great mass of our people; the unusual literator [*sic*] can . . . protect himself."[62] *All* the judges, in other words, agreed that the state could act against books that promoted lust. They disagreed only on the criteria for deciding whether a book *did* promote lust. They disagreed on whether there could be or should be two standards: one for young people and the general public and another for the educated elite.

Obscenity was a major issue in England too.[63] A number of nineteenth-century statutes had strictures against obscenity. From the beginning of the century the Society for the Suppression of Vice worked hard to ferret out and prosecute those who marketed such horrors as an "obscene tooth-pick case," inside of which was a "filthy" picture of a man and woman in an "obscene situation, attitude and practice" (in 1812); in 1820 William Moore was convicted for selling snuffboxes with images of "carnal copulation."[64] But a giant step forward (or backward) came with the passage of Lord Campbell's Act in

1857—the first "serious attempt by the legislature to regulate the distribution and circulation of obscene publications."[65] The preamble expressed the aim of the statute: "to give additional Powers for the Suppression of the Trade in Obscene Books, Prints, drawings, and other Obscene Articles." Under the law, magistrates and justices of the peace could grant a constable or police officer "Authority by Special Warrant," which entitled the holder of the warrant to enter a store or house and seize the offending object.

As in the United States, the war against obscenity heated up because of the rise in literacy and the development of a mass market for books, periodicals, and newspapers. Dirty books are no problem for people who cannot read. Of course, there had been (and continued to be) dirty pictures, but cheap novels and magazines made the problem so much worse. St. John-Stevas quotes a remarkable passage from Dickens, written in 1867. Dickens praises a novel by Charles Reade but also claims that if Dickens had been the editor of a "periodical of large circulation," he would not have allowed certain passages to get through his moral filter: "What was pure to an artist might be impurely suggestive to inferior minds (of which there must necessarily be many among a large mass of readers)"; the writer's intent might well be "perverted in such quarters."[66] Lord John Campbell, the lord chief justice who gave his name to the obscenity act, had fulminated against obscenity in the House of Lords in 1857. The problem was not just "indecent books of a high price," where the cost "was a sort of check"; there were also "periodical papers of the most licentious and disgusting description," which came out "week by week" and were "sold to any person who asked for them."[67] Lord Campbell himself presided over the trials in May 1857 of two men charged with violating the law. The two men were sentenced to prison. His Lordship was horrified that the obscene material in this case had been sold on the London streets for as little as one penny.[68]

Lord Campbell's Act was broadly interpreted in the courts. The courts held that anything was obscene under the act if it tended to "deprave and corrupt those whose minds are open to such immoral influences and into whose hands a publication of this sort may fall."[69] These were the words of Lord Cockburn, frequently quoted and approved of later on. The act was applied not just to ordinary pornography but also to pamphlets on birth control and to a whole parade of books by famous authors. Lord Cockburn's "test" was also cited and approved in a number of American cases in the later nineteenth century.[70] In England George Bernard Shaw's play *Mrs. Warren's Profession* (1894) was kept off the public stage for some thirty years (it met with a similar fate in the United States). Mrs. Warren's profession, of course, was owning and running brothels. There were no dirty words in the play and no sex or violence, but the theme was too shocking for the censors. In the twentieth century the British censors lost none of their zeal. *Ulysses* was banned and burned in England. Home Office and Customs officials worked zealously and tirelessly to keep foul literature from corrupting the young in Shakespeare's homeland. Shakespeare himself, of course, did not entirely escape the zeal of the purists.

Censorship of alleged obscenity continued deep into the twentieth century and is certainly not completely dead. As we have seen, there were two consistent and persistent themes. One was protecting the corruptible (children and the ordinary person), and, second, in a way a subtheme of the first, preventing bad books and pictures from whipping up lust. These themes are closely related to my argument in earlier chapters. They embody a double standard: What the elites can see and read is not what the masses can see and read. The masses are too easily led astray. What keeps society from falling apart is the insistence on moderation, the denial of legitimacy to vice and sin, and a double standard—whether between women and men or between the masses and the respectable elites. The same ideology that insisted on circumscribing sex, exiling it to the bedrooms of nice married people, demanded suppression of any books, plays, or pictures that violated this norm of privacy and repression.

THE SILVER SCREEN

In the early twentieth century a new and powerful entertainment medium burst onto the scene—motion pictures. Very early on, they became enormously popular. Within a short space of time nickelodeons were everywhere, at first in the big cities and then also in the smaller towns. By 1907 Chicago alone had more than a hundred nickelodeons.[71] Every year, more and more people became addicted to the moviegoing habit.

The authorities quickly took note of this new medium, and there was an almost indecent rush to censor the movies.[72] In some places censorship of the movies went beyond censorship of other media—newspapers and magazines. Why? Because movies were considered exceedingly dangerous. They had an almost fatal attraction for ordinary people. The nickelodeons were cheap, and they were found in every neighborhood. A survey in New York in 1910 found that 72 percent of all moviegoers were workers and their families; this group made up only 2 percent of the audience for the regular (and more expensive) theaters.[73] The movies were vivid, thrilling, seductive. They were thus a serious threat to good morals and traditional values. The very atmosphere of the movie theater was unwholesome. As a former police commissioner of New York pointed out in 1911, movies were shown "in darkness." In these shadowy places, full of "young children from fourteen to sixteen," the "procurer" could easily do his dirty work. This made movie theaters a "terrible menace to the morals of young girls."[74] The darkness, wrote Louise de Koven Bowen, gave "cover for familiarity and sometimes even for immorality."[75]

But the greater threat was not what happened in the darkness of the theater. The greater threat came from the content of the movies. Children, even before walking in the door, Bowen wrote, were enticed by "lurid advertisements and sensational posters." And the films were "demoralizing"; boys saw the "gentlemanly burglar, the expert safe-blower, the daring train robber"; these images gave him ideas of "what a hero ought to be." The audience looked on "crime of all kinds" and also "scenes of brutality and revenge." Bowen mentioned a movie that showed the body of a man, robbed by Gypsies, hanging by a rope over a precipice, "plucked at by vultures."[76] An early movie that created an uproar was *The Unwritten Law: A Thrilling Drama Based on the Thaw-White Case*, of 1907; in a number of cities the police refused to allow this movie to be shown.[77] Such movies convinced many good citizens of the need for rigid, rigorous censorship to stop movies from conveying such terrible images and messages.

In 1908 the mayor of New York City, George McClellan, went so far as to revoke all the nickelodeon licenses in the city—more than 550 of them. This rather panicky move did not survive a court test, but it was a straw in the wind.[78] The National Board of Censorship of Motion Pictures had been established as early as 1909. It reviewed movies and made recommendations to local censorship groups. The Board conceived of itself as duty bound to condemn material that might have a "deteriorating tendency on the basic moralities or necessary social standards."[79] Chicago was the first city to try its hand at formal, legal censorship. A city ordinance of 1907 gave the chief of police power to censor movies. He had authority to ban "obscene or immoral" movies. The ordinance was challenged in court after the chief withheld his approval from two movies, one called *James Boys* and one called *Night Riders*. In *Block v. City of Chicago*[80] the Illinois Supreme Court upheld the ordinance and gave the idea of censorship a ringing endorsement. Movies, said the court, cost very little and they attracted children and people of "limited means," people who did not go to plays in "regular theatres." (This was, of course, quite true). The moviegoers, then, were "classes whose age, education and situation in life specially entitle them to protection against the evil influence of obscene and immoral representations." The banned films in the *Block* case were crime movies, and they could well have harmful effects on "youthful spectators."

The urge to censor soon spread to other cities and states. In Pennsylvania a state board of censors was empowered to ban movies that would "debase or corrupt the morals." The Ohio Board of Censors was told to approve only movies that were "moral, educational or amusing and harmless." In an important decision the United States Supreme Court, in 1915, upheld Ohio's law on grounds similar to those given by the Illinois Supreme Court. Movies were dangerous and seductive and could be "used for evil." The audiences included children. Sometimes they excited a "prurient interest." There are "some things which should not have pictorial representation in public places and to all audiences." What about freedom of speech? The concept, the Court felt, did not apply to movies at all; to be sure, movies might be "mediums of thought," but so was the "circus, and all other shows and spectacles." The "guaranties of free opinion and speech" did not apply to the "multitudinous shows which are advertised on the bill-boards of our cities and towns."[81] A law review article, published in 1915, considered it a "startling . . . novelty" to claim that norms of freedom of speech had any application to "the product of a mechanical device on a curtain in a motion picture theatre."[82] Entertainment was not political debate but something altogether different. It was clear to the courts (and to a lot of moral leaders) that the state had the right—and the duty—to regulate, control, and censor movies.

In a New York case from 1917 a movie company sued the commissioner of licenses of the city of New York for refusing to allow a certain movie to be shown.[83] The movie was *The Hand That Rocks the Cradle*, and the subject was birth control. The heroine, the wife of a doctor, was an advocate and imparted "unlawful knowledge" about birth control to poor women, who benefited from the advice. The court thought that there would be a "sorry future in store for human liberty" if the "ignorant and uninformed" were told that "the laws which they do not like may be defied, and that lawbreakers deserve to be glorified as such." The commissioner had the perfect right to decide whether the movie was "decent." In any event, decency was to be measured "by standards in vogue among highly civilized people and not those that may prevail among the Fiji or South Sea Islanders. Lewd men or women have no sense of decency."[84]

In general, the Supreme Court and almost every other court upheld censorship of the movies.[85] Often the courts stressed the potential impact of movies on children. Movies were capable of exerting a powerful influence. As one writer put it, the "vast haphazard, promiscuous . . . ill-chosen, output of pictures" could mold the minds and attitudes of the young. The screen is the "most open of all books," and it has enormous influence on people "in the most impressionable years of their life."[86] About 38 percent of girls "in a home for delinquents" blamed the movies (in part) for their problems. They began the "pathetic succession of steps in their careers" with "wild parties patterned after . . . the movies, then truancy, then running away from home." As one 17-year-old girl said, it was "these love pictures" that were "responsible" for getting her "in trouble." The love pictures made her want to flirt with "some man on the corner. . . . The best thing I like are wild parties. Movies were the first thing that made me go astray."[87] Movies were "an education along the left-hand or primrose path of life" for these girls. For boys the movies were also pernicious; gangster movies seduced them into lives of vice. In short, for both sexes the road to delinquency was "heavily dotted with movie addicts."[88]

Not every city or state had a formal censorship board. Where they were lacking, private groups tried to fill in the gaps, campaigning against bad or immoral movies. In St. Louis, for example, attempts to create a censorship board failed in the years after 1913. But a private campaign put constant pressure on the police department and its morality squad. Hundreds of films were edited or banned. The usual reasons were given: The movies were immoral, seductive, and unfit for mass audiences.[89] Free speech junkies objected to censorship on general principles; the industry itself, along with various liberals, leftists, and labor unions, worked to oppose censorship but without great success.

The critiques of the movies in the early twentieth century sound prudish, heavy-handed, and elitist, at least to our current tastes. Of course, the controversy over movies has never died out. We hear in some ways similar complaints today—too much sex and violence and the idea that Hollywood is spreading bad values across the land. But the movies that were banned and censored in, say, 1915 seem to us completely tame and innocuous, even timid. The campaigns against them would strike most people today (of course not all) as incomprehensible, like something from another planet. With regard to sex and indecency, between the attitudes of 1907 and the attitudes of 2007 there is an absolute yawning chasm.

Or, take attitudes toward race. The most famous movie of its day (1915) was *Birth of a Nation*. It did arouse controversy, partly on the grounds that it would incite race hatred and violence.[90] The movie glorified the Ku Klux Klan, and its picture of the South in the years after the Civil War was wildly distorted and racist to the core. No studio today could or would make a movie so retrograde or one that painted the Ku Klux Klan in rosy colors. But the movie came during the high-water mark of American racism, the age of lynching and full segregation. Race was also a factor in the movement to ban boxing films. Boxing movies were extremely popular with audiences. Some of them reenacted boxing matches. Others were live films of actual bouts. Boxing in general had many enemies and was illegal in most states—condemned as brutal, savage, disgusting, and, as usual, dangerous to the morals of children and the working classes. Moreover, many famous boxers were black, and there was particular venom directed against matches in which a "Caucasian brute and an African biped beast" took part—as one congressman put it.[91]

But the bulk of condemned movies were considered too hedonistic or sexually immoral. Indeed, some movies were fairly salacious for their times. Movies such as *The Inside of the White Slave Traffic* attracted thousands of people—and tremendous controversy.[92] A movie about white slavery was bound to upset the moral guardians of society. Movies of this type seemed to make vice and immorality seem glamorous. True, sin and crime almost always lost out in the end, and the movies *claimed* that they condemned evil, sin, and wrongdoing. But even so, the movies were mentioning the unmentionable. And in a sense, the moralists were right to be disturbed. As with advertising and the mass media in general, the movies were in fact deeply subversive—and they were subversive in ways that no censor could possibly hope to touch.

This is because the movies, even without nudity, drugs, or sex, even when they tried to preach the old-time morality, were in fact deadly enemies of the old-time morality. The movies offered escape, adventure, glamour. They opened a window into a world of wealth and sophistication. More basically, the movies, like the media in general, appealed to the *individual*, to the solitary watcher in the theater, and the message primarily was a message of pleasure, fun, consumption, self-fulfillment. Of course, not all movies could be described in these terms. Some movies showed, sympathetically, the trials and tribulations of everyday life; some attacked corruption or exposed the oppression of workers.[93] But most movies—and the most popular ones—were not of this type. Audiences liked comedies, and they also liked dramas that showed the lives and habits of glamorous people—beautiful women reclining in a beautiful bed, wearing a beautiful robe, and eating a beautiful breakfast served on a silver tray by a black maid in uniform; or men in tuxedos, mixing cocktails for themselves from gleaming, cut-glass decanters, sharing their drinks with women who wore furs, jewels, and evening dress. Nothing in the movies conformed to the quaint nineteenth-century ideal of moderation in all things. Nothing seemed to stress the Protestant ethic. By showing people a dream world, a world of endless horizons, the movies also helped to breed a culture of envy and desires.

So it is not surprising that moral crusaders turned their wrath against this medium. Hollywood, for its part, was terrified of censorship, which could cripple their business. Hollywood was also afraid that the censor's ban could keep them from recovering money invested in particular movies. The danger was real enough. Between 1915 and 1920 attempts were made to give Congress control over movies. A bill was introduced in Congress in December 1915 to create a "Federal Motion Picture Commission"; under this bill, no film could be licensed if it was "obscene, indecent, immoral, inhuman, or depicts a bull fight or a prize fight" or would "tend to impair the health or corrupt the morals of children or adults, or incite to crime."[94] None of these bills passed, but drug and sex scandals in the 1920s helped fuel the censorship movement, and quite a few states and cities continued to have censorship boards.[95] In response, the studios set up the Motion Pictures Producers and Distributors Association in 1922; its president was Will Hays, a Republican, who had been postmaster general in the Harding administration. The "Hays office" imposed a rigorous code on the movies: no dirty words; no "indecent movements"; crime must never pay; lustful kissing was banned; "sex perversion," drug traffic, and "white slavery" were not even to be mentioned. In general, the movies were supposed to present "correct standards of life."[96] The work of the Hays office was supplemented by other amateur and unofficial watchdogs, notably the Catholic Church. Anything obscene or even just plain vulgar fell under the ban. As a result, as H. L. Mencken put it, the movies were "cribbed, cabined and confined by regulations that would now seem oppressive in a Baptist female seminary."[97]

Despite the work of the Hays office, the movies continued to arouse controversy during the 1930s. The flood of gangster movies—films such as *Little Caesar*—aroused a kind of moral panic. There were the usual charges of corrupting the young, "poisoning the minds of the youth," and even of serving as a "kindergarten of crime."[98] One critic claimed in 1934 that the movies were "breaking down the home and destroying all the principles that fathers and mothers have been endeavoring to instill into their children." Movies were "insidious," full of "vulgarity"; they wrecked the moral teachings of "home, church, and school."[99] The Catholic Church was especially active in the struggle against harmful and indecent movies. The cardinal of Philadelphia declared in 1934 that movies were the "greatest menace to faith and morals in America" and that "one hour spent in the darkened recesses of a movie picture theater" could "undo years of careful training."[100] Catholics formed the Legion of Decency in 1934. Good Catholics were supposed to pledge not to see movies that the Legion condemned. Vast numbers of the faithful took this pledge.[101]

All of this—in the end, of course, a losing battle—was in line with a time-honored trend in American social life. Propriety—today we would call it prudery—was an essential pillar of the moral order. Anything sexual was banned from open, public discourse. Respectable men did not talk about such things. Respectable women were, in turn, supposed to be shielded from impropriety. Women in general—certainly middle-class women—were yet another category of people who had to be protected from corruption. The true woman of virtue was delicate and modest; she lived in a kind of bubble, where the dirt and grime of the ordinary world never entered. This was, of course, sheer fantasy.[102] But it was significant fantasy, and it was supported by custom and law. Hence a Georgia statute in the late nineteenth century made it a crime to "use obscene and vulgar language in the presence of a female."[103] If and when a trial touched on delicate or indecent subjects, the judge sometimes chased women out of the courtroom.[104] Women in New York City were not allowed to attend prizefights. In 1913 a girl "in male garb" in New York City tried to sneak into a prizefight and nearly set off a riot.[105] A "sex hygiene" movie of 1927, *Is Your Daughter Safe?* which was advertised as a "sensational sex expose film," was "for men only" and "boys under 16 [were] not admitted." The movie was banned in New York, Maryland, Ohio, Virginia, and Portland, Oregon.[106] Open and notorious impropriety, especially if it had a mass audience, had to be suppressed; it was a threat to the image of women that the upper reaches of society had constructed.

American prudery and censorship may seem somewhat extreme. But censorship of the movies was not just an American habit. The program of censorship in Great Britain was perhaps even more vigorous than anything in the United States. As usual, the censors were extremely worried about the impact of sexual material on the mass public. The censors were also quite protective of the royal family and of authority figures in general. George Bernard Shaw's play *The Doctor's Dilemma* could not be made into a film (1935–1936); the play was "absolutely unsuitable" material, because it reflected badly on doctors.[107] In Germany, which had a thriving film industry, censorship began in Prussia as early as 1912. As in England and the United States, the movies were condemned as a threat to the morals of children and adolescents and to the mass public as well. Movies had a "mesmerizing influence on its young patrons" and were dangerous for the "criminally inclined or morally weak."[108] The Reichslichtspielgesetz of 1920[109] was a general censorship law that applied to the whole German empire. No movie was to be shown if it threatened "public order or security" (*öffentliche Ordnung oder Sicherheit*) or if it injured religious feelings or was contrary to morality or harmed relations with other countries. Movies of scientific or artistic distinction could be shown to specific audiences. Under this law children under 6 were altogether forbidden, and young people under 18 could be barred from movies that were likely to harm their moral development or their good health or that might lead to "overstimulation of the imagination of young people" (*eine Überreizung der Phantasie der Jugendlichen*).

Movies were of course censored during the Nazi period on grounds far broader than immorality. But the restoration of democracy after World War II did not mean that allied forces or the German elites gave up the fight to control the content of movies. In 1949 the occupation authorities replaced state censorship with a form of self-censorship, which the industry itself would run, after the American model of the Hays office.[110] In 1951 a tremendous controversy arose over the movie *Die Sünderin*, which was widely condemned as immoral. Not surprisingly, it became a tremendous hit. The main character was a former prostitute; she performs euthanasia on her dying lover and then commits suicide. The churches were appalled by the movie; critics accused the movie of corrupting the infant democracy and weakening its moral resolve; moreover, it was said, "women and youth" were "most susceptible to the attractions and 'insidious' influences" of this sort of film.[111] Each European country has its own history of censorship, each no doubt subtly different but sounding common themes. The impulse to censor movies is by no means completely gone. Bertolucci's *Last Tango in Paris* (1972), for example, a movie that was praised by many critics, was condemned as obscene and totally banned in Bertolucci's home country, Italy.

Note that, everywhere, censorship laid heavy stress on movies, books, and plays that could be seen or heard or fall into the hands of women and children. A secondary theme was protection of the masses in general from corruption. But when it came to adult men, law and practice were curiously ambivalent. A truly respectable man, in theory, was not that different in behavior from a truly respectable woman. It was both harmful and wrong, however, to evoke his "lustful thoughts." Implicitly, the standard was this: Whatever in books or movies might encourage or stimulate masturbation was pornographic and dangerous. Yet side by side with this view was quite a different belief: Men had powerful sexual instincts, and they simply had to have sexual outlets by hook or by crook. Arguably, then, an underground supply of dirty books and a certain number of well-run houses of prostitution were a kind of social safety valve. In the first part of the twentieth century, at the same time that *Mrs. Warren's Profession* or Dreiser's *American Tragedy* were fighting for their lives in court, burlesque houses were open for business and raking in huge amounts of money. Big audiences of men watched women in scanty costumes dance and sing, with lyrics drenched in sexual innuendo. In the 1920s came that great American invention, the striptease. There were repeated campaigns against the evils of burlesque, to be sure. But the fact that it survived was probably an important social indicator. Somehow, it seemed less of a threat to society to tease and arouse the "prurient interests" of an audience of men than to write and mount a serious play about prostitution or a serious novel about men and women who embrace adultery. Most of the men in the burlesque houses were working-class men, but professional men and middle-class men were scattered throughout the audience. And many of these men seemed quite willing to admit that they liked what they heard and saw.[112] Dirty jokes and the striptease existed below the level of polite society. What polite society could not tolerate was a shocking play by George Bernard Shaw or a novel by James Joyce. These were more dangerous precisely because they undermined the very pillars of that same polite society.

SHOW AND TELL

I have used the term *Victorian compromise* to describe a certain kind of arrangement in the living law of the nineteenth century. The adjective *Victorian* is commonly used to mean a kind of prudery, a reluctance to talk about sex in public forums. Mainstream novels in the nineteenth century never spoke openly about sex. A visitor from outer space who read Dickens, George Eliot, even Willkie Collins and the "sensation" novelists, might dimly suspect that getting married had something to do with having babies (for the most part). But the visitor would learn absolutely nothing about how this was actually done or even that a woman needed a man to make herself pregnant. Pornography was plentiful, but it was illicit and strictly underground. The *Oxford Dictionary*, which appeared in the late nineteenth century, was a massive and scholarly enterprise; it aimed to be completely exhaustive—a total, historically accurate dictionary of the English language. It included all sorts of dialect, regional, obsolete, and obsolescent words, but, on the other hand, it omitted two common words in the English language—the "four letter words" *fuck* and *cunt*. For the learned editors printing these words was simply impossible. They were so taboo that no decent book had a right to print or utter them. Here was one case where scholarship had to bend its knee to propriety.[113]

Whatever the reasons, the Victorian age was an age of extraordinary prudery, and this was in some ways even more striking in the United States than in Victoria's England. In the United States aspects of the age of prudery lasted long after Victoria herself was dead and buried. The United States is a country where in the movies for a long time even *married* people (on film) had to sleep in twin beds. It was a country where at one time whole hosts of words became taboo, where people talked about wearing "unmentionables," where some people even used the word *limb* instead of *leg*. The word *leg* was never "mentioned before ladies"; apparently it had too many sexual over-tones.[114] H. L. Mencken dates the "palmy days of euphemism" to the years from 1820 to 1880,[115] but the attitude lasted much longer, especially outside the big, bad cities. It is certainly far from dead in the United States, especially in the Bible Belt.[116]

It is easy to sneer at Victorian prudery; moreover, a rich literature exposes the dark secrets of the Victorian underground. It can even be argued that the Victorians, here and abroad, were actually obsessed with sex; otherwise why was it so taboo? Why was everybody tiptoeing around the subject? There is a point to this argument, but it can be carried much too far. There is no easy way to measure how obsessed a society is with sex. In contemporary times (early twenty-first century) images of sex seem to leer at us everywhere, in every medium, and there is little left that would suggest tiptoeing; in short, there is plenty of evidence that our societies now are far more obsessed with sex.

In any event, Victorian prudery was in many ways a matter of surfaces. As I have argued all along, however, this distinction between surface and what was below the surface was not at all pointless and random; there was a purpose and a theory behind the distinction. A healthy society, as I have suggested and for reasons I have suggested, required a bland, blank bourgeois surface. And surfaces were everything. Taboos against open discussion of sex reinforced a form of privacy. Sex was, of course, a reality. Without sex, as everybody knows, the species would soon die out. (There seems no immediate danger.) But sex was a *private* affair. Sex was legitimate only for married men and women and only in the quiet precincts of their bedrooms.

Much later on, when censorship and prudery were already fighting a los-ing battle, in the 1960s, an interesting interchange took place in the course of a New Jersey obscenity trial. The real defendant in the case was a woman long since dead and always fictional: the infamous Fanny Hill. At one point the prosecutor, referring to a character in the book, asked a witness whether the "deflowering of virgins" was a "practice which is accepted by the people of today." Charles Rembar, Fanny's sly and able lawyer, pounced on this question: Didn't that depend on the circumstances, he asked. After all, how would the "the human race . . . survive if people were to reject the practice of deflowering virgins"?[117] Rembar had scored a direct hit. Probably people in the courtroom snickered. But traditional society did have an answer to his question. Yes, virgins were to be deflowered and *had* to be deflowered. Loss of virginity was a solemn and mystical ritual, performed on the wedding night, intimately and privately. But nobody but a husband had the right to deflower a virgin. Of course, this was a fantasy, but it was a fantasy at the heart of the Victorian compromise. In the eyes of millions of respectable people it was a *necessary* fantasy. Any book or picture that suggested otherwise was a threat to the social order and the very health of society.

The naked body itself was private. "Private parts" (the term is significant) were meant to be kept hidden. Nudity was taboo, as we have seen. Even nudity in works of art—paintings and sculpture—were suspect. In the 1840s the American Academy turned down *Cupid and Psyche*, a painting by William Page, because it was simply too nude.[118] There *were* naked bodies underneath all those layers of Victorian clothing, but nobody outside the immediate family had any right to catch a glimpse of these bodies. They were hidden behind buttons and flounces and cloth.

And perhaps not even the family could take a peek. Dr. Frank Lydston, who wrote about sex, vice, crime, and related matters in the early twentieth century, raised a serious question about what he called undue familiarity between husbands and wives. A "less intimate association of husband and wife would be better for . . . health and morals. The less knowledge they have of each other's physiology, the better for sentiment. Privacy is an individual right, in or out of matrimony."[119] Lydston even thought husbands and wives should never sleep in the same bed. This was a "pernicious" practice that could lead to sexual "excess."[120] Nudity, even during sex, was another bad idea. Krafft-Ebing thought that "shame" in the "exercise of the sexual functions" and "modesty" in "mutual relations" were the "foundations of morality." This is one reason that "the act" is performed "in private." "Savage races" still had sex openly, and such people were not "ashamed of their nakedness."[121] But of course, Europeans and Americans were not members of savage races.

In fact, many couples in the nineteenth and early twentieth century did manage to have sexual intercourse without getting undressed (beyond a certain unavoidable minimum). Alfred Kinsey, in the middle of the twentieth century, found that quite a few older couples still behaved this way. In Kinsey's famous study a third of the women who were born before 1900 claimed that they were usually or always "clothed" during sex. This was true for only 8 percent of women born in the 1920s. Kinsey himself was all for nudity. Humans, he argued, had evolved from animals, and animals, believe it or not, were totally naked during sex. From this it followed (for Kinsey) that wearing clothes "during coitus" was arguably "a perversion of what is . . . normal sexuality."[122]

For ordinary people, what militated against nudity during sex was sheer lack of privacy. Millions of working-class couples in England, for example, lived under appalling conditions, squeezed into wretched tenements and often sharing a single filthy, miserable room with children or a boarder. Under these conditions a "satisfactory sex life" was out of the question. To "copulate in the presence of others calls either for furtive cunning or brash heedlessness."[123] Having sex under these conditions rules out, at least for most people, elaborate romance or foreplay—and very likely nudity as well.

As I have argued, reputation was linked in the nineteenth century to propriety. Both reputation and propriety were, in a sense, clothing that people wore. Underneath was a naked reality, but the good person, the person who deserved respect, never let that naked reality show through—in public. If we believe the medical guidebooks, sex was dangerous, even toxic, except in small doses—toxic for the body, for the soul, and for society. Keeping sex under wraps was one way to discourage overuse, one way to encourage people to keep the doses small. We have seen some reasons why intelligent people could hold these views.

At times the United States seemed to be an outlier, an extreme case, among the richer Western nations. Many countries found it perfectly normal, and in fact desirable, to license prostitutes, to give medical examinations to prostitutes, or even to provide a supply of prostitutes for raunchy soldiers. This was the case in many European countries. To be sure, many of these countries had their own versions of the Victorian compromise. In France, for example, prostitution was, strictly speaking, illegal, but nonetheless "prostitution was policed and controlled throughout the country," with Paris leading the way.[124] Under an ordinance of the city of Buenos Aires, Argentina, in 1875, prostitutes were to submit to medical examinations twice a week. The licensing system had mixed results, but it was the first in a long line of regulations aimed at controlling prostitution.[125] In Mexico the Reglamento de Prostitución en México of 1867 called for prostitutes to register; they would pay monthly fees and submit each week to a medical examination.[126]

Even in Victorian England, Parliament, alarmed at the spread of venereal diseases among soldiers and sailors, enacted a law "for the Prevention of Contagious Diseases at certain Naval and Military Stations" in 1864.[127] Under this law, if a woman was thought to be a "common prostitute" (a fairly vague concept), the authorities could order a medical examination. The woman had no choice but to obey. If the examination showed that the woman was suffering from syphilis or gonorrhea, she could be sent to a specific hospital "for Medical Treatment" and kept there until the authorities discharged her. These laws applied only to military and naval enclaves (although some people wanted to make the act more general). A schedule attached to the law listed the locations (near military areas) where the law was to be in effect.[128] It seemed to be sound military policy to take steps to preserve the health of soldiers and sailors, to protect them against venereal diseases. In this law one sees the same underlying ethos as in the regulation of American red-light districts. Doctors were allowed to poke about in women's genitalia, but there was no provision that applied to the men or allowed doctors to look at *their* private parts. The regulation "reinforced a double standard of sexual morality"; it "justified male sexual access" to "fallen" women but "penalized women for engaging in the same vice as men."[129]

To most decent Americans, no doubt, foreign examples meant nothing. Or rather, they proved only how much better Americans were compared to foreigners. The Old World was a world of moral decay—a world sinking deeper and deeper into the cesspools of vice. France, in particular, was assumed to be the motherland of debauchery and loose morals. Any arrangements that regulated and controlled prostitution were, as we have seen, simply out of the question in the United States. In fact, reformers wanted abolition, not regulation. The same was true for other vices—drinking, for example. During World War I, soldiers were allowed to buy some kinds of wine and beer, but hard liquor was forbidden and taverns were off-limits. Nor were the soldiers officially allowed access to women. The French had a wartime system of licensed brothels (those with a blue light over the door were for officers; red lights were for ordinary soldiers). The British went along at first, then decided this was not acceptable; American soldiers were banned from brothels (a rule that turned out to be hard to enforce).[130]

The war, indeed, was a spur to the temperance movement in the United States. The climax, of course, was national Prohibition. The Eighteenth Amendment to the Constitution outlawed the "manufacture, sale, or transportation of intoxicating liquor." In fact, the "noble experiment" did not last very long. It was in trouble from the start. Millions of people wanted to drink and found a way to do so. It would be wrong to call Prohibition a dead letter, but enforcement was always porous, jagged, and sporadic, to say the least.

Why does the United States appear to be so perversely moralistic? Part of the reason may lie in the enormous power of religion in the United States—not any *particular* religion but religion in general. Waves of evangelism have from time to time swept across the country. But there is, I think, an additional cultural factor—one I have already mentioned. It is a kind of fragility, an unease, a kind of fear of falling. It is the notion that the country teeters on the verge of destruction, that it hangs in the balance, that doom is ahead if the country were to let down its moral and ethical guard. And the country was in danger precisely because it always insisted that it was classless, because it lacked a formal aristocracy, because it was so overtly egalitarian, because ordinary people voted and stood for office. Popular democracy raised one crucial question: Did ordinary people, in fact, have the sense and the brains to run a country? Did they have the virtue, the moral fiber, the integrity? The basic answer was yes. This was the American creed. But underneath, perhaps, were all these nagging doubts. And these doubts led to recurring epidemics of morality, recurring panics, recurring outbursts of extra morality.

European countries, on the other hand, have a long aristocratic tradition. Class structure is still strong in many of them. Their societies seem more comfortable with rule by elites, or, if not by elites, by experts. England, for example, prides itself on its vibrant democracy, its tradition of freedom. But its prime ministers, its members of the House of Commons, were always drawn from the same small, narrow band of upper-class men, regardless of party affiliation. Labor, of course, had its policies and ideologies, and the Tories had quite different policies and ideologies. But the party leaders, whatever their affiliation, were men from the same backgrounds. They had gone to the same schools, and they spoke with the same accents. Even Socialists were in a way members of the same exclusive club. The United States—more mobile, more disparate, more heterogeneous, a nation of wanderers, movers, immigrants, a restless and unbuttoned society—could not fall back on any such clubbiness.

Of course, American society was multilayered—at all times. And so were British society, French society, and other societies. My argument hardly rises above the level of a guess—hopefully an educated guess. In any event, as we shall see, the Victorian compromise and all its accompanying baggage altered dramatically in the late twentieth century.

THE ANATOMY OF PUBLIC PRUDERY

The ethos of censorship persisted until almost yesterday and is not yet gone. It shows itself, for example, in periodic waves of attempted book banning and the like. There are occasional panics about books in school libraries—books full of dirty words or (alleged) left-wing propaganda or books that spread disrespect for authority or that are too soft on homosexuals or that preach something called secular humanism. Long after censorship of books for adults had practically ceased to exist, high school book burnings kept right on going.[131]

Censorship always had a rationale, and the rationale seemed particularly important for children and young people, hence the persistence of censorship for children: rating systems in movies, for example, or the absolute frenzy over child pornography in a period that treats adult pornography (for the most part) with a yawn. Schools have to be not just a drug-free and a gun-free zone but definitely a sex-free zone.

Consider, for example, the rather remarkable case of *Cleveland v. LaFleur*, decided by the Supreme Court in 1974.[132] Jo Carol LaFleur was a junior high school teacher in Cleveland. Under a school board rule, if a school teacher became pregnant, she had to take maternity leave without pay in her fourth month of pregnancy. LaFleur was pregnant, but she felt fine; she did not want an unpaid leave; she wanted to keep on teaching until the end of the school year.

The dispute between LaFleur and the Cleveland authorities went all the way up to the United States Supreme Court, which decided the case in her favor. The precise legal issues do not concern us, but the facts of the case are significant. What was the point of the school board's rule? Why did they want a perfectly healthy, pregnant, married woman to leave the classroom? The only

reason given, that made any sense at all, was the urge to keep "physically unfit teachers out of the classroom."[133] The Court rejected this reason. Pregnant
women are not per se physically unfit. The record in the case, however, gave
tantalizing hints of other reasons. For example, the rule would "save pregnant
teachers from embarrassment at the hands of giggling schoolchildren" when the
teacher would begin to "show."[134] And the Chesterfield County School Board,
which also had a mandatory leave rule, thought it was necessary to "insulate
schoolchildren from the sight of conspicuously pregnant women"; some of the
kids might say things like "My teacher swallowed a watermelon."

But what would the children be giggling about? Why should a pregnant
woman give rise to embarrassed laughter? And why should children be insu-
lated from the sight of pregnant women? One answer immediately suggests
itself: A pregnant woman is walking proof of sexual intercourse. Perfectly legitimate sexual intercourse, yes; sex that is necessary for the very survival of
the species, but sex nonetheless. And sex was something to keep hidden, to
keep away from the eyes and ears of young children. Of course, the Cleveland
rule carried this notion to ridiculous extremes. Many children must have seen
their own mothers in late stages of pregnancy. But that was safely and securely
distant, confined to the home.

Other cases from the same period, turning on school board rules, reinforce
the impression one gets from the *LaFleur* case. Many school districts had rigid
rules about how to deal with married high school students. It is perfectly legal
to get married at 16 or 17 in most states so long as the parents consent. Despite
this fact, in some jurisdictions married students were not allowed to continue
in high school. In other places married students were allowed to stay in school
but were subject to rules about what they could and could not do outside the
actual classroom. In one district, for example, married students were barred
from the baseball team and from the high school prom. In a number of cases
married (male) students brought lawsuits because the rules kept them from
playing on high school sports teams.

What was the point of these rules? One case (1975) talked about "integrity" and a "wholesome atmosphere." Married students were setting a bad example. If you let a married student play on a team, he might discuss "marital
intimacies" and there could be bad "locker room talk."[135] There is a certain
naïveté here—the locker room talk of unmarried male athletes, I would imag-

ine, would almost certainly be far worse; in fact, married students would be unlikely to talk at all about marital intimacies, whereas the local studs and machos would be bragging and swaggering all over the premises. Married students, according to the school board of Waterloo, Iowa, "are more likely to have undesirable influences on other students during the informal extracurricular activities." Their "personal relationships" are "different from those of non-married students" and this could have a negative effect on other students.[136] In one parish in Louisiana married students were to enroll only in "academic subjects"; there were to be no "extracurricular activities whatsoever," the married students were supposed to "leave the school campus without loitering" as soon as classes were over, and, perhaps most telling, "physical education course requirements" were "waived" for these married students.[137] (No risk of locker room talk in this parish!).

What the school boards were really afraid of was openly embracing the idea of teenage sex. The ideal was chastity, strict morality, respect for authority. As with a pregnant, married schoolteacher, married students were simply too blatant an advertisement of sex. Of course, school board officials must have known, especially by the 1960s and 1970s, that not all adolescents were pure and innocent, that adolescence was a period of raging hormones, and that sex among high school students was nothing particularly rare. But these cases demonstrate once again the social importance of *surfaces*. Sex was a secret, undercover world. It was important for society to keep it that way—especially among young people. Schools, churches, and other key institutions of society had to uphold society's standards. Dirty books might be available in a bookstore but not in a school library. Students who regularly, legitimately, had sexual intercourse were out of place in a school.

Because women become pregnant after sexual intercourse, pregnancy itself was somewhat taboo. Jo Carol LaFleur was not the only woman to run up against this issue. In 1953 Lucille Ball, star of the incredibly popular TV show *I Love Lucy* and a married woman, became pregnant, as women are wont to do. According to one account, TV executives "refused to allow anyone on the . . . program to say 'pregnant' on the air, fearing that the word would conjure up, in the minds of viewers, images of a man and woman having sexual intercourse."[138]

By this time, of course, these attitudes were out of date and even slightly ridiculous. They were the last vestiges of the Victorian compromise. Jo Carol

LaFleur won her case. Married students went to court to protest against the rules that worked against them. Often they won their cases. The world had changed radically by this time. It had begun to change in the late nineteenth century. The first major move was an attack on the Victorian compromise—but from the right wing, from the forces of morality. Then, in the last half of the twentieth century the whole system fell apart. In the next chapters I explore this changing world.

CHAPTER 8

INTO THE
TWENTIETH CENTURY

DECLINE AND FALL

The years after 1870 were tough years for the Victorian compromise, which began to unravel in a serious way. The story is of course extremely complicated. In the first stage the enemies of the compromise grew stronger and mounted a sort of zero tolerance campaign. Powerful forces refused to accept the cozy compromises that the system embodied. Laws against vice, sexual misconduct, drugs, alcohol, and all sorts of bad behavior tightened considerably after 1870; the campaign against vice raged on unabated during the first twenty years or so of the twentieth century.

To be sure, many people in the United States had never really accepted the idea that a certain amount of vice, a certain amount of hard liquor and gambling, a certain amount of extracurricular sex could or should or must be tolerated. It would be wrong to think of what happened after the 1870s as simply a conservative reaction, a revolt of traditionalists against loose morals, a right-wing turn of the screw. The politics of reform made strange bedfellows; outraged clergymen, good government progressives, public health junkies, eugenicists, and feminists were among those who were sleeping in this particular bed. The warriors in the battle against vice, sin, and debauchery fought under all sorts of banners. What bound them all together was the belief in victory. It was both possible and desirable to wipe these evils off the face of the earth.

The reformers did not agree, for example, that people (especially men) needed an outlet for their "animal instincts," needed something more than plain vanilla marital sex. They thought that sexual misbehavior was not natural behavior and that it was almost unavoidable; it was, if anything, a kind of primitive throwback. The march of civilization should put an end to vice, perversion, debauchery. As Jane Addams said, the human race had the duty to "free itself from the survivals and savage infections of the primitive life from which it started."[1] Addams (according to Barbara Hobson) believed that prostitution was a "prehensile tail that would wither away as society evolved." Society was capable of perfecting itself, and destroying the "social evil" once and for all.[2]

Many foot soldiers in the war on vice were moralists, plain and simple. Perhaps all of them were moralists to some degree. But others made more pragmatic arguments against the Victorian compromise. Vice was infectious, contagious—and dangerous. Toleration made no sense. This was somewhat akin to the fear that lay behind movements to censor books and movies. In addition, the war on vice had science on its side, especially the new "science" of heredity—and its branch, the "science" of eugenics. If you believed in eugenics, if you thought prostitutes, criminals, and paupers bred true, then on these grounds, too, it made no sense to tolerate vice. You could draw a dramatic lesson from this gloomy science. Not only was toleration wrong policy, but the state also had a positive duty to prevent the rotten underclass from breeding. And this meant controlling their sexual behavior.

In 1874 Richard L. Dugdale paid a visit to some of New York's county jails. He was surprised to find a whole cluster of prisoners who were, it seemed, blood relatives. Members of the "Juke" family (not their real name) were dismal descendants of a single rotten line. Dugdale published his sensational findings in 1877. He argued that the "dangerous classes" were "breeding like rats in their alleys and hovels" and that they threatened to "overwhelm the well-bred classes of society." Families like the Jukes, with their children and grandchildren and great-grandchildren, formed a kind of dynasty of crime and morbidity.[3] Generations of paupers, idiots, prostitutes, criminals, and tramps inevitably grew out of what the first bad seed had sown.[4] Oscar McCulloch,

writing in the late nineteenth century, described another long line of degenerates, which he called the tribe of Ishmael. They were descended from a
"half-breed woman" whose sons married "three sisters from a pauper family."
The family produced a crop of murderers, bastards, and prostitutes. Most
of the descendants were diseased. The children died young. They lived "by
petty stealing [and] begging."[5] Henry M. Boies, a member of the Pennsylvania Board of Public Charities, wrote in 1893 that "criminals and paupers . . .
are degenerate; the imperfect, knotty, knurly, worm-eaten, half-rotten fruit of
the race. . . . Hereditary drunkenness, insanity, suicide, epilepsy, idiocy, deaf-
mutism, cancer, syphilis, gout, rheumatism, tuberculous or scrofulous diathesis
in the blood" were all symptoms of "degeneration, likely to be intensified by
propagation in succeeding generations." "Degeneracy" bred true and always
led to the "decay of republics."[6]

By the early nineteenth century these views were widely held, along with
beliefs in superior and inferior races. The eugenics movement was flourishing.[7]
Eugenic ideas led to laws to prevent the degenerate from marrying and having children.[8] Millions came to believe with Dugdale that crime, degeneracy,
prostitution, and feeble-mindedness ran in families. One obvious solution to
the problem was surgical. Sterilization might prevent the Jukes and similar
families from breeding like rabbits and sending their rotten progeny swarm-
ing through the cities.[9]

Indiana in 1907 was the pioneer state to mandate sterilization. Institutions
in Indiana that housed "confirmed criminals, idiots, rapists and imbeciles" had
to add "skilled surgeons" to their staffs. These skilled surgeons could desex
inmates if they were considered hopeless cases.[10] Many states followed with
their own eugenic statutes. Under a California law of 1909 an inmate of a state
prison could be sterilized if he gave "evidence" through his actions and his
record that he was a "moral and sexual pervert."[11] For some reason California
made heavier use of this statute than most other states. In the first third of the
twentieth century California was to sterilization what Texas is today to capital
punishment: the absolute champion.

Not everybody, of course, accepted the premises of the movement—certainly not the candidates for sterilization themselves. A number of lawsuits
challenged the practice. Some courts were horrified at the practice and disal-
lowed it. But most of the states went along. In the famous case of *Buck v. Bell*

(1927), the United States Supreme Court put its stamp of approval on eugenic sterilization. Carrie Buck was described as a "feeble minded white woman," 18 years old, who lived in the State Colony for Epileptics and Feeble Minded in Virginia. Carrie's mother, it was said, was also feeble-minded, and so too was Carrie's (illegitimate) baby. Oliver Wendell Holmes Jr. wrote for the majority, upholding the statute. In the course of his opinion he uttered his famous line, "Three generations of imbeciles are enough."[12]

In *The Blood of the Fathers*, a play written in 1911 by Dr. Frank Lydston, author of popular sex and hygiene manuals, the hero of the play, Dr. Gilbert Allyn, firmly believes in the genetic basis of crime and degeneracy. Alas, Allyn becomes infatuated with the adopted daughter of a rich society couple. He finds out that her biological parents were a bank robber and a drug addict. He knows that this is risky business, that the woman has dangerous and defective blood; still, totally besotted by love, he goes ahead with the marriage. At the end of the play, Kathryn, the young wife, is exposed as a kleptomaniac; at a society ball she steals a diamond. Distraught, she kills herself. Her husband's reaction would strike the modern reader as callous and unnatural. Kathryn, he feels, had found the only way out of her biological trap. He exclaims: "Poor Kathryn! . . . You set things right—. . . . The blood of the fathers!—And our children yet unborn—and our children's children—they, too, thank God, are saved—and in the only way."[13]

Gilbert (and Lydston) seemed convinced that there was, in fact, no way out: no way to overcome the rot that inhered in the germ plasm. One of Willkie Collins's last novels, *The Legacy of Cain*, turned on a similar question: Is the daughter of a convicted murderess, who died on the gallows, bound to inherit her mother's fatal flaws?[14] The eugenics movement and popular ideas about heredity did not in themselves argue against the logic of the Victorian compromise. But they gave one more argument to those who felt disinclined to tolerate vice and crime. And they at least suggested that good people did not have to accept the status quo. They could take action.

The Victorian compromise protected elites and respectable people. The collapse of the Victorian compromise should not be taken to mean that this policy was abandoned. In part, when the Victorian compromise collapsed, some losers simply became winners. The forces of morality, always strong and vocal, now had enough power to win the upper hand. But people were mostly arguing about means, not ends. The moralists wanted to protect traditional American values; this meant, in practice, protecting elites or, in general, respectable people. The state of the union, however, had changed. In the late nineteenth century hordes of foreigners poured into the country. They brought their loose morals with them (or so it seemed). They also produced a huge crop of babies. They threatened to out-breed the old-line Americans. This was a world in flux. It was a world of cities and factories, not a world of farms and small towns. In every generation some people think that the country or the world or both are sliding into chaos. The late nineteenth century was no exception.

The rejection of the Victorian compromise arose out of a toxic brew of fears, anxieties, and regrets. The new policy was zero tolerance. Governments at all levels beefed up their laws against victimless crime. As I noted, in the 1870s Congress made it a federal crime to send obscene material through the mail (including information about contraception).[15] The states added their two cents to the war against obscenity. As of 1920 Florida law banned books, movies, and pictures "containing obscene language" and "obscene prints, figures, pictures manifestly tending to the corruption of the morals of youth."[16] New York law applied to books and pictures that were "obscene, lewd, lascivious, filthy or disgusting"; the law also banned "any slot machine or other mechanical contrivance with moving pictures of nude or partly denuded female figures."[17] Young people were particularly vulnerable and at risk. As Anthony Comstock put it, "Place a dry sponge upon a plate containing water, and soon the water is absorbed and the sponge is expanded. . . . So surround the child with a corrupt literature, and the traits of character in the stories soon develop in the life of the child."[18] As we have seen, campaigns against pornography date far back into the nineteenth century.[19] But now they ratcheted upward. Organizations such as the New York Vice Society or the Watch and Ward Society in Boston worked feverishly to prevent "smut" from defiling the morals of the American public.[20]

Between 1860 and 1880 there was also a wave of laws against abortion.[21] Before this time the legal status of abortion was somewhat confused and ambiguous. Some states did not regulate abortion at all, or the legality of abortion turned on quickening (i.e., whether the mother felt life moving inside her). The Connecticut statute of 1821, for example, made it a crime to give a woman "any deadly poison, or other noxious and destructive substance" in order to produce a "miscarriage," provided that she was "quick with child."[22] Other states had more general laws. Apparently, the practice of abortion became more common in the second half of the twentieth century. Medicines for "female troubles" were hawked in shops and advertised in the press. Abortionists who catered to wealthy women earned huge sums of money. Between 1860 and 1880, however, most states either made abortion totally illegal or tightened their laws considerably. There was a concerted campaign against the practice—and the practitioners.[23]

The notorious Madame Restell (her real name was Ann Lohman) was among the most successful abortionists. She peddled "female monthly pills" and "Preventive Powders." Madame Restell lived in a "large mansion on Fifth Avenue," five stories high. Her office was in the basement; the rest of the house was a palace of luxury, filled with "statuettes, paintings, rare bronzes, ornamental and valuable clocks, candelabras, silver globes, and articles of *vertu*."[24] Madame Restell plied her trade for many years, serving upper-class women with unwanted pregnancies. In the end, hounded by Anthony Comstock and facing a possible jail sentence, Madame Restell had to admit defeat. She retired to the elegant bathroom in her mansion, undressed, entered the bathtub with its casing of black walnut woodwork, and slit her own throat. So ended the career of the "wickedest woman in New York."[25]

Doctors were leaders in the battle against abortion. It was part of their campaign against quacks. Certainly, many abortionists *were* quacks who raked in money from the sale of "Lunar Pills," "French Periodical Pills," and the like. Druggists sold such products as ergot, tansy, pennyroyal tea, and other nostrums, including "Ergo-Kolo Monthly Remedy" and "Emmenagogue," a safe method of "re-establishing or restoring the menstrual periods." "Cottonwood bark" was "used extensively by negroes." "Elamef" ("female" spelled backward) was another of the abortion drugs.[26] Some doctors acted as abortionists themselves; others prescribed some of these marvelous medicines; but the organized and high-toned members of the profession were eager to drive the abortionists out of business. They were also anxious to get rid of midwives and other rivals to their practice. A study of twenty-seven midwives who advertised in foreign newspapers in New York in the early twentieth century found that twenty-three of the twenty-seven agreed to perform abortions; two of the four who refused gave the names of midwives who would do the job.[27] Winning the battle against midwives and others would put all power over childbirth and natal care safely in the hands of male doctors. A parallel campaign went on in England in the middle of the nineteenth century, also led by doctors. The reformers blasted abortionists as a "loathsome parasitical race which preys upon the follies and vices of mankind. They are slayers of the body and polluters of the mind."[28] To be sure, many abortion nostrums were worthless; in addition, botched attempts at abortion killed or seriously injured hundreds of women. Between January 1, 1907, and June 30, 1909, the records of the coroner's office in New York City showed seventy-two deaths from abortion.[29] The battle against illegal abortions was not by any means pointless. There were pragmatic as well as moral and religious objections.

But abortion had deeper social implications. After all, purely *medical* considerations would dictate only that abortion should be safe and legal, put into the hands of trained, antiseptic doctors. But this was not the path of the law. Abortion became in essence illegal. Some evidence suggests that strict abortion laws were yet another instance of late-nineteenth-century moral panic. Among the women who had abortions there were some who were poor, unmarried, and uneducated. On the other hand, a good many others were married women, often quite well-off. Certainly, this was true of Madame Restell's clientele and the clientele of other high-class abortionists. James McCabe condemned both abortion (he called it murder)[30] and, significantly, contraception in general. He wrote that it is "fashionable . . . not to have more than one, two, or three children." Men and women "mean . . . to enjoy the blessings of the married state, and to avoid its responsibilities." The "appalling truth" was that "so many American wives are practicers of the horrible sin of 'prevention' that in certain sections of our country, the native population is either stationary or is dying out."[31] As another writer put it in 1869, "women of fashion" were the ones "most guilty" of getting an abortion; "the poor Irish seldom, if ever, resort to the practice." Babies interfere "with the round of dissipation of the stylish woman," and having babies "compels her, for a time at least, to live a life somewhat secluded."[32]

In other words, elite men faced a shocking and dangerous situation. The lower classes, the immigrants, the huddled masses, were busy *making* babies; white middle-class women were busy killing or *preventing* babies. What did this mean for the future of the country? Married women who had no children

or a child or two at most were betraying their womanhood; they were choosing
pleasure over duty; far worse, they were damaging their own society, which
needed their babies, their germ plasm, their stock of good genes, to carry on
true American values. The waves of new immigrants were enemies of old-line
American culture, enemies of traditional morality (or so it seemed). They were
also in line with the new "science" of eugenics and the growing pseudoscience
of race, inferior breeds who would lower standards of life in America. The Juke
family had no qualms about reproducing.

Abortion, during the palmy days of Madame Restell, was part of the Victorian compromise. Women who had abortions were hardly advertising that
fact. If an otherwise respectable woman was unmarried, an abortion—and
the *reason* for the abortion—was of course a scandal. For a married woman
it was somewhat less so, but certainly abortion had to be kept totally private
and secret. Then abortion became a crime; and there was a serious attempt to
stamp it out. This meant abandoning one aspect of the Victorian compromise.
Protecting elites from scandal was a valid goal, but now other, more important
considerations overwhelmed this goal.

THE WAR AGAINST SEX

During the late nineteenth century and early twentieth century, laws about
sexual behavior changed in rather dramatic ways. Some states tightened their
laws against adultery. In New York, where adultery had not even been a crime,
a 1907 law filled in the gap. Adultery was defined as the "sexual intercourse
of two persons, either of whom is married to a third person." The law made
adultery a misdemeanor, punishable by fine or a short spell in jail.[33] This law
was the brainchild of the National Christian League for the Promotion of
Purity. Supposedly, many married men in New York were "living in adulterous intercourse with women." Lax laws, it was claimed, made New York a
magnet for sinners.[34]

In an important move almost all states raised the so-called age of consent.
As we have seen, sex with a woman *below* the age of consent was defined legally
as rape, even if the female was a willing or even eager partner in crime. A child
could not legally consent to sexual intercourse. This was a general proposition
not many people would disagree with. The devil was in the details. At common
law the age of consent was awfully low—10 years. In the late nineteenth and

early twentieth century states raised the age of consent dramatically—to 16 in many states, to 18 in others.[35] This seems (to some of us) to err in the opposite direction. In California, where the age of consent was 18, teenage sex was, in essence, criminalized—for the male at least. The female was, by definition, a victim, imposed on by men.[36]

The low age of consent had protected *men*. If a man—or an adolescent male—had sex with a girl of, say, 15, he was guilty at most of fornication, and often not even that. Raising the age of consent, like criminalizing abortion, lifted, to a degree, a shield of protection from men who had sex with teenage girls, or boys of whatever class who did the same. It was thus also a loosening of the Victorian compromise. Of course, the girl in each case had been "ruined," but if she was a servant (in England) or a seamstress or a factory girl, only she and her family cared; society as a whole most certainly did not. But after the law changed, the woman was now a victim, regardless of her actual role in the whole seamy affair—in other words, it was all *his* fault. This, then, was part of the general campaign of zero tolerance. This was not solely an American campaign. It also affected Britain in many ways, and it even extended to the empire. In 1909 a general directive to the colonial service told British administrators in Africa and Asia to stop taking native women as concubines.[37] And in the homeland the Criminal Law Amendment Act of 1885 raised the age of consent from 13 to 16; in part this was the reaction to sensational stories in the *Pall Mall Gazette* about sexual exploitation of young girls.[38]

Whatever the intention, the law in action, at least in the United States, had little or nothing to do with what later would be called the white slave trade, or with prostitution in general. Age of consent law had most of its impact on working-class and immigrant families. Some working-class parents and immigrant parents found statutory rape a useful legal tool. They could use it to force men to "do the right thing" and marry the girls they had "ruined." In a sample of New York City cases on statutory rape, middle-class families were simply missing. They made their own arrangements or turned to private maternity homes (when the girl became pregnant).[39]

THE "SOCIAL EVIL"

A key target of the campaign against vice was prostitution, the "social evil." In the late nineteenth and early twentieth centuries prostitution—its causes and cures—was much discussed. From the eugenics standpoint, of course, it was the Jukes and similar families who bred prostitutes. One might even argue that some women were doomed to degeneracy from the moment of conception. Others felt, to be sure, that the prostitute was simply a sinner; she had made a wicked choice, but perhaps she could be redeemed. Throughout the nineteenth century and into the twentieth century, thousands of earnest, sincere reformers tried to pick up the "fallen woman" and help her to a better life.

If, however, the fallen woman was a dominant image of the prostitute in the nineteenth century, the twentieth century replaced this, in part at least, with a different image: the "white slave," innocent victim of evil men. The white slaver was a predator who kidnapped women, literally or figuratively, imprisoned them, literally or figuratively, in a brothel, ravished them, and forced them to live a life of sin and debauchery.[40] The two images, of course, could coexist. A lot depended on who was doing the imaging. But the *proportions* did seem to change in the twentieth century, the age of a heightened purity campaign. In any event the red-light district now seemed more dangerous than ever. It was hard to accept the district as a kind of male safety valve. It was rather a cesspool of vice, a social swamp, a festering sore on the body politic. No decent society could tolerate white slavery, the sexual traffic in human beings. No decent society could tolerate red-light districts. They were spreading disease throughout the whole society.

Disease here was not just a metaphor. The social evil infected men with real diseases, venereal diseases, insidious diseases, which ruined thousands of innocent lives and wrecked thousands of innocent families. Something drastic had to be done to prevent the propagation of vice.

One of the tools in the war against vice was the famous Mann Act, passed by Congress in 1910, the so-called White Slave Traffic Act.[41] This law, as we saw in Chapter 5, made it a crime to transport a woman across state lines for prostitution, "debauchery," and "other immoral purposes." Courts extended the meaning of the law, but the root notion clearly referred to commercialized sex. Before the law passed, there was a tremendous outburst of publicity about the evils of white slavery. Newspapers, magazines, and vice commission reports repeated horror stories about white slavery. In New York City, for example, a young girl of 15 was abducted by a "cadet," who took her to a hotel "under pretext of attending a concert." There he gave her a drugged glass of soda. The next day he "told the frightened and bewildered victim that he would take her home," but instead he moved her to a brothel "and sold her to the madam."[42] White slavers were usually described as dark, villainous, foreign men. The victims were sweet, young white girls fresh off the farm.

The Supreme Court upheld the Mann Act in 1913.[43] Critics of the law warned about blackmail, as we have seen; and indeed, there is some evidence that confirms this suspicion—the Mann Act gave blackmailers a rare opportunity to make dirty money.[44] But this blemish was not enough to curb the enthusiasm of the moral reformers. After all, if a man was afraid of blackmail, all he had to do was live a clean, pure life. Abstinence was the key. The wages of sin were death—and disgrace.

It is hard to tell how much reality lay behind the noise and uproar over white slavery. Surely there were men who took advantage of women, abused them, exploited them. On the other hand, respectable people found it impossible to admit—or even to imagine—that a woman might actually *choose* to make a living selling her body. It was much easier to assume that evil men, mostly foreigners of course, were responsible and that the women were enslaved. People also found it hard to face the fact that part of the problem lay in a cruel and callous system of economic exploitation. Many of the vice commission reports admitted, quite candidly, that masses of working girls in the cities earned pitifully small salaries—starvation wages. These women had no honest way to keep body and soul together.

Thousands of young women worked in shops, offices, and factories. Most of them led drab, relatively hopeless lives—like the life of Dreiser's Sister Carrie. All around these girls were glittering signs of wealth and enjoyment and luxury. In a society that put more and more value on consumption, a society drenched with advertising, a society where everybody went to the movies and saw (or thought they saw) how rich people lived, the young women in the cities were easy prey for men who could show them a good time and give them a bit of money. The city was full of traps and pitfalls, full of overt and subtle temptations. Hidden dangers, for example, lurked in the dance halls. Hotel accommodations were "easily secured in the same building or nearby"; girls who went to the dance halls were expected to "drink with their partners," and for respectable girls the "constant companionship night after night with immoral women," dressed in beautiful gowns, was an additional peril.[45] The

dark world of movie theaters was another place of danger. Temptations were
everywhere. In Glasgow, Scotland, in the early twentieth century, there were
reports of young girls who were seduced in Italian ice-cream parlors and temperance hotels (of all places).[46]

The conventional story also assumed that once a girl or woman was ruined,
once she was in the sex trade, she had no way out. She was trapped in a downward spiral. At the end of the road there was nothing but disease and death. It
was hard to admit that some women actually chose to *leave* the life and were
successful in doing so.

White slavery was a special problem. But prostitution in general was an
even more serious problem. In the early twentieth century a powerful "red light
abatement movement" sprang up. The vice commission reports presented in
great detail facts about the social evil running rampant in the cities. In the
decade of World War I, huge campaigns got under way to get rid of the vice
districts, close them down, board up or tear down the brothels, put an end
to the houses of assignation, shut the corrupt saloons, and destroy the social
evil once and for all.[47] The Minneapolis Commission, for example, was one
of those that argued for abolition. The red-light district did not "restrain and
check vice; rather, it sanctions, encourages and propagates vice." Yes, there
were those who defended the system of segregation; there were those who argued that the district was like a "boil which gathers to a head the impurities
of the blood and protects the rest of the body from disease." But this metaphor, the commission felt, was fundamentally wrong. Rather, the vice district
was "a cancer poisoning every drop of blood and sending the virus to the very
extremities."[48]

Religious leaders, medical experts, and reformers in general shouted this
idea from the rooftops. Dr. Howard Kelley, speaking on behalf of the Pennsylvania Society for the Prevention of Social Disease, called the segregation
system "intolerable"; it "corrupts the police"; it "introduces a plague spot of
vice." Under this system a "man hungry with lust is never satisfied," and this
man, "who enters the segregated district for an immoral purposes carries his
immorality and his physical disease wherever he goes."[49] Physical disease—
venereal disease—was a common theme. David Starr Jordan, president of
Stanford University, in a statement before the Public Morals Committee of the
California Assembly in 1911, called the issue "not a question of morals, primar-

ily" but rather a question of "self-protection of civilization itself." Prostitutes harbored "slow-maturing diseases caused by the presence of minute but deadly plants in the blood tissues." These diseases, "the Red Plague," were "terrible to men, horrible beyond suggestion to women and children." The "vilest" of these diseases could be "communicated through towels, drinking cups and the like to people wholly innocent," causing "blindness, sterility, and . . . many other ills." Medical inspection of brothels was "a dangerous farce. It seems to give a guaranty of immunity when no immunity exists."[50]

The time had come to change course. As the vice commission report for New Jersey put it, it was time to abandon the "old conception" that prostitution, the oldest profession, would stay with human beings forever. "Commercialized prostitution can and eventually will be done away with."[51] But to do this, reformers had to renounce the double standard—the idea that men were animals who had to have sex, by hook or by crook, and that the vice districts were a necessary evil. This was an uphill battle, of course. As Jane Addams said, both good and bad men "prize chastity in women" (and "good men require it of themselves"), but almost all men "are convinced that it is impossible to require it of thousands of their fellow citizens, and hence connive at the policy of the officials who permit commercialized vice to flourish." For reasons of public health, if nothing else, there had to be a "single standard of morals for men and women"; "illicit intercourse is neither necessary nor advantageous to the health and vigor of any male or female."[52] The reformers emphasized, or revived, the idea that men should control their impulses. Self-control was a sign of enlightenment: "The lower the individual in the scale of civilization the more conspicuous as a rule is his sexual power." Indeed, "the sexual appetite grows with feeding." For "men of the very noblest types . . . indulgence in the sexual act is notably infrequent."[53] It is true, as one Viennese professor put it, that "healthy men" had a strong sex drive. He also thought that modern society unduly stimulates the sex drives (his rather odd list of villains included a sedentary life, lack of exercise, and warm beds, along with such conventional villains as immoral pictures and dances and bad literature). But restraint, the professor believed, was "physiologically possible." It was men's duty to make a titanic effort to make reason their master, rather than brute instinct. Blind, brute, insensate behavior would lead to the destruction of society.[54]

Dr. Frank Lydston agreed. True, nature had designed the human male to be "primarily polygamous," unlike the "gorilla, chimpanzee, and other anthropoids who are monogamous." But to curb this "hunger" for sex, "Christian communities" had "wisely and properly put polygamy under the ban, and inhibited . . . man's polygamous instincts." Unfortunately, this "control" was far from perfect.[55] According to Abraham Flexner, writing in 1914, civilization had "stripped for a life-and-death wrestle with tuberculosis, alcohol and other plagues." It was now "on the verge" of a struggle "with the crasser forms of commercialized vice," and "sooner or later" it had to "fling down the gauntlet to the whole horrible thing."[56]

The campaign against the red-light districts did result in significant *legal* changes. States drafted and passed tough legal instruments designed to get rid of these "cancers." The laws, very notably, grabbed onto the old concept of nuisance and refashioned it for a brand new purpose. Under these laws private citizens could bring actions to "abate" brothels and other disorderly houses by labeling them nuisances.[57] The first of these laws was adopted in Iowa, and it served as a kind of model for abatement and nuisance laws adopted in most of the states.[58] In Portland, Oregon, there was the so-called Tin Plate Ordinance. Every house had to have a tin plate giving the name and address of the owner. This was, of course, designed to "intimidate landlords who would not want to be publicly associated with prostitution."[59] In city after city private citizens and the authorities tried to sweep the city clean. And, indeed, some of the most famous vice districts, such as Storyville in New Orleans, passed into history. Vice, of course, quickly found ways to get back into business. Willoughby Waterman, writing in 1932, thought that the same number of women as before were "lured into the profession."[60] Prostitution, driven out of its districts, simply spread into other areas of the cities. The "bawdyhouse," as one scholar put it, was "replaced by the hotel room, the tenement apartment, the roadhouse and the cabaret."[61]

The social hygiene movement aimed to rid the country of prostitution, not just the bawdy houses. They would have liked to put an end to the double standard. The men were as guilty as the women. Nobody would sell sex if there were no buyers. During World War I the Commission on Training Camp Activities of the federal government drafted a "Vice Repressive Law." This proposal would have defined prostitution broadly; under its terms the customers were as guilty of a crime as the women.[62] A number of states adopted laws that followed this model. The Ohio version, for example, made it "unlawful" to "engage in prostitution, lewdness or assignation or to aid or abet prostitution, lewdness or assignation by any means whatsoever." Prostitution was defined as "the offering or receiving of the body for sexual intercourse for hire," or even "the offering or receiving of the body for indiscriminate sexual intercourse without hire."[63] Bascom Johnson, of the American Social Hygiene Association, explained that "amateurs" had to be targeted, not just professional prostitutes. He was referring to women who "are supplementing their incomes, or securing . . . luxuries" by building up "a select clientele."[64] Moreover, he argued, "progress" depended on including in the sweep of the laws "all males whose payments make prostitution possible" and anybody, male or female, who was "sexually indiscriminate," even when no money changed hands.[65]

Two dreaded diseases—syphilis and gonorrhea—were the strongest arguments of the reformers. These were what a man reaped when he sowed "wild oats."[66] By the end of the nineteenth century medical science had come to understand much better what these diseases were and how they were spread. Knowledge of the facts strengthened the movement to control these plagues.[67] These diseases did not just afflict fallen women and their customers. The men spread the diseases to their innocent wives and to their children. The sins of the fathers were passed on to their wives, sons, and daughters. This was the theme of Henrik Ibsen's shocking play, *Ghosts*, written in the late nineteenth century. Alving, a man of supposedly impeccable reputation (already dead at the beginning of the play) brings about the destruction of his family through his secret vices. The son inherits his father's loathsome disease. At the end of the play the son goes blind, and the curtain falls.[68]

According to the New York Social Hygiene Society in a 1906 pamphlet, every year in the United States 770,000 "males reach the age of early maturity, that is, they approach the danger zone of initial debauch." At least 60 percent of these men will "become infected with venereal disease." Many of them will "carry this infection into the family." There is "evidence to show that 80 per cent. of the deaths from inflammatory diseases peculiar to women, 75 per cent. of all special surgical operations . . . and over 60 per cent. of all the work done by specialists in diseases of women" were caused by or stemmed from "gonococcus infection." Half of these women were "rendered absolutely and irremediably sterile"; many were "condemned to life-long invalidism." From

70 to 80 percent "of the ophthalmia which blots out the eyes of babies" was the result of "gonococcus infection"; syphilis, for its part, was "the only disease which is transmitted to the offspring in full virulence."[69]

Society could not afford to compromise with so great and dangerous an evil. As Ibsen's play made clear, reform could not work unless it targeted the men who used prostitutes for sex as well as the prostitutes themselves. These men were "damaged goods."[70] They should be forced to choose between their reputation—and the health of their families—and their vices. At least this was the hope of moral campaigners. In this regard they probably had little or no success. There is no evidence that police departments arrested men and charged them with criminal offenses, even in those states that made buying as well as selling sex a crime. Vice, as we will see, lost a battle or two but ultimately won the war.

Illicit sex was not the only target of the moral campaigns. Gambling and drink were also targets. Congress passed a law in 1895 to bar lottery tickets from the mails.[71] The most difficult and important struggle was the struggle against the evils of drink, but it achieved phenomenal success. National Prohibition was in many ways the crown jewel of the campaign against vice.[72] The Eighteenth Amendment to the Constitution, the Prohibition Amendment, went into effect in January 1920. Significant drug laws, at least on the federal level, also basically date from the early years of the twentieth century. There were sporadic laws earlier, mostly directed against opium dens and the like. But drug sale and use per se were not criminalized. In 1909, however, Congress passed the Opium Exclusion Act. The Harrison Narcotic Drug Act of 1914 was another important step.[73] By 1925 federal authorities were arresting more than 10,000 men and women a year for drug violations.[74]

What lay behind the mighty campaign against the Victorian compromise and against vice and sin in general? Surely, many factors. Venereal diseases *were* a threat. Women *were* subject to sexual predation, even if there was little truth to the more lurid tales of white slavery. Nobody doubts that drunkenness and drug addiction—and addiction to gambling, perhaps—were and are serious social problems. But one attractive theory sees a culture crisis at the roots of the antivice campaign.[75] Society was changing rapidly—too rapidly for comfort. Many people felt as though they were on a speeding train, rushing helter-skelter toward a cliff. Their whole world was tottering on its base.

Immigrants from weird places were pouring into the country. The moral su-
perstructure was collapsing. Crime, vice, and debauchery were spreading like
dry rot. Compromise and laissez-faire were no longer acceptable. The white
Protestant race seemed to be losing its grip; losing its dominance. Something
had to be done.

In the early twentieth century many Americans also began to think about
closing the great gates of entry. Nobody wanted the huddled masses, except the
huddled masses themselves and their relatives who were already here, jammed
into tenements in New York. The Chinese had already been excluded.[76] More
general immigration controls were just around the corner, in the restrictive
laws of the 1920s. These laws were designed to stem the floods of Italians,
Greeks, Jews, and Slavs who swarmed into the ports of entry.[77] Behind immigration reform was the notion of keeping American culture and American
values intact—saving them from the threat of the outsiders. This goal of preserving one image of the past, of saving a traditional culture, lay behind the
war on vice as well.

People pointed the finger of blame at foreigners, immigrants, and radicals—at evil men and at degenerates who washed up on American shores. It
was easy to declare war on these bad people. A more subtle enemy and a more
subtle war lurked in the shadows, but it was easy to overlook. This was the
war between parents and children, between people raised in one tradition
and their children who lived in a different world. Signs of this war between
generations peeps out from the controversy over censorship of movies and in
the general concerns over seduction and debauching of the young. It appears
in the campaign against white slavery, in images of the moral and physical
dangers of the city. The white slave, after all, was depicted quite typically as
a young farm girl, fresh from the countryside, who comes to the big city in
search of money and adventure. The crusade against white slavery never confronted the motives that drove young girls to the city in the first place. The
crusade against teenage sex refused, in turn, to admit that young girls from
good families might be capable of consensual sex.

Each campaign—against prostitution or against gambling or drink—had its
own dynamic. But what joined the campaigns together was this sense of crisis,
this sense of cultural decay. And the sense of crisis above all was what doomed
the Victorian compromise and the assumptions on which it was based.

THE TRIUMPH OF SIN

In 1920 national Prohibition was just beginning its short and ignoble career. After a turbulent decade or so, the "noble experiment" ended abruptly. The Eighteenth Amendment was essentially canceled. Prohibition slunk off the stage of history under a barrage of hisses and catcalls. The crusade against vice had reached some sort of high point between 1910 and 1920. From then on it was downhill all the way. In hindsight it seems fairly clear that the war against vice and sin was doomed from the beginning. In the last two generations of the twentieth century the whole structure collapsed like a house of cards. Dramatic legal (and social) change took place in the last half of the twentieth century. From the standpoint of many honest and respectable people, what resulted was the triumph of sin.

Take, for example, pornography. For most of our history it was simply assumed that the state could and should ban dirty books and pictures. This tendency was carried to great lengths in the nineteenth century and in the early twentieth century. Today, it seems almost incredible that bluenoses and some courts could pin the label of obscenity on works of art and information that seem totally innocuous. Describing or advocating contraception was a dangerous move. Films did not dare even to *mention* the fact that some men made love to other men and that some women made love to other women. Pictures or descriptions of sexual intercourse, even if mild and decorous, even covered with fig leaves, were totally taboo.

Many of the cases sound the theme of corruption of the young. There was, of course, no single litmus test to decide what made a book or a picture obscene. One definition, often repeated, put it this way: A book is obscene "if it has a substantial tendency to deprave or corrupt its readers by inciting lascivious thoughts or arousing lustful desire."[78] Obviously, lascivious thoughts and lustful desires could not be evils in themselves. A married man (or woman) surely was entitled to have lascivious thoughts and lustful desires. These lustful desires were essential to human survival. And every man (or woman) above a certain age was apt to feel these lustful desires and lascivious thoughts. Still, they were not supposed to act on these impulses. That right was reserved for married people in their bedrooms.

In the first half of the twentieth century the old taboos were very much alive and were at least sporadically enforced. Cases kept coming up, which suggests a certain decay in the standards. And occasional cases swam against the tide—the *Ulysses* case, for example. Battles over obscenity continued to rage in the 1940s and 1950s. Was D. H. Lawrence's book *Lady Chatterley's Lover* obscene? The book was published in 1928 privately in Italy. Nobody dared bring out this book in the United States—at least not the unexpurgated edition—until 1959, when Grove Press took this bold step. The postmaster general of New York thought that Lady Chatterley was definitely obscene. Grove Press took the matter to federal court. The district judge held that the book could not be banned.[79] Lawrence's novel had "literary merit"—even the postmaster general admitted as much—and critics treated the book as a serious work of art. Grove Press, said the court, was a "reputable publisher with a good list." The Press advertised and promoted the book "as a serious work of literature." Grove made no attempt "to appeal to prurience or the prurient minded," made no attempt "to pander to the lewd and lascivious." What was important here was "not the effect upon the irresponsible, the immature or the sensually minded" but the impact on "the average man of normal sensual impulses." Some passages, to be sure, if "taken in isolation," might "tend to arouse shameful, morbid and lustful sexual desires in the average reader." But these passages were "an integral . . . part of the development of theme, plot and character." The court also recognized that times were changing. Much was "now accepted" that "would have shocked the community to the core a generation ago." At this "stage in the development of our society," then, this "major English novel" was not legally obscene.

The postmaster general appealed, but in vain. The court of appeals affirmed the decision of the district court.[80] The steamy descriptions of sex between Lady Chatterley and her randy gamekeeper, Mellors, were essential to the unfolding plot and the themes of this distinguished novel. The decision was unanimous; but one of the circuit judges, Leonard Moore, went along obviously only as a reluctant fellow traveler. He had nothing but contempt for the praise heaped on the book. "The public," he said, had "avidly purchased thousands (probably millions) of copies," but only because they were "anxious to read in print certain words which they can so easily see written in public toilets and other public places." Authors "of the so-called school of 'realism'" vied with each other to describe things that "could be observed by peeking through hypothetical keyholes and by hiding under beds." The "eager public, possibly bored by the monotony of monogamy," relished the idea of enjoying "vicariously—and quite safely—bold but rather impractical daydreams of a life which could be found in fictional actuality in these books."

This antediluvian screed did have a serious point. To such a man as Leonard Moore, *Lady Chatterley* breached the unwritten laws of propriety; it crossed and confounded the boundary between the public and the private. It did this by legitimating dirty words (otherwise to be found in "public toilets") and scenes visible only through "keyholes" or by "hiding under beds." The real danger, of course, was that this same "eager public" (bored with "monogamy") might decide that "vicarious" thrills would not do. Jane Public might go looking for her own version of Mellors, and millions of respectable American Mellors might go looking for their own Lady Chatterley. What would happen, then, to family values and to propriety itself? Moore emphasized, in other words, the *social* importance of taboos. But the fact that he concurred—even grudgingly—showed that the battle was as good as lost.

Lady Chatterley's victory—or maybe it was Mellors's victory—was not the end of the war. Literary hits that broke Victorian rules were still in trouble. More than sixty cases in twenty-one states turned on the status of Henry Miller's book *Tropic of Cancer* as late as the 1950s and 1960s. Some state courts held that the novel was obscene (not an entirely unreasonable conclusion). Other courts found the book strong medicine but legally acceptable. One federal case, in the Ninth Circuit in 1953, dealt with both *Tropic of Cancer* and *Tropic of Capricorn*, another Miller opus; the books had been "printed in Paris" and "intercepted at an American port of entry."[81] The judge thought that these books were obviously and completely obscene. "Practically everything that the world loosely regards as sin is detailed in the vivid, lurid, salacious language of smut, prostitution, and dirt." The book leads the reader "through sex orgies and perversions of the sex organs." "Nothing has the grace of purity or goodness." Mere "literary merit" does not "lift the reader's mind clear of . . . sticky slime." In fact, the "literary merit" of the books "carries the reader deeper" into this slime.[82] But this was by now a rearguard action. In the end, Miller won the battle; by 1964 it was clear that Miller's books could not be outlawed in America.[83] Readers no longer had to rely on the naughty French people to publish and ship books like Miller's or *Lady Chatterley.*

Freedom of speech, of course, is a basic right guaranteed by the First

Amendment to the Constitution and the bills of rights of various states. But in the nineteenth century obscenity cases said little or nothing about freedom of speech. It was taken for granted that freedom of speech did not apply to obscenity or pornography. Freedom of speech meant vigorous political debate, arguments over religion, policy, and the like. Sex talk was entirely different. By the middle of the twentieth century, however, the issue of freedom of speech began to occupy center stage in cases about obscenity and pornography.

The United States Supreme Court had uttered not one word about this relationship—between freedom of speech and obscenity—until that time. In the 1940s New York banned a novel by the famous critic Edmund Wilson, *Memoirs of Hecate County*. Wilson's book ended up in court and eventually before the United States Supreme Court. The case did raise an issue of freedom of speech. But in the end nothing was decided. The Court was evenly split, four to four, and the practice in such a case is to issue no opinion at all.[84]

The first real decision in an obscenity case came ten years later, in 1957, in *Roth v. United States*.[85] The Supreme Court decided that the right of free speech did not cover obscenity. But what was obscenity? The Court ventured on a (rather conventional) definition: "material which deals with sex in a manner appealing to prurient interest." If these words are taken literally, then the state could censor or ban any book, picture, or play that aroused lustful thoughts—which were apt, for example, to give a man an erection. No one ever puts it this bluntly, of course, but the implication is clear. (The reader or observer of obscene material is usually assumed to be a man; nice women either do not buy these books or fail to be aroused by them.) Once again one can ask, What is so terrible about lust? It is an absolute biological necessity. A married man, snuggled up against his lawful wife in a big, soft comfortable bed has every right—perhaps even a duty—to indulge in his "prurient interests." In short, the definition in *Roth* not only was conventional but also continued the tradition of treating sex in a traditional way, as a private, secret matter. The *Roth* definition was compatible with inherited notions of respectability. Social surfaces must remain smooth and sexless, like the conventional picture of heaven, where people play harps and wear white robes and animal instincts are only a memory.

But *Roth* did not end the matter. Behind the bland words was perhaps a realization that times were changing. *Roth* was not a unanimous decision; and although it has never been actually repudiated, in hindsight we can see the case as the end of a line rather than a beginning. And *Roth* at least stood for the proposition that obscenity cases *did* implicate free speech. Except for this point, *Roth* resolved nothing. The cases continued to come up.[86] Outside the quiet chambers of the Supreme Court, a sexual revolution was raging in the country. One of its minor consequences was an increased demand for sexual candor in print. Respectable publishers began to bring out the novels that had been earlier under a ban. In the case law after *Roth*, the Supreme Court fumbled and stumbled, trying to find a workable definition of obscenity or pornography in a world that was shedding its prudery at a rapid rate and in which the argument from freedom of speech seemed more and more persuasive to authors, publishers, and readers. The Court never really succeeded. It never came up with a satisfying body of doctrine. Events and attitudes completely passed the Court by. As they struggled with the issue, pornography was winning its war outside, especially in big cities. In much of the country pornography in essence had been decriminalized.

To be sure, obscenity laws are still on the books. But in much of the country there is not the slightest effort at enforcement. Courts—and legislatures—recognize that obscenity is here to stay. In California, for example, the penal code still defines obscenity as material that "appeals to the prurient interest" and that, "taken as a whole, depicts or describes sexual conduct in a patently offensive way." But the statute also refers to "contemporary statewide standards," and these standards, as anybody with the slightest knowledge of San Francisco and Los Angeles must know, are extremely loose. Besides, no work that has "serious literary, artistic, political, or scientific value" is obscene under California law. And if this is not enough to make the statute completely toothless, the statute then adds, somewhat slyly, a rather astonishing proviso. If it appears "from the nature of the matter" or the way it is distributed that it is "designed for clearly defined deviant sexual groups" (sadomasochists, for example), then it is to be "judged with reference to its intended recipient group."[87] One can imagine what Anthony Comstock might make of this kind of law.

The pornography story is only one of many parallel stories about the triumph, so to speak, of vice. The history of the Mann Act is instructive. The act had been much abused. The government used it as a way to get people it wanted to get if their private lives left something to be desired (not a rare situation). In the 1940s the great comedian Charlie Chaplin went on trial for violating the Mann Act. A woman named Joan Barry claimed that Chaplin paid her to travel to New York and have sex with him. J. Edgar Hoover, head of the FBI, had taken it into his head that Chaplin was a dangerous radical and had to be deported. At the trial Chaplin was acquitted, but he did in fact leave the United States.[88] By 1970, however, the fire had almost completely gone out of the Mann Act. Few people were ever charged or convicted. In the 1970s and 1980s the law was drastically restructured. Terms such as *white slavery* and *debauchery* vanished. The new version applied to both men and women, and it applied only to transportation across state lines for "sexual activity for which any person can be charged with a criminal offense." Since in most states fornication and adultery were no longer crimes, people like young Caminetti, who crossed state lines for a small bout of consensual sex, no longer had anything to fear.[89]

The fate of laws against fornication and adultery is also instructive. State after state wiped these crimes off their statute books.[90] If consenting adults wanted to have sex, then so be it; the state would not interfere. Even in states where the laws remained theoretically in force, enforcement was exceedingly rare. In practice, these laws were dead letters.

Strictures against contraception also largely disappeared. In the second half of the twentieth century, writing about birth control, talking about it, or advocating it were no longer under any sort of cloud. In 1950 sales of condoms reached $100 million a year. Condoms were on sale in hundreds of drugstores. And in 1960 the Food and Drug Administration approved an oral contraceptive—the Pill—for sale.[91]

One state, in particular, had lagged behind the trend. As late as the 1960s, Connecticut still had laws on its books that basically made it a crime to sell contraceptives and even to give out birth control advice. A long and frustrating campaign to get rid of this law ended up, finally, in the United States Supreme Court. In *Griswold v. Connecticut* (1965),[92] the Supreme Court struck down the statute. What is particularly notable is the basis on which the Court acted. The main opinion, written by William O. Douglas, claimed to find a right of "privacy" hidden somewhere in the Bill of Rights. Of course, nothing in the Bill of Rights dealt directly with condoms, diaphragms, and birth control pills. But Douglas, in a famous passage, said that the fundamental rights had "penumbras" and "emanations" and that these penumbras and emanations implied constitutionally protected "zones of privacy."

It is easy to sneer at these mythical and mystical concepts, but the zeitgeist, not logic, makes the laws. *Griswold* was the father of a long line of later cases, and its position in the pantheon of Court cases is firmly established. The case boldly created a new area of constitutional litigation. But Douglas's opinion, radical though it seemed, had certain elements that looked backward. Douglas talked about the "intimate relation of husband and wife" and the "sacred precincts" of the marital bed. If you took this language seriously, then Douglas was in a way affirming a much older notion of privacy. Sex was something private, something between husbands and wives. The vice, then, of the Connecticut statute was that it interfered with this intimate, private relationship.

If one reads the case this way, then a later case, *Eisenstadt v. Baird* (1972)[93] takes on greater significance. Massachusetts had a statute that was less extreme than Connecticut's. Contraceptives were legal, but only for married people. Yet the Supreme Court struck down this statute too. Justice William Brennan described the right of privacy as "the right of the *individual,* married or single, to be free from unwarranted governmental intrusion." And, in the landmark case of *Roe v. Wade,* decided the next year, the Supreme Court voided all state laws that restricted abortion and insisted that the right of privacy included a woman's right to choose to abort, at least in the early months of a pregnancy.[94]

Roe v. Wade was controversial when it was decided, and the controversy has never died down. Abortion has become an extremely hot issue politically. Millions of people condemn the decision; millions think of abortion as a form of murder, and for many of these people abortion is not just one more political issue—it is in fact the issue of issues. The Republican Party has essentially committed itself to getting rid of *Roe v. Wade.* But the case also has its defenders, who also number in the millions and perhaps form a majority. Despite all the turmoil, despite the cases and statutes that have nibbled about the edges, at this writing (2007), *Roe v. Wade* still stands.[95]

The *legal* restrictions on sex outside marriage have been largely abolished. The same can be said of the *social* restrictions for the most part. Indeed, this trend undoubtedly came first and *led* to the legal changes. In the nineteenth century "living in sin" was a scandal, something no decent woman could possibly do without losing her place in good society. By the 1970s, however, cohabitation had become so common in the United States and abroad that it almost amounted to a way of life. Cohabitation was the issue in a famous California case, *Marvin v. Marvin* (1976).[96] Michele Triola had lived for years with the movie star Lee Marvin. After the relationship broke up, she claimed a share of his (very large) earnings. According to her, she and Marvin had entered into a contract. She had agreed to give up her own career, move in with him, and run his household; in return, he had promised her a slice of his income. What stood in her way was a long line of cases in which courts refused to enforce "immoral" contracts. But the California Supreme Court turned its back on this line of cases. Cohabitation, said the court, had become "pervasive" in society. The "mores" had radically changed; old "moral considerations . . . have apparently been . . . widely abandoned." The old legal barriers to such a lawsuit were thus no longer operative. Michele was entitled to sue her former lover and enforce the agreement—assuming, of course, that she could prove her case.[97]

The court was certainly correct in its assessment of the "mores"—correct or, perhaps, prophetic. In more than 50 percent of the marriages celebrated between 1990 and 1994 in the United States, the couple had lived together before getting married.[98] In some European countries the trend has gone even further; in parts of northern Europe not even pregnancy and childbirth are enough to induce a cohabiting couple to drag themselves to the altar. In Sweden in 2000 more than half of all births took place outside marriage; "illegitimate" births were also astonishingly high in Norway and Denmark and, surprisingly, constituted almost a third of all births in Catholic Ireland and Austria. Unquestionably, the "engine driving the rise in nonmarital child-bearing . . . is the rise in cohabitation."[99] There is also a growing trend to give legal recognition to "domestic partnerships." This stage has already been reached in some countries, for example, Sweden.[100]

Domestic partnership in fact hardly raises an eyebrow anymore in most parts of the United States, except perhaps in some stretches of the Bible Belt. Marriage is no longer quite so sacred; society tolerates committed relationships of all sorts now. These partnerships and relationships are, to be sure, much more controversial if the partners happen to be two men or two women. But even here law and society have changed in ways that once seemed totally unthinkable. For more than a generation there has been a strong gay rights movement, perhaps modeled on the success of the civil rights movement, but surely in large part an independent development. Like the feminist movement, the struggle to decriminalize homosexual behavior is common to the whole developed world. In England success came with the Sexual Offences Act of 1967.[101]

Most of the states, especially in the north, the midwest, and the west, revised their penal codes and got rid of laws against the "infamous crime against nature." These laws followed the laws against adultery and fornication into the dustbin of history. To be sure, some states resisted the trend. Most of these states were in the southern United States. *Bowers v. Hardwick* (1986)[102] arose under the sodomy law of Georgia. Michael Hardwick, a gay bartender in Atlanta, was arrested for committing an act of "sodomy." He was not actually prosecuted, but neither did the state drop the case officially and Hardwick brought a civil action in the federal courts, claiming that the sodomy law was unconstitutional. He based his argument on the line of cases from *Griswold* on—in short, on his constitutional right of privacy. The Supreme Court, by a vote of five to four, refused to strike down the statute. Ironically, the Georgia Supreme Court, in 1998, basing their decision on the *Georgia* constitution rather than the federal constitution, took the step that the United States Supreme Court had been unwilling to take; Georgia's justices declared the local sodomy statute null and void.[103] And *Bowers v. Hardwick* itself was not destined to survive very long. In 2003, in a case arising out of Texas, one of the states that retained laws against sodomy, the Supreme Court flatly overruled *Bowers v. Hardwick*. The Court declared the dozen or so surviving sodomy laws unconstitutional. The two gay men who acted as petitioners in the case were "entitled," as Justice Kennedy put it, "to respect for their private lives."[104]

At one time, gambling was in general illegal. In 1895 Congress, as I have mentioned, banned the interstate sale of lottery tickets. The Supreme Court upheld this law in 1903.[105] Rigid laws against gambling were in effect in most states and cities. These laws were not always strictly enforced, but open and notorious gambling was not allowed and there were no public casinos, no American Monte Carlo. In the twentieth century the barren desert state of Nevada built up an amazing economy by breaking ranks and allowing casino gambling. Nevada took advantage of the federal system to carve out its own niche—not only legalized gambling but also easy divorce, prostitution, and quick and easy marriage.[106] Millions of people flocked to the gambling palaces in Las Vegas and Reno, reveling in the dramatic kitsch that sprang up like a fantastic mirage in the midst of a dry and profitless landscape. For decades Nevada was something of an anomaly. But in the late twentieth century gambling spread from this desert stronghold like an infectious plague. First, there was Atlantic City in New Jersey, then riverboats on the Mississippi, casinos on Indian reservations, and for a time, gambling on the Internet.[107] State after state established a lottery. These schemes, once interstate pariahs, were now favorites of state government, which hawked and hyped them from one end of the country to the other.

The trends have been unmistakable and have moved powerfully in one direction. Law and society tolerate levels of vice—indeed, open and notorious vice—that would have been considered totally unacceptable two generations ago. Of course, developments with regard to each aspect of the story have never been without complications. There were always ups and downs and ins and outs, always resistance and backlash. The laws against use and sale of narcotics not only remain in place but are also stronger and harsher than ever. Prostitution is still a flourishing business—but, except in Nevada, it is not really legal anywhere. The culture wars have never really ended. Millions of earnest citizens have fought and are still fighting to preserve traditional values. They have lost many battles, but they refuse to concede.

The biggest changes in law and society have been changes with regard to sexual behavior and, generally speaking, with regard to decency. As late as the 1930s, New York City mounted a serious campaign against its burlesque houses, which offended respectable people with their stripteases and raunchy humor.[108] Movie censorship was at its height. But all this seems almost quaint in the early years of the twenty-first century. Today, sex is all over TV; women's magazines run stories about ways to improve techniques of sexual intercourse; in books, plays, and movies, sex is discussed and depicted in finger-licking detail, and more and more, explicit sexual behavior forms the basis of plots on comedies and dramas alike; and it saturates the so-called reality shows. Women on *Sex and the City*, a popular TV program of the early twenty-first century, can and do talk about such things as anal intercourse or the size of their boyfriends' penises. In the last half of the twentieth century the sexual content of the media had grown so dramatically that it was possible to say that "sexual repression" had been "replaced by sexual obsession."[109]

Yet all along earnest and sincere people have decried and continue to decry the sexual content that has flooded the media. Many people still think that sex education in the schools is wrong and that abstinence is the best policy—in fact the only policy—for avoiding teenage pregnancy, sexually transmitted diseases, and a host of other pathological conditions. Sometimes politics makes strange bedfellows. A strong wing of the feminist movement joined traditional moralists in a battle against pornography. Catherine MacKinnon has argued that pornography is one of the main pillars on which a massive system of male domination rests. Indianapolis adopted a strict antipornography ordinance, inspired by MacKinnon; the ordinance banned the "graphic sexually explicit subordination of women, whether in pictures or in words." But a federal court declared the ordinance unconstitutional in 1985, on free speech grounds.[110] The war on abortion has, of course, never ended, as I noted, and there is no sign that it will ever end.

And despite the millions of couples who live together without bothering to get married, traditional marriage still has powerful champions. Gay people are visible on TV and in the movies, many cities prohibit discrimination on the basis of sexual orientation, and in some places openly gay men and women have been elected to public office. But hatred and discrimination and just plain disgust for the "gay lifestyle" still abound, and the movement along the road to legitimacy and acceptance has been neither neat nor easy. During the McCarthy period, there were witch hunts against "perverts" in government. Gay men and women were supposed to be vulnerable to communist blackmail because of their sexual orientation. Gay marriage is particularly controversial. The Massachusetts Supreme Court handed down a decision that validated gay marriage. This set off something close to moral panic in much of the country. Congress and most of the states leaped to the defense of marriage in the old sense of one man and one woman. Almost without exception, referenda against gay marriage win by large majorities in the states. Yet "civil unions," which are marriages in almost everything but name, seem much more acceptable. At any rate every aspect of the permissive society has been and will continue to be contested.

The so-called sexual revolution dealt a painful defeat to crusaders for purity. Much of what they had accomplished between 1870 and 1920 ended up on the rubbish heap of history. The revolution was only in part a revolution in behavior—more significant, perhaps, was a revolution in attitudes. In part, what happened was that what was once hidden became open and notorious. What was private emerged into the public—and demanded recognition, demanded legitimacy.

This demand was one of the points of the famous Kinsey report.[111] Alfred Kinsey, in 1948, published the results of his research on the sex life of American men. A second volume, in 1953, reported on the female of the species. Kinsey's work stirred up a hornet's nest at the time; today, the work does not shock anymore. In some ways time has not been kind to Kinsey's reputation as a scientist; some critics have cast doubt on his data; some have even labeled his work as essentially little better than junk science. But clearly these two volumes carried a powerful and explicit message. Kinsey's message was this: Dirty behavior was, in fact, as common as dirt. Masturbation was, in essence, universal among men and extremely widespread among women.[112] Fornication, adultery, homosexual behavior, even sex with animals—all of these were far more widespread than anyone had dared to suggest. Indeed, Kinsey went so far as to claim that if one took the law seriously and literally, some 95 percent of the men in the United States were sexual offenders. The laws, in short, were both tragic and absurd. An honest attempt to enforce them would put almost the whole population—male and female—in jail. But of course nobody had any intention of enforcing the laws as such.

Books such as Kinsey's, no matter how big a splash they make, are symptoms, not causes. Kinsey was preaching a message whose time had come. His life work was an attack on Victorian taboos—on the implicit theory that what society needed above all was a heavy dose of secrecy and privacy. His books were a full frontal attack on the idea that society would suffer from free, frank discussion of sex and vice. He also implicitly attacked those theories and institutions that once had shielded the reputation of elites. What was shocking about his books was not the idea that lowlifes, prostitutes, or the lumpenproletariat broke the rules and indulged in illicit sex. What was shocking was the idea that *nobody* or almost nobody, including the vast armies of the middle classes, really obeyed those rules. The emperor had no clothes, and Kinsey was the one who pointed out that fact to a shocked and embarrassed public.

REPUTATION IN THE POST-KINSEY AGE

These profound changes in sexual attitudes and mores in the last half of the twentieth century produced new definitions of what it meant to be respectable. The boundaries of acceptable behavior were moved some distance. The impact was enormous—on criminal law, family law, and elsewhere in the legal order. And there was an impact on the way the legal system *behaved*, as well as on the way it was supposed to behave. In Chapter 10 I will make some guesses as to what brought about these changes.

The impact of legal change is, of course, hard to measure. Take, for example, the law and practice of blackmail. People who flaunt their "infirmities" or secrets—people who "let it all hang out"—cannot, after all, be blackmailed. As I noted, during the McCarthy period, there were government crusades and purges against gays and alleged gays. The purges were led by cold warriors and right-wingers. Gay people, they claimed, were too vulnerable to blackmail. This point was made, for example, in the congressional report *Employment of Homosexuals and Other Sex Perverts in Government*. McCarthy himself played this theme; and the Reverend Billy Graham had praise for those who exposed "the pinks, the lavenders, and the reds" who apparently infested the civil service.[113] The gay rights movement helped to kill any such blackmail at its source: the secrecy of the closet. It was harder, too, to blackmail parents of illegitimate children; the legal disabilities and social stigma of bastardy had been largely shucked off. The same could be said for the scandal of cohabitation. In most of the country "living in sin" no longer meant anything. Perhaps blackmail is, in fact, a declining occupation. Traditional blackmail has probably lost *some* of its market. People who want to make money out of secret information may not even *need* to use blackmail. They can peddle their information, selling "their sordid story to tabloid newspapers or TV shows."[114]

It is still true, of course, that reputation depends on the person and the situation. You cannot defame a rock star by accusing him of having sex with legions of groupies. A much milder charge could kill the career of a minister of the gospel. Morality is not dead. It has simply been redefined. An arrest for a felony, a charge of rape, an accusation of stock fraud—all of these still carry tremendous stigma in most circles.

The situation at the end of the twentieth century and the beginning of the twenty-first, then, was roughly this: The old system of protection of reputation, a system that largely benefited the elites, the respectable members of society, has largely collapsed. First, it was buffeted by the revolt against the Victorian compromise. Then, in a startling about-face, the triumph of vice dealt it a series of hammerlike blows. The old code of morality has been largely (of course not entirely) dismantled. An openly gay congressman, a divorced president, rich industrialists with mistresses, men and women who live together without bothering to get married—none of this spells public doom or scandal any longer. On the other hand, elites, famous people, stars, prominent citizens no longer have any safe haven. Indeed, as we will see, they have in a sense almost *no* right to privacy at all.

BREACH OF PROMISE AND ITS RELATIVES

As the twentieth century progressed and the permissive society began its triumphal career, the old action of breach of promise and its relatives, alienation of affection and criminal conversation, lost their hold on society. These actions had for a long time aroused controversy. Even in the nineteenth century, as we have seen, there was a constant barrage of criticism against them. A few flamboyant and scandalous cases fueled the fire. In Kentucky in 1893 Madeleine Pollard brought a breach of promise case against a congressman, W. C. P. Breckenridge. Pollard was 28 years old; Breckenridge was 56. She told a sordid story: For nine years she had had an affair with the congressman. He promised to marry her after his wife died; instead, he married another woman. Breckenridge never denied the affair, but he did deny the promise. And Pollard, he claimed, had not exactly been an unsullied dove when their affair began. A jury found for Pollard and awarded a rather fat verdict of $15,000.[115]

In 1922 a dancer named Evan Burrows Fontaine sued Cornelius Vanderbilt Whitney for breach of promise; Whitney, she said, was the father of her baby. She asked for a million dollars. Whitney's lawyer called it a "blackmail plot."[116] A legal soap opera followed. Fontaine, it seemed, had once been married to a sailor; the marriage was annulled. Whitney's legal team argued that the annulment was invalid; it was based on perjured testimony. Fontaine's lawsuit, then, was based on a false premise. At least one judge bought this argument, and at one point Fontaine was even jailed, apparently for perjury. An appeals judge reversed the trial court judge who had ruled against the annulment, but in the end it was all in vain: The breach of promise suit failed.[117] There was a kind of sad, ironic coda to this business: Evan Fontaine was appearing at a "beach front cabaret" in Atlantic City; later she placed some of her goods in storage, never to be reclaimed; she disappeared into the bottomless well of American obscurity. In 1931 her goods were auctioned off because she had failed to pay the storage fees. An "unidentified woman" bid $6 to buy a poem, which was "apparently inspired" by Evan's "blighted romance."[118]

In both of these cases a young woman brought an action against an older, richer man. This was, in general, the way the media reported breach of promise cases in the twentieth century. The image was the gold digger and her rich, gullible prey. The plaintiff was usually young but hardly chaste and innocent. Sometimes she was not even young but a mature woman of the world. Ida May McNabb, a 40-year-old widow with three children won a jury verdict of $30,000 in 1915 from a man described as a wealthy mine owner. She had a "marriage contract" that he had been stupid enough to sign.[119] A jury as late as 1936 awarded a quarter of a million dollars to Lilian Mandel, who sued the department store heir Frederick Gimbel for breach of promise. She was 22 years old and was working as an assistant buyer in a gown shop in 1917 when she met Gimbel (who was then 25).[120] The difference in social class is striking here, as is the fact that a jury of her peers thought she deserved a sizable verdict.

A lawsuit in New York in 1917, brought by a young woman named Honora O'Brien, is a striking example of what critics objected to—it also illustrates the erratic behavior of some juries.[121] Honora O'Brien was 29 years old. John Bernard Manning, the defendant, was 84. He was a man of "considerable vigor" but "partially palsied." He was also very, very rich—worth between $15 and $20 million, a staggering fortune in those days. It was a whirlwind courtship; the wedding was supposed to follow "in a few days." But instead, old Mr. Manning backed out.

The jury awarded O'Brien $200,000—an amazing amount for a civil suit of this type, or any type. Evidence that "aroused a feeling against the defendant" may have influenced the jurors. Manning apparently "strangled his daughter's pet dog" and was "expelled from the stock exchange for altering some certificates." He also lied about the plaintiff in an "inexcusable" and "vicious" way on the stand. Manning appealed his case. The appeals court thought that the damages were out of line. O'Brien had not suffered very much—"no loss of social position, no loss of a chance to marry some one else." Was she marrying

Manning for his money? Probably. But this made no legal difference. Even if a woman was marrying for "mercenary motives," she did not forfeit her right to recover. The court ordered a cut in the damages, to $125,000 but otherwise, perhaps reluctantly, affirmed the decision.

In many of these cases—the cases that made the newspapers and the cases appealed and reported—the jury seemed surprisingly willing to believe the plaintiff's story and award her substantial damages. Juries in such cases seemed immune to the relentless drumbeat of attacks on this particular cause of action. Perhaps the jurors were prejudiced against rich, foolish defendants. Perhaps they believed that the women had legitimate grievances. Juries were made up of fairly ordinary people—more likely to mesh with the plaintiff in income and class than with the defendant. Legislators were another story. They answered more to the needs and wants of elite men. By the 1930s the image of the plaintiff, for elites, was no longer the image of the innocent flower, seduced and abandoned. It was the image of the heartless gold digger. The rich and famous were not predators but prey. The women, not the men, were the seducers. No longer was this an action to protect the reputation and honor of respectable women. It had become a blackmail device, an abuse.

To be sure, only the most notorious and lurid cases made the columns of the newspapers. These cases did give off the rancid smell of blackmail—or at least the smell of a gold digger at work.[122] The point of the law had been to protect "respectable" women—and, not incidentally, to save from disgrace their fathers, brothers, and other members of her family. How the law operated in practice is difficult to tell.[123] In many reported American cases the social class of the plaintiffs remains obscure. Even the reported cases, atypical as they were, were probably on the whole less sensational—and less dubious—than the literature would suggest.[124] In any event, in both England and the United States criticism became more and more strident over the years. An English journal, *The Spectator*, in 1893 called the trials "demoralising spectacles" that served "no good end."[125] An American jurist, writing in 1929, called breach of promise cases "lurid and sensational," dear to the heart of the yellow press. A lawsuit for breach of promise "does nothing but harm" and "can and does function as an instrument of blackmail."[126] Harriet Spiller Daggett, writing in 1935, called the action a "dishonorable sword for a class of women who are trading on their sex"; the "great majority" of the plaintiffs were "unscrupulous women fortune hunters."[127]

Many people—and many jurists and legislators—now felt that a virtuous, respectable woman would never invite disgrace and humiliation by suing her ex-fiancé. Marriages were supposed to be based on love. If love flew out the window, so did the right to insist on marriage or to complain.[128] By the 1930s there was a serious and successful campaign in many states against breach of promise.[129] A number of states flatly abolished the cause of action. In the process they often also got rid of actions for seduction, alienation of affections, and criminal conversation.[130] In other states breach of promise survived but in a wounded and impotent form. An Illinois statute (1947) began by reciting that breach of promise actions had been "subject to grave abuses" and were "used as an instrument for blackmail by unscrupulous persons for their unjust enrichment." Under the new statute a plaintiff could recover only "actual" damages. There were to be no "punitive, exemplary, vindictive or aggravated damages." The statute also required the victim to give notice in writing within three months of the time the promise was breached, setting out the date the marriage was supposed to be performed, the damages incurred, and asserting whether the defendant was or was not "still willing to marry."[131] For many years breach of promise was dormant and all but dead. When in 1992 a (male) lawyer sued his ex-fiancée under the statute, asking for some $40,000—the "costs of the fur coat, the car, the typewriter, the engagement ring" and "even the champagne with which he toasted his bride-to-be"—it was newsworthy enough to make the *New York Times*.[132]

The blackmail argument was one of the main complaints against "heart balm" lawsuits. In Indiana, interestingly, Mrs. Roberta West Nicholson, the only woman in the Indiana legislature, led the campaign for abolition. She introduced a bill to rid Indiana of "itching palms in the guise of aching hearts." This "soft-voiced woman" on the floor of the Indiana house, wearing a "plain black dress offset by wide, ruffled collar and cuffs," denounced breach of promise as "a sordid and vulgar" affair. It debased the idea of marriage. Marriage was "a divine sacrifice, not a commercial agreement." Ninety percent of these lawsuits, she said, never reached court; they were "blackmail suits," plain and simple.[133]

By the time of the Mandel-Gimbel trial, New York state was also in the process of getting rid of breach of promise, and for good. The New York Court of Appeals sustained the abolition law. "Thoughtful people," said the court, had "long realized" that "scandals growing out of actions to recover damages for breach of promise . . . constitute a reflection upon the courts and a menace to . . . marriage" and could even be described as a "danger to the state."[134]

Still, this campaign would not have succeeded—as it did in a number of states[135]—unless the ethos underlying the breach of promise cases itself had not already been breached. Breach of promise was a failure, we are told; it did not conform to "changed *mores* concerning sex morality, the status of women, and the functions of the family."[136] The action, in other words, no longer served a useful purpose—at least in the opinion of middle-class men. Chastity was still, of course, a value for respectable women, but it had lost at least some of its currency. This was another reason that it was possible—and probably desirable—to get rid of breach of promise. After all, women of the 1930s were not as easily ruined as they had been in the nineteenth century.[137]

Alienation of affections was under attack for similar reasons. This cause of action, too, was supposed to be a vehicle for blackmail. In Los Angeles in 1897 David Davidson sued Henry Wormington for alienating the affections of Davidson's wife. Davidson found his wife with Wormington in Wormington's room "in a compromising position," or so he said. Wormington told a different story. He said that he was "disrobing for the night" when in came Mrs. Davidson and "partly divested herself of her clothing. . . . No sooner had she done so than a knock was heard at the door." Lo and behold, it was Davidson and "two companions." It was all a conspiracy (said Wormington) "for the purpose of extorting money from him." The Davidsons were "people of bad character." The judge "ordered a judgment entered in Wormington's favor, and against Davidson for costs of suit."[138]

Perhaps the truth here was somewhere in the middle. Most likely, Wormington was not quite so innocent as he made out. Probably he agreed to meet and have sex with Mrs. Davidson, unaware that she was setting a trap for him. Alienation of affections was, in theory, designed to protect the holy institution of marriage, in that it punished those who interfered with husbands and wives. But it was also—so people said—an open door to schemes like the Davidsons'. It was a way to extort money from respectable people—although usually, of course, these were respectable people who had something to hide.

Newspaper stories, as was their custom, only reported what was lurid and striking. They gave particular space to cases in which the defendant was rich or famous. Senator Ralph Cameron, of Arizona, was just such a defendant. Edward McFarlin sued the senator in 1921 for alienating the affections of McFarlin's wife. Cameron, according to McFarlin, had "detained and harbored" Marjorie McFarlin and had been "guilty of misconduct" with her on a New Haven railroad train among other places. McFarlin wanted $100,000 in damages. The senator—just elected in 1920—angrily denied the charges; this was a "blackmailing attempt to discredit him" now that he was about to enter the Senate. He would fight "with both fists," he said. He did in fact win the case—the statute of limitations had run out.[139]

Was the senator as innocent as he claimed? The McFarlins may have been blackmailers, but it does not follow that the senator was telling the truth. Even so, the McFarlins did not look much like victims. Such cases fed the campaign against alienation of affections, which for the most part went into the same discard pile as breach of promise.

Common law marriage had been in decline since the middle of the nineteenth century.[140] There were many reasons for this development, but perhaps an additional one was the idea that it, too, was a vehicle that scheming women used to get their hands on the money of wealthy men. The squabble over the estate of Abraham Lincoln Erlanger, a wealthy theater owner, was one such black mark against common law marriage. Erlanger had lived for years with a woman who called herself Charlotte Fixel-Erlanger; she was, she said, his common law wife and entitled to a widow's share of his estate when he died. Erlanger's will in fact left her nothing. His children claimed she was nothing but a mistress. Heaps of evidence were introduced on both sides. In the end, Charlotte won her case. The tumult over the Erlanger case helped administer the coup de grace to common law marriage in New York: The legislature abolished it in 1933.[141]

Criminal conversation was overtaken by the same fate that overtook breach of promise and alienation of affections. This was yet another heart balm cause of action. It was closely connected doctrinally and socially with the action for breach of promise. But only unscrupulous people (it was alleged) would stoop to this kind of lawsuit. Here, the gold diggers were men, not women. Indiana abolished the cause of action in 1935. "An Act to Promote Public Morals" swept aside breach of promise, alienation of affections, criminal conversation, and actions "for the seduction of any female person of the age of twenty-one years or more."[142] By the end of the 1930s nine states had followed suit. In 1939 California, like Indiana, made a clean sweep; it abolished alienation of affections, criminal conversation, "seduction of a person over the age of legal consent," and breach of promise of marriage (California Civil Code, § 43.5). There was another wave of abolitions in the 1970s and 1980s.[143]

In a few states where the legislature had not acted, the courts stepped in and "repealed" the action of criminal conversation.[144] In a divorce case in Idaho, the defendant, Mary Neal, counterclaimed and also asked for damages from her husband, Thomas Neal; he was having an affair with Jill La-Gasse. There had been no reported case of criminal conversation in Idaho since 1918, and the court simply "abolished" the cause of action.[145] Women were no longer the property of their husbands, said the court. Moreover, this kind of lawsuit might expose a person to "extortionate schemes," and it might "ruin" the "reputation" of the person accused.[146] In an earlier case the Idaho court had abolished alienation of affections.[147] The Supreme Court of Iowa did the same in 1981: "Suits for alienation . . . are useless as a means of preserving a family. They demean the parties and the courts. We abolish such a right of recovery."[148] By this point, about half the states had gotten rid of alienation of affections, either by statute or by court decision, and in many of the rest of the states procedural or other restrictions were placed on the action; in any event, this type of lawsuit had become, apparently, quite rare.[149] By the end of the twentieth century only a handful of states still preserved these ancient causes of action. In North Carolina, juries still seemed to love these cases—in one case a wrestling coach sued a man who had "engaged in sexual intercourse at a hotel" with his wife; the marriage broke up, and the jury awarded the coach $910,000 in "compensatory damages" and $500,000 in punitive damages.[150] In North Carolina carrying on with a married woman and breaking up her marriage still seems to be an extremely risky business, financially speaking. But elsewhere this cause of action is gathering dust on the shelves, even in states where it still, in theory, exists.

In other parts of the common law world the law of breach of promise and related causes of action traveled the same path. In Canada by the 1930s seduction and breach of promise "had all but fallen into disuse"; as Patrick Brode put it, in "true Canadian fashion, seduction seems to have gone away quietly instead of in a blaze of glory."[151] The Family Law Reform Act of 1978 ended all the heart balm torts in Ontario. In Manitoba the Equality of Status Act of 1982 did the same. The last province to abolish seduction as a cause of action was Saskatchewan, in 1990.[152] English developments, along parallel lines, were an influence in Canada. In England a 1970 statute provided that an "agreement between two persons to marry one another shall not . . . have effect as a contract giving rise to legal rights," and "no action shall lie . . . for breach of such an agreement."[153]

In general, actions for breach of promise or the equivalent are absent from civil law jurisdictions. The German, French, Spanish, and Italian civil codes generally do not allow such lawsuits, although the codes may provide for recovery of actual damages and the return of gifts (see, for example, German Civil Code, § 1298).[154] As I noted, German law once provided for *Kranzgeld*, more or less like breach of promise. The German courts, however, ruled in the 1970s that this idea offended basic German law and was no longer valid, in part because of changes in social norms; in 1998 it was wiped off the books.[155]

Thus this grab bag of legal actions fell victim to a double evolution. The original intent was protection of respectable women and their families, even if these women had slipped a bit. The tide turned against them when the dominant view asserted that now respectable (or quasi-respectable) *men* needed protection, even when they might have done something foolish or hasty. What completed the evolution was the second factor, perhaps even more powerful: the sexual revolution. It was no longer easy to ruin a woman. The two factors, working together, sealed the doom of breach of promise, alienation of affections, and criminal conversation.

CHAPTER 9

PRIVACY AND REPUTATION IN THE LATE TWENTIETH CENTURY

O NE OF THE chief arguments in this book has been that one can detect two concerns in American law in the nineteenth century—and to an extent the law of other countries. These concerns seem to contradict each other. The law expressed and enforced a strict code of traditional morality. Yet the law also protected the reputations of respectable people—even when they strayed somewhat from the straight and narrow path. I also tried to show how and why this happened. At many points the concept of *privacy* underlay the central argument—the idea that certain things (notably, the sexual side of life) had to be kept secret, kept private. Protecting reputation in an important sense meant protecting privacy, protecting the sanctity of the private realm, warts and all, especially or primarily for elite and respectable people. The actual law of "privacy," explicitly using the word, is largely a creation of the twentieth century. In this chapter I discuss some aspects of the law of privacy in its early phase and relate these aspects to the themes of this book.

At the end of the nineteenth century a new tort appeared in American law: the tort of invasion of privacy. Initially at least, the point of this tort was to protect the privacy—and the reputations—of the better sort of people.

A famous article written by Samuel D. Warren and Louis D. Brandeis, published in 1890 in the *Harvard Law Review*, launched the tort.[1] The two writers argued that the common law had the right and the duty to act to protect a person's privacy. Why was this a necessary and proper step? Because (said Warren and Brandeis) privacy was under attack from the mass media. The press was seriously misbehaving; it was "overstepping . . . the obvious bounds of decency." Gossip had become a commodity, a business. Irresponsible journals were threatening the reputations of respectable people. Details of "sexual relations" were "broadcast in the columns of the daily papers" to "satisfy a prurient taste." "Idle gossip, which could only be procured by intrusion upon the domestic circle," filled column after column in the daily press.

Warren and Brandeis were writing in the age of cheap, sensational mass-market newspapers, the age of Pulitzer and Hearst, and so-called yellow journalism.[2] This style was intense, vivid, accessible. The yellow press used photos and drawings to make stories more colorful. Newspapers covered grisly murders and executions and followed dramatic, lurid trials with great gusto. This was also the age of the first "candid" camera, the Kodak. The primitive cameras of the days before Kodak could not capture people and things in motion. To make a photographic portrait, the subject had to sit quietly and pose. The candid camera changed the situation dramatically. For the first time photographs of people could be taken without their permission—perhaps even without their knowledge.[3] The "latest advances in photographic art," as Warren and Brandeis put it, "have rendered it possible to take pictures surreptitiously." This added to the fears they expressed in their article—fears of "intrusion upon the domestic circle." The candid camera made the danger to privacy that much more palpable.[4]

Warren and Brandeis were men of impeccable honor and reputation. Presumably they had little to fear from gossip and the press. Neither of them had been touched by scandal. But they were nonetheless deeply concerned with threats to privacy. Why would invasions of privacy bother men of their stamp, who led lives beyond reproach? Would details of *their* sexual relations appeal to a prurient taste? One answer is yes: *Any* intrusion into the domestic circle would lead to scandal; *any* invasion of privacy would endanger the social fabric. Suppose (for example) that a person could peep through a keyhole and watch a married couple in the heavy throes of sexual intercourse. The couple was committing no crime, no sin; indeed, they were doing their duty. Yet they would be horrified at the loss of privacy. For them the veil of secrecy—of privacy—was essential to human dignity. And almost everyone would agree.

This is an extreme example of the basic point. But it illustrates how precious privacy can be. And beyond the embarrassment of individuals, there was also the larger social point: the belief that society in some way *depended* on privacy and secrecy—a point I have made many times. In addition, although Warren and Brandeis did not say so (and perhaps did not even think so), no doubt *some* respectable people in fact had dark and dirty secrets to hide. Even for these people, privacy—the veil of secrecy—was, as I have argued, a definite social good, an aspect of the social order that had to be protected.

Warren and Brandeis in their article advanced the claim that the common law, in an almost metaphysical way, already contained the seeds of a right of privacy. The common law was, in a way, already committed to this kind of protection—or so they claimed. There were raw materials, principles and precedents, in the toolshed of the common law from which the courts could craft a remedy for breach of the right of privacy. Nobody had recognized this before; but, they argued, those principles were nonetheless there, hidden in the folds and wrinkles of existing case law. More realistically, they were inviting courts to take the hint and invent such a tort. Not many courts actually followed their suggestions. More than twenty years later a treatise on the law of torts said it was still "not clear" whether "and to what extent the law will recognize . . . a so-called 'right of privacy.'"[5] In 1902 the highest court of New York, for example, refused to take up the invitation from Warren and Brandeis. A flour company and a box company had used a picture of the plaintiff, a young woman, in their advertising posters. They had not bothered to get her permission. The ads were "conspicuously posted and displayed in stores, warehouses, saloons and other public places." The plaintiff claimed that she was "greatly humiliated by the scoffs and jeers of persons who have recognized her face and picture"; she suffered "severe nervous shock" and "was confined to her bed." The court was unsympathetic. The "so-called 'right of privacy'" had no basis in the cases and "could not now be incorporated" into the law without doing "violence to settled principles of law."[6] The legislature of New York disagreed and responded by passing a law to protect privacy. It was a narrow law, however, and applied only to situations in which someone used the "name, portrait or picture of a living person" for advertising purposes without permission.[7]

Most of the early cases were, in fact, directed against advertisers who made unauthorized use of the plaintiff's name or picture, as in the New York case. The results were mixed. Some courts, such as the one in New York, refused to recognize this new cause of action.[8] Others embraced the idea. In the best known of these cases, *Pavesich v. New England Life Insurance Co.*, decided in Georgia in 1905,[9] the insurance company printed a picture of Paolo Pavesich and claimed that he had bought life insurance from the defendant, which Pavesich denied. In one odd case, Mrs. G. W. Stokes gave birth to twin boys, Siamese twins, joined from the shoulders down. The twins died, and Mr. Stokes hired a photographer, Douglas, to take a photograph "of the corpse in a nude condition." Douglas was to make twelve photos, give them to Stokes, and make no more. Instead, Douglas made additional copies from the negative and filed for a copyright. A jury awarded damages to the Stokes family, and the Court of Appeals of Kentucky affirmed.[10]

THE RED KIMONO:
THE SAGA OF GABRIELLE DARLEY MELVIN

Melvin v. Reid (1931), a California case, was one of the more notable cases that recognized a right of privacy.[11] The plaintiff was a woman who called herself Gabrielle Darley Melvin. Earlier in her life, Gabrielle Darley had been a prostitute who "followed the life of a sporting woman" in various towns in Arizona.[12] She fell in with a man named Leonard Tropp; he became her pimp and her lover. They moved to Los Angeles. There the romance went sour. Gabrielle had apparently given Leonard money to buy a diamond wedding ring. He bought a ring, but not for Gabrielle. Instead, it was intended for another woman—a woman he planned to marry. Gabrielle found this out, and she shot down Tropp on the street. She was arrested and tried for murder. This was in 1918.

The trial was fairly spectacular. Earl Rogers, a flamboyant criminal defense lawyer, represented Gabrielle. He put on a fantastic show. Gabrielle took the stand, and she told a pitiful story of love, abandonment, and betrayal. She said nothing about her career as a prostitute. When the prosecution tried to bring out certain nasty details, Gabrielle burst into tears. Rogers furiously condemned the prosecution and its "contemptible effort to influence the jury at the price of humiliating a pitiful young woman already bowed down by the weight of a terrible load of misfortune." Gabrielle claimed the revolver went off accidentally. Leonard, she said, had treated her roughly, and she was trying to defend herself. And, in any event, she did not really remember shooting him.[13] In his closing argument Rogers insisted that until she met Tropp, Gabrielle was "as pure as the snow atop Mount Wilson." Tropp, the cad, had "lured the soul-starved little waitress . . . to Los Angeles under promise of marriage," induced her to live a life of shame, cheated her out of her money, and was at the point of abandoning her for another woman. The jury promptly acquitted her.

Rogers's daughter, Adela Rogers St. John, a writer, covered the trial. Later, she wrote a short story based on the case and called it "The Red Kimono." It used incidents from Gabrielle's life, and it used her actual name. Dorothy Reid bought the story and produced a movie based on it. This film also was called *The Red Kimono*. It was shown in theaters in 1927.[14] The movie identified the heroine as Gabrielle Darley. The next year, Gabrielle, now calling herself Gabrielle Darley Melvin, brought suit against Reid and Reid's motion picture company. Her right of privacy, she claimed, had been invaded.

The plaintiff admitted many facts about her background, which she could hardly deny. And the trial, of course, was an open and notorious fact. But that was back then, she said; now, at the present time, she had become a new woman. She had married a man named Bernard Melvin. She had begun a new life. Her friends now treated her "as a lady of culture and refinement." All was going well, until, to her total shock, the movie appeared, using her real name, and she lost her hard-won respectability and reputation. The whole world knew her now as a killer and whore; she was exposed "to obloquy, contempt and ridicule"; she suffered "grievously . . . in mind and body," all to the tune of $50,000.

The California appellate court was entirely sympathetic. Here was a woman who had "abandoned her life of shame" and taken her place in "respectable society." What the producers of the movie had done (said the court) was truly reprehensible, not "justified by any standard of morals or ethics." They had indeed invaded Mrs. Melvin's privacy. She had a right to live her new life, her respectable life, free from this kind of publicity. The court did seem to be groping about for some legal hook on which to hang its opinion—anything at all. It cited, for example, the right to pursue happiness, as guaranteed by the California constitution. For our purposes, however, the court's general attitude toward Mrs. Melvin is the important point. The court was anxious to protect honor, decency, reputation—in precisely the way that Warren and Brandeis had wanted it done. It was also protecting a regime of second chances. The result of the case was, in a way, the functional equivalent of the (presumed) result of laws against blackmail: the right of decent people to start over again, to begin a new life, unencumbered by the debris of the old one.[15]

To be sure, Gabrielle Melvin had an unusual amount of such debris. The California court spoke the language of second chances; it spoke about the rights of a respectable person to start all over again. But the facts of the case were extreme. Mrs. Melvin had been a prostitute and had been on trial for murder. It is hard to be ruined more thoroughly than she had been at the time of her trial. A fresh start and a new life would not be easy under those circumstances. The fresh start notion always had its limits; whatever they were, Gabrielle Darley Melvin must have crossed over those limits. Perhaps another way to read the case is as a sign of the erosion of such limits. By 1931 there were abundant indications of a cultural shift, a change in the climate of opinion. Sexual and cultural mores were changing. It was much harder to ruin a woman once and for all.

In fact, Gabrielle Darley's case is full of ironies. Gabrielle stayed out of prison in the first place because she had a brilliant lawyer, who was able to spin a convincing tale. The jury was persuaded—Gabrielle Darley was an innocent flower, victimized by a human wolf. This was almost surely a blatant lie. She won her privacy case in the California appeals court with another bold argument and another blatant lie. She convinced the court that she had changed her life, that she was now a decent, respectable, bourgeois woman.[16] There is good evidence that she was, in fact, as phony as a three dollar bill. A journalist in Arizona argues that she was still working as a prostitute and a madam at the time of the trial in a town in Arizona. During her lifetime she had several husbands, but they had the distressing habit of turning up dead, just like her boyfriend Leonard Tropp had done.[17]

In short, almost everything about the case rings false. It also tells us something about legal sources. Judicial facts are not the same as real-life facts. The judges saw Gabrielle Melvin as a pillar of the community. Legally, then, she *was* a pillar of the community. Judges and juries "find" facts, and these facts are binding and conclusive in the world of the law. But reality is not the same as the facts that are found to be true. What is interesting is how eager a jury and a panel of judges were to believe in the picture that Gabrielle Darley Melvin presented to them. It fit their stereotypes of women, it soothed their ethical sense, and, in the case of the California court, it reinforced their belief in redemption and reform. Perhaps the court imagined that no former prostitute and murder suspect would have the gall to sue unless she was telling the truth.

Barber v. Time, Inc.,[18] a Missouri case from 1942, also echoed something of the tone of Warren and Brandeis. The plaintiff was "pretty Mrs. Dorothy Barber of Kansas City." The defendant magazine, *Time,* told the following story (under the heading of "Medicine"). Barber had an eating problem. Her appetite was insatiable; in the past year she had eaten enough "to feed a family of ten." Despite her gluttony, she had actually lost weight. Barber "grabbed a candy bar, packed up some clothes," and went to the hospital. A doctor thought possibly her pancreas was "functioning abnormally," burning too much sugar, and "causing an excessive flow of digestive juices, which sharpened her appetite." While he conducted laboratory tests, "Mrs. Barber lay in bed and ate." Accompanying the story was a picture of Barber in bed in a hospital gown.

A jury found for Barber and awarded damages. The appeals court was sympathetic. She had never given permission to the magazine to publish her picture or her story. A person should have the "right to obtain medical treatment at home or in a hospital for an individual personal condition . . . without personal publicity." True, Barber "may have been a matter of some public interest," because her condition was "unusual." But there was no reason to reveal "the identity of the person who suffered this ailment." The court also quoted, approvingly, from the comments to the Restatement of Torts: An action lies where an "intrusion" has "gone beyond the limits of decency," that is, "where intimate details of the life of one who has never manifested a desire to have publicity are exposed to the public."[19]

Like Gabrielle Darley, Dorothy Barber was trying to reform, to change her life. She was trying to conquer her eating disorder and reenter the society of ordinary, normal people. She had never manifested any desire to be a public figure. Legally—and socially—these cases raised two issues. First, who is a private citizen, and who is a public figure? And second, what is it that the public has a right to know, even about public figures, and what aspects of their lives can and should be legally protected? The nineteenth century had diligently tried to build a wall of protection around the lives and reputations of respectable people. It also put a wall of protection around things that were purely personal—things that were proper enough in their sphere but that were and should be private: the nude body, for example, and sex acts, no matter how legitimate and holy; and intimate details, such as the kind of underwear people might be wearing. In *Daily Times Democrat v. Graham* (1964),[20] the plaintiff, Flora Bell Graham, was a 44-year-old woman in Alabama, married with two sons. She lived "in a rural community" where her husband raised chickens. There she "led the usual life of a housewife . . . participating in normal church and community affairs." In 1961 she took her boys to the Cullman County Fair. As she came out of the fun house with her sons, "her dress was blown up by the air jets and her body was exposed from the waist down," except for "that portion covered by her 'panties.'" Unfortunately, a newspaper photograph snapped a picture of this exciting event and put it on the front page. Mrs. Graham "became embarrassed, self-conscious, upset and was known to cry on occasions." A jury awarded her something over $4,000. The appeals court affirmed. The photo was "embarrassing to one of normal sensibilities"; perhaps it was even "obscene." A person "involuntarily . . . enmeshed in an embarrassing pose" does not lose her privacy simply because she was "part of a public scene."

As we will see, for "public figures" (a quite elastic concept), the original right of privacy has been shrinking, and for *very* public figures it is practically gone. If we ask who is a public figure, this too is controverted. Clearly, a president or a prime minister is a public figure. But who else? High government officials, no doubt; probably movie stars and famous people in the world of entertainment. Famous leaders of business, science, or religion might also qualify. How much further does the concept go? What about people who become an "object of attention" but unwillingly? Even in 1931 there was an excellent argument that Gabrielle Darley's sensational trial had turned her into a public figure. In their original article Warren and Brandeis admitted that public figures had less claim to privacy than ordinary folks. Most of the cases, even in the early days of the right, recognized the same limitation. The right of privacy does not draw a curtain over anything in which the public has a legitimate interest—a right to know.

In the years since Warren and Brandeis, the definition of a public figure and the notions of what the public has a right to know have changed enormously. Reputation—for elites, for respectable people—remains enormously important for the career, for social standing. True, some behavior that once could kill a person's good name no longer does so or does so not quite so dramatically. But there is still a wide range of behavior that people would prefer to keep secret; and there is also, as before, a strong sense that some parts of life ought to be kept secret. But in the late twentieth century, at least with regard to prominent people, the public began to feel *entitled* to find out all the secrets, to see all, hear all, know all. Warren and Brandeis thought of their shiny new tort as a dragon, guarding the privacy of elites. The mass media and the insatiable curiosity of the lower orders threatened the privacy of men and women who belonged to Warren and Brandeis's class. In practice, however, the law did not work out the way they intended. Today, elite status does not entitle you to extra privacy or even ordinary privacy. In fact, elite status means, practically speaking, giving up a good deal of your privacy altogether—socially and legally as well.

This, at least, is the message of the cases in the United States. *Melvin v. Reid* and the case of Dorothy Barber now look like anomalies. The decisions—certainly from the 1930s on—backed away from the ethos that underlay Warren and Brandeis's argument. They wanted to shield prominent people. They wanted genteel respect for the privacy and decency of people like themselves. It did not happen. The modern mass media have brought about vast social changes—in attitudes, expectations, wishes, desires, and thoughts. The mass media have also made it possible for people to observe, watch, and spy on public figures—especially through television and perhaps now the Internet. The modern decisions no doubt reflect the norms of modern society. The result by now is something close to a *right* to know whatever there is to know about kings, queens, presidents, popes, and movie stars, sports heroes, rock stars, characters on TV soap operas, captains of industry, and famous people in general.

The twentieth-century story, then, is in part a story of the decline and fall of one form of protection of privacy and secrecy for the rich and the powerful.

In 1914 Daisy, Lady Warwick, once the mistress of King Edward VII, found herself strapped for cash and heavily in debt. The king had died in 1910, and his son, George V, was now king of England. Lady Warwick owned a raft of love letters, written by Edward VII. She embarked on an elaborate scheme to raise money—not by publishing the letters but by promising *not* to publish them. The government and the royal family managed to foil this genteel blackmail scheme. In August 1914 England went to war with Germany, and the government invoked a law—the Defence of the Realm Act—to squelch Lady Warwick, even to threaten her with prison. Lady Warwick had to admit defeat. The palace was anxious to keep the whole affair secret. The legal actions that had been taken disappeared from the official records. Indeed, the story did not come to light until some fifty years after it had happened.[21]

Clearly, the government—and the royal family—considered these letters embarrassing. This in itself was, in a way, a sign of changing times. Mistresses were one of the privileges of kings. Usually nobody cared very much. Victoria had been an exceedingly bourgeois queen; her son, Edward VII, was something of a throwback to the bad old days. His mistress, Mrs. Keppel, was present at his deathbed. But in the twentieth century the mass media had more capacity to spread gossip and scandal to ordinary people. This had been much less so in the eighteenth century or earlier. And there were people, too, who thought that kings were not exempt from bourgeois rules. Clearly, there was a market for Lady Warwick's letters. Today the sins and foibles of the royals are more and more an open book. It would be hard today to keep the lid on. Some tabloid would buy and publish the letters—and would sell a lot of newspapers doing so.

Big people did not lose their privacy overnight. It happened in fits and starts and in stages. Franklin D. Roosevelt successfully hid his wheelchair from the public.[22] The media obviously cooperated. People knew the president had polio and was handicapped. But they were never allowed to see exactly *how* disabled he was. When John F. Kennedy was president, no newspaper reported on his obsessive sexual encounters. In Britain the press was still muzzled—voluntarily—during the constitutional crisis of the 1930s. The new king, Edward VIII, demanded the right to marry a divorced American woman. Only when he gave up the throne for Mrs. Simpson did the British press tell the story. All this is dramatically different today. The president's health statistics are religiously reported. President Clinton's sordid sex life was front-page news. The tabloids in England spill tons of ink on the private lives of royals, on marriages and divorces and love affairs among the queen's children, especially the affairs of Prince Charles, his first wife, Diana, and his long-time mistress (now his wife) Camilla.

Presidents and kings are obviously public figures. But the concept of a public figure itself has been stretched beyond all recognition in the law. At times, courts almost seemed willing to label *anybody* a public figure if the public had any conceivable interest in the woman or man.[23] In hindsight it seems clear that the Warren and Brandeis *idea*—protection from the despicable snooping of the media—never got much past the starting post. Whatever a newspaper or a magazine or a TV station prints or shows or reveals must be of public interest, almost by definition; otherwise there would be no point in printing this news.

In the well-known case of *Sidis v. F-R Publishing Company* (1940),[24] the *New Yorker* magazine ran an article about William James Sidis. Sidis had been a child prodigy—a math whiz who graduated from Harvard at age 16. When Sidis was 11, a "distinguished" professor at MIT predicted that he would "grow up to be a great mathematician." And where was he now, as an adult, the magazine asked. Basically, he was nowhere. Sidis went to law school, graduated, took a teaching job in Texas, but then gave it all up. He turned into a something of a neurotic hermit and an avid "peridromophile"—a "collector of streetcar transfers" (Sidis had coined this word himself). At the time of the article, Sidis was 39 years old, living alone "in a hall bedroom" in Boston's "shabby south end." He worked as a "clerk in a business house." This one-time mathematical genius was "leading a life of wandering irresponsibility," and the "very sight of a mathematical formula" made him "physically ill."[25] Sidis was not pleased to return to the limelight. He brought a lawsuit against the *New Yorker*. On the whole, Sidis seemed much less of a public figure than Gabrielle Darley Melvin. The magazine had been "merciless in its dissection of intimate details of its subject's personal life," but the public apparently had a right to find out what had become of this former child prodigy. At least the court so held.

Later, in the 1970s, Mike Virgil, a well-known "body surfer," objected to an article in *Sports Illustrated*, "The Closest Thing to Being Born." It was an article about body surfing and the strange cast of characters who went in for

this sport. Mike was one of the strangest. He once extinguished a lighted ciga-
rette in his mouth. At a ski lodge he "dove headfirst down a flight of stairs,"
apparently to "impress" some "chicks." His wife reported that he ate "spiders
and other insects and things" but not meat, which (said Virgil) "takes up too
much energy."[26] A federal appeals court sent the case back down for retrial,
and the trial judge dismissed the case: Body surfing was a "matter of legitimate public interest." The article was neither "morbid" nor "sensational." The
"personal facts" about Mike Virgil were a "legitimate" attempt to explain his
"extremely daring and dangerous style of body surfing."[27]

Thus the cases have expanded the right of the public to know absolutely
and the right of the media to tell and tell and tell, and they have shrunk the
right of elites to private life. And not only elites—the right of anybody newsworthy. In an early case (1929), Thomas Jones and Lillian Jones were walking along a street in Louisville, Kentucky. Two men assaulted Mr. Jones and
stabbed him to death. According to the local newspaper, Mrs. Jones "hero-
ically attacked both men"; they got away. She was reported to have said that
she would have killed the "brutes" if she could. The newspaper printed her
picture and her husband's. She brought suit for invasion of privacy among
other things. But "the right to live one's life in seclusion" is lost, said the court,
when a person, "willingly or not, becomes an actor in an occurrence of public
or general interest."[28]

What survives most vigorously from the original tort is a *commercial* right:
Nobody can make money from your name or image in an ad, a pamphlet, a
brochure, without your permission. Recently, however, perhaps out of revul-
sion against lurid mass media, gossips, paparazzi, and peeping Toms, there is
something of a trend to limit the definition of a public figure and what the
public is entitled to know about them. Courts seem sympathetic to the idea
that ordinary people have a right to some protection for privacy and private
lives, even when they become entangled in extraordinary events.

A terrible crime was the background of one Kansas case from 1983.[29] Young
Jack Hanrahan, 12 years old, disappeared from his home. Later his dead body
was found. One day, a man named Horn was teaching a class of prospective
real estate brokers. During a break, his wife called him and repeated a rumor
she had heard: The police suspected the boy's father and were holding him for
questioning. Horn repeated the rumor to the class. Maybe he just wanted to

liven up the class of future brokers. The rumor turned out to be false. Later, Horn recanted, apologized, and so on; but Mr. Hanrahan, furious, filed a lawsuit. The trial court dismissed the case, but the appeals court sent it back to be tried. Hanrahan had frequently been in the newspapers because of his family tragedy, but that did not make him a public figure. Public figures are people "who seek to influence the resolution of public questions," said the court. All Hanrahan was trying to do was find out who killed his son.[30]

For people who are clearly in public life, however, privacy rights have come close to the vanishing point at times. For celebrities almost anything goes. This is most obviously the case if what someone reveals about them is true; as we will see, even certain classes of misstatements or lies have a kind of immunity. In the development of privacy law the United States stands somewhat apart from other Western countries. European countries grant much more right to privacy, even for public figures. Private facts about public figures cannot be revealed unless they have some relevance to official duties and the like. Everything else is forbidden.[31] This divergence between the United States and its sister democracies is perhaps only to be expected. Deference to authority, although much weaker than in the past, has more force in Europe than in the United States. I will return to this theme in Chapter 10.

One should be careful not to exaggerate the differences between Europe and the United States. So far as the formal law goes, they seem fairly sharp. On the ground the differences seem rather blurred. Gossip about celebrities is epidemic in every country. There are as many fan magazines, tabloids, and scandal sheets in England or Germany or Spain as in the United States. Most Americans would not recognize many or most of the names in these magazines, but they would also find a sizable coterie of international stars, and the themes—marriage, divorce, drunkenness, sexual cavorting, and so on—would be quite familiar.

THE CELEBRITY SOCIETY

This convergence in media trash on two continents should not come as much of a surprise. Developed countries all share a cultural feature that we can call celebrity culture. Basically, a celebrity is not simply a famous person. A celebrity is a famous and *familiar* person.[32] The mass media create celebrities. Their fame—and familiarity—are the result of movies, magazines, television, and the other mass media.[33] Television in particular breaks down the *apparent* barrier between elites and the mass audience. Elites tend to get redefined as celebrities.[34] Television is beamed into almost every home in the West, and it is suffused with images of the rich and famous—images of celebrities. Because we see the faces and hear the voices so constantly, we get the illusion of familiarity; we think we know these people, these heroes of politics, sports, and entertainment; we know what they look like, how they walk and talk, what they wear, how they comport themselves.[35] Soccer stars, the queen of England and her gaggle of wayward children, the pope, the Dalai Lama, prominent singers or actors—all these people are visible and audible in every way and every day.

Because we have this illusion of familiarity, because we seem always to be peering into the lives of the famous, it is easy for us to believe in the end that we have the *right* to learn about the lives of celebrities. We have a right to know about their private affairs, their personal habits, their pets, their tastes in food and wine, their views on every subject. And this can in a proper case include their diseases and physical infirmities, their sex lives, what church they belong to, number and gender of illegitimate children, identity of mistresses or boyfriends, and almost everything else about them.

Celebrity culture is extraordinarily important in our modern societies. And its essence is the illusion that we know the celebrity intimately. This point became dazzlingly clear after the death of Diana, Princess of Wales. She died on August 31, 1997, in the early hours of the morning in Paris, France; she was riding with her boyfriend in a Mercedes-Benz auto, which crashed into the wall of an underpass at great speed. News of this tragedy flashed around the world in a very short time. The "People's Princess" was dead. What followed was an amazing outpouring of grief. From ten to fifteen tons of flowers were heaped up against various London palaces. In a survey carried out by the British Film Institute, 50 percent of the people who were polled said that Diana's death had affected them personally.[36] Tens of thousands of people, all over the world, signed books of condolences. The Republic of Togo put Diana's face on a postage stamp. A memorial mural on the Lower East Side of New York cried out: "Diana, you will be greatly missed by all of us."[37]

Why was this death so moving? Why did it have so powerful an impact? What could Diana, daughter of an earl, ex-wife of the Prince of Wales, have possibly meant to the countless millions who mourned her? But Diana was a celebrity, indeed, one of the most celebrated women of her day. She was famous in a way utterly unlike the Princess of Wales in, say, 1800 or even 1900. People felt that they *knew* Diana. They knew her face, her voice, her clothes; they knew about her troubled marriage—they knew, or thought they knew, all about her thoughts, her hopes, her despairs. Her mother-in-law, Queen Elizabeth II, is a celebrity in her own right. Unlike Queen Victoria, she is not just a face on postage stamps and coins. She has been, from birth, constantly in the public eye. She is seen almost every day on TV. Her voice is familiar. The way she walks and talks, her dowdy clothes and her hats, all this is common knowledge to countless millions of people. We know she likes horses and dogs. We know how much grief her four wayward children have brought into her life.

The media have created these celebrities—this class of intimate strangers. It is television, for example, that helps give us the illusion of familiarity with intimate strangers. A TV program called *Lifestyles of the Rich and Famous*, quite popular for a while, claimed to take the audience inside the houses of these "rich and famous" people. It showed viewers what kind of kitchens they had, what was hanging on the walls, what kind of rugs they walked on, what chairs they sat in. They seemed more real to us, perhaps, than people who live down the street or in our apartment building in some big city. Yet the familiarity is lopsided. We know them, but *they* do not know *us*. We look at them, see them, watch them through what is, in effect, a one-way mirror.[38]

In the modern world billions of people surf the Internet, read fan magazines, go to the movies, attend sports events, and above all watch television. The big stars and the big people are so familiar that we are, as it were, on a first-name basis with them. The tabloids can talk breathlessly about Tom or Liz or Brad or Diana or Oprah or Angelina, and everybody knows who they are talking about. The *National Enquirer* sells millions of copies and is largely devoted to celebrity gossip. It has lost ground recently—but only because more respectable journals have stolen some of its thunder and copied some of its style.[39] *People* magazine and its counterparts are simply more chaste versions of supermarket tabloids. Gossip is no longer a whisper but a shout.

In every advanced society there are literally hundreds, maybe thousands of celebrities. Football players, rock stars, movie idols are like old friends, faces we recognize, people we know. And they are also, in most ways, very ordinary people. They have a talent, but the talent is usually only a heightened form of something everybody does. They dance, they sing, they act, they throw or hit a ball—of course they do it better than the rest of us, but there is nothing magical or otherworldly about their talent. And some people become celebrities because of sheer dumb luck: They win the lottery or give birth to quintuplets or are born the eldest son of the king of Spain or the queen of England. Some become celebrities because of sheer *bad* luck: victims of some terrible crime or attached to a Siamese twin or one of six children born at once. But what they have in common is that we *know* them, see them, understand them. Or think we do.

The world of the one-way mirror has transformed politics. To a large extent image replaces ideology. In fact, politics may be the most extreme example of celebrity culture. A basketball star, after all, has to shoot baskets. A rock-and-roll singer has to sing. But in politics image is almost everything. Party and policies still make a difference, of course, but the swing voters tend to swing on the basis of image. A successful candidate has to have charisma; also a good family life, sound religious principles, and a good deal of personal charm. A wooden speaker, a man or woman without the magic touch, is unlikely to win an election. Robert Bellah argues that political parties are "based on sentiment more than principle"; a "politics of personality," he feels, is "replacing a policy of reputation."[40] People vote on the basis of appearances and images projected through the media rather than on a hard-won reputation, which might rest on sound ideas and good works. Bellah is describing, in short, the celebrity society. Of course, politics is still a matter of reputation, but what has changed is the source of the reputation. It is a matter of sound bites, TV appearances, press conferences. The worst thing is to be stilted or boring. In a way the celebrity society has assimilated politics to entertainment. The president, as Neal Gabler put it, is the "entertainer-in-chief."[41]

Of course, the president has enormous political power. He can unleash the dogs of war, he appoints the upper bureaucracy and the judges, he determines the direction of national policy. But he is also and strikingly a national celebrity. He is on TV literally every day. We know, or think we know, everything about him: his walk, his talk, what he wears, where he lives, his family, his personal likes and dislikes, even his cats and dogs. We see him as he strides toward his helicopter or relaxes at Camp David or talks to visiting kings and heads of state. It is easy to forget that we watch him through the one-way mirror.

Other authority figures who historically were remote, even godlike, have become familiar too—have become, in other words, celebrities. This is true of the pope and the Dalai Lama,[42] and even, to a degree, the emperor of Japan. A celebrity society is a society that breaks down the (apparent) barriers between the leaders and the led, between the stars of stage and screen and the ordinary earthlings, between the high and the mighty, the rich and the famous, and everybody else. The social distance between the president and his voters or between the pope and his flock has diminished; it is more like the distance between sports idols and their fans.

In reality, of course, the barriers are still there. The president moves within a cocoon of secret service agents. Rich celebrities never go anywhere without their bodyguards. But these human barriers and physical barriers testify to the erosion of psychological and cultural barriers. *Those* barriers have become almost invisible. So much so, that some people forget that they exist at all. When we know "intimate details about a famous person," we "may be lured into a false sense of intimacy."[43] Hence we have the slightly addled but scary tactics of people who, for example, "stalk" the stars.[44]

Most stalkers stalk their former wives, girlfriends (or husbands and boyfriends), but the small group of star stalkers is of special interest. Mentally speaking, they tend to be damaged goods. They cross the boundary line between sanity and derangement. They also try to cross through the one-way mirror. Yet even normal people lose sight of the distance between themselves and their celebrities. This was, of course, what happened at the death of the Princess of Wales. People all over the world mourned a person they had never met and were never likely to meet. It struck them with the same force as a death in the family.

It follows that the essence of celebrity is a certain loss of privacy. The celebrities have to struggle to control the publicity, to monitor the images they project through the one-way mirror, to try to keep at least some parts of life truly private. This can be a battle—with tabloids, with tabloid television, and with the paparazzi.[45] Rogue photographers are constantly looking for fresh opportunities: a princess of Monaco taking a topless sunbath on a yacht or a movie star kissing on a beach. A German tabloid, *Das Bild*, had a tremendous scoop in 1994; it published a picture, taken with a telephoto lens, of Charles, Prince of Wales, totally naked. This was front-page news, together with the photo itself and a huge headline that shouted "Charles Naked!" The photo-graph, somewhat blurry, revealed nothing startling about the prince's private parts, but it did sell a lot of newspapers. The royal family huffed and puffed and expressed great indignation, but in the end took no action against *Das Bild*.[46] Back home in England, in 1992 the *Daily Mirror* printed topless photos of the Duchess of York and sold half a million extra copies of the paper.[47]

Privacy was once like a series of forts protecting a system of deference. Much of this line of defense has crumbled. It was apparently not beyond the pale to expose the seamy sex life of President Clinton. Loss of privacy for public fig-ures, however, does not necessarily mean loss of reputation. Gossip and tabloid news about the sex life of a rock star are probably not terribly injurious. But it would be a huge public scandal to accuse a bishop of sleeping with women—or men. A modern pope cannot afford to be surrounded by "nephews" or to live the high life of the Borgias and Renaissance popes.

What unites all celebrities is the sense of familiarity and the feeling that the people have a *right* to know, a right to have access to image and informa-tion. How this ideology became salient, how it spread, is a difficult historical question. Certainly, it owes an enormous debt to the media, especially televi-sion, the great modern one-way mirror. But television (and now, the Internet) only heightened a process that began with mass-market magazines and news-papers and gained speed and force with movies, newsreels, and radio. In some complex way the process is related to the collapse of older hierarchies. Modern developed societies are also wealthy societies. The middle class is enormous; most people have at least some money and (significantly) some leisure time to fill and kill. These, then, are *entertainment* societies. Hardly any industry is more important than the fun industry and its various components. The need for entertainment, the passion for entertainment, infects news, educa-tion, and politics. No right in modern society is more central than the right to be amused.

All developed societies are to a degree celebrity cultures. All are heavily focused on entertainment. Privacy law and practice have been reshaped in all of them, but the loss of privacy for public figures has probably gone farther in the United States than in Europe. European countries and their legal system place heavy emphasis on dignity, honor, and personal privacy.[48] This seems to be true even for public figures. Some of the differences may come from leftover habits of class consciousness and deference in Europe. It may be, however, that these transatlantic differences are slowly diminishing.

PRIVACY: THE CONSTITUTIONAL RIGHT

Celebrities may have lost much of their privacy, but in general, privacy is still an important value for the population at large—perhaps more valuable than ever. Privacy has had a distinguished career as a constitutional principle. We have seen how it evolved from *Griswold v. Connecticut* through *Roe v. Wade* and beyond.[49] But the constitutional right of privacy is in some ways the opposite of the Warren and Brandeis right. It is the right to make certain life choices freely, without state interference—even, if you please, the right to make these choices in an open and notorious way. The general public is also legitimately worried about the power of governments and big institutions to intrude into people's lives—and into privacy in this more modern sense. There is a curious tension here. The public loves the morbid and the sensational, but they hate surveillance and the technology of surveillance (except for criminals and terrorists, of course). They are intensely suspicious of anything that puts information, data, records, and the like in the hands of authorities.[50] They hate the fact that credit companies, banks, and hospitals can compile dossiers on them. They fret over wiretapping (again, except for criminals and terrorists). It bothers civil libertarians that the FBI has a gigantic computer database, which it can use not just to identify drug pushers and suicide bombers but also to ensnare people committing minor offenses.[51] We know that there are cameras here and there and everywhere, taking pictures and storing them—but for how long? It is alarming to think that government can read e-mail messages, tap into financial records, listen in on conversations.[52] People want to keep control of their lives. They want limits on the information other people (and Big Brother) can compile about them. They are especially finicky about medical records and financial information. Proposals for a national identity card are greeted in some quarters with about as much enthusiasm as a letter bomb. What is at stake is not primness or modesty or fears about one's reputation. It is the fear of Big Brother. It is fear that power to control our own lives is slipping away from us.

Thus two strands of evolution seem to be in conflict. One path leads toward permissiveness and the freedom to do what ones likes. The other holds

over our heads the *power* to squeeze and squash the individual soul. A kind
of sullen tension exists between the right to know and the right to keep other
people from knowing things that are none of their business.

One thing is clear: What Warren and Brandeis assumed—a kind of moral
distance between the elites and the masses—has lost a lot of its strength.
America always considered itself a classless society, whether it was one or not.
It was certainly never classless in terms of wealth, power, and dignity, but it
prided itself on a certain degree of *cultural* classlessness. One symptom is the
American disdain for intellectuals. No egghead could ever be elected president.
The president throws out the first baseball, but never goes to the opera. Political leaders can come from rich families, and they often do; but they cannot
seem snobbish or condescending.

The trend toward cultural classlessness is, if anything, more pronounced
today. Take clothing, for example. Clothes cost money, and the working man
and his family in, say, the late nineteenth century could not dress up the way
rich people could. The poor dressed in ragged or second-hand clothes. Farmers
and miners wore overalls. Yet already clerks and other members of the lower
middle class tried to dress more or less like their betters, as much as they could.[53]
In England and in the United States many people imitated or tried to imitate
the general cut and style of the clothing that their betters tended to wear.

The American style of dress, wrote one author, was "so inornate and so
uncostly, that it is attainable by men of all classes above the very poor."[54] Of
course, elite behavior set the tone and the standard.[55] Rich people had their
tailors and dressmakers and wore custom-made clothing. The rest of the
population wore mass-produced, ready-to-wear clothing, but the clothes were
more or less copies of the clothing of the rich. The situation today is complex.
Obviously, only very rich women wear designer gowns. But in the crazy world
of fashion the rich often imitate the styles of the street. What young people
wear is particularly influential. Some kinds of clothes are definitely classless.
Blue jeans come out of working-class culture. They were originally clothing
for miners, then for farmers, and now for everybody. By the 1970s jeans had
become almost a uniform.[56] On a college campus all the students dress more
or less alike; the untrained eye will have trouble picking out subtle differences
in cut and cloth and style. What is true in clothing is true in other aspects of
popular culture. In music jazz and rock-and-roll have roots in black society.

Both are now essentially classless and universal—and not only in American society. They, like blue jeans, have become global institutions.

In many ways the mass media *made* modern society; and they contribute to this blurring of cultural distance. The mass media create the illusion that we actually *know* the celebrities we see and hear and read about almost every day. As they lose their privacy, they also lose the sense of distance and remoteness.

PRIVACY AND SPACE

Modern law endlessly discusses privacy; nineteenth-century law almost never did. Yet as a *social* value privacy was important in Victoria's day, and in a very literal sense. Victorian prudery, as I have argued, was itself a form of privacy protection. Taboos about sex drew a curtain over private life. This was in many ways a shield for respectable elites. But privacy has above all a spatial element. Victorian elites, in their homes, had space to pursue private lives. Still, in England (much more than in the United States) that privacy was never absolute. Even in middle-class homes a small corps of maids, cooks, and other servants bustled about. In a striking passage in her book *Aurora Floyd*, Mary Braddon in 1863 advised gentlefolk to be careful what they said and did in front of servants: "Your servants listen at your doors, and repeat your spiteful speeches in the kitchen. . . . They . . . understand every sarcasm, every inuendo, every look. . . . They understand your sulky silence, your studied and over-acted politeness. The most polished form your hate and anger can take is as transparent to those household spies as if you threw knives at each other. . . . Nothing that is done in the parlour is lost upon these quiet, well-behaved watchers from the kitchen."[57] Braddon, of course, talked only about the parlor, not the bedroom; in that room the rich were perhaps most vulnerable of all.

The poor, of course, lacked privacy for other reasons. In their huts, hovels, and cottages they had to share space with children and often with other adults. Yet for both rich and poor Victorian culture acted as a kind of curtain; maybe there was little or no privacy at home, but a curtain of secrecy separated home from the larger world. It is for this reason that Catherine MacKinnon, for example, has argued that privacy acts as an instrument of male supremacy; it hides the abuse and oppression of women. It is a "sword in men's hands presented as a shield in women's." In fact, she argues, for women, "the measure of the intimacy has been the measure of the oppression."[58] Women, in other words, were left without power and autonomy, behind the curtain of silence. In the private sphere men could abuse women without fear of legal or social consequences.[59]

There is no doubt a good deal of truth to this assertion. Scholars dispute, however, whether law and society were as tolerant of abuse of women as MacKinnon seems to suggest. In any event there was dramatic change in the twentieth century. Wife beating is taken much more seriously. The same can be said for sexual abuse. Legally, at one time, no man could be convicted of raping his own wife. A woman's marriage gave a man blanket sexual consent; as soon as she said "I do," rape became a legal impossibility. Contemporary jurists found this doctrine repellent. A New York court held in 1984 that marriage did not give a man the "right to coerced intercourse on demand."[60] Most states have done away with the marital exemption for rape.[61] In England the House of Lords declared in 1991 that the exemption no longer applied.[62] The state, in other words, can rip aside the curtain. In general, the modern state has greater powers to intervene in family life—in cases, too, of child abuse and elder abuse. All this is part of the retreat from privacy in its classic sense. Society today—and this is a major theme of this part of the book—no longer hesitates to peep into dark corners of family and social life. No curtain of absolute secrecy protects hidden pathologies.

CHAPTER 10

DEFAMATION IN CONTEMPORARY TIMES

T HE LAW OF DEFAMATION is the branch of law most directly concerned with protecting reputation. It has deep historical roots and is at the same time a branch of living law. How much impact defamation has on society is not at all easy to say. Many people—and certainly people who work for the media—are acutely aware that it exists. The actual *number* of defamation cases in court, though, is not great. Also, there is not much empirical research on the subject. What little there is focuses almost necessarily on appealed cases. Only appealed cases get reported. For what it is worth, studies show that plaintiffs lose most of these cases.[1] One researcher, who looked at libel cases reported between 1974 and 1984, found that plaintiffs won only 10 percent of the cases and perhaps even less.[2] Newspapers and other media companies were the most popular defendants. If they lost at the trial stage, they were likely to win on appeal.[3]

Why do people sue if the chances of winning are so slight? Plaintiffs who sue tend to be men and women who are angry, frustrated, and hurt. In an Iowa study plaintiffs in libel actions were interviewed; these plaintiffs complained about "reputational harm," about harassment, embarrassment, threatening phone calls. Some lost business as a result of defamation. Plaintiffs wanted vindication: "Somebody's got to pay." One plaintiff said, "I didn't care about the money; I wanted the [defendant] to suffer embarrassment." Many said they just wanted to clear their name.[4] Some thought that, win or lose, they might at least stop the defendant from doing more bad things.[5]

Legal doctrines make the plaintiff's lot more difficult. Truth is now a complete and total defense. The defendant must have told an out-and-out lie. There are some minor exceptions—the old antidueling statutes, for example, still alive in a few states but probably never used.[6] In some places it is still against the law to insult the flag or to insult members of the National Guard or to insult or abuse election officials. A few statutes specifically refer to insults. In Montana it is a "basic personal right" to be protected from "personal insult, defamation, and injury to . . . personal relations," and the same is true of California.[7] Louisiana has a statute regulating the "African dip." This was an obnoxious practice at amusement parks or carnivals; black men sat on seats above a vat of water; they were paid to shout insults at white people passing by. The customers would throw balls at a target; if the customer hit the target, the black man was dumped into the vat of water. This practice is now happily extinct (we hope), but Louisiana law still instructs the (black) people sitting on the "target seat" not to use "foul or insulting language" and to be "properly dressed."[8]

None of these statutes seem particularly significant or of any importance in the living law. There is basically no defense against insults or obnoxious rumors. Libel, in general, has to hurt your pocketbook, not just your feelings. This at least is the basic thrust of the law—with exceptions, of course. On the whole, the courts allow American society "to remain a cacophony of sometimes rude . . . opinionated, shrill, unreasonable, and unreasoning voices that sometimes make statements that are flat-out wrong." Society, for whatever reasons, tell us to put up with "verbal incivility."[9]

Yet defamation law, the rules about libel and slander, are extremely sensitive to current social norms. In the long trajectory of history defamation has changed dramatically—shifted almost 180 degrees. It began as a field of law that had, as it primary goal, protecting elites, governments, kings, and presidents against criticism from troublemakers, most of whom were much lower down on the social scale. Today, it is almost the opposite. Elites have much less protection than ordinary citizens. I take up these two points in turn.

First, in the nineteenth century and into the twentieth century it was defamation to accuse a respectable woman, for example, of sexual misconduct. Chastity and virtue were at the very heart of respectability. In a case from 1921 Henriette Coquelet had dinner in Baltimore with her husband, Lieutenant Henry Coquelet, a wounded war veteran. The lieutenant felt sick, and they decided to stay overnight in Baltimore (they lived in Washington, D.C.). A clerk at the Union Hotel, however, refused to rent them a room. He declined to say why, although the reason was obvious. They had no baggage, and she was wearing a "fluffy French dress." The clerk plainly thought they were not actually married. Mrs. Coquelet sued on the basis of this (implied) slur. She lost the case—the clerk had said nothing slanderous, and the court refused to make the necessary inferences.[10] Madame Coquelet got no money, but at least she told the world her story. She was a respectable married woman, misunderstood and maligned.

And today? No problem: The clerk would have simply rented them the room. This is the age of *Marvin v. Marvin*; millions of people cohabit. Is it also still slanderous to say that a woman fools around or that a married woman is having an affair? Or is it libelous to print it? At one time, as we saw, these were crimes in some states. Under a Washington state statute, originally passed in 1909, it was a misdemeanor to say any "false or defamatory words" that could "impair the reputation" of a woman "for virtue or chastity."[11] Many other states, including New York, had similar statutes. But most of these statutes have now disappeared. Early in 2005 there was a campaign to get rid of the Washington statute, one of the survivors. Senator Jeanne E. Kohl-Welles introduced a bill to repeal the law, which she called "patronizing," an old vestige of the "double standard."[12] To be sure, a lie about a woman's sex life can still be hurtful and perhaps quite damaging. Standard legal texts still call it defamation to accuse a woman of extramarital sex. But the case law on this point in recent years is actually quite skimpy.[13] In general, many "forms of sexual activity once regarded as particularly egregious are today thought of in many quarters as not justifying special legal condemnation."[14]

Moreover, in the age of civil rights and black pride, is it still defamation to claim (falsely) that somebody has black blood? This was a devastating libel at one time, especially in the South. Is this still the case? There is little authority on this question. In 1983 a Georgia newspaper published an obituary of

Paulette Thomason, 38, and said that "services will be at 1 p.m. Thursday at Cascade Hill Funeral Home in Atlanta." The story was not particularly accurate. For one thing Paulette was not actually dead. She was also a "Caucasian female," and the Cascade Hill Funeral Home catered to a black clientele. This subjected her (she said) to ridicule and contempt. She lost her case. People, said the court, have their biases and prejudices, but this does not mean that the law is obliged to "give them effect."[15]

Is it defamatory to say that someone is lesbian or gay in the age of gay pride? This too was once clearly defamatory. In 1952 Neiman-Marcus, the department store, sued the authors of a book that claimed that some female models were "call girls—the top babes in town," that the (male) dress and millinery designers were " the nucleus of the Dallas fairy colony," and that "most of the sales staff are fairies, too." A federal court thought that these words were defamatory and denied a motion to dismiss.[16]

This was more than fifty years ago. Sodomy has now been decriminalized. Same-sex relations between consenting adults are legal in every state. Does that change the situation?[17] Yes and no. Many men—probably the majority—would resent being called a fag and would find it harmful. In a 1984 case members of a singing group, the Good Rats, talking about a man named Matherson, claimed that Matherson "really freaked out" when "somebody started messing around with his boyfriend." Matherson sued. Many "public officials," the defendants argued, "have acknowledged their homosexuality and, therefore, no social stigma may be attached to such an allegation." But the court disagreed; many gays express "pride in their status," but still, in some circumstances, a "false charge of homosexuality" could be quite harmful. The plaintiff was, in fact, a married man.[18] Most courts have agreed.[19] As a Missouri court put it in 1993, attitudes "change slowly and unevenly. . . . Despite the efforts of many homosexual groups to foster greater tolerance and acceptance, homosexuality is still viewed with disfavor, if not outright contempt, by a sizeable proportion of our population." In this case the defendant told a reporter that the plaintiff, Janet Nazeri, "lives with . . . a well known homosexual and has lived with her for years."[20]

A lot depends on context, as I have pointed out. This particular defamation might be more hurtful in the Bible Belt than in, say, Manhattan or Hollywood. And calling a schoolteacher or a scoutmaster gay strikes a blow at the very heart of their professional life. Indeed, for the schoolteacher or the scoutmaster, a secret gay life might still lead to blackmail.[21]

DEFAMATION AS A CONSTITUTIONAL ISSUE

This brings us to the second point: the reversal of fortune for powerful elites. Today, not only is truth a total defense, but in some cases even *untruth* gets legal protection—indeed, constitutional protection. Defamation has emerged rather suddenly as a constitutional issue. The Constitution, of course, protects freedom of speech, but nobody ever imagined that freedom of speech protected defamers and slanderers. But then came the great case of *New York Times v. Sullivan* in 1964.[22] Here, the Supreme Court plainly changed the rules of the game.

The facts of the case were (as usual) important. Sullivan, the plaintiff, was an official of Montgomery, Alabama. The civil rights movement was struggling against segregation and white supremacy in Alabama and in the rest of the South. A full-page ad in the *New York Times* ("Heed Their Rising Voices") asked for contributions to the movement. The ad unfortunately made some mistakes—none of them particularly earthshaking, but still mistakes of fact. For example, the students (said the ad) sang "My Country 'Tis of Thee" at the Alabama state capitol; in fact, they sang "The Star-Spangled Banner." The ad said that students who protested at the capitol were expelled from school; in fact they were expelled for a sit-in at a segregated lunch counter. Sullivan brought a defamation action in an Alabama court, and (to nobody's surprise) the all-white jury (after the local judge charged them in a very biased way) awarded Sullivan a great deal of money from all the defendants, including the *New York Times*.

The Supreme Court overturned this award. The Court stressed the enormous value in society of "vigorous debate" about significant issues. When people carry on these vigorous debates, it is hard to avoid some "erroneous" statements. People who criticize the government cannot be expected to "guarantee the truth" of every single statement of fact they might make. Therefore the rule should be this: No public official may collect damages for defamation, even when the defendant gets things wrong, unless the defendant made his statement knowing that it was false or "with reckless disregard of whether it was false or not." In other words, the Supreme Court raised the bar for defamation suits against public officials very, very substantially.

New York Times v. Sullivan was a turning point in the law of defamation. At one time, as I said, even truth was no defense; sedition was part of the living law, and defamation protected the high and mighty against criticism. What congressmen said, for example, on the floor of Congress or what a judge said in the courtroom was privileged, and no defamation action was possible.[23] Later, truth became pretty much an absolute defense; and sedition shriveled and died—revived, if at all, only in wartime.[24] And it was standard doctrine that freedom of speech and freedom of the press did not prevent actions for libel and slander.

The *Sullivan* case was not totally unprecedented. Earlier there had been a certain sensitivity to criticism of public officials. For example, in an 1890 Massachusetts case the defendant, Collier, hinted that Malcolm Sillars, a member of the Massachusetts House of Representatives, had taken a bribe. He said that Sillars had "had a change of heart" about a certain bill and ended up voting for it. "Sometimes," Collier added, "a change of heart comes from the pocket." Sillars sued, but unsuccessfully. "It is one of the infelicities of public life," said the Massachusetts court, "that a public officer is thus exposed to critical and often to unjust comments." These have to be tolerated unless they are explicit. In this case the comments were (for the court) not explicit enough; they did not flat-out state that the plaintiff had taken a bribe.[25]

Sullivan, of course, went far beyond this. Now truth was not the only defense for those accused of slinging mud at a public official. An honest mistake was now an additional defense. And the new rule was not just another doctrine; it was a principle of constitutional law.

No doubt the social context of the case—the struggles of the civil rights movement—was close to the minds and hearts of the justices. The plaintiffs were trying to smash the movement through defamation cases. They were trying to punish and intimidate civil rights workers. The Supreme Court—the Court of *Brown v. Board of Education*[26]—was determined to kill segregation and help the civil rights movement. Perhaps a case coming from some other context would have found the Court less eager to drag defamation law into the realm of constitutional doctrine.

Later events, however, clearly suggest that the case had meaning beyond the politics of civil rights. The principles, intuitions, urges, and thoughts underlying *New York Times v. Sullivan* transcended this context. The case stripped officials of much of their immunity—and by extension, much of their privacy.

The Court could have confined the case to its facts. It could have restricted it to a narrow band of elected officials. But the Court soon made it clear that the case had broader significance. Three years after *Sullivan* the Supreme Court stretched the doctrine to cover public figures in general—a category far broader than public officials. In two related cases the plaintiff was not a public official at all, and one of the cases had nothing to do with race.[27]

Wally Butts, athletic director of the University of Georgia, was one of the plaintiffs. An article in the *Saturday Evening Post* accused him of conniving to fix a football game. Not surprisingly, Butts was outraged and brought a lawsuit. Butts, despite his title, was not a state employee; his boss was a private corporation, the Georgia Athletic Association. (Why the athletic director of a state university should have this private status is an interesting question.)[28] Butts claimed that the story was a lie, and he won in the lower courts. The Supreme Court affirmed but made clear that *New York Times v. Sullivan* applied in principle to people such as Butts. He won only by showing that the magazine had been more than careless or sloppy; its failures went far beyond that.

In the companion case, decided together with *Butts*, Edwin Walker, the plaintiff, a former general, had taken an active role in trying to prevent a black student from enrolling in the University of Mississippi in 1962. An Associated Press story said that Walker had "taken command" of a violent crowd, encouraging violence and giving the crowd "technical advice on combating the effects of tear gas." Walker sued and won, but here the Supreme Court reversed. *New York Times v. Sullivan* applied; Walker was a public figure. He could sue only if the defendant had recklessly or maliciously lied. Wrong charges in themselves would not do.[29]

In a quite remarkable passage the Court argued that any distinction between government and the private sector had now been "blurred." There was a certain "blending of positions and power" so that "individuals . . . who do not hold public office at the moment are nevertheless intimately involved in the resolution of important public questions." Or, perhaps their "fame" gave them power to "shape events in areas of concern to society at large." These "public figures" have "ready access . . . to mass media." Citizens have a "legitimate and substantial interest in the conduct of such persons." The Court thus stripped away the protective armor of the football coach and ex-general, just as it had stripped away the armor of elected officials.

In an important social sense the Court was right. In a celebrity society political officeholders are not the only public figures. Other public figures set the agenda, mold public opinion, start trends and fashions, and end them. Millions of Americans could not name their congressman or state senator to save their souls; but the same millions could run off a string of dozens and dozens of names of movie stars, rap musicians, sports figures, television personalities, and other people famous or notorious in all sorts of ways. And not only their names but a rich menu of details about these public figures: who is married to whom, who is carrying whose baby, who is on a diet and who is losing weight, how many of them have become Scientologists or are studying Kabbalah, and so on.

The boundaries of the *Sullivan* case were never quite clear. Courts have struggled for years with such concepts as reckless disregard for truth. They have wrestled with the definition of a public figure. Could *anybody* who was in the public eye for whatever reason become a public figure? The Supreme Court hesitated. The John Birch Society, a right-wing organization close to the lunatic fringe, blasted a civil rights lawyer, Elmer Gertz, in the society's magazine. It said Gertz had a criminal record and had framed a policeman, helping out in the "Communist War on Police"; Gertz was, in general, a "Leninist" and a stooge of the communists. Gertz sued for defamation. The defendant invoked *New York Times v. Sullivan* and said Gertz could not win unless he showed "actual malice." But the Court disagreed. Gertz was not a public figure and had to meet a lower burden of proof.[30] In *Dun & Bradstreet v. Greenmoss* (1984)[31] the Court refused to stretch the doctrine to cover "ordinary" cases of defamation. Dun & Bradstreet had published erroneous information about Greenmoss's business; and he sued. The Court allowed Greenmoss's lawsuit; there were no public figures and no issues of great public interest.

And what of the involuntary public figure? What of families of victims of horrible front-page crimes? There are, according to the courts, three distinct categories: full-blown public figures, limited-purpose public figures, and involuntary public figures. Courts have also propounded various tests to determine who fits in what category and why. The courts have not been anxious to strip away legal armor from ordinary people and leave them naked before their defamers. Private citizens do not become public figures even if they happen to be "connected to newsworthy stories." A private citizen can therefore win a case without showing actual malice or reckless disregard for truth.[32]

An important case in 1979 involved a scientist, Ronald Hutchinson. Hutchinson had a research grant to study anger in monkeys. Senator William Proxmire of Wisconsin, who loved to make fun of research grants—he used to award a mock prize, which he called the "golden fleece" award—had a merry time sneering at this research. He called it a study of why monkeys clench their jaws and made fun of Hutchinson's work on the floor of the Senate—and also in a newsletter and a press release. The Supreme Court held that Hutchinson was not a public figure and had the right to sue Proxmire.[33] In *Quincy Wilson v. Daily Gazette Company*, a West Virginia case from 2003,[34] the plaintiff was a high school athlete, a top football and basketball player, who at age 17 had won an athletic scholarship to West Virginia University. The newspaper repeated a story that Wilson had exposed himself to the audience after a basketball game. The trial court thought Wilson was a public figure, but the appeals court reversed. Wilson was "a private individual at the time of the alleged defamatory publications."[35]

The cases are—no surprise—not entirely consistent. Sometimes the right of the public to know something significant overrides the poor plaintiff's right to privacy. Consider, for example, John Neff, a fan of the Pittsburgh Steelers. In 1973 *Sports Illustrated* published a picture of fans who were drunk, screaming and howling. Neff was one of these yobs. His fly was open (although not, as the court pointed out demurely, "to the point of being revealing"). Neff sued, but to no avail. The court thought that there was "legitimate public interest in the behavior of sports fans.[36] In a South Carolina case decided in 1998, the plaintiff was arrested and charged with a terrible crime (dousing a woman with gasoline and setting fire to her mobile home). The police later released him. He never actually stood trial. A newspaper, however, published a story about what happened, including a statement that he had been raped in jail. His suit, for invasion of privacy, was also unsuccessful. Violence in jail was a "matter of public significance."[37]

Whether or not the cases bring some clarity to the idea of a public figure, they do illustrate the final collapse of the Warren and Brandeis conception of privacy. The elite—celebrities, in any event—have been stripped naked and their reputations are at the mercy of journalists, paparazzi, and almost everybody else. Privacy protection is mostly for ordinary people, not public figures.

But then, the very concept of an elite has changed. For Warren and Brandeis it was clear who were members of the elite. They were political, religious, and social leaders. They were professional men, lawyers and doctors. Public figures may all be elites, but not all elites are public figures. In a celebrity society loss of privacy, as we have seen, is part of the essence of celebrity; to *be* a celebrity is to dedicate oneself and one's image to the public. Even a celebrity's sex life is something the public has a right to know about, or at least to find out about when the news leaks out. Tommy Lee, a drummer for a rock-and-roll group, married Pamela Anderson, a sexy television star. They took pictures of themselves on their honeymoon, including pictures of "sexual touching." The pictures were stolen and peddled to the eager tabloid press. The couple was brazen enough to sue. But the pictures, said the court, were "newsworthy." They were part of an article on this couple's sex life, which was, it seems, a "legitimate subject" for public consumption.[38]

LIBEL AND SLANDER REVISITED

Despite *New York Times v. Sullivan* and other developments, defamation is still a living field of law. It performs a valuable function. Warren and Brandeis were not entirely wrong to worry about the irresponsible press. Defamation is still a weapon against abuse. The press makes up a good percentage of the defendants in defamation cases. Print media range from the good gray *New York Times* and other sources of serious reportage and social commentary down to gossip magazines, semipornographic rags with hints on how to improve your love life, supermarket tabloids about aliens from outer space, and every conceivable voice and point of view, howling and mewling and sneering and shouting noisily in public space—a cacophony of raucous noises, wild, sometimes vicious and hard-hitting, sometimes prurient, galling, offensive, much of it sheltered cozily under the expansive wings of the First Amendment. The line between vigorous criticism on the one hand and libel and slander on the other is still fuzzy and is likely to remain fuzzy. So is the line between pointless, meddlesome gossip and matters of genuine public concern. So is the line between parody and satire on the one hand and insult and defamation on the other.[39] Defamation actions can be used, and sometimes are used, as weapons of attack or revenge—to get back at ideological or political enemies or even to try to stifle criticism of the government and powerful institutions. What impact libel and slander cases have on policy debates, on freedom of the press—and on the privacy rights of everyone, from public figures to ordinary citizens—is exceedingly hard to say. The scandal magazines are sued again and again— sometimes successfully. Everybody agrees (in principle) that nothing should be allowed to stifle political debate. But much of what defamation is about today is hardly political and hardly debate. It *is* about privacy and reputation.

New York Times v. Sullivan was a federal case, and it was decided on the basis of the federal Constitution. The individual states are therefore obliged to pay attention. Under the Illinois constitution, as we have seen, truth was a defense in a defamation case only when the material was "published with good motives and for justifiable ends." In *Farnsworth v. Tribune Co.*, decided in 1969, Myrtle Farnsworth, an osteopath, sued the *Chicago Tribune* for libel.[40] The *Tribune* had called Farnsworth a quack. A jury found for the *Tribune*, and Farnsworth appealed. Her complaint was that the trial judge had failed to instruct the jury about Illinois's constitutional rule. The appeals court disagreed. The Illinois constitution itself was now unconstitutional. This was because of the principle of the *Sullivan* case. Dr. Farnsworth was not, perhaps, a public figure, but medical "quackery" was "an area of critical public concern." In matters of "public interest and concern," it was wrong to force a defendant to prove not just truth but also "good motives and . . . justifiable ends."

Vestiges of criminal libel, long moribund, could not survive the new climate of opinion. Even in England, its original home, J. R. Spencer, writing in 1977, referred to the law as dormant. In 1940 there had been ten trials for criminal libel; by 1975 there were none at all.[41] Shortly afterward, Sir James Goldsmith created a stir by invoking the law of criminal libel against the satirical magazine *Private Eye*.[42] "Defamatory truth," Spencer argued, brought two important values into collision: "truth and privacy." Truth, he thought, was "the more important and should prevail." He suggested limiting criminal libel to two situations: "poison-pen" writings by "deranged persons" and the work of the "character assassin," who "invents a deliberate lie about another in order to damage him."[43]

In the United States criminal libel cases had become exceedingly rare.[44] A few years after *New York Times v. Sullivan* the Supreme Court was asked to decide whether such statutes were valid at all. Garrison, a district attorney of Orleans Parish, Louisiana, who was embroiled in a dispute with local judges, held a press conference, at which he made some wild charges against the judges. He called them lazy and inefficient; he said that they took too many long vacations and that they were hampering his attempts to enforce the vice laws, refusing to "authorize . . . funds" for closing down "clip joints." This raised "interesting questions about the racketeer influences on our eight vacation-minded judges." Under Louisiana law a statement made with "actual malice" could constitute criminal libel, even if it were true. Garrison was arrested, charged with criminal libel, and convicted. The Supreme Court reversed the conviction. Garrison's wild accusations were protected under the *Sullivan* rule because they were criticisms of public officials. Louisiana could not constitutionally punish true statements about officials, even those made with "malice," and it could not punish false statements, unless they met the *Sullivan* standard, that is, that they were made knowingly or recklessly. The local statute, which allowed punishment for true statements made with "actual malice," was therefore unconstitutional.[45]

The high court of Pennsylvania reached a similar result in 1972. The publisher of a weekly Italian newspaper had published a strong attack on James Buchanan, including the statement that he ran a club "well known as a hangout for sex deviates."[46] As the court pointed out, under the *Sullivan* rule, even a true statement about a public official or a public figure would not support a civil suit (and never mind why it was made); and even if it was false, so long as it was not made recklessly or knowingly, the suit had to fail. If so, how was it possible to justify a *criminal* case—with a possible jail sentence—for saying something true simply because the person who told the truth had bad motives? Criminal libel statutes are still on the books in a few states. But they seem doomed; as soon as somebody tries actively to get rid of them, the courts will consign them to oblivion.[47]

The American cases come in full constitutional dress, but the general principle seems to be broader than American constitutional doctrine. The English courts have also "recognized the importance of . . . free political speech" in situations where the "defamatory statements were published in good faith."[48] And the European Court of Human Rights (ECHR), in a line of decisions, has upheld the same principle in the teeth of local statutes about criminal libel. In *Lingens v. Austria* (1986), the defendant published articles in *Profil*, a Vienna magazine, attacking the Austrian chancellor, Kreisky, for protecting a former Nazi, accusing the chancellor of opportunism, of immoral and undignified behavior, and the like. Kreisky brought a private prosecution for criminal libel. Truth, under Austrian law, was a defense to such a prosecution. But Lingens could not prove his accusations. He was fined by the Austrian courts. Lingens complained to the ECHR. The Austrian decision, he said, "infringed his freedom of expression." The ECHR agreed and overturned his conviction. "The limits of acceptable criticism are . . . wider as regards a politician . . . than as regards a private individual." The politician "knowingly lays himself open to close scrutiny," and the politician must "display a greater degree of tolerance."[49]

The ECHR made a similar ruling in a Spanish case, *Castells v. Spain.*[50] Miguel Castells, who lived in the Basque region of Spain, published an article in 1979 bitterly attacking the central government; he accused the government of all sorts of crimes against Basque nationalists, including murder—the government was guilty of the "ruthless hunting down of Basque dissidents" and "their physical elimination." Castells was prosecuted for insulting the government under the Spanish Criminal Code. Castells, too, turned to the ECHR and won his case. The "limits of permissible criticism," said the court, were "wider with regard to the Government than in relation to a private citizen, or even a politician." In still another ECHR case an Icelander called Icelandic policemen (in print) "beasts in uniform" and "brutes and sadists" who acted out "their perversions" on innocent citizens. The European court thought that the issue he raised was one of "serious public concern," the language he used was not "excessive," and criminal proceedings would discourage "open discussion" of important issues.[51]

In Germany, for example, as I noted, fundamental laws call for the protection of honor and dignity and the rights of personality.[52] A striking case in 1973 arose out of a sensational crime—an attack on a munitions depot. The plaintiff had been convicted as an accomplice. He had been a friend of one of the attackers (moreover, the friendship had a "homosexual component"). The plaintiff had served a term in prison and was about to be released. There were plans to broadcast a television program, reenacting the crime. The plaintiff argued that the program would adversely affect his reintegration into society. The program was apparently completely accurate and truthful. Nonetheless, the court came down on the plaintiff's side. The attack on the depot was old news, and fanning the flames again would be a "severe incursion" on the plaintiff's personal rights.[53] In an even more striking case a German court issued an injunction preventing a horror movie from being shown. The movie was based on a real and shocking incident: Armin Meiwes killed and ate a man, who had volunteered for this gruesome fate through the Internet. Meiwes complained that the movie violated his privacy rights. The court conceded that Meiwes was some sort of public figure; nonetheless, he had the right to prevent the movie from being shown.[54] Almost certainly, in the United States freedom of the press (and television) would have trumped the plaintiff's claims about honor and dignity. An American court would probably not have been sympathetic to Princess Caroline of Monaco, who complained about unauthorized photographs that showed her doing such exciting things as shopping, skiing, or playing tennis; one "blurry portrait," however, did show her wearing a swimsuit and stumbling at the Monte Carlo Beach Club.[55]

In sum, there is widespread agreement that citizens of democracies should have free rein to criticize officials, governments, and public figures. There is some disagreement, however, on limits and boundaries. The United States seems to permit greater incursions into the private lives of public figures and defines public figures more broadly than Europe and other Western democracies. These countries worry more about invasions of privacy[56]—even for the likes of Princess Caroline of Monaco or elected officials. A Canadian court, for example, was afraid that *New York Times v. Sullivan* could make the reputation of people in public life too "vulnerable." The principle of that case could destroy the "delicate balance between freedom of expression and protection of reputation." People in public life would lack any way to defend themselves against "defamatory falsehoods," except for those "rare cases" of "actual malice." There would be danger, then, that "honest and decent people" would be discouraged "from standing for public office."[57]

In an Australian case decided in 1988,[58] a "well-known Australian cricketeer," Gregory Chappell, sought an injunction against a television station. The station was planning to repeat a story, originally published in "Australia's sleaziest newspaper," about Chappell's sex life—specifically, that he committed adultery with Samantha Hickey and had "engaged in sexual activities of an unusual nature" (the court, somewhat primly, never specified what these were). The station argued that the public "expects high standards of behaviour by cricketers" (does it?) and that "there is a legitimate public interest in the misconduct in private of such public figures"; indeed, public figures "do not have a private life." The Australian court disagreed. Unless the private action of a public figure "affects the performance of his public duties," which was not the case here, the media cannot invoke a defense of this kind.

Perhaps these differences are differences only in detail, and it is easy to exaggerate them. The United States seems more willing to immunize free-swinging attacks on public figures. This may be because the United States is a more extreme case of a celebrity society. It may also be less traditional, more crass and bumptious, and hence less concerned with issues of dignity, honor, and deference, which do have something of the flavor of old Europe, with its traditions and its hierarchies. But this, of course, is rank speculation.

All modern countries have moved more or less in the same direction. All of them are raunchy and permissive compared to the way they were a century ago. There are also important regional differences within a country. The United States, in particular, is big and sprawling. What goes in San Francisco could still be taboo in Mississippi. Countries also differ with regard to social norms. The United States is not invariably more permissive and freewheeling. Revealing that a United States senator kept a mistress might well kill his career. In France, on the other hand, important men might be *expected* to have mistresses. In Quebec a gay man—and something of a hellion who (among other things) snorted cocaine—was a candidate for leadership of the Parti Québecois. After the revelations his standing shot up in the polls.[59] This would hardly happen in the United States, even (say) in San Francisco. And only yesterday, it seems, Quebec was reputed to a rural backwater, dominated by the Catholic Church. Time and place make a difference.

CENSORSHIP

The libel laws at times work in a way like private laws of censorship. Official, legal censorship—of movies, books, plays, and magazines—once so prominent, as we have seen, has just about run its course. In England film censorship is history. James Ferman, the last "chief film sensor, or classifier as he preferred to be known," quit in 1999 after twenty-three years. In his final report he said that "no sexual image has been cut from any mainstream cinema film since 1989."[60]

In the United States, as I noted, the Supreme Court never solved the problem of defining obscenity. Free speech, in theory, does not extend to what is truly obscene. Communities may crack down on sexually explicit stuff that is "utterly without redeeming social value." But the courts have found redeeming social value in rather unexpected places. Finally, after all its years of controversy, that hoary classic, *Memoirs of a Woman of Pleasure*, better known as *Fanny Hill*, received the ultimate stamp of approval: In 1966 the Supreme Court of the United States gave the book its blessing.[61] For almost 200 years this book was an underground classic, passed on from clammy hand to clammy hand. In the nineteenth century nobody doubted that it was illegal, obscene, pornographic.[62] But now the Supreme Court solemnly decided that Fanny had redeeming social value.

Justice Brennan wrote the main opinion. He repeated older doctrine: A book was obscene if it appealed to a "prurient interest in sex," was "patently offensive" in the light of community standards, and "utterly" without value. But a book was obscene only if it suffered from all three of these defects. Experts testified that *Fanny Hill* was literature, not pornography (although anybody who actually read the book might conclude that *both* were the case). Brennan's opinion still bore traces of older censorship law; no evidence suggests (he said) that the "the book was commercially exploited for the sake of prurient appeal, to the exclusion of all other values." William O. Douglas, concurring, objected to the point about commercial exploitation. He could not understand how a book "that concededly has social worth" could still be banned "because of the manner in which it is advertised and sold. However florid its cover, whatever the pitch of its advertisements, the contents remain the same." Douglas also remarked that universities and libraries had placed "an unusually large number of orders" for *Fanny Hill*, and the Library of Congress had requested the right to create an edition in Braille.

Despite Douglas, exploitation did seem to matter to the Court. In *Ginzburg v. United States*,[63] decided almost at the same time as the *Fanny Hill* case, the Court, by a narrow five to four vote, upheld the conviction of Ginzburg for violating federal obscenity laws. He had distributed three publications: *EROS*, a "hard-cover magazine of expensive format," *Liaison*, a "bi-weekly newsletter;" and *The Housewife's Handbook on Selective Promiscuity*, a "short book." These publications were deliberately advertised as "erotically arousing." Ralph Ginzburg had been "pandering" to the lusts of his audience. It did not help Ginzburg's case that he wanted to distribute his material from Blue Ball, Pennsylvania. Ginzburg went to jail.

To a degree, the justices in the *Ginzburg* case seemed to be in a kind of time warp. The majority opinion quoted from a 1940 case, *United States v. Rebhuhn*.[64] In that case Judge Learned Hand and the Second Circuit sustained a conviction for sending "printed obscenity through the mails." The "offending matter" consisted of "circulars which advertised books for sale"; the books were (arguably) obscene, and the circulars were sent out "at random" to thousands of addressees. The books (said the court) might have been lawfully sold to "laymen who wished seriously to study the sexual practices of savage or barbarous peoples, or sexual aberration"; they were for the most part not "obscene per se." But the defendants had "indiscriminately flooded the mails with advertisements, plainly designed merely to catch the prurient." The circulars distributed were "no more than appeals to the salaciously disposed."[65]

When it was an issue of obscenity or pornography, citing a case from 1940 was almost as bad as citing a case from the days of the Roman Empire. *Ginzburg* in hindsight looks like the dying embers of a dying theory—the theory that censorship was needed to protect the morals and character of young people and ordinary folk. Soon the juggernaut of a permissive society rolled over the carcass of orthodox legal doctrine. Laws against pornography and obscenity may still exist. But do they matter? In practice, almost anything goes. Hardcore pornography of all shapes and sizes is freely available in big and little cities. And in the age of the Internet, no community, however remote or puritanical, is beyond the reach of the worldwide web of trash. There are still some controls over prime-time network TV. The FCC insists that the "seven dirty words" do not reach ears that might be sensitive.[66] A woman's breast seen for a second or two in the commercial zone in the midst of a football game set off a storm of protest. Child pornography is a major issue, on the Internet most notably, but this is partly because "smut" is so incredibly pervasive. Nobody censors movies anymore, but they have evolved a rating system; children cannot see a movie rated R without an adult sitting next to them, and they are absolutely barred from the few movies rated NC-17. What people say and do in movies rated R would have caused a universal ban one generation ago. And, in general, for consenting adults over 18, there are basically no limits at all. In 1969, when Charles Rembar wrote *The End of Obscenity*, he predicted that, when censorship ended, so would "distorted, impoverished, masturbatory concentration on representations of sex." Pornography, "which is in the groin of the beholder," would "lose its force."[67] Rembar was dead wrong. The sheer scale of pornography—on the Internet, for example—dwarfs anything he might have imagined. Prurient interest seems to be a growth stock.

Blackmail is still a crime. It has always been rare, as crimes go, compared to assault or robbery or forging a check.[68] Certainly there are and have been few arrests for blackmail, judging by police reports. The Los Angeles Police Department reported exactly one arrest for blackmail in 1917–1918 and 1921–1922; in other years there were none at all.[69]

Blackmail does, however, crop up once in a while in the newspapers. I mentioned earlier the case of young Autumn Jackson, who claimed in 1997 to be the daughter of the comedian Bill Cosby.[70] She wanted him to recognize her as his child, and she asked for a great deal of money (some $40 million); otherwise, she said, she would go straight to the tabloids. Cosby admitted an affair with her mother but denied that he was her father. She never got her $40 million; instead she was tried and convicted of extortion in federal court.[71] She spent more than a year in federal prison; at that point an appeals court overturned her conviction on a technicality.[72] In 1992 John Michael Fountain, a "former Harvard University student," was sentenced to a year in jail and three years of probation for trying to blackmail a doctor. Fountain had demanded $10,000 in cash to be "delivered to a West Hollywood garage." Otherwise, he would reveal that the doctor had AIDS.[73] And in 1999 a football player in Iowa—a "6-foot-5-inch, 240-pound linebacker"—was charged with blackmail; the young man, it was said, threatened a "news media smear campaign" against a coach, charging him with "N.C.A.A. violations and the sharing of Hawkeye secrets with opponents" and warning that he would go public unless the football player got his scholarship back.[74] In 2001 a lawyer was convicted of "trying to extort $310,000 from movie heroine Erin Brockovich and her employer Ed Masry in exchange for not going to the tabloids with allegations that she was a bad mother and had an affair with Masry."[75] Note that the threat in these recent cases is to "go to the tabloids." One might ask, Why not go straight to the tabloids, which would surely pay for the dirt? Presumably, because the tabloids would not pay enough. Or, perhaps, because the accusations were untrue.[76] In any event, in an age where the tabloids, television, and the Internet see all and tell all, blackmail, where it exists, is subtly different from blackmail in the age of secrecy, privacy, prudery, and second chances.

THE CONSUMER SOCIETY

Any discussion of social change in the late twentieth century has to give pride of place to the mass media. Television is especially potent and ubiquitous. On television you can listen to a preacher, hear the news in Mandarin, watch an opera, observe a master chef make sushi, see a soap opera, follow developments on the Weather Channel, and many more things. But entertainment trumps everything else; even uplifting programs live or die by their success in attracting an audience, and that in turn depends on whether people find the uplift entertaining. And the same is true for news programs. Modern developed societies, as I pointed out, are entertainment societies. Fun, leisure activities, sports, music—in the aggregate, these may well be the largest industry in the United States, an industry that reaches almost everyone. It is also one of the country's biggest export products. There is a global, insatiable hunger for American trash—movies, music, and so on. And entertainment is dominant, too, in other Western countries.

Fun is a consumption good, a consumer product. Consumption is the key to modern economic life. Advertisers spend billions of dollars every year hawking their products. In Western society, in Japan, in all developed countries, advertising is absolutely pervasive. Newspapers and magazines survive through the sale of ads; so too do commercial television and, more and more, the Internet. There is advertising on buses, billboards, sometimes even in the sky. Advertising, *all* advertising, conveys two messages; the first, the overt message, begs people to buy some particular product; the second, implicit message is a message of individualism, consumption, and pleasure. After all, why *should* you buy this product? Because it will make you richer, sexier, happier; because you will have whiter teeth or stronger muscles; because this clothing will make you look more glamorous; because this beer or this car will give your dreary life a jolt of new energy.

In the past, as society became more and more mobile, people could move from place to place, changing, if they so desired, their very identity. In contemporary times, in the age of advertising, the consumer society at its core is somewhat analogous. A consumer society is a makeover society. Advertising constantly hints (or, at times, shouts) that we can change our looks, our personalities, that we can recast every element of our being. Psychology and self-help books by the dozens are eager to instruct us on how to make a new and improved human self. Plastic surgery is a booming industry. And millions of people claim to be born again; they claim to have undergone a kind of plastic surgery of the soul.[77]

At the center of modern life is the *individual*, the unique, unduplicated self. Advertising is the servant of this cult of the individual—and one of the motor forces that engendered it. The message of advertising is a message of cultural mobility, rebirth, improvement. And the message is directed at *you*, the individual, the buyer, the consumer. What is true of advertising is also true of the self-help books, the psychological counseling, the new evangelism. All of these, then, are in an important sense archenemies of traditional values. A case can be made that capitalism itself is at the root of this transformation; it thrives on getting and spending and consuming. Modern capitalism has created vast affluence; it has also created, and must create, a hunger for raw consumption, for spending the dollars that the middle class earns, for filling the leisure time they have, with product after product, activity after activity. It has created what one writer has called, somewhat hyperbolically, the desiring self. The human being has become "an insatiable, desiring machine," an "animal governed by an infinity of desires." This "capitalist concept of self" has become "the reigning American concept."[78]

Of course, capitalism did not begin yesterday; consumption capitalism looks very different from the pinch-penny capitalism of the Protestant ethic. One can argue that in a way the Protestant ethic and nineteenth-century market capitalism, in the moments of their triumph, were sowing the seeds of destruction at least with regard to the ethos that led to that triumph. Success in business depended on thrift, hard work, discipline, and enormous self-control. But big business meant big money, and big money supported an upper class, high society, and a leisure class: people who engaged in what Veblen called conspicuous consumption. It also generated envy and emulation among members of the middle class. The fluidity of the lines between the haves and the have-nots made the position of elites socially and culturally precarious—at least, they might have thought so.

Moreover, one can surely argue that as capitalism developed, along with the social and political institutions it created, it also fostered the modern personality—the individualism of today, the sense of uniqueness, the striving for self-realization. Traditional society and even the society of the Victorian compromise rested on hierarchies, elites, separation between the masses and the classes; and this was, perhaps, doomed from the start.

Market capitalism meant mass production, and mass production depended on (and created) a consumer society—a society of men and women who lusted in their heart for goods. Advertising campaigns inflamed the desire to buy, buy, buy. The mercantile and manufacturing barons of the nineteenth century believed in frugality. The guidebooks and the etiquette books spoke about saving, hard work, self-discipline. A century later this message was pretty much obsolete. Now the message was to consume and to spend. We are told, for example, to dress for success, to spend money on appearance; if you spent, dressed, and acted like people who had "made it," then you were more likely to make it yourself. "White-collar men," for example, "needed to show that they understood the language and the symbols of the successful business class in order to join it."[79] Even more important was the message of self-realization. Market society became, by its very nature, permissive. It focused attention away from moderation, self-control, discipline, and saving. It downplayed notions of deferring gratification. Why scrimp and save to buy a car when you can buy one now and pay it off in installments? The same for a house, for a trip to the Caribbean, for a color television set, and so on. The development of the self, personal happiness, doing your own thing—that was the core. Each individual was a unique and uniquely worthy being. Of course, in this society, as in any other, there were winners and losers. Not all losers accepted their lot with grace and resignation. Grace and resignation were not part of the consumer society. Losing could and often did lead to pathology and crime.

What I have been describing seem to be the major trends. There are, as always, countertrends. And, I might point out, some of the overt messages on TV, and in the media in general, are *not* messages of consumption and individual pleasure but the opposite: messages of traditional values. Indeed, preachers and evangelists shout and fulminate over the airwaves and on television. They broadcast endless jeremiads against modern lust and decay. Religious conservatives find so many aspects of modern life deeply abhorrent: smut, promiscuity, abortion, gay rights, radical feminism, and the loosening of family bonds. They use the tools of modernity, but they try to turn these tools to their own specific ends. Yet in one sense their messages undermine themselves. This is because they use—and *have* to use—the channels of mass culture. They too have to appeal to the *individual*; in a way they have to embrace the ethos of individualism, even when they ask the individual to submerge his or her self in the interest of some higher goal or in allegiance to metahuman authority.

Religious faith in the United States is strong and intense, but it is also extremely personal, extremely individual. No one religion in the United States is the country's true faith. There is extraordinary religious diversity. And Americans are, on the whole, rather tolerant of other peoples' religions. They see religion as something quite personal; it is, as it were, a kind of commercial product, something that depends on individual choice. One person's path to personal, spiritual satisfaction is not the same as somebody else's. What is important, then, is not whether a religion is true, whatever that might mean, but whether it fills your particular needs. Millions of Americans actively shop around for a church that will bring them what they want. Intense religion in this society is in many ways only another form of expressive individualism. America is exceptionally religious—compared to other Western countries. Yet American religion, politically and socially powerful, coexists with a radically permissive society, a society supremely conscious of individual rights and wants and needs.

CHAPTER II

A SUMMING UP—
AND A CAUTIOUS LOOK
AT THE FUTURE

IN THE NINETEENTH CENTURY moderation in all things
was one of the keystones of character and reputation. In
theory, men and women were held to exacting standards. As we have seen, the
standards themselves were the point, the crux; they were considered essential
to society, even if not all men and women could live up to them all the time.
The legal order and social norms protected the standards themselves in full
knowledge that they were ideals that could not be attained. Some aspects of
law and society in the nineteenth century made sense only if you assumed
the goal of protecting and upholding the reputation of elites, even though
they did not always deserve this protection. I examined the theories—mostly
implicit—that underlay both the standards and the fences around them.
There was a heavy dose of self-interest, of course, in the protective rules, but
elites no doubt sincerely believed that society might fall apart under other
arrangements.

In the late nineteenth century and early twentieth century this structure
of norms and beliefs and attitudes came under attack. A strong movement
arose to get rid of the Victorian compromise and replace it with a stern, strict
attitude toward sin and vice. In the end, this movement was a failure. In the

second half of the twentieth century what the reformers tried to accomplish fell apart in the age of the sexual revolution.

Of course, the social forces that lay behind these various developments were and are exceedingly complex. I have tried to explore some of them. I looked at the influence, initially, of such factors as social and geographic mobility and at the rise of representative government. Later, immigration and demographic changes, the revolution in science and technology, and the rise of the mass media all played a major role, as did capitalism itself and its handmaiden, advertising. In the second half of the twentieth century expressive individualism and the consumer ethos came to dominate social life in the developed countries of the West.

These massive developments have had an impact on reputation and on ways of defending and protecting it. It is of course still true that people respect an honest man more than a liar and a cheat or a philanderer, but the rules of sexual behavior have certainly changed. Similarly, people still have the general right to sue someone who spreads hurtful lies about them. But exactly what makes a lie hurtful shifts with the tides of history. The focus has moved from protection of elites to a situation in which elites have the *least* protection from criticism, insults, false rumors, and invasions of privacy.

In an important sense, privacy is a modern invention. Medieval people had no concept of privacy. They also had no actual privacy. Nobody was ever alone. No ordinary person had private space. Houses were tiny and crowded. Everyone was embedded in a face-to-face community. Privacy, as idea and reality, is the creation of modern bourgeois society. Above all, it is a creation of the nineteenth century. In the twentieth century it became even more of a reality. The middle-class home is full of private spaces. Parents, for example, believe that a child needs his or her own room if at all possible.

Yet paradoxically, that room, that private space—and indeed the whole house—has been invaded by the media. First came radio, then TV, now the Internet. Of course, the family can control what comes in: They can shut off the sets and the computers; they can pull out the plugs. Nobody is forced to watch TV or surf the net. Many parents monitor (or try to monitor) what children hear and watch. In a basic sense this is a losing battle. The very fact that radio and television and the Internet are *there*, inside the house, that voices and images are available at the flick of a switch, has a profound effect on privacy, at least in the sense of being alone or being left alone. Hordes of young people in 2007 are never alone in the sense of Walden Pond or a quiet corner to themselves. They walk the streets babbling on their cell phones, they log on to the computer as soon as they get home, they sit for hours glued to the TV set, they listen to music through headsets while they jog or do homework. They talk all day long to friends and schoolmates. They also absorb sounds and voices and faces and images from far away. The media bombard them with these faces and voices and images; the media drill these into their heads.

We live in what one might call the Peeping Tom society. It is a prying, gossiping society. Gossip has always been an important social phenomenon. But gossip was at one time mostly about people in your own circle, people you knew personally. This kind of gossip, of course, survives and always will. There was also a certain amount of political gossip. Now, however, there is also celebrity gossip—tons of it. Gossip about the rich and famous or about the aristocracy was common in the hothouse culture of Versailles or the other palaces of Europe. But now it is everybody's province. The modern age began, perhaps, with cheap mass-circulation newspapers. Then came Hollywood fan magazines. Then the supermarket tabloids. Gossip is a significant factor on TV and in newspapers as well. The pages of these magazines and tabloids are full of tales about famous people. In a society that admires or even worships celebrities, celebrities have no privacy; on the other hand, celebrities can almost literally get away with murder. Movie stars have affairs, marry and divorce time and again, and have children out of wedlock; they grant interviews about drug habits, their sex life, their religious beliefs, and everything else. Male sports stars brag about how many women they have serviced or admit that they are gay or go to drug rehabilitation centers in a blaze of publicity. Nobody seems to mind. The Peeping Toms relish each detail.

For ordinary people, too, the rules have changed. Millions of people today cohabit (and are "open and notorious" about it) or freely confess to various mental and psychological failings.[1] Behavior and situations that were once taboo or stigmatic have lost their bite. Bankruptcy and divorce carry much less of a stigma. Legally there is no longer such a thing as a bastard child, and socially, too, nobody seems to care much, in most places, whether a person's parents were married or not. Old hierarchies and old moral norms have crumbled and have been replaced by newer, more subtle ones. In short, in the last two decades

society has redefined the very concept of *respectability*. It now allows a much
wider, or at least different, range of behavior.[2] People are more willing to accept
a blemish or two in a candidate's past—provided that he or she has recanted
or turned over a new leaf. But they surely want to *know* about this.

The mass media, as I pointed out, reinforce a sense that we have a *right* to
know. We see, or think we see, so much on television—everything, in fact, that
might interest us. If a hurricane ravages Louisiana, if mudslides kill hundreds
in the Philippines, if a tsunami wreaks havoc in Thailand, we expect to see
footage, vivid images, reports, full coverage. Seeing everything gives rise to a
culture of expectations, hence the right to know everything. Government is,
in principle, not supposed to have secrets (national security excepted). Congress passes the Freedom of Information Act.[3] Adopted children demand, and
get, the right to find out who their "real" parents are. Patients have the right
to know the truth, the whole truth, and nothing but the truth about their
medical conditions. They have a right to know all the risks and side effects
of medical procedures.

PRIVACY AND ITS DISCONTENTS

Privacy has been one of the main themes of this book: secret lives, secret
places. Another theme has been about the way the concept has changed over
the years. It has been and remains an important value, even in its older, classic
sense. The lavatory door is still closed. Only porn stars have sex in front of an
audience. To be sure, people do expose more of themselves in public—body
and soul—than the Victorians ever did. That fact is visible on any beach in
the summer. People talk openly about sex. Sex education is taught in some
schools, although this is still controversial. The movies regularly use four-letter
words. The sex laws have been almost totally revamped.

The camera and the computer are both seductive and intrusive. Some
people—how many is hard to say—almost lustfully embrace the chance to
expose themselves to the world. They wallow in the loss of privacy. They are
willing, quite literally, to go naked in public. A small but significant number
of people are willing to tell everything—and on national TV or the Internet;
they air their disputes and arguments on television and let Judge Judy decide,
or talk openly about their sex lives on the trash talk programs, such as that
great social document, *The Jerry Springer Show*.[4] Some lust for their fifteen

minutes of fame on reality television. A few even install cameras in their homes so that the rest of the world (for a price) can watch them eat, drink, dress and undress, or even have sex. Perhaps the pioneer in this dubious enterprise was a young woman in Washington, D.C., Jennifer Ringley, who began to live her life under the eye of the camera in the late 1990s. She was 20 years old at the time. "Jennicam" had a seven-year run; at one time it was getting millions of hits every week.[5] She started a trend. In Tampa, Florida, in 2001, customers who were willing to pay could get a "24-hour look at the lives of four college-age residents," thanks to four Internet cameras placed inside their house.[6] In the world of the one-way mirror some people are more than willing to cross over to the other side. And hundreds of amateurs send pictures of themselves to pornographic websites.

But these people are still a minority. To be sure, a *very* large number of people seem willing and eager to watch and listen to people who are less inhibited than they are, as they expose their dirty laundry in public or foul their own nests.[7] But most members of this audience would vehemently reject the idea of cameras in the house, in the kitchen, in the bedroom. Nudity in public or in front of the public is still a huge taboo for most of us. So is psychological nudity. We are far too private to expose ourselves.

We also place great stock in *anonymity*. Anonymity can be defined as a "state of privacy in the public sphere."[8] A woman sitting in a café in a city where nobody knows her is not private in the way that she is private in her bedroom with the shades drawn, but she is anonymous. Anonymity is, as the quote suggests, a kind of public privacy, paradoxical as this might seem. In many circumstances, as Gary Marx has pointed out, anonymity is an important aspect of the "autonomy of the person." The "decision to reveal" your name, identity, and so on "can be viewed as a kind of currency exchange . . . as trust in a relationship evolves."[9] Marx believes that Americans have "particularly strong expectations" of anonymity. This is one reason that they reject the idea of identity cards, for example.[10] Marx does wonder whether this trait is contradicted by the "California-inspired pseudo-*gemeinschaft* of 'hi, I'm Bill your waiter.'"[11] But "Bill" or "Mike" or "Susan" does not really tell you much; there are tens of thousands of Bills and Mikes and Susans. Indeed, when a business firm or a bank calls you, leaves a message and a number, and says "Ask for Diane," they are solving a problem: how to pinpoint the person you are supposed to respond to without actually identifying her. She could be Diane Anybody. Or perhaps not even Diane at all.

ENTER THE COMPUTER

This book has been, on the whole, an essay in history. I began roughly with the beginning of the nineteenth century and traced certain developments from there to now. I tried to explain certain features of law and society: how we got to where we are, and why a particular path was taken. The question is, Where do we go from here?

Nobody, of course, knows the answer to this question. We do see some trends that are, to say the least, unsettling. Technology has been a major engine powering the story I have tried to tell in this book. Cameras and television sets have been featured players, and we are now in the age of the computer and the Internet. These have made or may make the biggest difference of all.

The average person, as I pointed out, likes his privacy, expects privacy, demands privacy, along with a certain degree of anonymity. The average person, however, seems perfectly willing to invade the privacy of other people—especially famous people. These two attitudes seem a little bit contradictory or inconsistent. They may also be contradictory in practice. The technology of invasion of privacy is definitely a double-edged sword.

We have to begin with the technology of surveillance. Computers and other devices can spy, scan, monitor, and control to a degree never before possible in human history. Is the home still a castle? Can people today really shut the front door, pull down the blinds, and feel safe and private? In the old days the home was a sanctuary—at least for the middle class. In the 1920s and 1930s families often shared telephones, and a nosy neighbor could listen in on a party line. Then came the power to wiretap. Wiretapping raised serious and persistent legal and social questions. When and how was the government allowed to use this new technology? The first case on the subject, decided in 1928, was *Olmstead v. United States*.[12] Olmstead, the government charged, was a leader in a "conspiracy of amazing magnitude" aimed at bringing liquor from Canada into the thirsty regions of Washington state. Olmstead was violating the Prohibition laws on a grand scale. The government built its case by wiretapping his phones and the phones of his associates. His lawyers argued that there could be no greater "invasion of . . . privacy of life . . . than to have one's private and confidential communications intercepted and overheard by promiscuous government agents." The wiretapping was an illegal "search and seizure," forbidden by the Bill of Rights.

Nonetheless, the Supreme Court upheld his conviction, five to four. A search, according to Chief Justice Taft, had to be "of material things—the person, the house" or a person's "papers or . . . effects." Many states, however, had laws against wiretapping on their books. And Congress in 1934, in the Federal Communications Act, added its say and banned the interception of messages.[13] In 1967 the Court repudiated *Olmstead*; in this case, *Katz v. United States*,[14] the defendant had the bad habit of using a public phone booth to send "wagering information by telephone from Los Angeles to Miami and Boston, in violation of a federal statute." The government bugged this phone booth. "The Fourth Amendment," said the Court, "protects people, not places." Inside his glass phone booth, Katz had "an actual . . . expectation of privacy," and this expectation was "reasonable." A person who enters a phone booth and shuts the door "is surely entitled to assume that the words he utters into the mouthpiece will not be broadcast to the world."

This was hardly the last word on the subject. Where exactly does a person have a reasonable expectation of privacy? Not, said the Supreme Court, in a greenhouse where marijuana is growing if the sides and roof are more or less open and a helicopter is buzzing overhead.[15] And if you are a drug dealer in Laguna Beach, California, and you leave plastic trash bags in front of your house to be collected, the Fourth Amendment is not going to protect your trash from search.[16] The Fourth Amendment and its limits are the subject of a huge legal literature, quite a bit of state and federal legislation, and a heavy load of cases, not all of them easy to sum up or reconcile with each other. Still, wiretapping was historically used mostly to catch lawbreakers, and this was also the case when the authorities searched a house without bothering to get a warrant—another controversial subject in the literature on criminal justice.[17] Most people probably approved of wiretapping, searching houses, and other tools and weapons in the war on either organized or disorganized crime. The victims were mafiosi, drug pushers, and the like; the issue hardly seemed to affect the average person. But is this still the case? In December 2005 the *New York Times* revealed that the president of the United States, George W. Bush, had authorized the National Security Agency to wiretap within the United

States without a warrant from any court. The excuse was national security or the war on terror. The limits of the power seemed vague, to say the least. Terrorists are a much more shadowy group than drug pushers. The net of discovery has to be cast much more widely. Wiretapping—and snooping and surveillance in general—in the early twenty-first century were now matters that could affect a much broader group of people.[18]

Hence, as of now (2007), surveillance is a greater risk than it was in the days of *Katz*. As Gary Marx pointed out, in the 1980s (and the situation has deteriorated since then), life gave us fewer and fewer places "to run or to hide." There is no escape "from the prying eyes and ears and whirring data-processing machines of government and business." Every time we enter a shopping mall or a bank or a subway, we "perform before an unknown audience."[19] Privacy—or at least anonymity—becomes in a way impossible. The candid camera was a new invention in the late nineteenth century and one that, as we saw, gave nightmares to Warren and Brandeis. It was one factor that started them on their search for a legal response to invasion of privacy. But these cameras were, by our lights, extremely primitive. Today, cameras can take pictures from satellites high above the earth; they can capture tiny details—maybe even anthills—thousands of feet below. In the twenty-first century cameras are ubiquitous. The popular television program *Candid Camera* featured hilarious pranks and jokes that were recorded by hidden cameras.[20] Today, everybody is a character on *Candid Camera*. Heat sensors, and who knows what other sorts of devices, can penetrate anywhere, can see through walls and doors and roofs, can snoop into every nook and cranny of our homes. Physical barriers to entry no longer matter in many ways. Justice Douglas, in the *Griswold* case—the case that launched the modern constitutional law of privacy—in his invective against the Connecticut statute, talked about the dangers that police might invade the "sacred precincts" of the bedroom. In the twenty-first century, are there any sacred precincts left?

In the 1980s—a period that seems, in many ways, very long ago—Gary Marx warned that "important American values" were threatened by computerized records. The "idea of 'starting over' or moving to a new frontier" was in danger.[21] Starting over, historically speaking, depended on a slow, sluggish, and inaccurate flow of information. It was possible to break away from the old life and start a new life, a life where the past would not catch up with you.

And the law would, to a degree, protect this right—this was the concept, for example, behind the law of blackmail. There was real privacy and real anonymity, at least in certain areas of life. Of course, as I pointed out, this privacy and anonymity were not always so benign. Privacy could hide, for example, violence and pathology behind the curtain of family life. And, I might add, the narrow moral code of the day meant that a lot of things had to be hidden that need not be hidden today. But clearly, people put high value, then and now, on privacy and anonymity. Escaping your past is much harder in the twenty-first century. There is too much information on file.

It seems as though everything is recorded. As Robert O'Harrow puts it:

> When you wake up and sign on to the Internet . . . companies record where you go, the pages you access, anything you order or buy. . . . Suppose you turn on your TiVo machine? That act is being recorded. . . . You use your debit card for breakfast. . . . Or you hop in your car and pass through E-Z Pass. There are cameras at the parking garage, subway station, and, of course, the bank and Starbucks.[22]

Computers—government computers, business computers, institutional computers—gather or can gather incredible amounts of data; it is possible to store these data for long periods and maybe forever at practically no cost; and this mountain of data can be searched and accessed and cross-referenced cheaply and quickly, simply by entering the right keystrokes. Today, then, technology has the power to threaten or destroy our inherited values.[23]

To quote Gary Marx again, in the new society "one's past is always present." This makes possible the creation of a "class of permanently stigmatized persons."[24] FBI files and the like can haunt a person for a lifetime. Under Megan's Law, sex offenders can become, in effect, permanent social pariahs. This statute takes its name from a horrific crime in New Jersey; a man with two prior convictions for sex offenses raped and strangled a little girl who lived nearby. The New Jersey law, passed in 1994, was a response; other states quickly followed. Sex offenders, once out of prison, must register with the authorities; in some states there are restrictions on where they can live; in some states the neighbors have to be informed that a monster is living in their midst.[25] The scarlet letter was crude by comparison.

Businesses find it useful to gather as much information as they can about their customers. When a customer accesses Amazon, the online bookseller, she is told what books she is likely to want; the computer has sized up the customer—usually fairly well. This seems fairly benign. Other kinds of watching, recording, and data gathering may be less so. The war on terror, which went into high gear after the attack on the World Trade Center in 2001, is the reason, or excuse, for a massive increase in government surveillance and, at least potentially, a massive intrusion into the lives of American citizens. In almost indecent haste Congress passed the USA PATRIOT Act.[26] The title of this law reflected the new habit, which George Orwell would have admired, of constructing acronyms that could do duty as propaganda. "USA PATRIOT" stands for "Uniting and Strengthening America by Providing Appropriate Tools Required to Intercept and Obstruct Terrorism." This long, elaborate statute vastly increased the government's power to poke about in the affairs of the citizens. Later came the Department of Homeland Security, with its absurd color-coded alerts.

The frenzy over national security strengthened trends that were already under way. At this writing, metal detectors are everywhere. People who want to fly from Los Angeles to Denver have to take off their shoes, belts, and jackets and release their laptop computers from their cases; then they pass through a device that peeks inside their bodies and their belongings. They cannot carry manicure scissors, tweezers, liquids and gels, and other deadly weapons except as part of their checked luggage. Probably, for most people, taking off their shoes before flying to Las Vegas is only a minor annoyance. For some people, much worse is in store. Their names are on the "no fly" list, and they cannot get on the plane at all. Some of these people are innocent, ordinary folks who have the bad luck of sharing a name with a possible terrorist.[27] The United States is probably the worst offender, at least so far as airline passengers are concerned, but other countries also are screening, watching, filming. Some of them have their own home-grown terrorists, like the IRA and the militant Basques in Spain; militants all over the world, from Bali to Israel and the London underground, have increased the sense of insecurity and have called forth more or less extreme reactions. The ministers of justice of the European Union, at a meeting in Brussels in February 2006, decided that telephone companies would have to store data about telephone calls (though not the content of the calls) for at least six months; the data would be useful (they said) in the fight against terrorists and organized crime.[28]

A war on terror has no obvious ending; but even without a war on terror the problem of surveillance and intrusion shows every sign of getting worse year by year. Catching terrorists is only one of many goals that seem to call for spying and detecting. There is a war on drugs. There is a war on child pornography. There is a war on illegal aliens. All these wars can be used and are used as a reason or excuse for massive incursions into what were once zones of personal privacy. There is no shortage of literature deploring these developments and the "death of privacy" in our times.[29] The CEO of Sun Microsystems Inc. has been quoted as saying, "You have zero privacy. Get over it."[30] How real is the threat to privacy, and what can be done about it?

In one sense the main argument of this book has had to do with *leeways*. It was about places where the legal system was somewhat plastic, where it had a little bit of stretch and give—or, if you will, a little bit of heart and forgiveness, at least for respectable people. What I have discussed in the main were *formal* leeways—second chances, as it were. But just as important, and probably more so, were *informal* leeways. These were leeways that had no official basis. They arose from social norms, or they simply arose from human laziness and imperfection. Law enforcement is and always has been sporadic, partial, and, like all human institutions, somewhat inefficient. There are laws against speeding. But most speeders get away with their violations. There are laws against drunk driving. But only a tiny handful of drunk drivers get caught. Millions of people cheat on their income taxes. Most of them never get audited.

Modern technology has the power to destroy these leeways. An efficient radar-computer system could catch *every* driver who went faster than the speed limit; society could design a system, too, that could spot every single drunk driver. It might be possible to design a computer program that could find every owner of a pizza parlor, car wash, or body shop who cheated on a tax return, every waiter who declared only part of his tips, all painters and carpenters who moonlighted on weekends and were paid in cash, and so on. Another computer system could detect and snitch on workers who played solitaire on the job or peeked at naked bodies on the screen. In theory, these systems and programs would simply enforce laws and rules that are already on the books and that most people agree *should* be there. And yet . . . and yet . . . do we want total, 100 percent enforcement? Or do we want leeways? The leeways, in a sense, have been precious to people, have been a part of their lives; they expected them and relied on them. Perhaps these leeways act as a force for the good.

Thus two huge privacy problems crop up in contemporary times. The first is the capacity to snoop and intrude in the name of some overriding policy. The snoopers are officials (the government or the police) or big institutions (corporations, universities, hospitals). The capacity to snoop is in part technological (hidden cameras, for example). It is in part simply based on the power of government and big institutions to force people to comply with legal orders. One key strategy of the war on drugs, for example, has been to demand that "American workers prove their abstinence from illegal drugs by urinating into small plastic bottles."[31] The war on terror has brought about a major escalation in all these tendencies.

The second problem is the capacity to squeeze leeways out of the system. This is of course closely related to the first problem. A report in September 2004 let us know that Chicago was about to adopt a "highly advanced system of video surveillance." It would make people "safer," according to His Honor the Mayor. Anyone "walking in public," he said, "is liable to be almost constantly watched."[32] This could certainly cut down on jaywalking if the city chose to get rid of this particular leeway; but it might unsettle most people to know that they could no longer dart across the street. Big companies, too, have ways of controlling employees they never dreamt of before. They may routinely monitor e-mail, computer files, and employee phone calls. One survey found that nearly two-thirds of all companies "engaged in some form of electronic surveillance in the workplace."[33]

Not everybody, of course, would admit that all this is really a problem. The mayor of Chicago no doubt honestly thought that people would be safer and better off under the eyes of the cameras. The United States government argues for its right to snoop, in the interests of national security. There are terrorists out there who want to murder us with anthrax pellets or dirty bombs; therefore nothing should be allowed to hamstring the government. Many people—myself included—feel that the government has gone too far, that we need more controls over the controllers, more oversight over the overseers. Other people disagree.

There is also a third privacy problem. It is terribly convenient to buy online with credit cards, even to do your banking online; it is convenient to have your medical records computerized. But all this means that somebody—a company, the government—could potentially compile a kind of dossier on you, your life, and your works, terribly complete and with devastating accuracy. There is talk about building "aware" houses—marvelous homes that are wired and computerized, homes that can "interact with the occupants and with outside systems," that can "recognize the people that live in it," can "adapt" to them, and "learn from their behavior."[34] No doubt there are advantages, but, on the whole, do we really want to live in houses this smart? Smart homes may be just around the corner. Smart passports are already here and functioning. Smart identity cards or driver's licenses are probably the next step. All this information floating about has spawned new forms of criminality. One of the worst is identity theft. In some ways the identity thief is the modern analog of the confidence man. The confidence man, as we saw, thrived in the soil of a mobile society. Plenty of confidence men are still around today, but they have been joined by a corps of new thieves who steal your Social Security number, your passwords, your credit card numbers and thrive in the soil of a computerized society.

The Internet can create new pockets of privacy—and skullduggery—even as it threatens traditional privacy. New opportunities for anonymity abound. A person can surf the web for pictures and texts in at least apparent privacy and anonymity. He can communicate with other people who share his tastes and chat with them under the benign cover of a pseudonym. A famous cartoon in the *New Yorker* showed a dog at a computer, talking to another dog, and the caption reads, "On the Internet, nobody knows you're a dog."[35] And nobody knows that you're a minor, or old and fat, or a man rather than a woman, or somebody who lives in Wichita, Kansas.

Perhaps I can mention a fourth privacy problem: the problem of the Peeping Tom society. New technology puts powerful tools for invading privacy into the hands of ordinary people. This problem is not entirely new. The candid camera struck terror into the hearts of Warren and Brandeis. What would they say about cameras in cell phones, for example? It might be dangerous, today, to have a neighbor—or an enemy—who was too sophisticated, too knowledgeable about technology. You might end up with your sex life on video.

A man in Louisiana secreted tiny cameras in the attic of his next door neighbor—a married woman—and spied on her. He was caught, arrested, fined, and put on probation.[36] Dan Boyles Jr., of Texas, a precocious 17-year-old, had sexual intercourse with a 19-year-old girl, Susan Leigh Kerr, after quietly arranging with some friends to have their passion videotaped. Only a few people actually saw the tape, but gossip about it was rampant at the schools they attended. Susan sued and won a judgment for $1 million.[37]

In these cases the voyeur was caught and punished. There are, after all, technological solutions to privacy problems. And there are legal solutions—rules that forbid egregious invasions of privacy, as in the case of these hidden cameras. With regard to the behavior of government and large institutions, some of the *legal* solutions are already on the books. Some are relatively new. Congress has constantly tinkered with wiretap laws: In 1986 Congress passed the Electronic Communications Privacy Act, and in 1988 the Video Privacy Protection Act, to prevent stores that rent or sell videotapes from disclosing the names of the videos a person rented or bought. This was in response to an incident during hearings about the (failed) nomination of Robert Bork to the United States Supreme Court. Reporters searched out data on what movies Bork had rented.[38] There are laws that try to protect financial records, bank information, and so on. Under the Health Insurance Portability and Accountability Act of 1996,[39] the Department of Health and Human Services has promulgated privacy regulations that are supposed to safeguard medical records. In 2004 Congress passed a "Video Voyeurism" law.[40] This law made it a crime to "capture an image of a private area of an individual without their consent" if this is done "knowingly" and "under circumstances in which the individual has a reasonable expectation of privacy." (A private area was defined as the "naked or undergarment clad genitals, pubic area, buttocks, or female breast"; the female breast was further defined as "any portion of the female breast below the top of the areola"). These laws are responses, among other things, to the nasty use of little cell-phone cameras, which can be smuggled into toilets, locker rooms, and other places where cameras on the whole do not belong. A number of other countries have tried to deal with this issue as well. South Korea's government, we are told, has "ordered manufacturers to design new phones so that they beep when taking a picture."[41]

In criminal justice, restrictions on searches and seizures are of venerable date. The Fourth Amendment to the Constitution bans "unreasonable" searches and seizures and provides that search warrants are not to be issued except "upon probable cause."[42] On the scope and meaning of the Fourth Amendment, there is a huge volume of law and a huge literature—what can be searched and how, what "probable cause" means, and whether illegally

seized evidence can nonetheless be admitted as evidence.[43] A huge volume of
law also deals with when a warrant is needed, when a warrant can be ignored,
and so on. The question is, Do these safeguards work? *Can* they work? What
other safeguards are needed?

The leading European nations are, if anything, even more concerned with
this issue. The European Union issued a general directive in 1995: Member
states had a duty to "protect the fundamental rights and freedoms of natural
persons, and in particular their right to privacy with respect to the processing
of personal data." The directive specified, in general terms, how this was to be
done, although with significant loopholes.[44] How effective will this be? In the
United States some experts see "glaring omissions and gaps" in privacy protection. The laws are "complicated and confusing." Decisions "turn on technical
distinctions that can leave wide fields of information virtually unprotected."[45]

Whether things will improve or get worse is of course something we cannot predict. We see only a step or two in front of us; the rest of the future is
shrouded in mystery. Privacy as a legal and social concept has had a complicated history. Privacy touches on deep aspects of the human personality—at
least on the personality of our own times. Issues of privacy and anonymity
will certainly continue to be of the very first importance.

IN THIS BOOK I have tried to explore some of the many ways in which law
protected or tried to protect reputation. My discussion began with the traditional moral code of the nineteenth century and the legal arrangements that
both supported it and allowed it to be subtly evaded. The code called for punishment of deviance. But it also, paradoxically, allowed deviations, explicitly
and implicitly, and chiefly for the benefit of respectable society, especially (but
not exclusively) men. This was the age of the Victorian compromise, with its
byways and detours and leeways. Rules about blackmail, seduction, and breach
of promise and bits of the law of defamation—these were all part of the pack-
age of relevant norms. The Victorian compromise included a strong component
of *privacy* as well. Victorian prudery was an insistence that certain aspects of
life had to be kept secret. This too was functional—part of the subterranean
plan to protect society by protecting its best citizens from scandal. Even the
beginnings of the tort of invasion of privacy, expressed in the classic article by
Warren and Brandeis, fit neatly into this overall schema.

The cozy arrangements of the Victorian compromise began to break down in the late nineteenth century. Powerful forces attacked it—forces that aimed to stamp out vice altogether, and demanded an end to hypocrisy and degeneracy. At first these forces scored a number of brilliant successes—new laws that cracked down on vice and sexual behavior that they disapproved of. Ultimately, however, their efforts were a dismal failure.

In the late twentieth century, because of the so-called sexual revolution, because of the pervasive influence of the media and the rise of consumer society, the pendulum swung drastically in the other direction. Now law and society defined respectability to allow a much wider range of behaviors. The nineteenth-century code was seriously weakened. Public figures lost a good deal of their privacy rights. The media were everywhere and in every home; the media blurred the distinction between public and private space and between public and private figures. If the nineteenth century was a world of privacy and prudery, a world of closed doors and drawn blinds, both literally and figuratively, then the world of the twenty-first century is the world of the one-way mirror, the world of the all-seeing eye.

NOTES

CHAPTER 1

1. Reputation is also an important item in the law of evidence. A person who is accused of committing a crime can and often does introduce character witnesses at the trial to testify to the defendant's reputation in the community. This reputation presumably is good evidence in that it suggests that such a man or woman could not really be guilty of the crime. Character evidence is important in criminal trials, but I will not deal with it here, except incidentally.

2. See, for example, Norman L. Rosenberg, *Protecting the Best Men: An Interpretive History of the Law of Libel* (1986). The emphasis in Rosenberg's book is on the relationship between defamation and politics; it covers such topics as seditious libel. I will also briefly touch on seditious libel. The focus of this book differs from Rosenberg's focus, but the topics of the two are closely related, as the title of Rosenberg's book makes clear.

One specific aspect of defamation is treated in Diane L. Borden, *Beyond Courtroom Victories: An Empirical and Historical Analysis of Women and the Law of Defamation* (Ph.D. dissertation, University of Washington, 1993).

3. A secret is a "piece of information that is intentionally withheld by one or more social actor(s) from one or more other social actor(s)." Kim Lane Scheppele, *Legal Secrets: Equality and Efficiency in the Common Law* (1988).

4. The legal treatment of sexual behavior, and its social meaning, plays an important role in this book. The starting point is the nineteenth century and traditional rules of morality. There are, of course, many ways of looking at the history of sexuality, sexual

behavior, and the law relating to these topics—one notable example, of course, is Michel Foucault's *A History of Sexuality: An Introduction* (1978); my claim is only that the story told here is another way of looking at developments from the early nineteenth century up to contemporary times.

5. For this concept, see Lawrence M. Friedman, *The Legal System: A Social Science Perspective* (1975), pp. 193–194.

6. There are, of course, many people who think that the law ought to punish hate speech or gross racial insults; on attitudes toward offensive speech, see Laura Beth Nielsen, *License to Harass: Law, Hierarchy, and Offensive Public Speech* (2004). Insults and provocative speech addressed to women can amount to sexual harassment under modern law, and many European countries do in fact punish hate speech; see, for example, the German Penal Code, § 130 ("Volksverhetzung").

7. James Q. Whitman, "Enforcing Civility and Respect: Three Societies," *Yale Law Journal* 109 (2000): 1279–1398. The matter is, however, not quite so clear, as we will see in Chapter 3 on defamation of character.

8. Robert C. Post, "The Social Foundations of Defamation Law: Reputation and the Constitution," *California Law Review* 74 (1986): 693.

9. Post, "Social Foundations of Defamation Law," p. 711.

10. See Lawrence M. Friedman, *Crime and Punishment in American History* (1993), pp. 195–197; and Karen Halttunen, *Confidence Men and Painted Women: A Study of Middle-Class Culture in America, 1830–1870* (1982).

11. Richard Wightman Fox, *Trials of Intimacy: Love and Loss in the Beecher-Tilton Scandal* (1999).

12. On honor, see Edward L. Ayers, *Vengeance and Justice: Crime and Punishment in the 19th Century American South* (1984), ch. 1; and Joanne B. Freeman, *Affairs of Honor: National Politics in the New Republic* (2001). There is a substantial literature on the concept of honor in various societies; see, for example, J. G. Peristiany and Julian Pitt-Rivers, eds., *Honor and Grace in Anthropology* (1992).

13. See Whitman, "Enforcing Civility and Respect."

14. See, for example, the analysis of working-class homicides growing out of barroom brawls in Jeffrey S. Adler, *First in Violence, Deepest in Dirt: Homicide in Chicago, 1875–1920* (2006), ch. 1.

15. See Ron Chernow, *Alexander Hamilton* (2004), pp. 695–709.

16. Jack K. Williams, *Dueling in the Old South: Vignettes of Social History* (1980), p. 26.

17. Bertram Wyatt-Brown, *Southern Honor: Ethics and Behavior in the Old South* (1982); Ayers, *Vengeance and Justice*; Kenneth S. Greenberg, "The Nose, the Lie, and the Duel in the Antebellum South," *American Historical Review* 95 (1990): 57–74; and Freeman, *Affairs of Honor*, ch. 4.

18. Len G. Cleveland, "The Crawford-Burnside Affair and the Movement to Abolish Dueling in Georgia," *Research Studies, Washington State University* 44 (1976): 241–247.

19. Because honor and honor codes were closely tied to aristocratic societies, some

scholars believe that honor as such has lost much of its power in the modern world; others insist that it has simply changed its form. Ludgera Vogt, *Zur Logik der Ehre in der Gegenwartsgesellschaft* (1995). The word "honor," of course, is still in common use.

20. Blackmail is dealt with in more detail in Chapter 5.

21. Breach of promise is discussed in Chapter 6.

22. See Friedman, *Crime and Punishment in American History*, p. 127.

23. The story of how American society regulated sexual behavior is an important component of this book, but the history of sexuality itself—the subject of a large and significant literature—is outside the scope of this narrative. See note 4.

24. Émile Durkheim, *The Division of Labor in Society* (1933), p. 103.

25. Bestiality was defined in Pennsylvania as sodomy, which included, along with the usual prohibition on oral and anal sex, "any person who carnally knows in any manner any animal or bird." *Pennsylvania Laws 1920*, § 8043, p. 760. Apparently carnal knowledge of a reptile or amphibian was unthinkable.

26. On this point, and in general, see Nancy F. Cott, *Public Vows: A History of Marriage and the Nation* (2000). Mormon polygamy was especially odious in the nineteenth century; see Sarah Barringer Gordon, *The Mormon Question: Polygamy and Constitutional Conflict in Nineteenth Century America* (2002).

27. Claude Martin and Irene Théry, "The PACS and Marriage and Cohabitation in France," *International Journal of Law, Policy and the Family* 15 (2001): 135, 136; Lawrence M. Friedman, *Private Lives: Families, Individuals and the Law* (2004), pp. 85–88; and Kathleen Kiernan, "Unmarried Cohabitation and Parenthood in Britain and Europe," *Law and Policy* 26 (2004): 33–55.

28. For the concept, see Robert Bellah, Richard Madsen, William M. Sullivan et al., *Habits of the Heart: Individualism and Commitment in American Life* (1985), pp. 334, 336.

29. Walter E. Houghton, *The Victorian Frame of Mind, 1830–1870* (1957), p. 353.

30. On this point, see, for example, William J. Novak, *The People's Welfare: Law and Regulation in Nineteenth-Century America* (1996).

31. Warren I. Susman, *Culture as History: The Transformation of American Society in the Twentieth Century* (1985), ch. 14.

32. Juanita Rose Hixson, "Show and Tell," *American Childhood* 36 (September 1950): 18–19. "Many animals are brought to class, such as snakes, worms . . . and cats" or the "skull of a cow, which one boy had found in a forest, and an eagle's claw . . . from Alaska"; one "little boy" had cut his hand and had stitches, which made him "one of the most popular boys of the week."

33. See Friedman, *Crime and Punishment in American History*, pp. 342–354.

CHAPTER 2

1. James Willard Hurst, *Law and Markets in United States History* (1982), p. 10.

2. James Willard Hurst, *Law and the Conditions of Freedom in the Nineteenth-Century United States* (1956).

3. Hurst, *Law and Markets*, p. 91.

4. This was the so-called doctrine of coverture. It was replaced, although gradually, as the states passed married women's property laws; see Lawrence M. Friedman, *A History of American Law* (3rd ed., 2005), pp. 146–148; and Norma Basch, *In the Eyes of the Law: Women, Marriage, and Property in Nineteenth-Century New York* (1982).

5. See Friedman, *History of American Law*, pp. 120–129; and James W. Ely Jr., *Railroads and American Law* (2001), ch. 1.

6. See Paul W. Gates, *History of Public Land Law Development* (1968).

7. See, in general, Novak, *The People's Welfare*.

8. L. Edward Purcell, *Immigration* (1995), p. 43.

9. Lacy K. Ford Jr., "Frontier Democracy: The Turner Thesis Revisited," *Journal of the Early Republic* 13 (1993): 144, 152.

10. David B. Grusky, *American Social Mobility in the 19th and 20th Centuries* (Ph.D. dissertation, University of Wisconsin, Madison, 1986), p. 24; Patricia Kelly Hall and Steven Ruggles, "'Restless in the Midst of Their Prosperity': New Evidence on the Internal Migration of Americans, 1850–2000," *Journal of American History* 91 (2004): 829–846.

11. Lawrence M. Friedman and Paul Davies, "California Death Trip," *Indiana Law Review* 36 (2003): 17–32.

12. For details, see the fine study by Alexander Keyssar, *The Right to Vote: The Contested History of Democracy in the United States* (2000).

13. Andrew Miles, *Social Mobility in Nineteenth- and Early Twentieth-Century England* (1999), pp. 177–178.

14. Frances Trollope remarked that "it is more than petty treason to the Republic, to call a free citizen a *servant*" and that young women "are taught to believe that the most abject poverty is preferable to domestic service." Frances Trollope, *Domestic Manners of the Americans* (1949 [1832]), p. 52.

15. F. Trollope, *Domestic Manners of the Americans*, p. 234. She decried the "vile and universal habit of chewing tobacco."

16. Anthony Trollope, *North America* (1951 [1862]), pp. 266–267.

17. On the whole notion of equality in American history, the fundamental work is J. R. Pole, *The Pursuit of Equality in American History* (2nd ed., 1993).

18. F. Trollope, *Domestic Manners of the Americans*, p. 121.

19. F. Trollope, *Domestic Manners of the Americans*, p. 301.

20. See Paul T. Ringenbach, *Tramps and Reformers, 1873–1916: The Discovery of Unemployment in New York* (1973); and Roger A. Bruns, *Knights of the Road: A Hobo History* (1980).

21. For an account of the short-lived bankruptcy act of 1841, see Edward J. Balleisen, *Navigating Failure: Bankruptcy and Commercial Society in Antebellum America* (2001). In general, the literature on the history of American bankruptcy law is quite rich. Among the more notable recent works are David A. Skeel Jr., *Debt's Dominion: A History of Bankruptcy Law in America* (2002); Bruce Mann, *Republic of Debtors: Bankruptcy in the Age of*

American Independence (2002); and Lee Thompson, *The Reconstruction of Southern Debtors: Bankruptcy After the Civil War* (2004).

22. Friedman, *History of American Law*, pp. 196–197.

23. In a mobile society commercial reputation was problematic and created a market for information on credit and reliability. Lewis Tappan in the 1840s created the Mercantile Agency, which provided credit information and "rapidly established itself as a national bureau of standards for judging winners and losers" in a society where trading "beyond the horizon precluded looking another man in the eye." Scott A. Sandage, *Born Losers: A History of Failure in America* (2005), pp. 100–101. On the role of credit relations in English society, see Margot C. Finn, *The Character of Credit: Personal Debt in English Culture, 1740–1914* (2003).

24. Sandage, *Born Losers*, p. 17.

25. On the history of American divorce and divorce law, see, for example, Glenda Riley, *Divorce: An American Tradition* (1991); Nelson M. Blake, *The Road to Reno: A History of Divorce in the United States* (1962); and Friedman, *Private Lives*, pp. 27–43.

26. John F. Kasson, *Rudeness and Civility: Manners in Nineteenth-Century Urban America* (1990), p. 43.

27. John F. Witt, "Narrating Bankruptcy/Narrating Risk," *Northwestern Law Review* 98 (2003): 309; Balleisen, *Navigating Failure*, p. 170.

28. Friedman, *Crime and Punishment in American History*, pp. 193–210.

29. Lawrence M. Friedman, "Crimes of Mobility," *Stanford Law Review* 43 (1991): 637–658.

30. Friedman, *Crime and Punishment in American History*, p. 198.

31. See Friedman, *Crime and Punishment in American History*, p. 186.

32. Herman Melville's novel, *The Confidence-Man* was published in 1857. The Oxford English Dictionary traces the expression to 1849.

33. James D. McCabe Jr., *Lights and Shadows of New York Life* (1872), p. 316; see also McCabe's treatment of confidence men in New York in *New York by Gaslight* (1882), p. 514.

34. McCabe, *Lights and Shadows of New York Life*, p. 319.

35. McCabe, *Lights and Shadows of New York Life*, p. 319.

36. Karen Halttunen, *Confidence Men and Painted Women* (1982), p. 193. Some tricksters made a living, on the other hand, by imitating people at the *bottom* of society rather than near the top. These impostors pretended to be objects of charity: "blind men one day, cripples the next, wounded soldiers the third, robbed immigrants the fourth, southern Union refugees the fifth, discharged laborers the sixth, and victims of a railway accident the seventh. They make up admirably; hide one eye, conceal an arm or leg, create a cicatrice, simulate a sore, counterfeit an agony, imitate a grief, in a manner that would yield them histrionic laurels." Junius Henri Browne, *The Great Metropolis: A Mirror of New York* (1975 [1869]), p. 462.

37. See Susan J. Matt, *Keeping Up with the Joneses: Envy in American Consumer Society, 1890–1930* (2003).

38. Charles Dickens, *American Notes for General Circulation* (1972 [1842]), p. 286.

39. Jeanne Fahnestock, "Bigamy: The Rise and Fall of a Convention," *Nineteenth-Century Fiction* 36 (1981): 47–71.

40. Australia figures also in another famous novel with a bigamy theme, Anthony Trollope's *John Caldigate* (1879). The hero, encumbered with debts, goes to Australia, where he makes his fortune. He then returns to England and marries young Hester Bolton. Euphemia Smith, a woman he met on the boat and who was his mistress in Australia, returns to England and claims that she and John were married in Australia; Caldigate is put on trial for bigamy. He is convicted but later released when it becomes clear that Euphemia was lying.

41. Mary E. Braddon, *Lady Audley's Secret* (1985 [1862]). In Braddon's other popular novel, *Aurora Floyd* (1863), bigamy crops up again. Aurora Floyd, the heroine, has been secretly married to a bounder, John Conyers; she leaves him and marries John Mellish. Conyers is conveniently murdered later on in the book, and Aurora is then free to legalize her second marriage.

42. Blackmail figures also in Anthony Trollope's *John Caldigate.* Euphemia and a group of co-conspirators at first demanded money from Caldigate; if he paid, they promised to keep quiet about Euphemia's alleged marriage and to leave the country.

43. June Sturrock, "Murder, Gender, and Popular Fiction by Women in the 1860s: Braddon, Oliphant, Yonge," in Andrew Maunder and Grace Moore, eds., *Victorian Crime, Madness, and Sensation* (2004), pp. 73, 81.

44. Lawrence M. Friedman and Issachar Rosen-Zvi, "Illegal Fictions: Mystery Novels and the Popular Image of Crime," *UCLA Law Review* 48 (2001): 1411–1430; Lawrence M. Friedman, "Public and Private Eyes," in Michael Freeman, ed., *Law and Popular Culture,* v. 7, *Current Legal Issues* (2005), p. 375.

45. Friedman, *Crime and Punishment in American History,* pp. 204–206; a vivid description of the role of the detective is George S. McWatters, *Knots Untied, or Ways and By-Ways in the Hidden Life of American Detectives* (1873).

46. Horst-Volker Krumrey, *Entwicklungsstrukturen von Verhaltensstandarden* (1984), pp. 22–23.

47. Kasson, *Rudeness and Civility;* see also Arthur M. Schlesinger, *Learning How to Behave: A Historical Study of American Etiquette Books* (1947); and Sarah E. Newton, *Learning to Behave: A Guide to American Conduct Books Before 1900* (1994).

48. Newton, *Learning to Behave,* pp. 49–50.

49. Newton, *Learning to Behave,* p. 58.

50. Fraser Harrison, *The Dark Angel: Aspects of Victorian Sexuality* (1977), p. 23.

51. See Nancy F. Cott, *The Bonds of Womanhood: "Woman's Sphere" in New England, 1780–1835* (1977).

52. Barbara Leslie Epstein, *The Politics of Domesticity* (1981), p. 78.

53. See Larry D. Kramer, *The People Themselves: Popular Constitutionalism and Judicial Review* (2004).

54. Gustave de Beaumont and Alexis de Tocqueville, *On the Penitentiary System in*

the United States and Its Application in France (1964 [1833]), p. 79.

55. On the American penitentiary system, see Adam J. Hirsch, *The Rise of the Penitentiary: Prisons and Punishment in Early America* (1992); on the parallel developments in England, see Michael Ignatieff, *A Just Measure of Pain: The Penitentiary in the Industrial Revolution, 1750–1850* (1978).

56. On the poorhouse, see Michael B. Katz, *In the Shadow of the Poorhouse: A Social History of Welfare in America* (rev. ed., 1996). See also the important book by David J. Rothman, *The Discovery of the Asylum: Social Order and Disorder in the New Republic* (1971).

57. These are the remarks of John Duer, in *Reports of the Proceedings and Debates of the Convention of 1821, Assembled for the Purpose of Amending the Constitution of the State of New York* (1821), pp. 569–570.

58. Horatio Alger Jr. was the author of dozens of wildly optimistic novels, the theme of which was that "prosperity was the inevitable reward of hard work" and that "your fate is determined by your personal attributes and your own behavior, not by whatever hardship or injustice the social order imposes." David K. Shipler, "Introduction" to a modern edition (2005) of Alger's *Ragged Dick or, Street Life in New York with the Boot-Blacks*, first published as a serial in 1867. On Alger's life and work, see Marcus Klein, *Easterns, Westerns, and Private Eyes: American Matters, 1870–1900* (1994), pp. 13–28.

CHAPTER 3

1. Francis Ludlow Holt, *The Law of Libel* (1816), p. 210.

2. Holt, *The Law of Libel*, pp. 211–212.

3. Charles K. Burdick, *The Law of Torts* (4th ed., 1926), p. 360.

4. On this, see *Youssoupoff v. Metro-Goldwyn-Mayer Pictures Ltd.*, T. L. R. 581 (Ct. of Appeal [1934]).

5. Burdick, *Law of Torts*, p. 352.

6. *Roberts v. English Mfg. Co.*, 155 Ala. 414, 46 So. 752 (1908). But, says the court, if the person who sent the letter "knew that some other person was in the habit of opening letters, or that in the ordinary course of business the contents of the letter would come to the knowledge of some third person," then there would be publication.

7. Whitman, "Enforcing Civility and Respect." Apparently, this is also true of some other European countries. See Elena Yanchwokova, "Criminal Defamation and Insult Laws: An Infringement on the Freedom of Expression in European and Post-Communist Jurisdictions," *Columbia Journal of Transnational Law* 41 (2003): 861–894.

8. One interesting exception might be mentioned. In Texas, as elsewhere, manslaughter was a less serious crime than murder. Manslaughter was defined as "voluntary homicide, committed under the immediate influence of sudden passion." As a general rule, insulting words or gestures were not enough to generate the sudden passion that converted murder into manslaughter—that is, unless they were "insulting words or conduct . . . toward a female relation of the party guilty of the homicide." *Paschal's Digest Laws of Texas 1866*, Articles 2250, 2251, 2253, and 2254.

9. Whitman, "Enforcing Civility and Respect"; see also Georg Nolte, *Beleidigungsschutz in der freiheitlichen Democratie* (1992), for a comparison of U.S. and German laws about defamation and insults.

10. This right is not, however, absolute; it exists "so long as it does not impair the rights of other people, or violate the constitutional order, or offend against laws of morality (*das Sittengesetz*)."

11. *Bradley v. Cramer*, 59 Wis. 309, 18 N. W. 268 (1884); in *Steele v. Southwick*, 9 Johns. 214 (N.Y., 1812), the court used the phrase "a writing published maliciously, with a view to expose a person to contempt and ridicule."

12. Curiously, in some respects more is known about defamation in the colonial period; see, for example, the elaborate discussion of slander cases involving women in Cornelia Hughes Dayton, *Women Before the Bar: Gender, Law, and Society in Connecticut, 1639–1789* (1995), pp. 285–328.

13. *Solverson v. Peterson*, 64 Wis. 198, 25 N. W. 14 (1885).

14. *Buckstaff v. Viall*, 84 Wis. 129, 54 N. W. 111 (1893).

15. The cases discussed in the text are libel cases—cases of statements that appeared in newspapers. As we saw, in slander cases recovery was more difficult. Statements that a court or a jury could label as defamation if printed would not be defamation if merely spoken. A "vocal utterance . . . is more prone to be the ebullition of fleeting passion, mere effervescence or lack of mental equipoise." *Ukman v. Daily Record Co.*, 189 Mo. 378, 88 S. W. 60 (1905).

16. *Price v. Whitely*, 50 Mo. 439 (1872).

17. Some might argue, the court said, that because truth is a defense, "general abuse" is not defamatory, since you cannot prove it to be true or not true. But often, "abuse" implies some bad or disgraceful conduct. So, in this case, to successfully defend on the basis of truth, the defendant would have to show that the mayor really did perform some "mean and disgraceful acts" of the type that would fit the description implied in the abuse. *Price v. Whitely*, at 442.

18. Harriet Martineau, *Society in America* (1962 [1837]), p. 103.

19. Charles Dickens, *American Notes for General Circulation* (1972 [1842]), p. 288.

20. Anthony Trollope, *North America* (1951 [1862]), pp. 501–502.

21. On this point, see Paul Starr, *The Creation of the Media: Political Origins of Modern Communication* (2004), p. 148.

22. *Berkoff v. Burchill*, 4 All ER 1008 (1996).

23. One judge, Millett, dissented vigorously. It was a "cheap joke," but people "must be allowed to poke fun at one another without fear of litigation." Also, "ugly people" often have "satisfactory social lives," mentioning Boris Karloff, and there is also a "popular belief" that "ugly men are particularly attractive to women."

24. *Zbyszko v. New York American*, 239 N.Y. Supp. 411 (App. Div., 1930).

25. *Holt v. Cox Enterprises*, 590 F. Supp. 408 (D. C. No. District Ga., 1984). Holt was also labeled a "limited public figure"; on this concept, see Chapter 9.

26. Burdick, *Law of Torts*, p. 350.

27. Dayton, *Women Before the Bar*.

28. Joseph H. Smith, ed., *Colonial Justice in Western Massachusetts (1639–1702): The Pynchon Court Record* (1961), p. 355.

29. Rosenberg, *Protecting the Best Men*, p. 24.

30. Dayton, *Women Before the Bar*, p. 327.

31. Zechariah Chafee Jr., *Government and Mass Communications*, v. 1 (1947), pp. 106–107.

32. Robert C. Post, "The Social Foundations of Defamation Law: Reputation and the Constitution," *California Law Review* 74 (1986): 691, 702.

33. Post, "Social Foundations of Defamation Law," p. 702.

34. Dayton, *Women Before the Bar*.

35. Borden, *Beyond Courtroom Victories*, p. 100. In addition, both men and women were plaintiffs in four other cases; all four were classified under "imputation of immorality."

36. *Brooker v. Coffin*, 5 Johns 188 (N.Y., 1809).

37. *Anonymous*, 60 N.Y. 262 (1875).

38. *Lewis v. Hudson*, 44 Ga. 568 (1872). The court also said that the words did impute a crime to Evelina, that is, fornication.

39. *Revised Statutes of Indiana 1888*, sec. 285. Technically, what the statute did was make the slander "accountable in the same manner as in the use of slanderous words charging a crime . . . which would subject the offender to death or other degrading penalties."

40. *Battles v. Tyson*, 77 Neb. 563, 110 N. W. 299 (1906).

41. *Cooper v. Seaverns*, 81 Kan. 267, 105 P. 509 (1909).

42. *Barnett v. Ward*, 36 Ohio St. 107 (1880). See *Battles v. Tyson*, 77 Neb. 563, 110 N. W., 299 (1906): A "female" accused of "want of chastity" is "driven beyond the reach of every courtesy and charity of life."

43. *Gates v. New York Recorder Co.*, 155 N.Y. 228, 49 N. E. 769 (1898); see Diane L. Borden, "Reputational Assault: A Critical and Historical Analysis of Gender and the Law of Defamation," *Journalism and Mass Communication Quarterly* 75 (1998): 98–111.

44. One judge dissented: Women have "long been prominent upon the stage," and to say that a woman was on the stage or worked as a dancer or singer could not be considered libelous per se. Coney Island, as the majority admitted, had some "reputable" places of "amusement . . . where women sing and dance to audiences composed of the best people."

45. Borden, *Beyond Courtroom Victories*, p. 100. There were seventy-one cases reported between 1897 and 1906 in which men were the sole plaintiffs; eight of these were classified under the heading of "imputation of immorality" and sixty-three under "imputation of business." Not only did women bring fewer cases than men, but they also usually sued another individual rather than a newspaper—a much more popular defendant for men.

46. *Lumpkins v. Justice*, 1 Ind. 598 (1849).

47. The case actually turned on the wording of the declaration, which the defendant

had demurred to. The court quoted the statute on incest, which seemed to refer only to brothers and sisters who were age 16 and older and who were aware that they were brother and sister. The declaration was faulty, because it failed to say explicitly that they were older than 16 and that they knew they were brother and sister.

48. *Marion v. Davis*, 217 Ala. 16, 114 So. 357 (1927).

49. See J. R. Spencer, "Criminal Libel: A Skeleton in the Cupboard," *Criminal Law Review* (1977): 383.

50. "The Trial of John Hunt and John Leigh Hunt," *State Trials* 31 (1811): 367. The charge was that the "tendency of the publication" would be to "alienate and estrange the minds of the British soldiers from the service." The jury found the men not guilty.

51. The case was *King v. Harvey and Chapman*, 2 Barnewall and Cresswell 257 (1823). The jury found the men guilty but recommended mercy; the case is also reported in *State Trials*, new ser., v. 2, p. 2.

52. 4 Bl. Comm., 150–151.

53. *King v. Harvey and Chapman*, at 269.

54. 4 Bl. Comm., 150–151.

55. Rosenberg, *Protecting the Best Men*, pp. 29, 35.

56. Rosenberg, *Protecting the Best Men*, p. 47.

57. Quoted in Marcia Speziale, *The Puritan Pariah or a Citizen of Somewhere Else: Defamation in Massachusetts, 1642 to 1850* (Ph.D. dissertation, Harvard University, Cambridge, Mass., 1992), p. 71.

58. *Respublica v. Dennie*, 4 Yeates (Pa.) 267 (1805).

59. *Commonwealth v. Clap*, 4 Mass. 163 (1808).

60. This was a criminal case, and Parsons pointed out that the victim—the person defamed—was not a party to the suit; therefore if the court allowed evidence of truth, that would incite the defendant to do even more defaming. Parsons did allow that there might be cases in which the defendant could defend himself by arguing that he had a justifiable purpose and was not malicious; and some evidence of "the truth of the words" might in these cases "tend to negate the malice and intent to defame." *Commonwealth v. Clap*, at 169.

61. *Parliamentary Debates*, ser. 3, v. 75 (1843), app. 3, p. 34.

62. *Parliamentary Debates*, ser. 3, v. 75 (1843), app. 3, p. 41; Lord Abinger voiced a similar sentiment (app. 3, p. 8) when he also mentioned the situation of a woman who was "guilty of some Indiscretion" early in life and somebody chooses to "rake up" the incident, many years later, when she is married and has a family.

63. *Parliamentary Debates*, ser. 3, v. 75 (1843), app. 3, p. 34.

64. 54 & 55 Vict. ch. 51 (1891).

65. 6 & 7 Vict. ch. 96, § 6 (1843).

66. Samuel Merrill, *Newspaper Libel: A Handbook for the Press* (1888), p. 74.

67. The Sedition Act is 1 Stat. 596 (1998); see Stanley Elkins and Eric McKitrick, *The Age of Federalism: The Early American Republic, 1788–1800* (1993), pp. 700–703; and James Morton Smith, *Freedom's Fetters: The Alien and Sedition Laws and American Civil Liberties* (1956).

68. Quoted in Rosenberg, *Protecting the Best Men*, p. 84.

69. Rosenberg, *Protecting the Best Men*, pp. 86–88.

70. Merrill, *Newspaper Libel*, p. 62.

71. *Maine Revised Statutes 1883*, Tit. xi, ch. 129, p. 926. The punishment was imprisonment for less than a year or a fine up to $1,000.

72. See, for example, *General Statutes of Minnesota 1923*, ch. 97, § 10122, p. 1394; see also *State v. Shippman*, 88 Minn. 441, 86 N. W. 431 (1901).

73. *New Jersey Revised Statutes 1937*, § 2:146-1. At present, the New Jersey Constitution (Article I, § 6) provides that in "all prosecutions for libel" the defendant must be acquitted if the statements were true and were "published with good motives and for justifiable ends."

74. *Minnesota Revised Statutes 1923*, § 10113, p. 1394.

75. The Constitution of 1970 retained the same wording, Article I, § 4; but its meaning has been severely restricted; see Chapter 10.

76. Chafee, *Government and Mass Communications*, p. 80.

77. This was possible, for example, in Massachusetts. I am indebted to George Fisher for this observation.

78. P. T. Barnum, *Struggles and Triumphs; or, Forty Years' Recollections of P. T. Barnum* (rev. ed., 1875), pp. 64–65. Barnum, according to his account, did not suffer in jail. His room was "papered and carpeted; I lived well; I was overwhelmed with the constant visits of my friends; I edited my paper as usual." His release, at the end of the sixty days, was "celebrated by a large concourse of people." In the courtroom an "ode, written for the occasion was sung"; there was a "sumptuous dinner" and later a procession, complete with "the roar of cannons" and bands playing "Home, Sweet Home."

79. *Palmer v. City of Concord*, 48 N.H. 211 (1868); similar language can be found in *State v. Henderson*, 1 Rich. 179, 30 S. C. L. 179 (So. Car., 1845), but the conviction of the defendant was reversed on other grounds.

80. *Commonwealth v. Bonner*, 50 Mass. (9 Metc.) 410 (1845).

81. There are sometimes references in the literature to obscene libel, material whose tendency was "to deprave and corrupt the minds of persons reading it." Merrill, *Newspaper Libel*, p. 86. This was a more important concept in England than in the United States; see Colin Manchester, "A History of the Crime of Obscene Libel," *Journal of Legal History* 12 (1991): 36–57. The leading case was *Rex v. Curl*, 2 Str. 788, 93 ER 849 (1728); this case concerned publication of a book called *Venus in the Cloister, or the Nun in Her Smock*. As one of the judges put it, such behavior simply had to be punished, as it was "an offence against the peace, in tending to weaken the bonds of civil society, virtue, and morality." Curl was convicted and "afterwards set in the pillory, as he well deserved."

82. See Chernow, *Alexander Hamilton*, pp. 695–709; and Freeman, *Affairs of Honor*, pp. 159–198. Hamilton's oldest son, Philip, died as a result of a duel several years before his father's fatal encounter with Burr. Chernow, *Alexander Hamilton*, pp. 650–655.

83. *Code of Virginia 1873*, ch. 145, § 2, p. 995.

84. On the history and meaning of the statute, see *Chaffin v. Lynch*, 83 Va. 106, 1 S. E. 803 (1887).

85. The statute goes back to 1822. It also was an antidueling statute. See George W. Jarecke and Nancy K. Plant, *Seeking Civility: Common Courtesy and the Common Law* (2003), p. 84.

86. *Rolland v. Batchelder*, 84 Va. 664, 5 S. E. 695 (1888).

87. *Davis v. Woods*, 95 Miss. 432, 48 So. 961 (1909).

88. *Moseley v. Moss*, 47 Va. (6 Gratt.) 534 (1850).

89. The "truth of the insulting words," said the court, had to be "admissible in mitigation of damages." The court did concede that there might be exceptional cases in which "the truth of the words would be irrelevant." Suppose, for example, that the defendant insults the plaintiff by "taunting him with some secret bodily infirmity . . . or . . . the lewdness of his wife or daughter." Evidence of these things as true would simply make the situation worse for the poor plaintiff and "gratify the malice of the defendant." The court, therefore, should be able to "exclude evidence wholly irrelevant to the merits of the controversy, especially when absurd or indecent . . . or wantonly offensive to the feelings and reputations of third persons." *Moseley v. Moss*, 47 Va. (6 Gratt.) 534, 546 (1850).

90. Clement Gatley, *Law and Practice of Libel and Slander* (1924), p. 159.

91. Chafee, *Government and Mass Communications*, pp. 80–81.

92. Timothy W. Gleason, "The Libel Climate of the Late Nineteenth Century: A Survey of Libel Litigation, 1884–1899," *Journalism Quarterly* 70 (1993): 893–906.

CHAPTER 4

1. Charles E. Rosenberg, *No Other Gods: On Science and American Social Thought* (revised and expanded ed., 1997), p. 6; see Anita Clair Fellman and Michael Fellman, *Making Sense of Self: Medical Advice Literature in Late Nineteenth-Century America* (1981), pp. 91–112.

2. E. Anthony Rotundo, *American Manhood* (1993), p. 74.

3. F. S. Brockman, "A Study of the Moral and Religious Life of 251 Preparatory School Students in the United States," *Pedagogical Seminary* 9 (1902): 266, 268. Interestingly, of the sixty-six men who listed sexual intercourse as their worst temptation, only seventeen had "yielded" to it.

4. J. Richardson Parke, *Human Sexuality: A Medico-Literary Treatise* (4th rev. ed., 1909), pp. 379–380. Brockman rather sensibly remarks that possibly "in certain cases" young men overestimate the "evil physical results" of masturbation; but, he adds, "When one is brought to *think* that his mind is gone, he is not far from in as bad fix as the man whose mind is gone." Brockman, "Study of the Moral and Religious Life," p. 271.

5. Quoted in Rosenberg, *No Other Gods*, p. 82.

6. Rosenberg, *No Other Gods*, p. 77.

7. Quoted in Fellman and Fellman, *Making Sense of Self*, pp. 91–92.

8. Fellman and Fellman, *Making Sense of Self*, pp. 100–101.

9. Fellman and Fellman, *Making Sense of Self,* p. 92.

10. Friedman, *Crime and Punishment in American History,* p. 127.

11. See, for example, David Flaherty, "Law and the Enforcement of Morals in Early America," in Donald Fleming and Bernard Bailyn, eds., *Law in American History* (1971), p. 203.

12. Here one might mention Ariela Dubler's work on the nineteenth-century campaign against dower, the ancient and restrictive doctrine on the rights of widows in their late husband's estate. Dower had many disadvantages, and there were many arguments against it. One argument was that dower was inconsistent with the idea that the family was "a sacred, private space shielded from the invasive reach of the state"; it was an "invasion of the private family home after a husband's death," and this was "destructive of the core of women's gender-specific place within the family." Ariela Dubler, "In the Shadow of Marriage: Single Women and the Legal Construction of the Family and the State," *Yale Law Journal* 112 (2003): 1679.

13. George L. Mosse, *Nationalism and Sexuality: Respectability and Abnormal Sexuality in Modern Europe* (1985), p. 54.

14. In one county in Virginia, of 240 indictments for crimes between 1801 and 1810, there were exactly zero for fornication or adultery. Edward M. Steel, "Criminality in Jeffersonian America: A Sample," *Crime and Delinquency* 18 (1972): 154–159. In Marion County, Indiana, between 1823 and 1860, only 2.4 percent of the total number of prosecutions were prosecutions for sexual offenses, mostly fornication and adultery. David J. Bodenhamer, *The Pursuit of Justice: Crime and Law in Antebellum Indiana* (1986), p. 140.

15. Donna Dennis, "Obscenity Regulation, New York City, and the Creation of American Erotica, 1820–1880" (Ph.D. dissertation, Princeton University, 2005), pp. 129–130.

16. See, in general, Elizabeth Pleck, *Domestic Tyranny: The Making of Social Policy Against Family Violence from Colonial Times to the Present* (1987); and Linda Gordon, *Heroes of Their Own Lives: The Politics and History of Family Violence: Boston, 1880–1960* (1988).

17. Elizabeth Foyster, *Marital Violence: An English Family History, 1660–1857* (2005), p. 72.

18. Foyster (*Marital Violence,* p. 205), writing about the British situation and taking a somewhat longer historical perspective, argues essentially that what happened in the nineteenth century was a shift from community involvement in the problem of domestic violence—the involvement of friends, servants, neighbors, parents, and the like—to a situation in which police, doctors, magistrates, and others played a significant role. But "chastisement" in the privacy of the home probably did not reach the eyes and ears of the authorities very often in the United States (and probably not in England) and did not usually evoke much of a response.

19. *State v. Rhodes,* 61 N.C. 453 (1868).

20. See Reva B. Siegel, "The Rule of Love: Wife Beating as Prerogative and Privacy," *Yale Law Journal* 105 (1996): 2125.

21. Allen Steinberg, *The Transformation of Criminal Justice: Philadelphia 1800–1880* (1989), p. 69.

22. Steinberg, *Transformation of Criminal Justice*, p. 69.

23. Similarly, slave owners were rarely prosecuted or convicted for the crime of abusing slaves. This happened only in truly shocking cases, where the treatment was so inhuman that the slave died. As Michael Hindus put it, "Only the most atrocious or public murders [of slaves], frequently committed by men of low standing, resulted in conviction." Michael Hindus, *Prison and Plantation: Crime, Justice, and Authority in Massachusetts and South Carolina, 1767–1878* (1980), p. 134.

24. Carolyn Ramsey, "Intimate Homicide: Gender and Crime Control, 1880–1920," *University of Colorado Law Review* 77 (2006): 101–191.

25. Harrison, *Dark Angel*, p. 66.

26. *Laws of Nevada 1877*, ch. 43, p. 82; *Laws of Maryland 1883*, ch. 120, p. 172.

27. The Divorce and Matrimonial Causes Act, 20–21 Victoria, ch. 85 (1857).

28. Lawrence Stone, *Road to Divorce: England, 1530–1987* (1990), p. 161.

29. 20–21 Vict., ch. 85, § 27; see John Fraser MacQueen, *A Practical Treatise on Divorce and Matrimonial Jurisdiction* (1858), pp. 30–36.

30. Harrison, *Dark Angel*, p. 9.

31. *General Statutes of Minnesota 1913*, § 8702, p. 1921.

32. On this point, see Chapter 6.

33. For some of the material in this and the following paragraphs, I am indebted to Irene Shih, J.D. (Stanford, 2005).

34. Under a Virginia law of 1924, no white could marry anybody except someone who had "no trace whatsoever of any blood other than Caucasian." *Laws of Virginia 1924*, ch. 371. See Peggy Pascoe, "Miscegenation Law, Court Cases, and Ideologies of 'Race' in Twentieth-Century America," *Journal of American History* 83 (1996): 44–65; and F. James Davis, *Who Is Black?* (1991). An interesting comparative study is G. Reginald Daniel, *Race and Multiraciality in Brazil and the United States: Converging Paths?* (2006).

35. James M. O'Toole, *Passing for White: Race, Religion, and the Healy Family, 1820–1920* (2002). The "black blood" had been kept a family secret until a scholar revealed it in a book published in 1954. O'Toole, *Passing for White*, p. 2.

36. *Estate of Ernest J. Torregano*, 54 Cal. 2d 234, 352 P. 2d 505 (1960).

37. Ernest Torregano's will recited that he had no children and that he was a widower (he had remarried, and this wife had died before him); he left one dollar to anyone who might contest his will "or assert any claim to share my estate by virtue of relationship." Despite this, the California Supreme Court held that his daughter had a right to his estate.

38. Ariela J. Gross, "Litigating Whiteness: Trials of Racial Determination in the Nineteenth-Century South," *Yale Law Journal* 108 (1998): 148–149.

39. *Bryan v. Walton*, 33 Ga. Supp. 11 (1864); Gross, "Litigating Whiteness," p. 129.

40. The story of the Rhinelander trial is recounted in Earl Lewis and Heidi Ardizzone, *Love on Trial: An American Scandal in Black and White* (2001).

41. A woman who told her story in *Ebony* magazine in 1951 ("I'm Through with Passing") explained that she started passing to get a "secretarial job which was available

. . . in downtown Chicago." Quoted in Gayle Wald, *Crossing the Line: Racial Passing in Twentieth-Century U.S. Literature and Culture* (2000), pp. 136–137.

42. Friedman, *Crime and Punishment in American History*, pp. 34–35.

43. *Records and Files of the Quarterly Courts of Essex County, Massachusetts* (v. 2, 1656–1662) (1912), p. 432.

44. See, for example, *California Penal Code 1872*, sec. 266a; *Revised Statutes of Indiana 1877*, v. 2, p. 466, which uses the phrase "Every person who shall live in open and notorious adultery or fornication."

45. *Laws of Florida 1868*, pp. 96–97.

46. *Laws of Florida 1874*, p. 41.

47. There were other statutory patterns. In North Carolina, under an old statute going back to 1805, it was a misdemeanor for "any man or woman, not being married to each other" to "lewdly and lasciviously associate, bed, or cohabit together."

48. *Luster v. State*, 23 Fla. 339, 2 So. 690 (1887).

49. *Wright v. State*, 5 Blackf. 358 (Ind., 1840).

50. *B. Richardson and Another v. State*, 37 Tex. 346 (1872).

51. *State of Missouri v. W. H. Phillips*, 49 Mo. App. 325 (1892); see *General Statutes of Missouri 1865*, ch. 206, § 8, p. 816, which criminalized not only "open and notorious adultery" but also those who "lewdly and lasciviously abide and cohabit with each other" and also those guilty of "open gross lewdness or lascivious behavior" or any "open and notorious act of public indecency, grossly scandalous."

CHAPTER 5

1. James Lindgren, "Unraveling the Paradox of Blackmail," *Columbia Law Review* 84 (1984): 670–717.

2. Leo Katz, *Ill-Gotten Gains: Evasion, Blackmail, Fraud, and Kindred Puzzles of the Law* (1996), p. x.

3. "Society would be better off, and human rights more secure, if our blackmail legislation were terminated." Walter Block, "Trading Money for Silence," *University of Hawaii Law Review* 8 (1986): 73.

4. Michael D. Rips, "To Ask Is Not Always to Extort," *New York Times*, July 18, 1997, p. A29. The Jackson-Cosby affair is also treated in Chapter 10.

5. Breach of promise is treated in Chapter 6; similiarly for the Mann Act, discussed in Chapter 8.

6. The novel was published in 1935. Some of the suspects were, in fact, blackmailed by Madame Giselle, but in the end it turned out that the killer had a somewhat different motive. It would be a serious breach of custom (with regard to mystery novels) for me to say who this was and what the motive might have been.

7. Among these are Katz himself, *Ill-Gotten Gains*, pp. 133–145; Richard Epstein, "Blackmail, Inc.," *University of Chicago Law Review* 50 (1983): 553–566; and the various essays that appeared in a symposium in the *University of Pennsylvania Law Review* (v. 141),

in 1993; included was an essay by Richard Posner, "Blackmail, Privacy and Freedom of Contract," *University of Pennsylvania Law Review* 141 (1993): 1817–1847.

8. Lindgren, "Unraveling the Paradox of Blackmail," p. 672. "Selling the right to go to the police involves suppressing the state's interests. . . . And selling the right to inform others of embarrassing (but legal) behavior involves suppressing the interests of those other people."

9. Scott Altman, "A Patchwork Theory of Blackmail," *University of Pennsylvania Law Review* 141 (1993): 1644–1645.

10. Clayton J. Ettinger, *The Problem of Crime* (1932), pp. 28–29. When a "man of high station" is found lavishing money and jewels on a "pretty empty-headed girl from the tenements," the blackmailer's game "is an easy one." What follows is a "shake-down." A "man of means and social prominence . . . usually pays rather than suffer the penalties inseparable from publicity."

11. Scheppele, *Legal Secrets*, pp. 304–305.

12. Ken Levy, "The Solution to the *Real* Blackmail Paradox: The Common Link Between Blackmail and Other Criminal Threats," unpublished, 2006. I am grateful to Levy for providing me with the text of his article.

13. Ronald H. Coase, *Blackmail* (Occasional Papers No. 24; University of Chicago Law School, 1988), p. 22.

14. Quoted in Mike Hepworth, *Blackmail: Publicity and Secrecy in Everyday Life* (1975), pp. 21–22.

15. I am indebted for some of the material on the history of blackmail to Alex Lue, a Stanford Law student, and his paper, "Blackmail: American Style" (2002); and to research by Samantha Wakefield, Barbara Merz, and David Oyer.

16. California Penal Code, §§ 518 and 519.

17. "Another Black-Mailing Plot," *New York Times*, June 23, 1881, p. 5.

18. "Black-Mailers in New-Haven," *New York Times*, October 2, 1881, p. 2. There are many other examples. Under the headline "One Man Held for Blackmail," the *Los Angeles Times* reported (March 4, 1922, sec. II, p. 10) indictments against men who sent "Black Hand" letters to Los Angeles businessmen, "demanding large sums of money on threats of death."

19. *Oklahoma Statutes Annotated 2002*, Tit. 21, § 1488. Blackmail is a felony, and it can carry up to a five-year prison sentence or a fine up to $10,000 or both.

20. *General Statutes of Minnesota 1923*, ch. 97, § 10119, p. 1395.

21. See Antony E. Simpson, "The 'Blackmail Myth' and the Prosecution of Rape and Its Attempt in 18th Century London: The Creation of a Legal Tradition," *Journal of Criminal Law and Criminology* 77 (1986): 101–150.

22. *King v. Jones*, 1 Leach 139, 168 E.R. 171 (1776).

23. *King v. Hickman*, 1 Leach 278, 168 E.R. 241 (1783). Hickman was sentenced to death but reprieved in 1784 and "received his Majesty's pardon on condition of being transported to Africa for fourteen years."

24. In *King v. Knewland and Wood*, 2 Leach 721, 168 E.R. 461 (1796), Sarah Wilson, "a young woman just arrived from the country," wandered into an auction, where she was forced by threats to bid on some knives and forks; she insisted she was poor, had almost no money and no need to buy the stuff, but the two defendants threatened to take her before a magistrate. She gave them a shilling out of fear of being brought before a court of justice. Was this robbery? No, said Justice Ashhurst; fear of injury to character was not enough for a robbery case, except for cases where there are "insinuations against . . . character . . . by accusing [a man] . . . of sodomitical practices."

25. There is an exhaustive treatment of the subject: Angus McLaren, *Sexual Blackmail: A Modern History* (2002).

26. H. G. Cocks, *Nameless Offences: Homosexual Desire in the Nineteenth Century* (2003), p. 125.

27. Cocks, *Nameless Offences*, p. 126.

28. *Laws of Georgia 1816*, No. 178.

29. *Laws of Illinois 1827*, No. 145.

30. Alice Kramer Grief, "Criminal Law: A Study of Statutory Blackmail and Extortion in Several States," *Michigan Law Review* 44 (1945): 465.

31. 18 U.S.C. § 873.

32. *UK Statutes 1968*, ch. 60, § 21. The act does not apply if the person has "reasonable grounds for making the demand" and if the "use of the menaces is a proper means of reinforcing the demand."

33. Article 171. Interestingly, if the demand *was* successful (*si ha conseguido la entrega de todo o parte de lo exigido*), the punishment was two to four years in prison; if unsuccessful, four months to two years. See Angeles Jareño Leal, *Las Amenazas y el Chantaje en el Codigo Penal de 1995* (1997), pp. 88–95.

34. *Code Penal*, Title I, ch. 2, sec. 2, Article 312-10.

35. McLaren, *Sexual Blackmail*, p. 39; Cocks, *Nameless Offences*, pp. 115–135.

36. This subject is treated in Alexander Welsh, *George Eliot and Blackmail* (1985). According to Welsh, "blackmail or a related action" figures in every one of George Eliot's novels after *The Mill on the Floss* and in many novels by such notable writers as Anthony Trollope and Wilkie Collins (p. 3). And, as I mentioned, blackmail has been a constant theme in mystery stories.

37. Cocks, *Nameless Offences*, p. 117.

38. *London Times*, January 20, 1931, p. 9; January 21, 1931, p. 11; and February 10, 1931, p. 17. The prosecutor said the jury could, if it wanted, hear the name, address, and identity of the victim, but the "jury intimated that they had no desire to know." *London Times*, January 20, 1931, p. 9. But they did apparently see him and learned his "name and rank" during the trial. *London Times*, February 10, 1931, p. 17.

39. *London Times*, February 10, 1931, p. 17.

40. *London Times*, February 10, 1931, p. 17.

41. McLaren, *Sexual Blackmail*, p. 19.

42. Cocks, *Nameless Offences*, p. 128.

43. McLaren, *Sexual Blackmail*, p. 229.

44. 36 Stat. 263 (act of March 26, 1910); see, in general, David J. Langum, *Crossing Over the Line: Legislating Morality and the Mann Act* (1994). On the meaning of "immoral purpose," see Ariela R. Dubler, "Immoral Purposes: Marriage and the Genus of Illicit Sex," *Yale Law Journal* 115 (2006): 756–812.

45. Langum, *Crossing Over the Line*, ch. 5; the case was *Caminetti v. United States*, 242 U.S. 470 (1917).

46. "Blackmail Rich Men by White Slave Act," *New York Times*, January 13, 1916, p. 1; McLaren, *Sexual Blackmail*, pp. 86–92.

47. Quoted in Langum, *Crossing Over the Line*, p. 78.

48. Blackmail could even creep into ordinary actions for divorce. A woman in a divorce case could conceivably drag in the name of some famous or wealthy person and claim that he had committed adultery with her. In 1927 California passed a law to stop this form of "legal blackmail." Any "allegation or averment" in a divorce case was no longer "privileged" unless it was "sworn to" and was made "without malice" and by a person who had "reasonable and probable cause for believing the truth of such allegation." A violator might be open to a lawsuit for defamation. *Laws of California 1927*, ch. 866, pp. 1881–1882; McLaren, *Sexual Blackmail*, p. 94.

49. *Williams v. Ohio*, 32 Ohio App. 124, 167 N. E. 609 (1929).

50. *People v. Parker*, 307 Mich. 372, 11 N. W. 2d 924 (1943).

51. John D'Emilio and Estelle B. Freedman, *Intimate Matters: A History of Sexuality in America* (1988), pp. 292–293.

52. McCabe, *New York by Gaslight*, pp. 524–525; McCabe has a similar discussion in *Lights and Shadows*, pp. 658–661.

53. McCabe, *Lights and Shadows*, pp. 659–660.

54. McCabe, *Lights and Shadows*, p. 660.

55. Theodore Dreiser's *An American Tragedy* (1925) tells the story of a young man who murders his pregnant girlfriend. She stood in the way of his ascent up the ladder of success and a convenient marriage with a girl from a wealthy family. The book was based on the trial of Chester Gillette, who murdered Grace Brown at Big Moose Lake, New York, in 1906. The case is described in Craig Brandon, *Murder in the Adirondacks: "An American Tragedy" Revisited* (1968). The only difference between Grace Brown and a blackmailer is that Grace wanted a wedding, not hush money. The case was also the inspiration for the well-known movie *A Place in the Sun*, starring Montgomery Clift and Elizabeth Taylor (1951).

56. Allan Pinkerton, *Thirty Years a Detective* (1884), pp. 227–236.

57. Nonetheless, it is possible and maybe even probable that the victims in the United States were by no means always the rich. Certainly, almost everybody who considered himself or herself decent and respectable or had that reputation had some reason to be afraid of a charge of blackmail. Only people who had absolutely no money were, in a sense, immune.

58. Dennis, *Obscenity Regulation*, pp. 92–100.

59. Matthew Hale Smith, *Sunshine and Shadow in New York* (1880), pp. 132–133.

60. *New York Times*, February 8, 1897.

61. For example, in *State v. McKenzie*, 182 Minn. 513, 235 N. W. 274 (1931), all we learn is that the victim, Logelin, "had been guilty of disgraceful conduct and was in fear of exposure."

62. *People v. Williams*, 127 Cal. 212, 59 P. 581 (1899).

63. *State v. Coleman*, 99 Minn. 487, 110 N. W. 5 (1906).

64. Friedman, *Private Lives*, pp. 68–70. There was a similar system in England, where adultery was also the sole feasible grounds for divorce. Colin S. Gibson, *Dissolving Wedlock* (1994), pp. 96–97.

65. Posner, "Blackmail, Privacy, and Freedom of Contract," has an elaborate classification of blackmail into seven categories, depending on what the victim had done—whether it was a crime, a tort, a disreputable or immoral act that was not illegal, or an act or condition that was a "source of potential shame, ridicule, or humiliation."

66. *People v. Sexton*, 132 Cal. 37, 64 P. 107 (1901); the crime in *People v. Sanders*, 188 Cal. 744, 207 P. 380 (1922), was the illegal sale of liquor.

67. *State v. Barr*, 67 Wash. 87, 120 P. 509 (1912); the defendant, Harry Barr, accused John C. Robery "of having committed the crime of adultery with one May Barr, a married woman." Since Harry and May had the same last name, they were likely either husband and wife or close relatives.

68. *People v. Watson*, 307 Mich. 378, 11 N. W. 2d 926 (1943).

69. There is dispute, of course, about how much *actual* social mobility existed in the United States—how easy it was to move up the ladder. But social mobility was an American dream, myth, ideal—however you want to phrase it. And there were, in contrast to some Old World societies, no *formal* barriers to upward mobility, at least not for white men; see Chapter 2.

70. See Lawrence M. Friedman, *The Republic of Choice: Law, Authority, and Culture* (1990), pp. 101–106.

71. Bigamy is also what I have called a crime of mobility; see the discussion in Chapter 2. That is, it is a characteristic of a mobile society. The same is true of blackmail. Blackmail would be rare or nonexistent in a traditional society, where people stayed put their whole lives. A guilty or embarrassing past is almost impossible under such circumstances. See Friedman, "Crimes of Mobility."

The mobility point is implicit in some of the discussions of blackmail. See, for example, Posner, "Blackmail, Privacy and Freedom of Contract," p. 1821: "Suppose the blackmailer's victim is a person who had been convicted of a crime . . . and eventually . . . pardoned. Years later the blackmailer appears on the scene." One can ask, under what social circumstances is such a scenario *possible*? And the answer points, of course, to a society in which people (especially men) are extremely mobile and in which it is possible to move and start over again.

72. McLaren, *Sexual Blackmail*, p. 82.

73. Jana L. Pershing, "To Snitch or Not to Snitch? Applying the Concept of Neutralization Techniques to the Enforcement of Occupational Misconduct," *Sociological Perspectives* 46 (2003): 153.

CHAPTER 6

1. *Laws of Illinois*, 1899, p. 148.

2. *General Code of Ohio*, 1921, § 13026, p. 5084 (any "male person over eighteen years of age" who has "sexual intercourse under promise of marriage with a female person under eighteen years of age and of good repute for chastity" could be jailed or imprisoned for up to three years).

3. *Laws of New York 1909*, ch. 524; the phrase "under promise of marriage" appears in other statutes, for example, *Wyoming Compiled Statutes 1910*, sec. 5907, p. 1373; *Pennsylvania Statutes 1920*, sec. 8042, p. 760 ("seduction of any female of good repute, under twenty-one years of age . . . under promise of marriage").

4. *Criminal Code of Alabama, 1907*, ch. 289, sec. 7776, p. 922.

5. *Code of Georgia 1882*, sec. 4371, p. 1148.

6. Patrick Brode, *Courted and Abandoned: Seduction in Canadian Law* (2002), pp. 79–91.

7. *People v. Nelson*, 153 N.Y. 90, 94–95, 46 N. E. 1040 (1897).

8. H. Gerald Chapin, *Handbook of the Law of Torts* (1917), p. 469; Lea VanderVelde, "The Legal Ways of Seduction," *Stanford Law Review* 48 (1996): 867, 883–891; Jane E. Larson, "'Women Understand So Little, They Call My Good Nature "Deceit"': A Feminist Rethinking of Seduction," *Columbia Law Review* 93 (1993): 374–472.

9. Brode, *Courted and Abandoned*, pp. 133–134.

10. *Simpson v. Grayson*, 54 Ark. 404, 16 S. W. 4 (1891).

11. Burdick, *Law of Torts*, pp. 343–346; on the early history of this tort, see Brode, *Courted and Abandoned*, pp. 3–11.

12. The tort is considered in detail in Susan Gonda, *Strumpets and Angels: Rape, Seduction, and the Boundaries of Consensual Sex in the Northeast, 1789–1870* (Ph.D. dissertation, University of California, Los Angeles, 1999); see VanderVelde, "Legal Ways of Seduction."

13. *Briggs v. Evans*, 27 N.C. 16 (1844).

14. *Patterson v. Hayden*, 17 Ore. 238, 21 P. 129 (1889).

15. Under the *New York Field Code* in the middle of the nineteenth century, the law took a further step: It allowed a woman to sue "for her own seduction" and recover damages. See VanderVelde, "Legal Ways of Seduction," p. 891. Most courts were reluctant to allow this action in the absence of statute, but there were exceptions. The issue is discussed generally in M. B. W. Sinclair, "Seduction and the Myth of the Ideal Woman," *Law and Inequality* 5 (1987): 33–102.

16. William W. Sanger, *The History of Prostitution: Its Extent, Causes, and Effects Throughout the World* (1895), p. 494.

17. *Tennessee Code 1858*, §§ 4612 and 4613.

18. *Commonwealth v. Stratton*, 114 Mass. 303 (1873).

19. Mary Frances Berry, who examined reported cases in the South in the late nineteenth century, found no such cases; when black women were "seduced or by force or voluntarily cohabited with white men without marriage, the law took little if any notice." Berry did find three cases in which a black woman sued a black man for seduction. Mary Frances Berry, "Judging Morality: Sexual Behavior and Legal Consequences in the Late Nineteenth-Century South," *Journal of American History* 78 (1991): 849.

20. Slave women (and men) were not permitted to marry at all, although many did enter into long-term relationships. After the end of slavery the Southern states—and not only the Southern states—banned "miscegenation." In 1913 thirty of the forty-eight states had some sort of law against miscegenation. Friedman, *Private Lives*, p. 54. See also Peter Wallenstein, *Tell the Court I Love My Wife: Race, Marriage, and Law—An American History* (2002).

21. Nor, as a practical matter, raped. Of course, technically even a prostitute could be raped, but juries had other ideas; on this point, see the discussion in Harry Kalven Jr. and Hans Zeisel, *The American Jury* (1966), pp. 249–254. Legally, the only issue in rape (other than the intercourse itself) is consent. But the juries that Kalven and Zeisel studied were sensitive to anything they considered "contributory behavior" on the woman's part. The study makes it quite clear that a jury would not convict a man of rape if the victim was a woman who went to bars or got into cars with men or had a history of sexual activity.

22. The case is *State v. Green Horton*, 100 N.C. 443, 6 S. E. 238 (1888).

23. *People v. Gould*, 70 Mich. 240, 38 N. W. 323 (1888).

24. *Wright v. State*, 31 Tex. Crim. 354, 20 S. W. 756 (1892).

25. Edward H. Savage, *Police Records and Recollections: Or Boston by Daylight and Gaslight for Two Hundred and Forty Years* (1873), pp. 221–222.

26. On this trial, see Lawrence M. Friedman and Robert V. Percival, *The Roots of Justice: Crime and Punishment in Alameda County, California, 1870–1910* (1981), pp. 239–244. Carolyn Ramsey has shown that women who killed abusive husbands or lovers were also often acquitted or given mild sentences. Ramsey, "Intimate Homicide," p. 101.

27. On this famous case see Nat Brandt, *The Congressman Who Got Away With Murder* (1991); see also Robert M. Ireland, "The Libertine Must Die: Sexual Dishonor and the Unwritten Law in the Nineteenth-Century United States," *Journal of Social History* 23 (1992): 27–44.

28. Friedman, *Crime and Punishment*, pp. 397–398.

29. On common law marriage, see Michael Grossberg, *Governing the Hearth: Law and the Family in Nineteenth Century America* (1985), pp. 69–75; Ariela R. Dubler, "Wifely Behavior: A Legal History of Acting Married," *Columbia Law Review* 100 (2000): 957–1021; Friedman, *Private Lives*, pp. 17–27.

30. *Askew v. Dupree*, 30 Ga. 173 (1860).

31. See Stephen Robertson, "Making Right a Girl's Ruin: Working-Class Legal

Culture and Forced Marriage in New York City, 1890–1950," *Journal of American Studies* 36 (2002): 199–230.

32. For example, in *Iowa Statutes Annotated* (1880), v. 2, § 3861, p. 975.

33. See Chapter 8.

34. The English study used a nineteenth-century database consisting of 322 breach of promise cases. Men were plaintiffs in a small number (8%). Moreover, although most of the women won their cases (more than 80% were successful), of the twenty-five male plaintiffs, only seven won their suits. Susie L. Steinbach, *Promises, Promises: Not Marrying in England, 1780–1920* (Ph.D. dissertation, Yale University, 1996), pp. 210, 214. Another study gives rather similar figures (also for England): 97 percent of the plaintiffs were women, and they won 70 percent of their cases; men were 3 percent of the plaintiffs and tended to win little or nothing. Ginger S. Frost, "'I Shall Not Sit Down and Crie': Women, Class and Breach of Promise of Marriage Plaintiffs in England, 1850–1900," *Gender and History* 6 (1994): 224–248.

35. Brode, *Courted and Abandoned*, pp. 118–119.

36. *Olson v. Saxton*, 86 Ore. 670, 169 P. 119 (1917).

37. So did the male plaintiff in *Clark v. Kennedy*, 162 Wash. 95, 297 P. 1087 (1931).

38. *New York Times*, January 20, 1884, p. 2.

39. *Kelly v. Renfro*, 9 Ala. 330 (1846).

40. *New York Times*, September 17, 1884, p. 1.

41. Frost, "I Shall Not Sit Down and Crie," pp. 225 and 233. The plaintiff and defendant had had sex in a quarter of the cases, and in three-quarters of these, she became pregnant.

42. I am indebted to Amiram Gill for this information.

43. *Civil Code of New York* (1865), pt. 3, Title I, § 44. Under § 1859, the "damages for the breach of a promise of marriage rest in the sound discretion of the jury."

44. The language is from *Johnson v. Smith*, 3 Pitts. Rep. 184, 188 (1873). The fact that the couple had sex would act neither as "aggravation or mitigation of damages." But of course the practice was exactly the opposite. Consenting to sex *enhanced* the woman's damages, and having a baby, still more so.

45. Frank H. Keezer, *A Treatise on the Law of Marriage and Divorce* (2nd ed., 1923), p. 60.

46. *Osmun v. Winters*, 26 Ore. 260, 35 Pac. 250 (1894).

47. *Bennett v. Beam*, 42 Mich. 346, 4 N. W. 8 (1880).

48. *Van Storch v. Griffin*, 77 Pa. 504 (1875).

49. On the damages in nineteenth-century English cases, see Steinbach, *Promises, Promises*, p. 211. Many of the recoveries in England were quite modest, but a few were substantial.

50. 114 Me. 75, 95 A. 409 (1915).

51. A superior court judge awarded a new trial, and the case was apparently settled. "Is It Settled?" *Los Angeles Times*, July 22, 1887, p. 1.

52. *Ladies' Magazine and Literary Gazette*, 3 (October 1830), p. 459.

53. Quoted in Brode, *Courted and Abandoned*, p. 116.

54. In the operetta the judge saves the day by offering to marry the defendant himself.

55. See Charles J. MacColla, *Breach of Promise: Its History and Social Considerations* (1879). The long subtitle promises "a glance at many amusing cases."

56. *Carney v. McGilvray*, 152 Miss. 87, 119 So. 157 (1928). Cordelia P. Carney was 59; Duncan McGilvray was 69. She lost her case at the trial court level, but the Supreme Court of Mississippi reversed the decision for faulty instructions to the jury, among other things. Cordelia was immensely distant from the model nineteenth-century plaintiff; she was not young, not particularly innocent, and not at all in love.

57. I am indebted to Markus Wagner for this information.

58. This material is from Arlene J. Díaz, "Women, Order, and Progress in Guzmán Blanco's Venezuela, 1870–1888," in Ricardo D. Salvatore, Carlos A. Aguirre, and Gilbert M. Joseph, eds., *Crime and Punishment in Latin America* (2001), pp. 56, 61–69.

59. See Susan Staves, "Money for Honor: Damages for Criminal Conversation," in Harry C. Payne, ed., *Studies in Eighteenth-Century Culture* (1982), v. 11, p. 279.

60. "Jacob Vanderbilt Sued," *New York Times*, February 15, 1890, p. 8.

61. *New York Times*, June 22, 1893, p. 3; June 24, 1893, p. 8; June 28, 1893, p. 1.

62. *Doe v. Roe*, 82 Me. 503, 20 Atl. 83 (1890).

63. Similarly, in a criminal conversation case in 1895 in Minnesota, Mary Kroessin brought an action against Wilhelmina Keller because of Keller's "adulterous acts" with Kroessin's husband. The Minnesota court held that no such action could be brought. *Kroessin v. Keller*, 60 Minn. 372, 62 N. W. 438 (1895).

64. *Duffies v. Duffies*, 76 Wisc. 374, 45 N. W. 522 (1890).

65. *Foot v. Card*, 58 Conn. 1, 18 A. 1027 (1889).

66. *Sims v. Sims*, 79 N.J. L. 577, 76 A. 1063 (1910).

67. *New York Times*, August 29, 1930, p. 13. On this affair, see Tonie Holt and Valmai Holt, *In Search of the Better 'ole: A Biography of Captain Bruce Bairnsfather* (1985), p. 152.

68. Laura Hanft Korobkin, *Criminal Conversations: Sentimentality and Nineteenth-Century Legal Stories of Adultery* (1998). On criminal conversation in Canada, see Brode, *Courted and Abandoned*, pp. 121–132.

69. On bigamy see Friedman, *Crime and Punishment*, pp. 197–201. It is worth mentioning that in the nineteenth century in most states divorce was more difficult to get and more expensive than it is today, and this surely was a factor that influenced the amount of bigamy.

70. Gordon, *The Mormon Question*, pp. 22–23, 27; see also Edwin B. Firmage and Richard C. Mangrum, *Zion in the Courts: A Legal History of the Church of Jesus Christ of Latter-Day Saints* (1988).

71. See Gordon, *Mormon Question*, p. 33.

72. T. B. H. Stenhouse, *A Lady's Life Among the Mormons* (1872), p. 76. The subtitle was: "A Record of Personal Experience as One of the Wives of a Mormon Elder."

73. Quoted in Jeffrey Nichols, *Prostitution, Polygamy, and Power: Salt Lake City, 1847–1918* (2002), p. 14.

74. Gordon, *Mormon Question*, p. 55.

75. J. H. Beadle, *Life in Utah, or the Mysteries and Crimes of Mormonism* (1870), pp. 356, 357, 376.

76. J. W. Buel, *Mysteries and Miseries of America's Great Cities* (1883), p. 477. Buel accused the Mormons of even worse crimes. He gives an account of a woman named Mrs. Maxwell, who toyed with apostasy; she was found out, tortured, and murdered by an elder of the church with the approval of the church leadership. The elder who executed her stabbed her and virtually disemboweled her while she was still alive, "her screams of agony seeming to whet the elder's atrocious appetite." Buel, *Mysteries and Miseries*, p. 455.

The panic over the Mormons and their sexual proclivities has a certain resemblance to a common fantasy about black males, especially in the South: that these men were lustful, brutish, and that they were prone to ravish white women. This fantasy served as an ideological pillar of the dreadful epidemic of lynching that convulsed the South in the late nineteenth and early twentieth centuries. See Leon F. Litwack, *Trouble in Mind: Black Southerners in the Age of Jim Crow* (1998), pp. 280–312.

77. 12 Stat. 501 (act of July 1, 1862).

78. *Reynolds v. United States*, 98 U.S. 145 (1879). On the trial, see Gordon, *Mormon Question*, pp. 114–145. On Reynolds, see Bruce A. Van Orden, *George Reynolds: Secretary, Sacrificial Lamb and Seventy* (Ph.D. dissertation, Brigham Young University, 1986).

79. D'Emilio and Freedman, *Intimate Matters*, p. 162; see John C. Spurlock, *Free Love: Marriage and Middle-Class Radicalism in America, 1825–1860* (1988); and Hal. D. Sears, *The Sex Radicals: Free Love in High Victorian America* (1977).

80. McCabe, *Lights and Shadows of New York Life*, pp. 579–580.

81. Smith, *Sunshine and Shadow in New York*, p. 374. Junius Henri Browne, in *The Great Metropolis*, p. 436, quotes an estimate of 10,000 women in the city "who live directly and solely upon the wages of prostitution"; about twice as many more "lead unchaste lives, but preserve an outside show of respectability."

82. Sanger, *History of Prostitution*, pp. 584–585.

83. Sanger, *History of Prostitution*, pp. 566–573. Interestingly, Sanger was a bit squeamish about revealing these embarrassing facts, especially about the more luxurious houses. "It may be objected that the exposure of these mysteries imparts information which may lead the uninitiated into similar practices." But the information in his book was "not sufficiently definite for this end, and, certainly, nothing could be farther from the design of this work than to aid an immoral purpose" (p. 568).

84. Fernando Henriques, *Prostitution in Europe and the New World* (1963), p. 254.

85. Harrison, *Dark Angel*, pp. 217–218.

86. Christine Stansell, *City of Women: Sex and Class in New York, 1789–1860* (1987), p. 191.

87. *California Penal Code*, § 647(b). A person "agrees" to engage in prostitution when he or she "manifests an acceptance of an offer or solicitation to so engage."

88. *Illinois Revised Statutes 1845*, p. 174, § 127; identical language in, for example, *Colorado Revised Statutes 1877*, p. 296.

89. *Massachusetts Revised Statutes 1836*, ch. 143, §§ 5 and 6. I am indebted to George Fisher for this reference. See also *Connecticut General Statutes Annotated 1958*, § 53-235, which still contains a law against "common night-walkers," explicitly linked to "common prostitutes" and "lewd, wanton or lascivious persons" who "frequent the streets . . . or go . . . about with the intent to entice, allure or invite any one to sexual intercourse."

Interestingly, the term also still appears in the current Massachusetts statutes: "Common night walkers, common street walkers, both male and female, common railers and brawlers . . . [and] disturbers of the peace . . . may be punished by imprisonment in a jail or house of correction for not more than six months, or by a fine of not more than two hundred dollars, or by both." *Massachusetts General Laws Annotated*, ch. 272, § 53.

90. Daniel Davis, *A Practical Treatise upon the Authority and Duty of Justices of the Peace in Criminal Prosecutions* (1828), p. 260.

91. Savage, *Police Records and Recollections*, pp. 23, 106d.

92. Police Department, City of Boston, *A Record of the Enforcement of the Laws Against Sexual Immorality Since December 1, 1907* (n.d., perhaps 1913), pp. 9–10.

93. I am indebted to David Langum for this information on the history of the concept of night walking. The *New York Times*, October 21, 1856 (p. 1), reported that a "countryman" from Greene County complained that he was "fleeced" by a "female" who was a "Centre-street night-walker."

94. A St. Louis ordinance defined as a vagrant any "prostitute, courtesan, bawd or lewd woman, or any female inhabitant of any bawdy house . . . who shall be found wandering about the streets in the night time." *Revised Code of St. Louis 1907*, ch. 18, art. 6, § 1632(7), p. 896.

95. Police Department, City of Boston, *Record of the Enforcement of the Laws*, pp. 6–9. The report contains material also for years up to 1913; the general shape of the statistics is roughly similar, although arrests of common night walkers became more frequent. Presumably, men arrested in brothels got off with a fine in these later years, but the reports for those years do not say so explicitly.

96. For example, *Maine Revised Statutes 1903*, ch. 125, § 9, p. 931. In Maine, as elsewhere, prostitution itself was not criminalized; presumably the women were arrested on such charges as vagrancy.

97. *General Statutes of Massachusetts 1873*, ch. 87, § 6, p. 454.

98. *General Statutes of Massachusetts 1873*, ch. 165, § 2, p. 817.

99. The tenement house law is *Laws of New York 1901*, ch. 334, § 141, p. 920; see also *Criminal Procedure Code*, § 887; on the enforcement of the laws against prostitutes as vagrants and against the men who lived off their wages, see Research Committee of the Committee of Fourteen, *The Social Evil of New York City* (1910), pp. 70–77.

100. Friedman and Percival, *Roots of Justice*, p. 84.

101. *Report of the Major and Superintendent of the Metropolitan Police, District of Columbia, 1930*, p. 20; *Report of the Major and Superintendent of the Metropolitan Police, District of Columbia, 1929*, p. 20.

102. *People v. Cowie*, 34 N.Y. S. 888, 34 N.Y. Supp. 888 (1895).

103. *Laws of New York 1881*, ch. 187, p. 285. When the "house of refuge" was "ready for the reception of inmates," judges were authorized to commit "females, between the ages of fifteen and thirty years" who had been "convicted of petit larceny [*sic*], habitual drunkenness, of being common prostitutes, frequenters of disorderly houses or houses of prostitution" for a "term of not more than five years" (§ 8, p. 286).

104. Willoughby Cyrus Waterman, *Prostitution and Its Repression in New York City 1900–1931* (1932), pp. 12–13.

105. Mara L. Keire, "The Vice Trust: A Reinterpretation of the White Slavery Scare in the United States, 1907–1917," *Journal of Social History* 35 (2001): 5–41.

106. Ruth Rosen, *The Lost Sisterhood: Prostitution in America, 1900–1918* (1982), p. 78.

107. See Kevin J. Mumford, *Interzones: Black/White Sex Districts in Chicago and New York in the Early Twentieth Century* (1997).

108. Alexis de Tocqueville, that shrewd observer of the American scene, noted that there were in the United States "at the same time a great number of courtesans and a great many honest women." This "state of affairs" could lead to "deplorable individual wretchedness" but was no danger to the "body social," and it did not "weaken national morality. Society is endangered not by the great profligacy of a few but by the laxity of all. A lawgiver must fear prostitution much less than intrigues." Alexis de Tocqueville, *Democracy in America*, George Lawrence, trans., J. P. Mayer, ed. (1969), p. 598.

109. See Barbara M. Hobson, *Uneasy Virtue: The Politics of Prostitution and the American Reform Tradition* (1987), pp. 11, 23.

110. *Report of the Hartford Vice Commission, Hartford, Conn., July, 1913* (1913), p. 21.

111. *Report of the Little Rock Vice Commission, May 20, 1913* (1913), p. 10.

112. Craig L. Foster, "Tarnished Angels: Prostitution in Storyville, New Orleans, 1900–1910," *Louisiana History* 31 (4) (1990): 387–397.

113. Herbert Asbury, *Gem of the Prairie: An Informal History of the Chicago Underworld* (1986 [1940]), pp. 247–253.

114. Timothy J. Gilfoyle, *City of Eros: New York City, Prostitution, and the Commercialization of Sex, 1790–1920* (1992), p. 131. On prostitution in New York, see also Stansell, *City of Women*, pp. 171–192.

115. Pamela D. Arceneaux, "Guidebooks to Sin: The Blue Books of Storyville," *Louisiana History* 28 (1987): 397–405.

116. Asbury, *Gem of the Prairie*, p. 253. In return for the payments "the sisters were never molested and the name of the resort never appeared on any of the police lists of bawdy houses."

117. In 1836 Helen Jewett, a prostitute, was murdered in New York; her lover, Richard

Robinson, was put on trial for her murder. He was acquitted. The prosecution did not call as witnesses a number of men who frequented the brothel where Helen Jewett lived. They were "genteel men," and testimony might throw clouds around their "good name." Nor did any newspaper publish their names. Patricia Cline Cohen, *The Murder of Helen Jewett: The Life and Death of a Prostitute in Nineteenth-Century New York* (1998), pp. 322–323.

118. Joel Best, *Controlling Vice: Regulating Brothel Prostitution in St. Paul, 1865–1883* (1998), pp. 67–68.

119. Vice Commission of Chicago, *The Social Evil in Chicago* (1911), Appendix 21, p. 329.

120. Arceneaux, "Guidebooks to Sin," p. 397.

121. Best, *Controlling Vice*, pp. 59–60.

122. Best, *Controlling Vice*, pp. 24–25.

123. David J. Langum Sr., "James P. De Mattos: Feisty Frontier Lawyer and Politician Extraordinaire," *Western Legal History* 16 (2003): 21.

124. R. von Krafft-Ebing, *Psychopathia Sexualis* (English adaptation of the 12th German edition, 1906), p. 14. Krafft-Ebing, however, goes on to say that "Nevertheless, sexual consciousness is stronger in woman than in man. Her need of love is greater . . . but . . . is more spiritual than sensual."

125. Katherine Bement Davis, *Factors in the Sex Life of Twenty-Two Hundred Women* (1929), p. 74.

126. G. Frank Lydston, *Sex Hygiene for the Male and What to Say to the Boy* (1912), p. 35. Lydston, however, did denounce the "Lie of the Wild Oats," the "reef on which many a youth's life has been wrecked." G. Frank Lydston, *The Diseases of Society* (1906), p. 330; and Lydston, *Sex Hygiene*, p. 292.

127. Sanger, *History of Prostitution*, p. 489.

128. Sanger, *History of Prostitution*, p. 488.

129. Howard S. Gans, "Some Consequences of Unenforceable Legislation," *Proceedings of the Academy of Political Science in the City of New York*, 1 (1911): 568.

130. Harrison, *Dark Angel*, p. 264.

131. *Report on the Social Evil Conditions of Newark, New Jersey, to the People of Newark, 1913–1914*, pp. 154, 164–175.

132. Kathy Peiss, "'Charity Girls' and City Pleasures: Historical Notes on Working-Class Sexuality, 1880–1920," in Ellen Carol DuBois and Vicki L. Ruiz, *Unequal Sisters: A Multicultural Reader in U.S. Women's History* (1990), pp. 157, 162.

133. Frances Donovan, *The Woman Who Waits* (1920), p. 220.

134. David J. Pivar, *Purity and Hygiene: Women, Prostitution, and the "American Plan," 1900–1930* (2002), p. 45.

135. *Report of the Vice Commission of Minneapolis* (1911), p. 24.

136. Brenda Elaine Pillors, *The Criminalization of Prostitution in the United States: The Case of San Francisco, 1854–1919* (Ph.D. dissertation, University of California, Berkeley, 1982), pp. 148–152.

137. Friedman, *Crime and Punishment*, pp. 224–225; John C. Burnham, "Medical Inspection of Prostitutes in America in the Nineteenth Century: The St. Louis Experiment and Its Sequel," *Bulletin of the History of Medicine*, 45 (1971): 203.

138. *Report of the Vice Commission of Minneapolis*, pp. 51, 54. Examining just the woman, one doctor said, "is not fair." He also thought that examinations "usually result in graft."

139. Charles Loring Brace, *The Dangerous Classes of New York: And Twenty Years Work Among Them* (3rd ed., 1880), p. 126.

140. William McAdoo, *Guarding a Great City* (1906), pp. 72–73.

141. Marilynn Wood Hill, *Their Sisters' Keepers: Prostitution in New York City, 1830–1870* (1993), pp. 136–139.

142. Theodore A. Bingham, *The Girl That Disappears: The Real Facts About the White Slave Traffic* (1911), pp. 70–72.

143. In Madison, Wisconsin, in 1870 a brothel was raided and the resident "nymphs" were arrested; the customers went free. The legislature was in session, and one newspaper suggested sarcastically that the men had to be released "for fear one or both houses of the legislature would be without a quorum." Bonnio Ripp-Shucha, "'This Naughty, Naughty City': Prostitution in Eau Claire from the Frontier to the Progressive Era," *Wisconsin Magazine of History* 81 (1997): 45.

144. On this celebrated affair, see Fox, *Trials of Intimacy*. The most recent treatment is Debby Applegate, *The Most Famous Man in America: The Biography of Henry Ward Beecher* (2006); the Beecher-Tilton affair is treated at pp. 391–455.

CHAPTER 7

1. See, in general, on the growth of the franchise, Keyssar, *The Right to Vote*.

2. Friedman, *History of American Law*, pp. 279–280.

3. Lawrence M. Friedman, *American Law in the Twentieth Century* (2002), p. 476.

4. Lawrence M. Friedman, "Lexitainment: Legal Process as Theater," *De Paul Law Review* 50 (2000): 539–558; Stuart Banner, *The Death Penalty: An American History* (2002), pp. 24–52.

5. Banner, *Death Penalty*, p. 42.

6. On this development, see Friedman, *Crime and Punishment*, pp. 75–76, 168–171; and Banner, *Death Penalty*, pp. 144–161.

7. *Laws of Minnesota 1889*, ch. 20; John D. Bessler, *Death in the Dark: Midnight Executions in America* (1997), pp. 98–99.

8. *Louisiana Revised Statutes 1856*, pp. 53–54, §§ 28 and 29.

9. See, for example, *Abrams v. United States*, 250 U.S. 616 (1919); the subject is discussed in Richard Polenberg, *Fighting Faiths: The Abrams Case, the Supreme Court, and Free Speech* (1987).

10. Upheld by the United States Supreme Court in *Whitney v. California*, 274 U.S. 359 (1927).

11. For example, § 130 of the German Penal Code, among other things, makes it a

crime (*Volksverhetzung*) to "incite hatred against a portion of the population" or to attack the "human dignity" (*Menschenwürde*) of some portion of the population by insulting or defaming them in such a way as to disturb the peace. Similar provisions appear in other European penal codes.

12. There is a huge literature on the history of obscenity. For the United States, see, among others, Felice Flanery Lewis, *Literature, Obscenity, and Law* (1976); for England, see Alan Travis, *Bound and Gagged: A Secret History of Obscenity in Britain* (2000); and Norman St. John-Stevas, *Obscenity and the Law* (1956).

13. See the discussion in Chapter 3.

14. Henry Ward Beecher, *Twelve Lectures to Young Men on Various Important Subjects* (rev. ed., 1890), p. 155.

15. Manchester, "History of the Crime of Obscene Libel," pp. 36, 43.

16. *Commonwealth v. Sharpless*, 2 Serg. & Rawle 91 (1815).

17. *Commonwealth v. Holmes*, 17 Mass. 336 (1821).

18. On this point, see Friedman, *Crime and Punishment*, pp. 63–65.

19. These statutes are *Florida Revised Statutes 1892*, Title 2, ch. 7, § 2620, p. 823; *Indiana Revised Statutes 1852*, v. 2, p. 441; and *Kentucky Statutes 1894*, § 1351, p. 535.

20. This was part of a general "act to provide revenue from imports," 5 Stats. 548, 566–567 (act of August 30, 1842), § 28: "The importation of all indecent and obscene prints, paintings, lithographs, engravings, and transparencies is hereby prohibited."

21. *United States v. Three Cases of Toys*, 28 Fed. Cas. 112 (D. C. S. D. N.Y., 1843); Dennis, "Obscenity Regulation," pp. 139–140.

22. Dennis, "Obscenity Regulation," pp. 144–145. Dennis's dissertation treats the whole subject of obscene literature and the legal reaction to it in detail.

23. April Haynes, "The Trials of Frederick Hollick: Obscenity, Sex Education, and Medical Democracy in the Antebellum United States," *Journal of the History of Sexuality* 12 (2003): 43.

24. Dennis, "Obscenity Regulation," discusses the conflict between federal and state regulation of obscenity.

25. Donna Dennis, "Obscenity Law and the Conditions of Freedom in the Nineteenth-Century United States," *Law and Social Inquiry* 27 (2002): 385.

26. 13 Stats. 504, 507 (act of March 3, 1865).

27. The statute is 17 Stats. 598 (act of March 3, 1873). See Gaines M. Foster, *Moral Reconstruction: Christian Lobbyists and the Federal Legislation of Morality, 1865–1920* (2002), pp. 48–54.

28. A Nebraska statute of 1887 (*Laws of Nebraska 1887*, ch. 113, § 3, p. 672), made it a crime to advertise any "medicine, drug, nostrum, or apparatus" that claimed to treat or cure "venereal diseases."

29. On Comstock, see Nicola Beisel, *Imperiled Innocents: Anthony Comstock and Family Reproduction in Victorian America* (1997); James A. Morone, *Hellfire Nation: The Politics of Sin in American History* (2003), pp. 228–241.

30. Morone, *Hellfire Nation*, p. 249.

31. Andrea Tone, *Devices and Desires: A History of Contraceptives in America* (2001), p. 25.

32. Tone, *Devices and Desires*, p. 30.

33. *Dunlop v. United States*, 165 U.S. 486 (1897).

34. *Dunlop v. United States*, at 500.

35. See Chapter 4.

36. Anthony Comstock, *Traps for the Young*, Robert Bremner, ed. (1967 [1883]), p. 14.

37. Comstock, *Traps for the Young*, pp. 7, 12–13, 47.

38. See, for example, Frances Fenton, *The Influence of Newspaper Presentations upon the Growth of Crime and Other Anti-Social Activity* (1911).

39. Quoted in Fenton, *Influence of Newspaper Presentations*, p. 81.

40. *General Statutes of Kentucky 1887*, p. 467; *Laws of Kentucky 1894*, ch. 2, p. 3, § 2. A less sweeping statute, *Laws of Nebraska 1887*, ch. 113, § 4, p. 673, made it a crime to "sell, give away, or show to any minor child" any newspaper or magazine "principally made up of criminal news, police reports, or accounts of criminal deeds, or pictures and stories of immoral deeds, lust or crime"; but it was also forbidden to "exhibit" such books or pictures "upon any street or highway, or any place within the view, or which may be within the view of any minor child."

41. Comstock, *Traps for the Young*, pp. 170, 176.

42. On this point, see Beisel, *Imperiled Innocents*, p. 177.

43. Lydston, *Sex Hygiene for the Male*, p. 117. The "wrong kind of reading goes far in populating and supporting the brothel," according to Lydston. He also denounced "the yellow journal," which gives the impression "that sexual immorality in high places is smart," and the "degeneracy of the modern stage." But "the cheap dance hall" was perhaps the "most pernicious" institution of all, converting "a healthful and decent exercise" into an "orgie [*sic*] of sex debasement and drunkenness." (pp. 119, 120, 126).

44. *People v. Seltzer*, 122 Misc. 329, 203 N.Y. S. 809 (1924). In the case the name of the book is misspelled as "Cassanova's Homecoming."

45. *Commonwealth v. Friede*, 271 Mass. 318, 171 N. E. 472 (1930).

46. Paul S. Boyer, *Purity in Print* (1968), pp. 192–195.

47. See, for example, pp. 286 and 362 of Walter Kelly, ed., *Erotica* (1854). *Erotica* was a collection of what were then considered "erotic" classics, among them *Petronius Arbiter*.

48. Lewis, *Literature, Obscenity, and Law*, p. 30. A 1906 edition of Krafft-Ebing's *Psychopathia Sexualis* (New York: Rebman Company) suddenly lapses into Latin (on p. 176) in a description of the "terrible acts" a 49-year-old man had committed with two girls, ages 9 and 10.

49. "'Satyricon' Placed in Banton's Hands," *New York Times*, October 15, 1922.

50. 30 N.Y. Supp. 361 (S. Ct., N.Y. County, 1894).

51. Quoted in Nicholas J. Karolides, Margaret Bald, and Dawn B. Sova, *120 Banned Books* (2005), p. 356. For a discussion of the actions in the United States and England

against this novel, see Charles Rembar, *The End of Obscenity: The Trials of Lady Chatterley, Tropic of Cancer and Fanny Hill* (1969), pp. 59–160.

52. *New York Times*, June 22, 1922. The case, apparently unreported, was *United States v. Kidd* (1922); the quotes are from the *Times* and from Chafee, *Government and Mass Communications*, p. 251. A post office inspector who brought the charges (according to the *New York Times*) told the court that "posing as a high school student, he had entered into negotiations with the book company for the purchase of the unexpurgated edition."

53. "Boston Booksellers Fined," *New York Times*, December 12, 1903. Three of the "leading booksellers" of Boston were found guilty of possessing and selling "obscene literature," on the complaint of the Watch and Ward Society. They each paid a fine of $100. Boccaccio and Rabelais were among the books seized.

54. *New York Times*, December 12, 1903.

55. Many of these laws, along with laws of Australia and New Zealand among others, are set out in an appendix to Stevas, *Obscenity and the Law*, pp. 217–259.

56. Stevas, *Obscenity and the Law*, p. 183.

57. Quoted in Stevas, *Obscenity and the Law*, p. 89.

58. Stevas, *Obscenity and the Law*, p. 91.

59. *United States v. One Book Called "Ulysses,"* 5 F. Supp. 182 (D. C. S. D. N.Y., 1933). A few years later, an English edition finally appeared. In 1923 English customs seized a shipment of 500 copies and consigned them to the flames. Stevas, *Obscenity and the Law*, p. 96.

60. In a well-known passage, Woolsey wrote that the "dirty words" in the book were "old Saxon words known to almost all men and, I venture, to many women." These words would be "naturally and habitually used" by the people Joyce was describing. And, yes, the characters do seem to think a lot about sex, but, after all, the "locale was Celtic, and . . . [the] season spring."

61. *United States v. One Book Entitled Ulysses by James Joyce*, 72 F. 2d 705 (C. C. A., 2nd Circuit, 1934).

62. In Manton's view literature existed "for the sake of the people, to refresh the weary, to console the sad, to hearten the dull and downcast, to increase man's interest in the world, his joy of living, and his sympathy." This judge, however, later became notorious as one of the few federal judges to be exposed as corrupt. Manton took bribes in a number of cases. He was tried, convicted, and spent seventeen months in prison. See Gerald Gunther, *Learned Hand: The Man and the Judge* (1994), pp. 504–510.

63. "Obscene libel" had been an offense since the eighteenth century. Libel here refers, not to defamation, but to the literal meaning of the word—a little book. Manchester, "History of the Crime of Obscene Libel," p. 36.

64. Donald Thomas, *A Long Time Burning: The History of Literary Censorship in England* (1969), pp. 189–190. An obscene snuffbox also figured in *United States v. Three Cases of Toys*, 28 Fed. Cas. 112 (1843).

65. 20 & 21 Vict. ch. 83 (1857); see Colin Manchester, "Lord Campbell's Act: England's First Obscenity Statute," *Journal of Legal History* 9 (1988): 223–241. The act, as I said, did

not entirely come out of the blue. The Vagrancy Act of 1824 made it a summary offense to exhibit obscene prints, and the public display and hawking of obscene material was also an offense under the Metropolitan Police Act of 1839 and the Town Police Clauses Act of 1847. Lynda Nead, *Victorian Babylon: People, Streets and Images in Nineteenth-Century London* (2000), p. 192.

66. Quoted in Stevas, *Obscenity and the Law*, pp. 56–57.

67. Quoted in Nead, *Victorian Babylon*, p. 150.

68. Nead, *Victorian Babylon*, p. 189.

69. On obscenity enforcement in England, see, in general, Travis, *Bound and Gagged*.

70. *United States v. Bennet*, Fed. Cas. No. 14,571, 151 U.S. 29.

71. Raymond J. Haberski Jr., "Reel Life, Real Censorship," *Chicago History* 29(2) (Fall 2000): 7.

72. See, in general, Richard S. Randall, *Censorship of the Movies: The Social and Political Control of a Mass Medium* (1968); Steven Starker, *Evil Influences: Crusades Against the Mass Media* (1989), ch. 6; and Lee Grieveson, *Policing Cinema: Movies and Censorship in Early Twentieth-Century America* (2004).

73. Starr, *Creation of the Media*, pp. 303–304.

74. Bingham, *Girl That Disappears*, pp. 59–60.

75. Louise de Koven Bowen, *Safeguards for City Youth, At Work and At Play* (1914), p. 14; see Andrea Friedman, *Prurient Interests: Gender, Democracy, and Obscenity in New York City, 1909–1945* (2000), p. 30.

76. Bowen, *Safeguards for City Youth*, pp. 14, 15.

77. Grieveson, *Policing Cinema*, pp. 37–58.

78. Friedman, *Prurient Interests*, p. 30.

79. Quoted in Starker, *Evil Influences*, p. 96.

80. 239 Ill. 251, 87 N. E. 1011 (1909).

81. *Laws of Ohio 1913*, p. 399; *Mutual Film Corporation v. Ohio Industrial Commission*, 236 U.S. 230 (1915).

82. "Freedom of Speech and Boards of Censors for Motion Picture Shows," *Central Law Journal* 80 (April 1915): 307. The writer added that if someone "inculcates obscenity, anarchy or revolution by motion pictures," this is "something for the other senses than the intellectual sense, which the state in the interest of decency, order and government may regulate or suppress" (p. 308).

83. *Universal Film Manufacturing Co. v. Bell*, 100 Misc. 281, 167 N. Y. S. 124 (1917).

84. The court also argued that courts had no power to review the commissioner's decisions.

85. One of the few exceptions was *Message Photoplay Co. v. Bell*, 100 Misc. 267, 167 N.Y. S. 129 (1917), decided almost exactly at the same time as *Universal Film Manufacturing Co. v. Bell* and on the same general subject—a movie about birth control. In *Message Photoplay* the movie was called, in fact, *Birth Control*. The company asked for a temporary

injunction to restrain the commissioner from revoking the license of a the movie was to be produced. The court granted the injunction.

86. Henry James Forman, *Our Movie Made Children* (1933), pp. 141, 177.

87. Forman, *Our Movie Made Children*, pp. 217–218.

88. Forman, *Our Movie Made Children*, p. 232.

89. Julie A. Willett, "'The Prudes, the Public and the Motion Pictures': The Mov Censorship Campaign in St. Louis, 1913–1917," *Gateway Heritage* 15 (4) (1995): 42–55.

90. See, for example, Gerald R. Butters Jr., "*The Birth of a Nation* and the Kansas Board of Review of Motion Pictures: A Censorship Struggle," *Kansas History* 14 (1991): 2.

91. Dan Streible, "A History of the Boxing Film, 1894–1915: Social Control and Social Reform in the Progressive Era," *Film History* 3 (1989): 235–257. The quote is from p. 245.

92. See, for example, Shelley Stamp Lindsey, "'Oil upon the Flames of Vice': The Battle over White Slave Films in New York City," *Film History* 9 (1997): 351–364.

93. Starr, *Creation of the Media*, pp. 313–314.

94. Quoted in Lucius H. Cannon, *Motion Pictures: Laws, Ordinances and Regulation on Censorship, Minors, and Other Related Subjects* (1920), pp. 125–126.

95. Cannon, *Motion Pictures*, provides a list and the texts.

96. On movie censorship and the Hays office, see David A. Horowitz, "An Alliance of Convenience: Independent Exhibitors and Purity Crusaders Battle Hollywood, 1920–1940," *Historian* 59 (1997): 553. This was not the first attempt at self-regulation. In 1917 the National Board of Review, acting together with the National Association of the Motion Picture Industry, announced a ban on "undraped figures" in movies; the motion picture "should be in no sense an art pandering to lasciviousness and passion. It must not deliberately or even unintentionally cater to sensuality." (But the movies could aim to present "life as it is lived," even "dangerous relationships.") *New York Times*, January 22, 1917, p. 9.

97. H. L. Mencken, *The American Language* (abridged ed., 1963), p. 360.

98. John Springhall, "Censoring Hollywood: Moral Panic and Crime/Gangster Movies of the 1930s," *Journal of Popular Culture* 32 (1998): 142.

99. Quoted in Horowitz, "Alliance of Convenience," p. 567.

100. Frank Walsh, *Sin and Censorship: The Catholic Church and the Motion Picture Industry* (1996), p. 102.

101. D'Emilio and Freedman, *Intimate Matters*, p. 281. See, in general, Walsh, *Sin and Censorship*.

102. What made the trial of Lizzie Borden in the 1890s so sensational was the fact that Lizzie, an upper-class woman, unmarried, presumably chaste, a churchgoer, was accused of bashing in the heads of her father and stepmother—revealing, in short, a writhing nest of corruption underneath the bourgeois surface. Lizzie was, as we all know, acquitted, despite the fact that she was probably guilty. The jury no doubt thought that no woman of her class could possibly do such a thing. On the cultural meaning of the trial, see Cara Robertson, "Representing 'Miss Lizzie': Cultural Convictions in the Trial of Lizzie Borden," *Yale Journal of Law and the Humanities* 8 (1996): 351.

103. *Georgia Code 1882*, § 4372, p. 1149.

104. For example, in the sensational Rhinelander-Jones annulment case in 1925, the judge cleared the courtroom of women before allowing Rhinelander's love letters to be read. Lewis and Ardizzone, *Love on Trial*, pp. 140–141.

105. *New York Times*, September 4, 1913, p. 20. The girl, 18 years old, was charged with "impersonating a person of the opposite sex" but was released by the judge after a "lecture on deportment."

106. Eric Schaefer, "Resisting Refinement: The Exploitation Film and Self-Censorship," *Film History* 6 (1994): 295.

107. Jeffrey Richards, "The British Board of Film Censors and Content Control in the 1930s: Images of Britain," *Historical Journal of Film, Radio, and Television* 1 (1981): 109.

108. Scott Curtis, "The Taste of a Nation: Training the Senses and Sensibility of Cinema Audiences in Imperial Germany," *Film History* 6 (1994): 451.

109. Text from Albert Hellwig, *Lichtspielgesetz* (1921); I am indebted to Markus Wagner for this citation.

110. See Heidi Fehrenbach, "The Fight for the 'Christian West': German Film Control, the Churches, and the Reconstruction of Civil Society in the Early Bonn Republic," *German Studies Review* 19 (1991): 42.

111. Fehrenbach, "Fight for the 'Christian West,'" p. 47.

112. On the evolution and significance of burlesque, see Friedman, *Prurient Interests*, pp. 62–94. Burlesque shows included, in addition to the women who danced and sang, comedians who told racy jokes.

113. Needless to say, the modern editions of the OED have filled in the gap; both words now appear in their proper place in the alphabet.

114. Mencken, *American Language*, pp. 357–358.

115. Mencken, *American Language*, p. 357.

116. And in the august pages of the *New York Times* "four-letter words" never appear, even when they are relevant to a news story; the *Times* even avoids the word *shit* in favor of euphemisms.

117. Rembar, *End of Obscenity*, p. 385.

118. D'Emilio and Freedman, *Intimate Matters*, p. 158. To be sure, there were plenty of obscene books and postcards, and saloons "often had paintings of nude women" on their walls. (p. 132).

119. Lydston, *Diseases of Society*, p. 354.

120. "The present custom of association of husband and wife is pernicious. Personal privacy is impossible to married persons occupying the same sleeping apartment. . . . Too intimate association is a direct cause of sexual excesses." Lydston, *Sex Hygiene for the Male*, p. 133. Obviously, Lydston was thinking of people with money; for the poor, "personal privacy," if it meant a separate room for husband and wife, was out of the question.

121. Krafft-Ebing, *Psychopathia Sexualis*, p. 2. This is also, he thought, one reason that higher civilization is fostered by "frigid climes"; in these places one simply *has* to wear clothes.

122. Alfred C. Kinsey, Wardell B. Pomeroy, Clyde E. Martin et al., *Sexual Behavior in the Human Female* (1953), p. 365. Most men, especially upper-class men, preferred naked sex; and males "prefer to have intercourse in the light," whereas "more females prefer it in the dark." Alfred C. Kinsey, Wardell E. Pomeroy, and Clyde E. Martin, *Sexual Behavior in the Human Male* (1948), p. 581.

123. Harrison, *Dark Angel*, p. 171.

124. Jill Harsin, *Policing Prostitution in Nineteenth-Century Paris* (1985), p. 80.

125. Donna J. Guy, *Sex and Danger in Buenos Aires: Prostitution, Family, and Nation in Argentina* (1991), pp. 50–62; on the medical regulation of prostitutes in Rosario, see Maria Luisa Múgica, *Sexo Bajo Control* (2001).

126. Cristina Rivera-Garza, "The Criminalization of the Syphilitic Body: Prostitutes, Health Crimes, and Society in Mexico City, 1867–1930," in Ricardo D. Salvatore, Carlos Aguirre, and Gilbert M. Joseph, eds., *Crime and Punishment in Latin America* (2001), pp. 147, 150.

127. 27 & 28 Vict. ch. 85; the act was amended in 1866, 29 Vict. ch. 35.

128. For example, Portsmouth and parts of Plymouth. These acts were controversial, and after much agitation by both male and female groups they were suspended in the 1880s. For a discussion, see Judith R. Walkowitz, *Prostitution and Victorian Society: Women, Class, and the State* (1980).

129. Walkowitz, *Prostitution and Victorian Society*, p. 3. An "earlier attempt," she says, to examine the soldiers themselves "failed because enlisted men violently objected and officers feared that compulsory examination would lead to the demoralization of their men." Prostitutes were, however, powerless and were presumably already "bereft" of "self-respect."

130. Gary Mead, *The Doughboys: America and the First World War* (2000), pp. 199–202.

131. See Donald J. Rogers, *Banned! Book Censorship in the Schools* (1988).

132. *Cleveland v. LaFleur*, 414 U.S. 632, 94 S. Ct. 791 (1974). For an account of the case, including the views of Jo Carol LaFleur, see Peter Irons, *The Courage of Their Convictions* (1988), pp. 305–329.

133. The school board advanced another reason: to ensure continuity in the classroom. But, as the Court pointed out, the rule did exactly the opposite: It guaranteed discontinuity.

134. See, on this point, Irons, *Courage of Their Convictions*, p. 309. In addition, Mark Schinnerer, who actually wrote the regulations when he was school superintendent in Cleveland (at the time of the trial he was retired), explained that he was a "strong believer that young children ought to have the mother there" and that working mothers were a social problem (pp. 309–310).

135. On these cases, see Lawrence M. Friedman, "Limited Monarchy: The Rise and Fall of Student Rights," in David R. Kirp and Donald N. Jensen, eds., *School Days, Rule Days: The Legalization and Regulation of Education* (1986), pp. 244–245; *Davis v. Meek*,

462 Fed. 2d 960 (C. A. 5, 1972); and *Indiana High School Athletic Association v. Raike*, 329 N. E. 2d 66 (Ind. App., 1975). The students won both of these cases.

136. *Board of Directors of the Independent School District of Waterloo, Iowa v. Green*, 259 Iowa 1260, 147 N. W. 2d 854 (1967).

137. *Estay v. Lafourche Parish School Board*, 230 So. 2d 443 (La. App. 1969).

138. Roger Streitmatter, *Sex Sells! The Media's Journey from Repression to Obsession* (2004), p. ix. The characters on the program "had to limit themselves to facial expressions, hand gestures, and coded phrases when making reference to the wacky redhead's swollen stomach."

CHAPTER 8

1. Quoted in Hobson, *Uneasy Virtue*, p. 154.

2. Hobson, *Uneasy Virtue*, p. 155.

3. See, in general, Ysabel Rennie, *The Search for Criminal Man: A Conceptual History of the Dangerous Offender* (1978). Dugdale's book was *"The Jukes": A Study in Crime, Pauperism, Disease and Heredity* (1877).

4. The Juke clan was not clearly identified; modern research has discovered who the founders of the clan in fact were—and has cast considerable doubt on Dugdale's thesis. It seems that "many family members were neither criminals nor misfits, and that quite a few were even prominent members of . . . society." Scott Christianson, "Bad Seed or Bad Science?" *New York Times*, February 8, 2003, sec. B.

5. Oscar C. McCulloch, *The Tribe of Ishmael: A Study in Social Degradation* (4th ed., 1891), pp. 2–3. McCulloch drew a lesson from his study of these miserable beings: Get rid of "public relief" and "private benevolence." Charity and public relief only produce "stillborn children . . . prostitutes . . . criminals" (p. 7).

6. Henry M. Boies, *Prisoners and Paupers: A Study of the Abnormal Increase of Criminals, and the Public Burden of Pauperism in the United States; the Causes and Remedies* (1893), pp. 266, 279, 286.

7. On the eugenics movement, see Mark H. Haller, *Eugenics: Hereditarian Attitudes in American Thought* (1963); Edward J. Larson, *Sex, Race, and Science: Eugenics in the Deep South* (1995); and Christine Rose, *Preaching Eugenics: Religious Leaders and the American Eugenics Movement* (2004).

8. Friedman, *Private Lives*, pp. 51–54.

9. See Philip R. Reilly, *The Surgical Solution: A History of Involuntary Sterilization in the United States* (1991).

10. *Laws of Indiana 1907*, ch. 215.

11. *Laws of California 1909*, ch. 720, p. 1093.

12. *Buck v. Bell*, 274 U.S. 200 (1927). Sadly, it appears that Holmes had his facts all wrong. Neither mother nor child was actually feeble-minded (and certainly not "imbeciles"). See Paul A. Lombardo, "Three Generations, No Imbeciles: New Light on Buck v. Bell," *New York Law Review* 60 (1985): 30–62.

13. G. Frank Lydston, *The Blood of the Fathers: A Play in Four Acts* (1912), p. 241.

14. In case some of my readers are fans of Collins but have not yet read this novel, I will refrain from giving the novel's answer.

15. The Comstock law also made it a crime to transmit information about contraception, which was by definition dirty stuff. See Andrea Tone, "Black Market Birth Control: Contraceptive Entrepreneurship and Criminality in the Gilded Age," *Journal of American History*, 87 (2000): 435–459.

16. *Revised General Statutes of Florida, 1920*, p. 2647, § 5438.

17. *New York Penal Law*, § 1141, in Cahill's *Consolidated Laws of New York, 1923*, p. 1442. Section 1142 (p. 1443) prohibited the sale of any drug or device "for the prevention of conception, or for causing unlawful abortion."

18. Comstock, *Traps for the Young*, p. 244.

19. See the discussion in Chapter 7.

20. See, in general, Boyer, *Purity in Print*.

21. On the anti-abortion campaign, see James C. Mohr, *Abortion in America: The Origins and Evolution of National Policy* (1978).

22. *Connecticut Revised Statutes 1821*, Title 22, § 14, p. 152.

23. Mohr, *Abortion in America*, ch. 6.

24. McCabe, *Lights and Shadows of New York Life*, p. 627. McCabe refers to her simply as "Madame ——," but it is obvious to whom he is referring.

25. Clifford Browder, *The Wickedest Woman in New York: Madame Restell, the Abortionist* (1988), pp. 182–183. That title was also given to her by Junius Henri Browne, in *The Great Metropolis*, p. 582. Another account of this notorious woman is Allan Keller, *Scandalous Lady: The Life and Times of Madame Restell* (1981).

26. Research Committee of the Committee of Fourteen, *Social Evil of New York City*, p. 114.

27. Research Committee of the Committee of Fourteen, *Social Evil of New York City*, p. 105; on the campaign to license and control midwives in New York, see pp. 101–111 of this report.

28. Quoted in John Keown, *Abortion, Doctors and the Law: Some Aspects of the Legal Regulation of Abortion in England from 1803 to 1982* (1988), p. 46.

29. Research Committee of the Committee of Fourteen, *Social Evil of New York City*, p. 114.

30. Dr. J. Richardson Parke, writing in 1909, called abortion the most "cowardly and brutal form of murder, committed for the most selfish of motives." As far as "moral guilt is concerned," the women who have abortions "might just as well take the rosy, smiling babe from the cradle, and strangle it, as to swallow the potion that stills forever the tiny heart they can feel beating beneath their own." Parke puts some of the blame on the "luxury and idleness among the rich," their "sexual erotism [*sic*] and sensuality," and the "monstrous aversion to motherhood . . . so universally prevalent among women." Parke, *Human Sexuality*, pp. 170–171.

31. McCabe, *Lights and Shadows of New York Life*, p. 629.

32. George Ellington (pseud.), *The Women of New York, or the Under-World of the Great City* (1972 [1869]), p. 410.

33. *Laws of New York 1907*, Penal Law, §§ 100–103.

34. Research Committee of the Committee of Fourteen, *Social Evil of New York City*, p. 99. This report, however, suggests a pretty feeble enforcement effort—through December 1919 only forty-eight cases were tried; there were twelve convictions, but these represented only eight cases, because in four of them there were two defendants. Four of those convicted paid a rather small fine; in five cases the sentence was suspended, and only three defendants went to jail—two for ten days, and one for thirty days. Research Committee of the Committee of Fourteen, *Social Evil of New York City*, pp. 99–100.

35. For example, *Laws of Kansas 1887*, p. 214, made it a crime to "carnally" know any "female under the age of eighteen years."

36. On this movement, see Mary Odem, *Delinquent Daughters: Protecting and Policing Adolescent Female Sexuality in the United States, 1885–1920* (1995); and Stephen Robertson, *Crimes Against Children: Sexual Violence and Legal Culture in New York City, 1880–1960* (2005), pp. 95–115, 179–199. See also Jane E. Larson, "'Even a Worm Will Turn at Last': Rape Reform in Late Nineteenth-Century America," *Yale Journal of Law and the Humanities*, 9 (1997): 1–71.

37. See Ronald Hyam, *Empire and Sexuality: The British Experience* (1990), p. 157.

38. Judith R. Walkowitz, *City of Dreadful Delight: Narratives of Sexual Danger in Late-Victorian London* (1992), pp. 81–83.

39. Robertson, *Crimes Against Children*, p. 107. In prior times, Robertson points out, working-class families used such devices as bastardy laws or accusations of fornication to reach the same kind of result—that is, forcing men who had ruined their daughters to marry the girl.

40. Peter C. Hennigan, "Property War: Prostitution, Red Light Districts, and the Transformation of Public Nuisance Law in the Progressive Era," *Yale Journal of Law and the Humanities* 16 (2004): 159; Frederick K. Grittner, *White Slavery: Myth, Ideology, and American Law* (1990); Brian Donovan, *White Slave Crusades: Race, Gender, and Anti-Vice Activism, 1887–1917* (2006).

41. On the history of the Mann Act, the most complete treatment is Langum, *Crossing Over the Line*.

42. Research Committee of the Committee of Fourteen, *Social Evil of New York City*, p. 66. A cadet is "the procurer who keeps up the supply of women for immoral houses" (p. 60). New York enacted two laws specifically aimed at cadets. One law made it a crime for a man to prostitute his wife by forcing or tricking her into a brothel; another made it a crime to "place any female in the charge or custody of any other person for immoral purposes, or in a house of prostitution with intent that she shall live a life of prostitution." *Laws of New York 1906*, ch. 138, p. 259; ch. 413, p. 1007.

43. *Hoke v. United States*, 227 U.S. 308 (1913). The defendants, Effie Hoke and Basile Economides, were accused essentially of transporting a prostitute, Annette Baden, from New Orleans to Beaumont, Texas. On the case, see Langum, *Crossing Over the Line*, pp. 61–64. As Langum mentions, there had been serious doubts about the validity of the act: Was this within the power of Congress, under the interstate commerce clause? Justice McKenna, speaking for the court, gave a resounding yes. If Congress can shut out of interstate commerce the "demoralization of lotteries, the debasement of obscene literature, the contagion of diseased cattle," why not "the systematic enticement to and the enslavement in prostitution and debauchery of women."

44. See, for example, "Blackmail Rich Men by White Slave Act," *New York Times*, January 13, 1916, p. 1; see the discussion in Chapter 5.

45. Research Committee of the Committee of Fourteen, *Social Evil of New York City*, pp. 54–55. The legislature of New York state amended the New York City charter in 1909 to give it the right to license any "public dancing academy." No liquor was to be sold or given away in any such academy. *Laws of New York 1909*, ch. 400, adding to the New York City charter §§ 1488 to 1494.

46. Linda Mahood, *The Magdalenes: Prostitution in the Nineteenth Century* (1990), p. 152.

47. Friedman, *Crime and Punishment in American History*, pp. 328–332; Thomas C. Mackey, *Red Lights Out: A Legal History of Prostitution, Disorderly Houses, and Vice Districts, 1870–1917* (1987).

48. *Report of the Vice Commission of Minneapolis to His Honor, James C. Haynes, Mayor* (1911), p. 90.

49. Dr. Howard A. Kelly, *The Influence of Segregation upon Prostitution and the Public* (1912), p. 12.

50. The statement is to be found in Franklin Hichborn, *Story of the Session of the California Legislature of 1911* (1911), pp. 174–175.

51. *Report on the Social Evil Conditions of Newark, New Jersey*, p. 22.

52. *Report and Prospectus of the Pennsylvania Society for the Prevention of Social Disease* (1911), p. 6.

53. Quoted in Dr. Maude Glasgow, "On the Regulation of Prostitution, with Special Reference to Paragraph 79 of the Page Bill," *New York Medical Journal*, 92 (December 31, 1910): 1322. Dr. Glasgow was opposed to "regulation of the social evil . . . a measure essentially foreign in its aspects and a byproduct of old world opinions on the question of woman's inferiority to man" (p. 1320).

54. Max Gruber, *Die Prostitution vom Standpunkte der Sozialhygiene aus Betrachtet* (1900).

55. Lydston, *Diseases of Society*, pp. 320–321.

56. Abraham Flexner, *Prostitution in Europe* (1914), pp. 401–402. Flexner was hardly naive about the chances of ultimate victory. But the campaign could end streetwalking "of a provocative character," get rid of the worst brothels, and put pimps out of business.

This would result in "very important gains," even though it would not end prostitution completely (pp. 400–401).

57. Hennigan, "Property War," p. 123.

58. Hennigan, "Property War," pp. 166–167.

59. Rosen, *Lost Sisterhood*, p. 29.

60. Waterman, *Prostitution and Its Repression in New York City*, pp. 156–157. Waterman thought that an effective policy to get rid of, or reduce, prostitution had to be one that would "effect a reduction in the sources of supply and demand." That seems unlikely on both scores.

61. Hennigan, "Property War," p. 196.

62. Hennigan, "Property War," pp. 185–186.

63. *General Code of Ohio 1921*, § 13031-13, p. 5088, and § 13031-14, p. 5089. Lewdness was to be "construed to include any indecent or obscene act," and assignation meant "the making of any appointment or engagement for prostitution or lewdness or any act in furtherance of such appointment or engagement."

64. Bascom Johnson, "Law Enforcement Against Prostitution from the Point of View of the Public Official," *National Municipal Review* 9 (1920): 429.

65. Johnson, "Law Enforcement Against Prostitution," p. 429.

66. Lydston, *Sex Hygiene for the Male*, p. 33.

67. D'Emilio and Freedman, *Intimate Matters*, p. 204. See Allan M. Brandt, *No Magic Bullet: A Social History of Venereal Disease in the United States Since 1880* (1987).

68. There were objections to the play, and in general, conservative people treated the topic of venereal disease as "filth." A series of articles on these diseases in the *Ladies Home Journal* in 1906 led to a huge number of cancellations by shocked subscribers. D'Emilio and Freedman, *Intimate Matters*, p. 207.

69. Price A. Morrow, *New York Social Hygiene Society: Origin of the Movement—Its Objects, Aims and Methods of Work* (1906), p. 2.

70. *Damaged Goods* was the title of a British movie of 1919, one of a series of propaganda movies about venereal disease. George Dupont, about to be married, finds out he has syphilis as a result of sex with a prostitute. He goes to a quack, gets married, and his wife has a baby infected with syphilis. Annette Kuhn, *Cinema, Censorship and Sexuality, 1909–1925* (1988), p. 55.

In Charlotte Perkins Gilman's novel *The Crux*, published in 1911, Vivian Lane is warned by a woman doctor not to marry Morton Elder, despite her promise to marry him, because he is suffering from syphilis. Vivian protests: "He told me he had done wrong. He was honest about it," and, moreover, she loved him. Dr. Bellair asks, "Will you tell that to your crippled children? . . . Will they understand if they are idiots? Will they see if they are blind?" Vivian listens to the advice and painfully renounces her fiancé. "Wickedness could be forgiven; and she had forgiven him, royally. But wickedness was one thing, disease was another. Forgiveness was no cure." *The Crux* (2003 reprint), pp. 129, 138.

71. The antilottery law was 28 Stats. 963 (1895); it outlawed importing or mailing

"any paper, certificate, or instrument" that represented a "ticket, chance, share, or interest in or dependent upon the event of a lottery." The Supreme Court upheld the statute as a valid exercise of the power of Congress over interstate commerce in *Champion v. Ames*, 188 U.S. 321 (1903), although by a narrow five to four margin.

72. On the movement that led to Prohibition, see Richard F. Hamm, *Shaping the 18th Amendment: Temperance Reform, Legal Culture, and the Polity, 1880–1920* (1995).

73. These laws were 35 Stats. 614 (act of February 9, 1909) and 38 Stats. 785 (act of December 17, 1919). See David F. Musto, *The American Disease: Origins of Narcotics Control* (1973).

74. Troy Duster, *The Legislation of Morality: Law, Drugs, and Moral Judgment* (1970), p. 19.

75. Notably, Joseph Gusfield, *Symbolic Crusade: Status Politics and the American Temperance Movement* (1963).

76. See Andrew Gyory, *Closing the Gate: Race, Politics, and the Chinese Exclusion Act* (1998); see 27 Stats. 25 (act of May 5, 1892) and 32 Stats. 176 (act of April 29, 1902).

77. There is, of course, a huge literature on immigration; see, for example, Elliott Robert Barkan, *And Still They Come: Immigrants and American Society, 1920 to the 1990s* (1996).

78. See, for example, *People v. Wepplo*, 78 Cal. App. 2d. Supp. 949, 178 P. 2d 853 (1947).

79. On the Lady Chatterley case, see Lewis, *Literature, Obscenity, and Law*, pp. 200–207. The case is *Grove Press Inc. v. Christenberry*, 175 F. Supp. 488 (D. C. S. D. N.Y., 1959). Christenberry was the postmaster of New York.

80. *Grove Press Inc. v. Christenberry*, 276 F. 2d 433 (C. A. 2, 1960).

81. *Besig v. United States*, 208 F. 2d 142 (C. A. 9, 1953). *Tropic of Cancer* was published in 1934; *Tropic of Capricorn* in 1939.

82. "It is claimed," said the judge, " that these books . . . are not for the immature of mind" and that "adults read them for their literary and informative merits," but this was not the correct "yardstick." Congress, in enacting the obscenity statute, "probably saw the impracticability of preventing the use of the books by the young and the pure." Moreover, "salacious print in the hands of adults . . . may well incite to disgusting practices and to hideous crime." *Besig v. United States*, at 146.

83. Lewis, *Literature, Obscenity, and Law*, pp. 208–209.

84. Justice Frankfurter took no part in the deliberations. The New York courts had held that the book was obscene; because the Supreme Court could not reach a decision, the New York decision remained in force. *Doubleday & Co. v. New York*, 335 U.S. 848 (1948).

85. *Roth v. United States*, 354 U.S. 476 (1957).

86. See, for example, *Paris Adult Theatre I v. Slaton*, 413 U.S. 49 (1973).

87. *California Penal Code*, § 311. There are similar provisions with regard to any "obscene live conduct." Elaborate provisions, however, lay down much more stringent rules with regard to sexual material involving minors.

88. Langum, *Crossing Over the Line*, pp. 190–194.

89. Friedman, *Crime and Punishment in American History*, p. 343.

90. On these various developments, see Friedman, *American Law in the Twentieth Century*, pp. 231–237.

91. Tone, *Devices and Desires*, pp. 200, 203.

92. *Griswold v. Connecticut*, 381 U.S. 479 (1965); see John W. Johnson, *Griswold v. Connecticut: Birth Control and the Constitutional Right of Privacy* (2005).

93. *Eisenstadt v. Baird*, 405 U.S. 438 (1972).

94. *Roe v. Wade*, 410 U.S. 113 (1973). The literature on this case and the political reaction to it are simply enormous; see, for example, David J. Garrow, *Liberty and Sexuality: The Right to Privacy and the Making of Roe v. Wade* (1994).

95. One crucial case was *Planned Parenthood of Southeastern Pennsylvania v. Casey*, 505 U.S. 833 (1992). The Court here upheld a number of legislative restrictions on abortion rights, but not all of them; and a bare majority of the Court reaffirmed a commitment to keep *Roe v. Wade*. The justices appointed by President Clinton—Justices Breyer and Ginsburg—were prochoice. Those appointed by George W. Bush (Chief Justice Roberts and Samuel Alito) are thought to be in favor of getting rid of *Roe v. Wade*, but at this writing (2007) there are still five justices who clearly would vote to uphold the case.

96. *Marvin v. Marvin*, 18 Cal. 3d 660, 557 P. 2d 106, 134 Cal. R. 815 (1976).

97. Michele did not actually win in *Marvin v. Marvin*. The California Supreme Court reinstated her case, which the trial court had thrown out, and sent it back for trial. In the end, she recovered only a paltry amount. But the principle of the case had attracted nationwide attention and was widely (although not universally) followed in other states.

98. Pamela J. Smock and Wendy D. Manning, "Living Together Unmarried in the United States: Demographic Perspectives and Implications for Family Policy," *Law and Policy* 26 (2004): 89–90.

99. Kiernan, "Unmarried Cohabitation and Parenthood," pp. 33, 40, 43.

100. Harry Willekens, "Long Term Developments in Family Law in Western Europe: An Explanation," in John Eekelaar and Thandabantu Nhlapo, eds., *The Changing Family: International Perspectives on the Family and Family Law* (1998), p. 47.

101. Sexual Offences Act, 1967, ch. 60: Section 1 of the law provided that "a homosexual act in private shall not be an offence provided that the parties consent thereto and have attained the age of twenty-one years." In 1954 the British Parliament had named a committee, headed by John Wolfenden, to review the laws against homosexual behavior and prostitution. The Wolfenden Report, which came out in 1957, recommended almost unanimously that the law should no longer punish homosexual acts between consenting adults.

102. *Bowers v. Hardwick*, 478 U.S. 186 (1986).

103. *Powell v. State*, 270 Ga. 327, 510 S. E. 2d 18 (1998). In 1993 the Kentucky Supreme Court had done something quite similar. *Commonwealth v. Wasson*, 842 S. W. 2d 487 (Ky. S. Ct. 1993).

104. *Lawrence v. Texas*, 539 U.S. 558 (2003).

105. *Champion v. Ames*, 188 U.S. 321 (1903).

106. See Gilman M. Ostrander, *Nevada: The Great Rotten Borough, 1859–1964* (1966), on the rise of this black sheep among the states.

107. In 2006 Congress passed a law, the Unlawful Internet Gambling Enforcement Act of 2006, to curb gambling on the Internet. This was Title VIII of Pub. L. 109-347. This act was attached rather awkwardly to a long statute on security for ports.

108. Andrea Friedman, "'The Habitats of Sex-Crazed Perverts': Campaigns Against Burlesque in Depression-Era New York City," *Journal of the History of Sexuality* 7 (1996): 203–238.

109. Rodger Streitmatter, *Sex Sells!* p. 234. The passage on *Sex and the City* is on p. 199.

110. *American Booksellers Association v. Hudnut*, 771 F. 2d 323 (C. A. 7, 1985). The judge who wrote the opinion, Frank Easterbrook, conceded that very likely "depictions of subordination tend to perpetuate subordination." But this "simply demonstrates the power of pornography as speech."

111. Kinsey et al., *Sexual Behavior in the Human Male*; Kinsey et al., *Sexual Behavior in the Human Female*; see Julia C. Ericksen, *Kiss and Tell: Surveying Sex in the Twentieth Century* (1999), pp. 48–61.

112. This would not have been news to those few people who actually kept up with the literature. See, for example, the discussion in Davis, *Factors in the Sex Life of Twenty-Two Hundred Women*, pp. 91–94. The majority of the women in Davis's sample had practiced masturbation at some point in their lives (p. 97).

113. K. A. Cuordileone, "'Politics in an Age of Anxiety': Cold War Political Culture and the Crisis in American Masculinity, 1949–1960," *Journal of American History* 87 (2000): 515–545.

114. McLaren, *Sexual Blackmail*, p. 282.

115. Paul E. Fuller, "An Early Venture of Kentucky Women in Politics: The Breckenridge Congressional Campaign of 1894," *Filson Club History Quarterly* 224 (1989).

116. *New York Times*, August 13, 1922, p. 1.

117. *New York Times*, October 12, 1923; October 4, 1925, p. 3; January 15, 1926; May 30, 1929, p. 24.

118. *New York Times*, March 31, 1931, p. 33.

119. *New York Times*, April 21, 1915, p. 4. The contract promised her all sorts of things, including a home, a share of his estate, and the money to educate her children. In the same year the newspapers reported a suit by a widow, Mrs. Vivian Clark, with a 14-year-old daughter, against Albert Froelich, a wealthy broker, who had jilted her (she said) and married another woman. *New York Times*, June 30, 1915, p. 22.

120. *New York Times*, April 2, 1936, p. 26. Frederick had been foolish enough to write love letters to Mandel. After the verdict the trial judge threatened to set the verdict aside unless Mandel agreed to a reduction of the award to $150,000. *New York Times*, April 16, 1936, p. 5.

121. *O'Brien v. Manning*, 101 Misc. 126, 166 N.Y. Supp. 760 (1917).

122. On breach of promise actions, see Chapter 6; see also Grossberg, *Governing the Hearth*, pp. 33–63. For Canada, see Rosemary J. Coombe, "'The Most Disgusting, Disgraceful and Inequitous Proceeding in Our Law': The Action for Breach of Promise of Marriage in Nineteenth-Century Ontario," *University of Toronto Law Journal* 38 (1988): 64–108.

123. In England, as I noted, many plaintiffs had been lower middle class or working class. See Frost, "I Shall Not Sit Down and Crie," p. 225.

124. See Mary Coombs, "Agency and Partnership: A Study of Breach of Promise Plaintiffs," *Yale Journal of Law and Feminism* 2 (1989): 1–23.

125. Quoted in Steinbach, "Promises, Promises," p. 248.

126. Robert C. Brown, "Breach of Promise Suits," *University of Pennsylvania Law Review* 77 (1929): 497.

127. Harriet Spiller Daggett, *Legal Essays on Family Law* (1935), pp. 91–92.

128. Rosemary Coombe quotes a Canadian journal article from 1859: "Wounded love does not console itself with 'damages.' Marriage ought not to be where love is not." A woman who brings such an action (for breach of promise) proves that she was not really in love and hence not in a "moral condition to marry"; she is thus "entitled to no damages, for she has incurred none." Coombe, "The Most Disgusting, Disgraceful and Inequitous Proceeding," p. 68.

129. See, for example, Nathan P. Feinsinger, "Legislative Attack on 'Heart Balm,'" *Michigan Law Review* 33 (1935): 979–1009.

130. *Laws of Pennsylvania 1935*, no. 189, p. 450, abolished both breach of promise and alienation of affections.

131. *Laws of Illinois 1947*, p. 1181.

132. David Margolick, "Lawyer, Hereafter Broken Heart, Sues to Mend It," *New York Times*, September 11, 1992, p. B8. The plaintiff, Frank D. Zaffere III, a "corporate lawyer" in Chicago, had been engaged to a "hostess in an Italian restaurant." Zaffere claimed he still loved her and was still willing to marry her, under certain conditions.

133. "Aching Hearts Are Itching Palms, Says Woman Legislator as Men Gallantly Pass 'Love Bill,'" *Indianapolis News*, February 1, 1935, p. 1.

134. *Fearon v. Treanor*, 272 N.Y. 268, 5 N. E. 2d 815, 817 (1936).

135. M. B. W. Sinclair argues against overemphasizing the success of the campaign in the 1930s, which, after all, ended up by abolishing breach of promise and related actions only in about half a dozen states. But there was another wave of abolitions later; and all of these actions today are more or less gone or unused. Sinclair, "Seduction and the Myth of the Ideal Woman," *Law and Inequality* 5 (1987): 90–91.

136. Feinsinger, "Legislative Attack on 'Heart Balm,'" p. 979.

137. Not everybody felt that the campaign against heart balm lawsuits was justified. Breach of promise was vigorously defended by Frederick L. Kane, a professor at Fordham Law School, in "Heart Balm and Public Policy," *Fordham Law Review* 5 (1936): 63–72. Kane found the evidence of blackmail flimsy and thought that the "agitation" for heart

balm laws was only "one aspect of a movement to destroy the concept and ideal of marriage as an outmoded tradition."

138. *Los Angeles Times*, May 13, 1897, p. 3.

139. "Blackmail, Says Cameron," *Los Angeles Times*, May 29, 1921, p. 13; Blaine P.
Lamb, "'A Many Checkered Toga': Arizona Senator Ralph H. Cameron, 1921–1927," *Arizona and the West* 19 (1977): 53.

140. See Friedman, *Private Lives*, pp. 44–46.

141. For a detailed account of the case, see Dubler, "Wifely Behavior."

142. *Laws of Indiana 1935*, ch. 208, p. 1009. That this statute was concerned above all
with reputation is demonstrated by the rather remarkable provisions in §§ 4 and 5 of the
act, pp. 1010–1011. These provisions made it unlawful in a divorce or custody action to file
a pleading "naming or describing in such manner as to identify any person as co-respondent or participant in misconduct of the adverse party"; instead "general language" had
to be used. (The judge could, on petition, allow identification, at the judge's discretion.)
It was also unlawful to elicit the identification of the co-respondent through testimony
or cross-examination.

143. For example, North Dakota abolished breach of promise, alienation of affections, criminal conversation, and the action for seduction in 1983. *North Dakota Code
Annotated*, § 14.02.06.

144. See, for example, *Irwin v. Coluccio*, 32 Wash. App. 510, 648 P. 2d 458 (1982).

145. The earlier case was *Watkins v. Lord*, 31 Ida. 352, 171 P. 1133 (1918). In this case an
action was brought by Lemuel Watkins against Thomas Lord for "debauching" the plaintiff's wife. A jury awarded damages of $2,500, and the Idaho Supreme Court affirmed.

146. *Neal v. Neal*, 125 Ida. 617, 873 P. 2d. 874 (1994). The lower courts had dismissed
the case. The Supreme Court of Idaho basically agreed, but oddly enough, it did reverse
and send the case back to be tried on a different theory than the one Mary Neal had advanced. This was a somewhat far-fetched claim of battery. She claimed that when she had
sex with her lying, cheating husband, not knowing about his affair, her consent to the sex
was "ineffective"; she would not have consented to the sex had she known what he was up
to, and consequently he had committed battery on her.

147. *O'Neil v. Schuckardt*, 112 Ida. 472, 733 P. 2d 693 (1986). The action was brought
against officials of the wife's church, a fundamentalist group that had split off from the
Catholic Church, for destroying the marriage and proselytizing the children.

148. *Fundermann v. Mickelson*, 304 N. W. 2d 790 (Iowa, 1981).

149. Some litigants tried to get around the laws abolishing these actions, but they
were usually rebuffed. See, for example, *Cherepski v. Walker*, 323 Ark. 43, 913 S. W. 2d 761
(1996). Cherepski claimed that a Catholic priest, Father Walker, had had an adulterous
affair with his former wife. Among other things he sued for intentional infliction of emo-
tion distress, but the court said that his lawsuit was really a claim for alienation of affection and that the Arkansas Code had abolished this action.

150. *Oddo v. Presser*, 156 N. Car. App. 360, 581 S. E. 2d 123 (2003). The appeals court,

in its decision, thought that there should be a new trial on the issue of compensatory damages, but on this point the Supreme Court of North Carolina (358 N. Car. 128, 592 S. E. 2d 195 [2004]) disagreed.

151. Brode, *Courted and Abandoned*, p. 186.

152. Brode, *Courted and Abandoned*, pp. 188–189.

153. Law Reform (Miscellaneous Provision) Act, 1970, ch. 33, § 1.

154. Article 42 of the Spanish Civil Code begins with the words, "La promesa de matrimonio no produce obligación de contraerlo," and Article 43 simply states that if there is no reason for breaking off the contract (*incomplimiento sin causa*), there is only an obligation to reimburse for expenses and costs associated with the promised marriage.

155. See BverfGE 32, 296 (1972).

CHAPTER 9

1. Samuel D. Warren and Louis D. Brandeis, "The Right of Privacy," *Harvard Law Review* 4 (1890): 193–220.

2. The term *yellow journalism* was "coined by a hostile critic as a damning label for the kind of high-voltage paper" published by Joseph Pulitzer and William Randolph Hearst. The term referred to a character in a comic strip, "a street urchin in a yellow shirt known as the 'Yellow Kid.'" Starr, *Creation of the Media*, p. 258.

3. See Robert E. Mensel, "'Kodakers Lying in Wait': Amateur Photography and the Right of Privacy in New York, 1885–1915," *American Quarterly* 43 (1991): 24–45.

4. There has been a good deal of discussion about the underlying assumptions and the social meaning of this classic article by Warren and Brandeis. For one interesting take on the article, see Stacey Margolis, "The Public Life: The Discourse of Privacy in the Age of Celebrity," *Arizona Quarterly* 51 (2) (1995): 81–101; there is also a vast legal literature on the birth and early childhood of the new tort, for example, Diane L. Zimmerman, "Requiem for a Heavyweight: A Farewell to Warren and Brandeis's Privacy Tort," *Cornell Law Review* 68 (1983): 291–367.

5. Chapin, *Handbook of the Law of Torts*, p. 288.

6. *Roberson v. Rochester Folding Fox Co.*, 171 N.Y. 538, 64 N. E. 442 (1902). The court cited *Atkinson v. John E. Doherty & Co.*, 121 Mich. 372, 80 N. W. 385 (1899). The widow of Colonel John Atkinson, "a wellknown lawyer and politician," sued the defendant, a cigar maker, for marketing the "John Atkinson cigar" with "a label bearing that name and a likeness of Col. John Atkinson." The appeals court denied that she had a cause of action.

7. *Laws of New York 1903*, ch. 132. The aggrieved person could obtain an injunction "to prevent or restrain" the use of the picture or recover money damages.

8. See *Hillman v. Cherry*, 30 R.I. 13, 73 Atl. 97 (1909).

9. *Pavesich v. New England Life Insurance Co.*, 122 Ga. 190, 50 S. E. 68 (1905).

10. *Douglas v. Stokes*, 149 Ky. 506, 149 S. W. 849 (1912).

11. *Melvin v. Reid*, 121 Cal. App. 285, 297 Pac. 91 (1931).

12. The quote and many of the details that follow are taken from Alfred Cohn and

Joe Chisholm, *"Take the Witness!"* (1934), pp. 259–269, a book about the career of Earl Rogers.

13. Cohn and Chisholm, *"Take the Witness!"* p. 263.

14. The actual title of the movie is *The Red Kimona*, but the California court, in its decision, uses the more conventional spelling. The film is of some importance in the history of American cinema. Dorothy Reid, the producer, was also one of the directors. Most of the movie concerned Gabrielle's travails in the year or so after her trial, but this part of the film (I believe) was almost entirely fiction. In one of the opening scenes, however, we see what purports to be a newspaper column about her, which explicitly uses the name "Gabrielle Darley," and the movie certainly claims to be based on truth.

15. The movie, ironically, makes a similar point, is completely sympathetic to Gabrielle, and condemns the narrow-minded people in society who refused to allow her to rehabilitate herself. In the movie Gabrielle, destitute because her scarlet past meant that nobody was willing to give her a job, returns in despair to New Orleans, apparently to work once more as a prostitute. But she is (conveniently) hit by a car before she can begin a life of shame. She ends up in the hospital. When she recovers, she takes a job at the clinic and is scrubbing the floor diligently when Fred, a chauffeur whom we met earlier in the movie and who is in love with her, comes in by chance and finds her. He is in uniform (World War I has begun); but presumably when the war is over they will marry and lead a respectable life together as husband and wife.

16. According to one account, after the appeals court had ruled in her favor and sent the case down to be tried, she had the case dismissed, on her own motion, early in 1933. This might mean she settled out of court. Cohn and Chisholm, *"Take the Witness!"* p. 269. Other accounts insist the case bankrupted Dorothy Reid.

17. Leo W. Banks, "Murderous Madam," *Tucson Weekly*, June 5, 2000. Banks's account has a number of obvious errors—he refers to his heroine as "Gabriell Dardley" and renders Leonard's last name as Topp, rather than Tropp. But much of the rest of his tale rings true.

18. *Barber v. Time, Inc.*, 159 S. W. 2d 291 (Mo., 1942).

19. But there was no invasion of privacy if one simply described "the ordinary goings and comings of a person or of weddings, even though intended to be entirely private." Thus the emphasis was on some vague boundaries of decency.

20. *Daily Times Democrat v. Graham*, 276 Ala. 380, 162 So. 2d 474 (1964).

21. Theo Aronson, *The King in Love: Edward VII's Mistresses* (1988), pp. 259–265; Theo Lang, *The Darling Daisy Affair* (1966). On Daisy's life, see Margaret Blunden, *The Countess of Warwick* (1967).

22. Incredibly, out of 35,000 still photographs of Roosevelt at his presidential library, only two (which somehow managed to survive) show him sitting in a wheelchair. Hugh C. Gallagher, *Roosevelt's Splendid Deception* (1985).

23. See, on this point, Zimmerman, "Requiem for a Heavyweight," p. 291.

24. *Sidis v. F-R Publishing Company*, 113 F. 2d 806 (2d Cir., 1940).

25. Jared L. Manley, "Where Are They Now? April Fool!" *New Yorker*, August 14, 1937, pp. 22–26. "April Fool" refers to the fact that Sidis was, in fact, born on the first day of April.

26. *Sports Illustrated*, 34 (February 22, 1971): 72.

27. *Virgil v. Time Inc.*, 527 F. 2d 1122 (9th Cir., 1975); *Virgil v. Sports Illustrated*, 424 F. Supp. 1286 (S. D. Cal. 1976).

28. *Jones v. Herald Post Co.*, 230 Ky. 227, 18 S. W. 2d 962 (1929); see Louis Nizer, "The Right of Privacy: A Half Century's Developments," *Michigan Law Review* 39 (1941): 541. In the *Jones* case the plaintiff claimed that she never said the words attributed to her. But the story, said the court, was "complimentary"; it did not hold her up to "contempt, hatred, scorn, or ridicule by her friends and acquaintances, or the public in general."

29. *Hanrahan v. Horn*, 232 Kan. 531, 657 P. 2d 561 (1983).

30. In the fairly well-known case of *Sipple v. Chronicle Publishing Co.*, 154 Cal. App. 3rd 1040, 201 Cal. R. 665 (1984), Oliver Sipple, described in one article as a "husky ex-Marine," deflected a gun that Sarah Jane Moore had aimed at President Gerald Ford. The *Chronicle* story, praising him as a hero, also made it clear that Sipple was gay. Sipple sued, claiming his parents and siblings learned "for the first time of his homosexual orientation" and that this constituted an invasion of privacy. He lost the case. First of all, the court doubted that his sexual orientation was all that private, because he had marched in gay parades and so on. Also, the publication was "not motivated by a morbid and sensational prying" but rather by "legitimate political considerations." Indeed, the story helped "dispel the false public opinion that gays were timid, weak, and unheroic figures." Hence Sipple, his story, and his sexual orientation were of genuine public interest.

31. Tilman Hoppe, "Gewinnorientierte Persönlichkeitsverletzung in der europäischen Regenbogenpresse," *Zeitschrift für Europäisches Privatrecht* (2000), 39–50.

32. See Lawrence M. Friedman, *The Horizontal Society* (1999), pp. 27–43; and Richard Schickel, *Intimate Strangers: The Culture of Celebrity* (1985).

33. On this point there is general agreement; see, in general, Graeme Turner, *Understanding Celebrity* (2004).

34. See Friedman, *Republic of Choice*, ch. 7.

35. Celebrity culture would not have been "possible without television." Television brought "intimacy: we were able to see moving images and hear voices—in our own homes. . . . We saw people that were previously remote and perhaps unknowable as ordinary humans." Ellis Cashmore, *Celebrity/Culture* (2006), p. 38. Graeme Turner thinks we can "map the precise moment a public figure becomes a celebrity. It occurs at the point at which media interest in their activities is transferred from reporting on their public role . . . to investigating the details of their private lives." Turner, *Understanding Celebrity*, p. 8.

36. Robert Turnock, *Interpreting Diana: Television Audiences and the Death of a Princess* (2000), pp. 32, 34.

37. Diana Taylor, "Downloading Grief: Minority Populations Mourn Diana," in

Adrian Kear and Deborah Lynn Steinberg, eds., *Mourning Diana: Nation, Culture and the Performance of Grief* (1999), pp. 187–189.

38. Lawrence M. Friedman, "The One-Way Mirror: Law, Privacy, and the Media," *Washington University Law Quarterly* 82 (2004): 319–342.

39. On the tabloids, see S. Elizabeth Bird, *For Enquiring Minds: A Cultural Study of Supermarket Tabloids* (1992); on the relationship between these marvelous cultural icons and the regular media, see Richard L. Fox and Robert W. Van Sickel, *Tabloid Justice: Criminal Justice in an Age of Media Frenzy* (2001).

40. Robert N. Bellah, "The Meaning of Reputation in American Society," *California Law Review* 74 (1986): 747.

41. Neal Gabler, *Life, the Movie: How Entertainment Conquered Reality* (1998), p. 108.

42. The current Dalai Lama is supposed to be a reincarnation of the previous Dalai Lama. Historically, the Dalai Lama was a mysterious being who lived in a palace in Lhasa. The current Dalai Lama is—meaning no disrespect—a media star. His face is familiar, he publishes books, he travels, he gives lectures. The pope is also a media star. This was particularly true of the late John Paul II; but it seems clear that the pope, whatever his personality, is bound to be a star in this day and age. Yet the pope was once known as the "prisoner of the Vatican."

43. Jeffrey Rosen, *The Unwanted Gaze: The Destruction of Privacy in America* (2000), p. 201.

44. Stalking is a new crime. The first antistalking law was passed in California in 1990: California Penal Code, § 646.9 (stalking can also be the basis of a tort action, California Civil Code, § 1708.7). Within three years the whole country was blanketed with laws against stalking. The issue first arose in 1989, when a deranged fan, Robert Bardo, murdered a television actress, Rebecca Schaeffer. See Joel Best, *Random Violence: How We Talk About New Crimes and New Victims* (1990), pp. 48–54. The California law makes it a crime for anyone "wilfully, malicious and repeatedly" to follow or harass a person and to make "a credible threat with the intent to place that person in reasonable fear for his or her safety." See also, for example, *Florida Statutes*, ch. 784.048. In California it is also a misdemeanor to make "repeated telephone calls with the intent to annoy another person at his or her residence." California Penal Code, § 646.9(a).

45. The term *paparazzi* comes from Federico Fellini's great film, *La Dolce Vita*. In that film, "Paparazzo" was the name of a photographer. Vincent Canby, "Trailing the Photographers Who Follow the Famous," *New York Times*, July 1, 1992, p. C18.

46. On the incident, see "German Paper Prints Nude Charles Photo," *Rocky Mountain News* (Denver), September 8, 1994, p. A70.

47. "Tabloids Claim Duchess Sales Lift," *Financial Times*, August 22, 1992, p. 4.

48. On this point, see James Q. Whitman, "The Two Western Cultures of Privacy: Dignity Versus Liberty," *Yale Law Journal* 113 (2004): 101.

49. *Griswold v. Connecticut*, 381 U.S. 479 (1965); *Roe v. Wade*, 410 U.S. 113 (1973).

50. Lawrence M. Friedman, "The Eye That Never Sleeps: Privacy and Law in the Internet Era," *Tulsa Law Review,* 40 (2005): 561–578.

51. Barry Newman, "How Tools of War on Terror Ensnare Wanted Citizens," *Wall Street Journal,* October 31, 2005, p. 1.

52. Jeffrey Rosen, "Out of Context: The Purposes of Privacy," *Social Research* 68 (2001): 209–220.

53. Diana Crane, *Fashion and Its Social Agenda: Class, Gender, and Identity in Clothing* (2000), p. 47; Stuart M. Blumin, *The Emergence of the Middle Class: Social Experience in the American City, 1760–1900* (1989), pp. 140–143.

54. Quoted in Michael Zakim, *Ready-Made Democracy: A History of Men's Dress in the American Republic, 1760–1860* (2003), p. 206.

55. But some upper-class women "did not take imitation as flattery; they resented it." Stansell, *City of Women,* p. 165.

56. Mark Caldwell, *A Short History of Rudeness* (1999), pp. 66–68. Caldwell points out that jeans are not entirely classless—you can, if you want to, spend $1,000 on designer jeans.

57. Mary E. Braddon, *Aurora Floyd* (1984 [1863], p. 149).

58. Catherine A. MacKinnon, *Toward a Feminist Theory of the State* (1989), p, 191.

59. Judith Wagner DeCew, *In Pursuit of Privacy: Law, Ethics, and the Rise of Technology* (1997), p. 84.

60. *People v. Liberta,* 64 N.Y. 2d 152, 485 N.Y. S. 2d 207 (1984).

61. See, for example, California Penal Code, § 262.

62. *R. v. R.,* [1991] 4 All E. R. 481.

CHAPTER 10

1. Marc A. Franklin, "Winners and Losers and Why: A Study of Defamation Litigation," *American Bar Foundation Research Journal* (1980): 457–500.

2. Randall P. Bezanson, "The Libel Suit in Retrospect: What Plaintiffs Want and What Plaintiffs Get," *California Law Review* 74 (1986): 790–791.

3. Marc A. Franklin, "Suing Media for Libel: A Litigation Study," *American Bar Foundation Research Journal* (1981): 797.

4. Roselle L. Wissler, Randall P. Bezanson, Gilbert Cranberg et al., "Resolving Libel Disputes Out of Court: The Libel Dispute Resolution Program," in John Soloski and Randall P. Bezanson, eds., *Reforming Libel Law* (1992), pp. 296–299.

5. Bezanson, "Libel Suit in Retrospect," pp. 794–795.

6. Or a statute such as *New Hampshire Revised Statutes,* § 644.4, which makes it an offense (a breach of the peace) to utter "insults, taunts or challenges" when these are "likely to provoke a violent or disorderly response."

7. *Montana Code Annotated,* § 49-1-101; California Civil Code, § 43.

8. *Louisiana Revised Statutes,* § 4:10.3.

9. Jarecke and Plant, *Seeking Civility,* p. 126.

10. *Coquelet v. Union Hotel Co.*, 139 Md. 544, 115 A. 813 (1921).

11. *Revised Code of Washington*, § 9-58.110.

12. Sarah Kershaw, "A 1909 Washington State Law Shielding a Woman's Virtue Is Being Challenged," *New York Times*, January 26, 2005, p. A13.

13. On this point, see *Matherson v. Marchello*, 100 App. Div. 2d 233, 473 N.Y. S. 2d 988 (1984).

14. Rodney A. Smolla, *Law of Defamation* (2nd ed., 1999), v. 2, § 7.18.

15. *Thomason v. Times-Journal Inc.*, 190 Ga. App. 601, 379 S. E. 2d 551 (1989).

16. *Neiman-Marcus Co. v. Lait*, 107 F. Supp. 96 (S. D. N.Y. 1952).

17. See Elizabeth M. Koehler, "The Variable Nature of Defamation: Social Mores and Accusations of Homosexuality," *Journalism and Mass Communication Quarterly* 76 (1999): 217–228.

18. *Matherson v. Marchello*, 100 App. Div. 2d 233, 473 N.Y. S. 2d 988 (1984). The Good Rats also said that they "used to fool around with" Matherson's wife; she acted also as a plaintiff in the case. The lower court had dismissed her claim. The appeals court thought that the statement about fooling around could have "been interpreted . . . to mean that Mrs. Matherson was having an affair. . . . Such charges are clearly libelous." The case was reversed and sent back for trial.

19. See *Plumley v. Landmark Chevrolet*, 122 F. 3d 308 (C. A. 5, 1997). George Plumley sued the car dealer and its salesman, Hamilton. Plumley was buying a used truck and revealed that he was suffering from AIDS. Hamilton said, "We just don't want your business," and called him a "faggot." The court held that this was slander per se.

20. *Nazeri v. Missouri Valley College*, 860 S. W. 2d 303 (Mo., 1993). The court did point out that at the time "engaging in deviant sexual intercourse with another person of the same sex" was a crime in Missouri, which is, of course, no longer the case today.

Because same-sex behavior has been decriminalized, some courts believe that it is not "slander per se" to call someone homosexual. This *can* be slander, but the plaintiff has to show actual damages. *Hayes v. Smith*, 832 Pac. 2d 1022 (Colo., 1991): The "community view toward homosexuals is mixed"; *Donovan v. Fiumara*, 114 No. Car. App. 524, 442 S. E. 2d 575 (1994).

21. As I noted in Chapter 5, during the McCarthy period there was a panic over "perverts" in government, said to be vulnerable to blackmail. Foiling blackmail against public servants was indeed one of the arguments for getting rid of criminal sanctions against same-sex behavior. See, for example, on Canada, David Kimmel and Daniel J. Robinson, "Sex, Crime, Pathology: Homosexuality and Criminal Code Reform in Canada, 1949–1969," *Canadian Journal of Law and Society* 16 (2001): 154.

22. *New York Times v. Sullivan*, 376 U.S. 254 (1964).

23. See the discussion in Burdick, *Law of Torts* (4th ed.), pp. 383–397.

24. The Sedition Act of 1918 made it a crime to print or write "disloyal" language about the government, among other things. 40 Stats. 553 (act of May 16, 1918).

25. *Sillars v. Collier*, 151 Mass. 50, 23 N. E. 723 (1890); Francis M. Burdick, *The Law*

of Torts (3rd ed., 1913), p. 380. See the discussion in *Burt v. Advertiser Newspaper Company*, 154 Mass. 238, 28 N. E. 1 (1891).

26. *Brown v. Board of Education*, 347 U.S. 483 (1954).

27. *Curtis Pub. Co. v. Butts*, 388 U.S. 130 (1967). The second case, *Associated Press v. Walker*, was decided together with Butts.

28. No doubt this was a device to make it possible to pay such people as Butts way more than professors, deans, university presidents, Nobel Prize–winning doctors and physicists, and other employees of state universities who are apparently of much less value than football or basketball coaches.

29. *Curtis Pub. Co. v. Butts*, 388 U.S., at 163–164.

30. *Gertz v. Welch*, 418 U.S. 323 (1974). This was a five to four decision; the dissenters in general thought that free speech, freedom of the press, and vigorous debate on subjects of public interest should proceed free, as much as possible, from the stifling effects of possible defamation actions. For a discussion of the background of the case, see Irons, *Courage of Their Convictions*, pp. 331–354.

31. 472 U.S. 749 (1984). There was no real majority here. There was a three-person plurality opinion, two concurrences, and a four-person dissent. The dissenters would have applied the *Gertz* rule to the case.

32. Rosenberg, *Protecting the Best Men*, p. 254. One commentator saw a distinction between the "social or political function" of speech, which the Court is eager to protect, and "the individual function of personal happiness," where the "claims of the right to privacy usually are seen as stronger than those of expression." Gary Kebbel, "The Different Functions of Speech in Defamation and Privacy Cases," *Journalism Quarterly* 64 (1984): 743.

33. *Hutchinson v. Proxmire*, 443 U.S. 111 (1979).

34. *Quincy Wilson v. Daily Gazette Company*, 214 W. Va. 208, 588 S. E. 2d 197 (2003).

35. In *Franklin v. Benevolent and Protective Order of Elks*, 97 Cal. App. 3d 915, 159 Cal. Rptr. 131 (1979), the plaintiff, Virginia Franklin, was a high school teacher in a public high school. She was involved in a fuss over a supplementary textbook she used. The Elks (through an "Americanism Committee") denounced her in materials sent to the national organization; the materials claimed that she had been fired from one school district and that sixty-two others had refused to hire her. (She was also accused of being a "director of the Northern California Civil Liberties Union," apparently a heinous offense in the eyes of the Elks.) She sued for libel. The court held that a public schoolteacher was not an official under *New York Times v. Sullivan* and that she was also not a public figure; she could therefore sue for libel without showing actual malice.

36. *Neff v. Time Inc.*, 406 F. Supp. 858 (W. D. Pa., 1976). The court did admit that the publication was "in utmost bad taste."

37. *Doe v. Berkeley Publishers*, 496 S. E. 2d 636 (S. C. 1998).

38. *Lee v. Penthouse International Ltd.*, 25 Media L. Rep (BNA) 1651 (C. D. Cal. 1997). The couple had, one must admit, a fairly weak case, because French and Danish editions of *Penthouse* and *Screw* magazine had already published the photos.

39. In one interesting case, Gwen Davis Mitchell wrote a novel, called *Touching*, about a nude encounter group session led by "Dr. Simon Herford, M.D." Mitchell had actually attended such a session, which a clinical psychologist, Paul Bindrim, had conducted. Bindrim brought a lawsuit against Mitchell, claiming she had libeled him. He won his case. Readers, thought the court, might guess that "Herford" was actually Dr. Bindrim, and they might also think that he had been libeled. Rodney A. Smolla, in *Suing the Press* (1986), pp. 139–147, found this disquieting. Smolla felt, in general, that the legal system was too willing to "entertain libel actions based on novels, docudramas, and movies" in a way that threatened "to severely dampen the American capacity for self-criticism" (p. 158).

40. *Farnsworth v. Tribune Company*, 43 Ill. 2d 286, 253 N. E. 2d 408 (1969).

41. Spencer, "Criminal Libel," pp. 383, 389.

42. Harry Thompson, "Goldsmith Quelled by the Comedians," *Sunday Times*, August 3, 1997.

43. J. R. Spencer, "Criminal Libel: A Skeleton in the Cupboard (2)," *Criminal Law Review* (1977): 472, 473–474. An action for criminal libel survives in some European systems. In Italy, for example, libel by the press can be a crime under some circumstances. If the accusation "is related to the private life of the defamed," his or her sex life, for example, or if it is "expressed in a derogatory or insulting way," then truth is not necessarily a defense. Vincenzo Zeno-Zencovich, "Damage Awards in Defamation Cases: An Italian View," *International and Comparative Law Quarterly* 40 (1991): 693. This is another instance in which European countries show more sensitivity to personal privacy than the United States does.

44. Gregory C. Lisby, "No Place in the Law: The Ignominy of Criminal Libel in American Jurisprudence," *Communication Law and Policy* 9 (2004): 433–487.

45. *Garrison v. Louisiana*, 379 U.S. 64 (1964).

46. *Commonwealth v. Armao*, 446 Pa. 325, 286 A. 2d 626 (1972). An act of 1939 made it a misdemeanor to publish "any malicious or defamatory libel, tending . . . to blacken . . . the reputation of one who is alive, thereby exposing him to public hatred, contempt or ridicule." The statute did not say that truth was an absolute defense, which, in the view of the court, was fatal to its validity.

47. Occasionally, these statutes may have a flicker of life. In 2002 two men were charged in Kansas with criminal libel. By law the mayor of Kansas City was supposed to live in Wyandotte County; the defendants claimed that the mayor lived in another county. The defendants were convicted and fined. Lisby, "No Place in the Law."

48. Peter N. Amponsah, *Libel Law, Political Criticism, and Defamation of Public Figures: The United States, Europe, and Australia* (2004), p. 56.

49. *Lingens v. Austria*, 8 EHRR 407 (1986). The European court ordered the Austrian government to pay damages to Lingens.

50. *Castells v. Spain*, 14 EHRR 445 (1992). On this and the Lingens case, see Amponsah, *Libel Law*, pp. 90–94.

51. *Thorgeirson v. Iceland*, 14 EHRR 843 (1992).

52. See Pawel Lutomski, "Private Citizens and Public Discourse: Defamation Law as a Limit to the Right of Free Expression in the U.S. and Germany," *German Studies Review*, 24 (2001): 571–592.

53. *Entscheidungen des Bundesverfassungsgericht* 35, no. 16, p. 202 (1973); see Whitman, "Two Western Cultures of Privacy," for a general discussion.

54. Mark Landler, "Cannibal Wins Ban of Film in Germany," *New York Times*, March 4, 2006, p. B9. The case is subject to appeal. Meiwes had been sentenced to life in prison, although with the possibility of release after fifteen years. "Der Kannibale," *Frankfurter Rundschau*, May 23, 2006.

55. See Thomas Crampton, "Oops, Did It Again? An Irish Bill Seeks to Protect Personal Privacy," *New York Times*, October 2, 2006, p. C6. The case concerning Princess Caroline is *Von Hannover v. Germany*, 40 EHRR 1 (2005); and the date of the case was June 24, 2004. The public, said the court, "does not have a legitimate interest in . . . how she behaves generally in her private life," despite the fact that she is "well known to the public."

56. On a general directive of the European Union instructing member states to protect privacy rights, see Chapter 11.

57. Quoted in Douglas F. Harrison, "Canada," in Nick Braithwaite, ed., *The International Libel Handbook: A Practical Guide for Journalists* (1995), pp. 60, 69.

58. *Chappell v. TCN Channel Nine Pty. Ltd.*, 14 NSWLR 153 (1988).

59. Clifford Krause, "Campaign Rule 1: Be No More Virtuous Than the Voters," *New York Times*, October 25, 2005, p. A4. The candidate in question was Andre Boisclair.

60. Travis, *Bound and Gagged*, p. 272. See also Walter Kendrick, *The Secret Museum: Pornography in Modern Culture* (1987).

61. *A Book Named "John Cleland's Memoirs of a Woman of Pleasure" et al. v. Attorney General of Massachusetts*, 383 U.S. 413 (1966).

62. See the discussion of obscenity and censorship in Chapter 7.

63. *Ginzburg v. United States*, 383 U.S. 463 (1965).

64. *United States v. Rebhuhn*, 109 F. 2d 512 (C. A. 2, 1940).

65. *United States v. Rebhuhn*, 109 F. 2d 512 (C. A. 2, 1940).

66. See Jeff Deman, "Seven Dirty Words: Did They Help Define Indecency?" *Communications and the Law* 20 (1998): 39–52.

67. Rembar, *End of Obscenity*, p. 492.

68. Posner, "Blackmail, Privacy, and Freedom of Contract," p. 1841. But obviously, we have no reliable information on how rare or common blackmail has been. This is a crime that must have always been radically underreported. Posner found only 124 published blackmail cases. Newspaper accounts suggest that this might have been the tip of the iceberg.

Joseph Isenbergh is undoubtedly right when he says that blackmail is not a "major day-to-day concern of the criminal justice system. . . . For all I know, there may be *no one* in an American jail convicted of what might be called 'classical' or pure 'informational' blackmail." Isenbergh, "Blackmail from A to C," *University of Pennsylvania Law Review* 141 (1993): 1909.

69. *Annual Report of the Los Angeles Police Department, 1917–18*, p. 16; *Annual Report of the Police Department of the City of Los Angeles, 1921–22*, p. 46.

70. See the discussion in Chapter 5.

71. Benjamin Weiser, "Defense Lawyer Weighs Paternity Suit in Cosby Extortion Case," *New York Times*, July 28, 1997, p. B3.

72. *New York Times*, June 10, 1999, p. B1. Judge Amalya Kearse, who wrote the opinion, thought that the trial judge should have let the jury consider whether Autumn Jackson honestly thought she was Bill Cosby's daughter and had a legitimate claim against him. The instructions were in error. The judge believed, however, that with proper instructions a jury *could* have found her guilty. A true daughter would not have asked for such a huge amount of money.

73. *Los Angeles Times*, January 10, 1992.

74. *New York Times*, August 30, 1999, p. D11.

75. *Los Angeles Times*, April 3, 2001, p. B1.

76. In 1990 a "con artist" was convicted of trying to blackmail an "anchorwoman by asking for $30,000 to help block the publication of X-rated photos of her." He claimed that a "woman . . . planned to sell nude photos of the anchorwoman taken from a sexually explicit videotape to a national magazine" but that he could block the sale. The tape, in fact, "did not exist." *Los Angeles Times*, July 27, 1990, p. P8. In 2003 a "North Sacramento woman pleaded no contest to charges that she had tried to blackmail eight men into paying her about $500,000 so she wouldn't report that they had raped her—a charge she made up." *Los Angeles Times*, April 23, 2003, pt. 2, p. 7.

77. Gary T. Marx, "Fraudulent Identification and Biography," in *New Directions in the Study of Justice, Law, and Social Control* (School of Justice Studies, 1990), p. 143.

78. William Leach, *Land of Desire: Merchants, Power, and the Rise of a New American Culture* (1993), pp. 385–386.

79. Matt, *Keeping Up with the Joneses*, p. 78.

CHAPTER 11

1. For what it is worth, I report on my impressions from a nonrandom sample of applications to Stanford Law School that I have read in recent years. In their personal statements, people freely confess weaknesses; they admit to psychological failings, adopt postures of victimhood, talk about their illnesses, their personal tragedies, and on and on. My guess is that even as recently as a generation ago, applicants would not have dreamt of writing such things down. The applicants clearly think that their true confessions will help them, not hurt them. They are probably right.

2. To be sure, the traffic is not entirely one way. Voters today are fairly tolerant of candidates who have been divorced—Ronald Reagan, for example—or were hell-raisers as kids or are recovering alcoholics. They are more willing to accept candidates who are

Jewish or Catholic, black or Hispanic, and in some parts of the United States even candidates who are gay or lesbian. But a person who has no religion at all or who has said openly that he or she is an atheist would have a tough time getting elected almost everywhere in the United States.

3. Freedom of Information Act, 80 Stats. 250 (act of July 4, 1966).

4. On a program (September 27, 2001), which I watched strictly for research purposes of course, a young man announced that he was a male prostitute and had been on this job for years (it was fun and exciting, he said, and the money was good), but he had not bothered telling this to his live-in girlfriend—at least not before the show. The girl in question then appeared, learned her boyfriend's secret, and promptly gave him his walking papers while the studio audience whooped and hollered and clapped in delight at the spectacle. Millions more were watching the show at home, no doubt. Of course, the young man and his girlfriend might have been actors (on this point, see Joshua Gamson, *Freaks Talk Back: Tabloid Talk Shows and Sexual Nonconformity* [1998]) but they were *presented* as real people. In either case, they were enjoying their brief stint in the limelight.

5. *The Truman Show*, a successful American movie (Paramount Pictures, 1998) concerned a young man, Truman Burbank, who lived his whole life under the eyes of television cameras. What he thought was his world was actually a sham—a stage set. The people he met every day were, in fact, actors. Poor Truman was the only person who did not know this—or know that outside a huge audience was watching every aspect of his life. In the end Truman manages to break through to the real world. The movie is, of course, pure fantasy, but it skillfully plays on a number of contemporary themes: fears and anxieties about surveillance—and the powers and seductions of the world of the one-way mirror.

6. Brenna R. Kelly, "3 Neighbors Protest Tampa Voyeur Web Site," *Tampa Tribune*, March 12, 2001, p. 2.

7. Such people are affected by what Bromwich has called the mood of broadcast intimacy. The mass media, he believes, "have been so naturalized in the lives of many that they . . . confer on experience a reality it would otherwise lack." David Bromwich, "How Publicity Makes People Real," *Social Research* 68 (2001): 146.

8. David H. Flaherty, *Privacy in Colonial New England* (1972), p. 2. Flaherty's book is a valuable study of privacy in a premodern era and community.

9. Gary T. Marx, "What's in a Name? Some Reflections on the Sociology of Anonymity," *Information Society* 15 (1999): 104.

10. The driver's license, however, is evolving into a sort of identity card for many purposes; attitudes, in other words, may be changing.

11. Marx, "What's in a Name?" p. 104.

12. *Olmstead v. United States*, 277 U.S. 438 (1928). Holmes and Brandeis wrote dissenting opinions.

13. Federal Communications Act, 48 Stats. 1064, 1103–1104 (act of June 10, 1934).

14. *Katz v. United States*, 389 U.S. 347 (1967).

15. *Florida v. Riley*, 488 U.S. 445 (1989).

16. *California v. Greenwood*, 486 U.S. 35 (1988). Justice Brennan dissented. The police "clawed through the trash" that Greenwood had put in "opaque, sealed bags. . . . Complete strangers minutely scrutinized their bounty, undoubtedly dredging up intimate details of Greenwood's private life and habits." This, Brennan thought, was "contrary to commonly accepted notions of civilized behavior."

17. *Mapp v. Ohio*, 367 U.S. 643 (1961); on the background of this case and what happened afterward, see Carolyn N. Long, *Mapp v. Ohio: Guarding Against Unreasonable Searches and Seizures* (2006).

18. James Risen and Eric Lichtblau, "Bush Lets U.S. Spy on Callers Without Courts," *New York Times*, December 16, 2005, p. A1. This represented a "major shift in American intelligence-gathering practices, particularly for the National Security Agency."

Interestingly, Justice White, concurring in the *Katz* case many years before, had argued that no warrant should be needed "if the President of the United States or his chief legal officer, the Attorney General, has considered the requirements of national security and authorized electronic surveillance as reasonable."

19. Gary Marx, *Undercover: Police Surveillance in America* (1988), pp. 222–223.

20. *Candid Camera* began as early as 1948 and lasted into the 1990s. The hapless participants could refuse to allow the footage to be shown on TV, but apparently few ever did refuse. At one time the British and Australians had versions of this program. A more recent television program that is somewhat similar is *America's Funniest Home Videos*.

21. Marx, *Undercover*, p. 223.

22. Robert O'Harrow Jr., *No Place to Hide* (2005), pp. 284–285.

23. "At least in large cities, one enjoys the illusion, and to a large extent the reality, of being able to move about with anonymity. That freedom is soon to be a thing of the past . . . [by virtue of] the rapid spread of technology for routinely monitoring public spaces and identifying individuals." A. Michael Froomkin, "Cyberspace and Privacy: A New Legal Paradigm? The Death of Privacy," *Stanford Law Review* 52 (2000): 1476.

24. Marx, *Undercover*, p. 223.

25. *Laws of New Jersey 1994*, ch. 128, 133.

26. USA PATRIOT Act, 115 Stats. 272 (act of October 26, 2001).

27. O'Harrow, *No Place to Hide*, pp. 227–231.

28. "EU-Justizminister weiten Telefonüberwachung aus," available at http://www .dw-world.de/dw/article/0,2144,1911350,00.html (visited February 22, 2006). There were also rules about cell phones. Peter Schaar, the EU official in charge of privacy issues with regard to data, criticized the decision, but presumably to no avail.

29. Simson Garfinkel, *Database Nation: The Death of Privacy in the 21st Century* (2000). This book was written, of course, *before* the attack on the World Trade Center and the war on terror.

30. Quoted in Froomkin, "Cyberspace and Privacy," p. 1462.

31. John Gilliom, *Surveillance, Privacy, and the Law: Employee Drug Testing and the Politics of Social Control* (1994), p. 1.

32. Stephen Kinzer, "Chicago Moving to 'Smart' Surveillance Cameras," *New York Times*, September 21, 2004, p. A18.

33. Rosen, *Unwanted Gaze*, p. 57.

34. Quoted in Susan W. Brenner, "The Fourth Amendment in an Era of Ubiquitous Technology," *Mississippi Law Journal* 75 (2005): 48–49.

35. Peter Steiner, *New Yorker*, July 5, 1993, p. 61.

36. Clay Calvert, *Voyeur Nation: Media, Privacy, and Peering in Modern Culture* (2000), pp. 198–199.

37. *Boyles v. Kerr*, 855 S. W. 2d 593 (Tex., 1993). Kerr had sued for negligent infliction of emotional distress; the Supreme Court of Texas reversed on the grounds that there was no general duty not to inflict emotional distress negligently. But the Court obviously thought that Boyles's behavior was dastardly and deserved punishment; they sent the case back for a new trial, presumably on invasion of privacy grounds.

38. Daniel J. Solove, *The Digital Person: Technology and Privacy in the Information Age* (2004), pp. 68–69.

39. Health Insurance Portability and Accountability Act, 110 Stats. 1936 (act of August 21, 1996).

40. 118 Stats. 3999 (act of December 23, 2004); 18 U. S. C. § 1801.

41. "Move Over, Big Brother," *Economist*, December 4, 2004, pp. 31, 32.

42. The warrant is also to be "supported by Oath or affirmation, and particularly describing the place to be searched, and the persons or things to be seized."

43. The current answer, on the whole, is no, on the basis of the famous case of *Mapp v. Ohio*, 367 U.S. 643 (1961), discussed in Long, *Mapp v. Ohio*.

44. This is Directive 95/46/EC of the European Parliament and Council, October 24, 1995. However, Article 13 of the directive allows member states to "restrict the scope" of their obligations in the interests of "(a) national security; (b) defence; (c) public security; (d) the prevention, investigation, detection and prosecution of criminal offences, or of breaches of ethics for regulated professions; (e) an important economic or financial interest of a Member State or of the European Union." These and other loopholes seem to leave an enormous amount of room to wriggle out of the general requirements.

45. Solove, *Digital Person*, pp. 208–209.

INDEX

Abortion, 179–181, 182, 309*nn*25,30; *Roe v. Wade,* 198, 314*n*95

Adams, John, 57, 144

Addams, Jane, 176, 187

Adultery: changing laws on, 77–79, 182, 197, 287*nn*44,47,51; double standard on, 72–73, 119; as grounds for divorce, 95–96, 291*n*64

Advertising: in consumer society, 253, 254, 255; and early right-of-privacy actions, 215–216, 318*nn*6–7

African Americans: fantasy about sexuality of, 296*n*76; libel for claiming relationship to, 237–238; and miscegenation laws, 106, 286*n*35, 293*n*20; passing by, 73–77, 286*nn*35,41; and seduction laws, 106, 293*n*19

"African dip" statute, 236

Age of consent, 111, 182–183, 310*n*35

Alabama: breach of promise, 112; defamation per se, 53; seduction statute, 101

Alger, Horatio, Jr., 40, 279*n*58

Alien and Sedition Acts (1798–1801), 56–57. *See also* Sedition Act (1918)

Alienation of affections: relation to breach of promise, 117–120; decline of, 208, 209–210, 211, 316*n*130, 317*nn*147,149–150

Altman, Scott, 83

An American Tragedy (Dreiser), 151, 290*n*55

Ana Veronica (Wells), 153

Anderson, Pamela, 244, 324*n*38

Anonymity, 261–262, 269, 328*n*10, 329*n*23

Argentina, prostitution, 168–169

Arkansas: prostitution (Little Rock), 131; "services" doctrine in seduction cases, 103

Atkinson, John, 318*n*6

Aurora Floyd (Braddon), 233, 278*n*41

Australia, privacy of public figures, 248–249
Austria, criminal libel, 246–247
Authority, respect for: in Europe, 225; and social stability, 66

Bairnsfather, Bruce, 119–120
Bairnsfather, Cecilia, 119–120
Baldwin, E. J., 115
Ball, Lucille, 173, 308*n*138
Bankruptcy laws, 27–28, 276*n*21
Barber, Dorothy, 219, 221
Barber v. Time, Inc., 219, 319*n*19
Barnum, P. T., 58, 283*n*78
Barr, Harry, 291*n*67
Barr, May, 291*n*67
Barry, Joan, 197
Bartlett, Charles, 91
Beam, Mary, 114
Beaumont, Gustave de, 38
Beecher, Henry Ward, 7, 139, 144
Bellah, Robert, 16, 228
Bennett, John M., 114
Berkoff, Steven, 45
Bernard, Francis, 54
Berry, Mary Frances, 293*n*19
Bestiality, 13, 275*n*25
Bigamy: and changed nature of marriage, 29, 121; as crime of mobility, 29, 32–33, 98–99, 120–121, 278*nn*40–41, 291*n*71; and divorce, 295*n*69
Bigelow, Hobart, 84
Bindrim, Paul, 325*n*39
Bingham, Theodore A., 138
Birth control. *See* Contraception
Birth of a Nation, 160
Blackmail, 81–100; alleging homosexual behavior, 88–89, 90–91, 204, 239, 285–286, 288*n*23, 289*nn*24,38, 323*n*21; breach of promise and related actions as vehicles for, 207, 208, 209, 210;

British cases, 87–89, 288*n*23, 289*n*24, 289*n*38; in contemporary times, 252, 326*n*68, 327*nn*72,76; controversy over criminalizing, 81–84, 287*n*3, 288*nn*8,10; as crime of mobility, 31, 32, 33, 278*n*42; crimes of victims of, 96–97, 291*n*65; defined, 84–87, 288*n*8; function of laws against, 97–100; and gay rights movement, 204; laws criminalizing, 86–87, 289*nn*32,33; and Mann Act, 89–90, 185; protection of victims of, 10, 66; as theme in literature, 32, 33, 82, 88, 289*n*36; U.S. cases, 89–91, 290*n*48; by women, 91–96, 290*nn*55,57
Blacks. *See* African Americans
Blackstone, William, 53
Blackwell, Elizabeth, 64–65
Block v. City of Chicago, 158
The Blood of the Fathers (Lydston), 178
Boccaccio, Giovanni, 150, 151, 152
Boies, Henry M., 177
Boisclair, Andre, 326*n*59, 249
Borden, Lizzie, 305*n*102
Bork, Robert, 270
Boullemet, Stephen, 75
Bowen, Louise de Koven, 157
Bowers v. Hardwick, 200
Boyles, Dan, Jr., 269–270
Brace, Charles Loring, 137
Braddon, Mary: *Aurora Floyd*, 233, 278*n*41; *Lady Audley's Secret*, 32–33, 278*n*41
Brandau, John, 111–112
Brandeis, Louis D., 214, 215, 220, 243–244
Breach of promise, 111–117; damage awards, 115, 294*n*49; decline of, 205–209, 211–212, 315*nn*119–120, 316*nn*128,130,132,135,137, 317*n*143; foreign equivalents, 116–117, 212, 318*n*154;

literary sources on, 116, 295*n*54; men suing for, 111–112, 294*n*34; and seduction, 113–115, 294*n*44; and social class, 115–116, 206–207, 316*n*123; victims protected by, 10, 114–115; and virginity, 113, 294*n*41

Breckenridge, W. C. P., 205

Brennan, William, 198, 250, 329*m*6

Briggs, Lewis, 103

Briggs v. Evans, 103

Brinckerhoff, George, 147

Brockovich, Erin, 252

Brode, Patrick, 211

Brown, Grace, 290*n*55

Brown, J. Aldrich, 29–30

Brown, Oliver, 59

Buchanan, James, 246

Buck, Carrie, 178, 308*m*12

Buck v. Bell, 177–178, 308*m*12

Buel, J. W., 122

Burbank, Truman, 328*n*5

Burchill, Julie, 45

Burlesque, 164–165, 201, 306*m*112

Burr, Aaron, 9

Bush, George W., 263–264, 329*m*8

Butts, Wally, 241

Cahill, Sophia, 112

California: age of consent, 183; alienation of affections case (Los Angeles), 209; defamation statute, 236; extortion/ blackmail statute, 84–85, 290*n*48; murder trial of Clara Fallmer (Oakland), 108; obscenity law, 196, 313*n*87; prostitution, 127, 129, 131, 136; sterilization of prisoners, 177

Cameron, Ralph, 210

Caminetti, Drew, 90

Caminetti v. United States, 89–90

Campbell, John, 155

Canada: breach of promise, 111–112, 116, 211–212, 316*m*128; seduction law, 102–103, 211–212

Canby, Vincent, 321*n*45

Card, Maria, 119

Carney, Cornelia P., 295*n*56

Caroline, Princess of Monaco, 248, 326*n*55

Castells, Miguel, 247

Castells v. Spain, 247

Catholic Church, and movies, 162

Celebrity culture, 225–231; entertainment focus of, 230; gossip in, 259; mass media as creating, 225–226, 227, 233, 320*n*35; politics in, 228; public figures in, 242; stalking in, 229, 321*n*55

Censorship, 143–174; of alleged obscenity, 144–156; of books, 151–154, 155–156, 302*nn*47–48, 303*nn*52–53,59–60; elites exempt from, 150–151, 154, 302*n*43; of movies, 156–164, 249, 304*nn*82,84–85; political, 143–144; and pregnancy, 171–172, 173, 307*nn*133–134, 308*m*138; rationale for, 156; and social class, 164–165; society protected by, 149–150; and Victorian compromise, 148–149. *See also* Obscenity

Chafee, Zechariah, Jr., 48, 49, 58, 62

Chaplin, Charlie, 197

Chappell, Gregory, 248–249

Chappel, Ray, 96–97

Character: evidence regarding, 273*m*; reputation vs., 20, 46

Charity girls, 135–136

Charles, Prince of Wales, 229–230

Chastity, accusations of lack of, as defamation, 49–53

Chicago: movie censorship, 157–158; red-light district, 131, 132, 133, 298*m*116

Christie, Agatha, *Death in the Clouds,* 82, 287*n*6

Clap, William, 55

Clark, Vivian, 315*n*119

Class. *See* Social class

Cleland, John, *Fanny Hill,* 145, 166–167, 250

Cleveland v. LaFleur, 171–172, 307*nn*133–134

Clinton, Bill, 223, 230

Clothing, and American cultural classlessness, 232, 322*n*55

Coase, Ronald, 83

Cocks, H. G., 89

Cohabitation, 16, 78, 198–199, 204, 287*n*47, 314*n*97

Collier, Constance, 119–120

Collins, Willkie: *The Legacy of Cain,* 178, 309*n*14; *The Moonstone,* 33

Common law: age of consent at, 111, 182; and breach of promise, 116, 211; defamation law's origin in, 41–42, 43, 47, 61; and obscenity, 145; and right of privacy, 214, 215

Common law marriage, 109–111, 210

Commonwealth v. Bonner, 59–60

Commonwealth v. Clap, 55, 282*n*60

Commonwealth v. Holmes, 145

Commonwealth v. Sharpless, 145

Comstock, Anthony, 147–148, 150, 151, 179, 180; *Traps for the Young,* 149

Comstock Law, 147, 148, 309*n*15

Confidence men ("con men"), 30, 31, 277*nn*32,36

Connecticut: abortion law, 179–180; alienation of affections case, 119; contraception law, 197–198, 264; prostitution, 131; slander cases, 47

Consumer society, 253–255

Contraception: condemned, 181l; information about, as obscene, 155, 179, 192, 309*nn*15,17; movies about, 158–159, 304*n*85; in second half of twentieth century, 197–198

Coombe, Rosemary, 316*n*128

Coquelet, Henriette, 237

Coquelet, Henry, 237

Cosby, Bill, 82, 252, 327*n*72

Coverture, doctrine of, 23, 276*n*4

Cowie, Nellie, 129

Credit, and reputation, 7, 27, 277*n*23

Crimes of mobility, 29–33; bigamy as, 29, 32–33, 98–99, 120–121, 278*nn*40–41, 291*n*71; blackmail as, 31, 32, 33, 278*n*42; and confidence men, 30, 31, 277*nn*32,36; and detectives, 34; in England, 32

Criminal conversation, 117, 118, 119, 120, 295*n*63; decline of, 208, 210–211, 317*nn*142–143, 146

Criminal law, functions of, 12

Criminal Law Amendment Act (England), 183

Criminal syndicalism, 144, 300*n*10

The Crux (Gilman), 312*n*70

Culture: assumptions of, 13–14; classlessness of American, 232; legal, 5. *See also* Celebrity culture

Cupid and Psyche (Page), 167

Curtis, Mary, 92–93, 94

Daggett, Harriet Spiller, 207

Daily Times Democrat v. Graham, 220

Daisy, Lady Warwick, 222

Dalai Lama, 229, 321*n*42

Damaged Goods, 312*n*70

Darley, Gabrielle. *See* Melvin, Gabrielle Darley

Davidson, David, 209

Dayton, Cornelia, 47

Death in the Clouds (Christie), 82, 287*n*6

Death penalty, 142–143

Defamation: accusations of unchastity as, 49–53; change in, in contemporary times, 235–239, 322*n*6, 323*nn*18–20; in

colonial period, 47–48, 280*n*12; in
England vs. U.S., 48–49, 245, 246;
gender difference in cases of, 49, 52,
281*n*45, 281*35; and *New York Times
v. Sullivan,* 239–241, 242, 245, 246,
248; and public figures, 239–244,
242*nn*30–32,35,38; seditious libel as,
53–54, 282*nn*50–51; as tort, 3, 41; types
of, 41–42. *See also* Libel; Slander
Defamation, law of, 41–62; American
vs. European, 42–43; common law
origin of, 41–42, 43, 47, 61; knowledge
about, 43, 280*n*12; reputation
protected by, 3, 6, 43, 46, 49, 273*n*2.
See also Libel; Slander
Defence of the Realm Act (England), 222
De Mattos, James, 133
Democracy, American: fragility of, 37–
40; progress of, 140–143
Dennie, Joseph, 54
Detectives, 33, 34
Diana, Princess of Wales, 226–227, 229
Dickens, Charles, 31, 45, 155; *Pickwick
Papers,* 116
Dickenson, Hezekiah, 47
Diggs, Maury, 90
Divorce: adultery as grounds for, 95–
96, 291*n*64; and bigamy, 295*n*69;
blackmail in actions for, 290*n*48;
double standard in laws on, 72–73;
and ethos of second chances, 28
The Doctor's Dilemma (Shaw), 163
Domestic partnerships, 199–200, 202
Domestic violence, 69–71, 285*n*18
Double standard: in accusations of
sexual misconduct as defamation,
52–53, 281*n*47; in adultery laws,
72–73, 119; in alienation of affection
cases, 118–119; and censorship, 156;
in penal code, 65–66; of Victorian
compromise, 11–12, 66–67, 72–73, 79

Douglas, William O., 197–198, 250, 264
Dower, 285*n*12
Doyle, Arthur Conan, *A Study in Scarlet,*
33
Dreiser, Theodore, *An American Tragedy,*
151, 290*n*55
Drug laws, 190
Dubler, Ariela, 285*n*12
Dueling, 8, 9, 60–61, 236, 284*nn*85,89
Duffies, Frank W., 118
Dugdale, Richard L., 176, 308*n*4
Dun & Bradstreet v. Greenmoss, 242,
324*n*31
Dunlop, John R., 148
Dupree, James, 110
Dupree, Uriah, 110
Durkheim, Émile, 12
Durries, Frank W., 118

Easterbrook, Frank, 315*n*110
Economy: free market, 22–23;
individualism fostered by, 17–18;
and morality, 37; role of credit, 7, 27,
277*n*23
Education: censorship and prudery in,
171–173; individualism fostered by,
18–19, 275*n*32; sex, 202, 260; and
socialization, 14
Edward VII (king of England), 222
Edward VIII (king of England), 222
Eighteenth Amendment, 170, 190, 192
Eisenhower, Dwight D., 91
Eisenstadt v. Baird, 198
Electronic Communications Privacy Act,
270
The End of Obscenity (Rembar), 251–252
England: age of consent law, 183;
blackmail law and cases, 85–89,
288*n*23, 289*nn*24,32,38; breach of
promise, 111, 207, 212, 294*n*34,
316*n*123; criminal conversation, 117,

120; defamation in, vs. in U.S., 48–49, 245, 246; divorce law, 72, 291n64; homosexual behavior decriminalized, 200, 314n101; libel in movie review, 45–46, 280n23; movie censorship, 163, 249; obscenity laws, 144, 154–156, 303n65; privacy of royal family, 222, 223, 229–230; prostitution, 135, 169, 307nn128–129; seditious libel cases, 53, 282nn50–51; slander statute, 49; social class structure, 170–171; social mobility in, in nineteenth century, 24, 25, 31–32; truth as defense in libel cases, 55–56, 282n62; wife beating, 71
Equality. *See* Social class
Erlanger, Abraham Lincoln, 210
Etiquette books, information on norms in, 35–37
Eugenics movement, 176–178, 308nn4–5,12
Europe: censorship of books, 153; cohabitation, 199; criminal libel, 246–248, 326nn54–55; equality in, in nineteenth century, 24, 25, 26; offensive speech laws, 42, 274n6, 279n7, 300n11; right of privacy, 225, 230–231; technology and privacy protection, 271, 330n44. *See also specific countries*
European Court of Human Rights (ECHR), 246–247
Everleigh sisters, 131, 132, 298n116
Evidence, law of, and reputation, 273n1
Executions, 142–143
Expressive individualism, 16, 19
Extortion, 84–85

Fallmer, Clara, 108
Fanny Hill (Cleland), 145, 166–167, 250
Farnsworth, Myrtle, 245
Farnsworth v. Tribune Co., 245

Ferman, James, 249
Fixel-Erlanger, Charlotte, 210
Flexner, Abraham, 188, 311n56
Florida: cohabitation, 78; fornication and adultery laws, 78; obscenity law, 145, 179
Fontaine, Evan Burrows, 205–206
Foot, Enos, 119
Foot, Laura, 119
Fornication, 50, 77, 78, 197, 281n38, 287n47
Fountain, John Michael, 252
Fourth Amendment, 263, 270–271, 330n42
Fox, John, 51
France: blackmail statute, 87; cohabitation outside marriage, 16; extramarital affairs, 249; immorality of, 169; obscene literature, 144; prostitution, 168, 169–170
Franklin, Virginia, 324n35
Freedom of Information Act, 260
Freedom of speech: and defamation, 239, 240; first Supreme Court cases on, 144; and movie censorship, 158, 304n82; and obscenity, 194–196; and pornography, 202, 315n110
Free love movement, 13, 124
Freud, Sigmund, 65
Froelich, Albert, 315n119

Gabler, Neal, 228
Gambling, 200–201, 315n107. *See also* Lotteries
Garmong v. Henderson, 115
Gates, Ida, 51–52, 281n44
Gender differences: in ideal roles, 37, 108; in punishment for killing spouse, 71, 293n26; in sexual desire, 73, 134–135, 299nn124,126. *See also* Double standard

George IV (king of England), 53, 282*n*51

Georgia: antidueling laws, 9; blackmail statute, 86; common law marriage case, 110; libel for alleging black blood, 237–238; privacy case, 216; racial passing case, 75–76; seduction statute, 101–102; slander case, 50, 281*n*38; sodomy statute, 200

Germany: criminal libel, 247–248, 326*nn*54–55; *Kranzgeld*, 116–117, 212; laws protecting personal dignity, 42, 280*n*10; movie censorship, 163–164; naturist/nudist movement, 68; offensive speech laws, 6, 42, 300*n*11

Gertz, Elmer, 242, 324*n*30

Ghosts (Ibsen), 189, 312*n*68

Gilbert, William, *Trial by Jury*, 116, 295*n*54

Gillette, Chester, 290*n*55

Gilman, Charlotte Perkins, *The Crux*, 312*n*70

Gimbel, Frederick, 206, 315*n*120

Ginzburg v. United States, 250–251

Girz, Louis, 90

Goldsmith, James, 245

Goosha, Philip, 129

Gossip: celebrity, 5, 7, 43, 225, 227, 230, 259; and defamation, 43, 48; media publishing, 214, 222, 244

Gould, William, 107

Government: concern about invasion of privacy by, 231; economic responsibility of, 23; fragility of democratic, 37–40; seditious libel laws protecting, 53–54; technology laws of, 270; wiretapping by, 262–264, 328*n*12, 329*n*18

Graham, Billy, 204

Graham, Flora Bell, 220

Green, Anna Catherine, *The Leavenworth Case*, 33

Griffith-Jones, Mervyn, 152

Griswold v. Connecticut, 197–198, 264

Grove Press, 193, 313*n*79

Haines, William, 146

Hamilton, Alexander, 9, 60

Hamilton, Philip, 283*n*82

Hand, Augustus, 154

Hand, Learned, 251

The Hand That Rocks the Cradle, 158–159

Hanrahan, Jack, 224–225

Harrison Narcotic Drug Act, 190

Hays, Will, 161–162

Hays office, 161–162

Hayward, Caleb, 55

Healy, Michael, 74, 286*n*35

Healy, Patrick, 74

"Heart balm" lawsuits. *See* Alienation of affections; Breach of promise; Criminal conversation

Hebb, Ellen, 102–103

Hickey, Samantha, 248

Hickman, Daniel, 85–86

Hildreth, George, 112

Hindus, Michael, 286*n*23

Hobson, Barbara, 176

Hoke v. United States, 311*n*43

Hollick, Frederick, 146

Holmes, Oliver Wendell, Jr., 178, 308*n*12

Holt, Darwin, 46, 280*n*25

Holt, Francis, 41–42

Homosexuality: blackmail alleging, 88–89, 90–91, 204, 239, 288*n*23, 289*nn*24,38, 323*n*21; decriminalizing, 200, 314*nn*101,103; defamation for alleging, 238, 323*nn*18–20; and domestic partnerships, 199–200, 202; and right of privacy, 320*n*30. *See also* Sodomy

Honor: laws protecting personal, 42, 280*n*10; and males, 8–9, 108–109, 274*n*14; in modern world, 274*n*19

Hoover, J. Edgar, 197

Horton, Green, 106–107

Houghton, Walter, 16

Hudson, A. M., 50

Hutchinson, Ronald, 243

Ibsen, Henrik, *Ghosts,* 189, 312*n*68

Idaho: alienation of affections, 211,
    317*n*147; criminal conversation, 211,
    317*nn*145–146

Ideal: in gender roles, 37, 108; moderation
    as, 36–37, 63–64, 161, 257

Identity cards, 261, 328*n*10

Illinois: blackmail statute, 86; breach
    of promise, 208; libel laws, 58, 245,
    283*n*75; prostitution statute, 127;
    seduction statute, 101, 105

I Love Lucy, 173, 308*n*138

Immigration, 182, 191, 258

Incest, 52–53, 281*n*47

Indiana: antipornography ordinance
    (Indianapolis), 202, 315*n*110; breach of
    promise, 208; criminal conversation,
    210–211, 317*n*142; fornication laws, 78;
    incest case, 52–53, 281*n*47; obscenity
    statute, 145; prosecutions for sexual
    offenses, 285*n*14; slander statute, 51,
    281*n*39; sterilization mandate, 177

Individualism: and consumer society,
    254; expressive, 16, 19; in modern
    world, 17–19, 275*n*32; and religion, 256

The Inside of the White Slave Traffic, 160

Insults: dueling as response to, 8, 9, 60–
    61, 236, 284*nn*85,89; laws against, 6,
    42, 144, 274*nn*6–7, 279*nn*7–8. *See also*
    Defamation

Iowa: attitude toward married students,
    173; prostitution as nuisance, 188;
    study of libel plaintiffs, 235–236

Iredell, James, 57

Ireland, censorship, 153

Is Your Daughter Safe?, 163

Italy: defamation, 325*n*43; movie
    censorship, 164

Jackson, Autumn, 82, 252, 327*n*72

James Boys, 158

Jefferson, Thomas, 57

Jenks, Almet F., 94

Jewett, Helen, 298*n*117

Joans, Hugh, 77

John Caldigate (A. Trollope), 278*nn*40,42

Johnson, Bascom, 189

Jones, Alice Beatrice, 76, 306*n*104

Jones, Lillian, 224, 320*n*28

Jones, Thomas, 85, 224

Jordan, David Starr, 186–187

Joyce, James, *Ulysses,* 153–154, 156, 193,
    303*nn*59–60

Kane, Frederick L., 316*n*137

Kansas: age of consent, 310*n*35; criminal
    libel, 325*n*47; slander per se, 51

Katz v. United States, 263

Kearse, Amalya, 327*n*72

Keller, Wilhelmina, 295*n*63

Kelley, Howard, 186

Kendrick, Llewellyn Winthorpe, 88

Kennedy, John F., 139, 222

Kentucky: breach of promise case, 205;
    obscenity law, 145–146, 150, 302*n*40;
    privacy case, 216

Kerr, Susan Leigh, 269–270, 330*n*37

Key, Philip Barton, 108

Kinsey, Alfred, 168, 203, 307*n*122

Kohl-Welles, Jeanne E., 237

Krafft-Ebing, Richard von, 134, 167,
    306*n*121

Kranzgeld, 117, 212

Kroessin, Mary, 295*n*63

LaDue, Charles, 108

Lady Audley's Secret (Braddon), 32–33, 278*n*41

Lady Chatterley's Lover (Lawrence), 152, 193–194, 313*n*79

LaFleur, Jo Carol, 171–172

LaGasse, Jill, 211

Last Tango in Paris, 164

Latter Day Saints. *See* Mormons

Law of defamation. *See* Defamation, law of

Lawrence, D. H., *Lady Chatterley's Lover,* 152, 193–194, 313*n*79

The Leavenworth Case (Green), 33

Lee, Tommy, 244, 324*n*38

The Legacy of Cain (Collins), 178, 309*n*14

Legal culture, 5, 13–14

Legal system: as continually changing, 5; status quo guarded by, 2–3; suspicion of masses evident in, 142–143. *See also* Penal code

Levy, Ken, 83

Lewis, Evelina J., 50, 281*n*38

Libel: decline of actions for, 245–249, 325*nn*43,46–47; defined, 41–42, 43, 280*n*11; for excessive ridicule or abuse, 45–46, 280*nn*23,25; for imputing sexual misconduct by women, 51–52, 281*n*44; in nineteenth-century newspapers, 43–45, 280*n*17; obscene, 144, 283*n*81, 303*n*63; publication necessary for, 42, 279*n*6; seditious, 53–54, 56–57, 61, 66, 282*nn*50–51; and social class, 62; truth as defense in cases of, 54–60, 61–62. *See also* Defamation; Slander

Lindgren, James, 81, 82–83, 288*n*8

Lingens v. Austria, 246–247

Longworth, Maria Theresa, 32

Lord Campbell's Act (England), 155–156, 303*n*65

Lotteries, 39–40, 190, 200–201, 312*n*71

Louisiana: "African dip" statute, 236; criminal libel, 245–246; double standard in adultery laws, 72–73; married students, 173; privacy invasion by videotape, 269; racial passing case, 75

Lumpkins, Robert, 52–53

Lydston, Frank, 134, 167, 187–188, 306*n*120; *The Blood of the Fathers,* 178

MacKinnon, Catherine, 202, 233–234

Madel, Lilian, 206

Maine: alienation of affections case, 118, 119; libel laws, 57–58, 283*n*71; prostitution, 297*n*96

Mann Act, 89–90, 184–185, 196–197, 311*n*43. *See also* White slavery

Manners: of Americans in nineteenth century, 25, 28, 31, 38, 276*n*15; publications on, 35–37

Manning, John Bernard, 206

Manton, Martin, 154, 303*n*62

Market society, 7, 48

Marriage: changed nature of, and bigamy, 29, 121; cohabitation outside, 16, 78, 198–199, 204, 287*n*47, 314*n*97; common law, 109–111, 210; gay, 199–200, 202; miscegenation laws, 106, 286*n*35, 293*n*20; and seduction laws, 101, 105, 107; sexual relations within, 64–65, 306*n*120; women's property rights in, 23, 276*n*4

Married students, rules restricting, 171–172

Martineau, Harriet, 44–45

Marvin v. Marvin, 199, 314*n*97

Marx, Gary, 261, 264, 265

Masry, Ed, 252

Massachusetts: blackmail statute, 86; *Fanny Hill* obscenity case, 145; prostitution laws, 127–128, 297*n*89;

punishment for fornication, 77;
seditious libel, 54; seduction case, 105;
slander case, 47; truth and libel cases,
55, 59–60, 282*n*60

Mass media: celebrity culture created
by, 225–226, 227, 233, 320*n*35; and
privacy, 258–259, 260–261, 328*nn*4–
5,7; privacy invasions by, 214, 229–
230; and privacy of public figures, 221,
222–224; and right to know, 260; and
social change, 253

Masturbation, 64, 148, 203, 284*n*4,
315*n*112

Matrimonial Causes Act (England), 71, 72

McAdoo, William, 137

McCabe, James, 30, 91–92, 125, 181

McCarthy period, 91, 144, 202, 204,
323*n*21

McClellan, George, 157

McCulloch, Oscar, 176–177, 308*n*5

McFarlin, Edward, 210

McFarlin, Marjorie, 210

McGilvray, Duncan, 295*n*56

McLaren, Angus, 87–88, 89

McNabb, Ida May, 206, 315*n*119

Mead, Rena, 29

Media. *See* Mass media; Newspapers

Meiwes, Armin, 248

Melvin, Gabrielle Darley, 216–219, 220,
319*nn*15–17

Melvin v. Reid, 216–219, 221

Memoirs of Hecate County (Wilson), 195

Memoirs of a Woman of Pleasure
(Cleland), 145, 166–167, 250

Men: accusations of unchastity of, as
defamation, 51–52; breach of promise
actions by, 111–112, 294*n*34; honor of,
8–9, 108–109, 274*n*14; ideal role of,
37, 108; privacy and male supremacy,
233–234. *See also* Gender differences

Mencken, H. L., 162, 166

Mercantile Agency, 277*n*23

Merrill, Samuel, 57

Michigan: breach of promise and
seduction, 114; seduction case, 107

Miller, Henry: *Tropic of Cancer,* 194;
Tropic of Capricorn, 194

Minnesota: blackmail statute, 85;
criminal conversation case, 295*n*63;
double standard in adultery laws,
72–73; execution law, 143; libel laws,
58; prostitution in St. Paul, 132–133;
prostitution in Minneapolis, 136, 137;
red-light district (Minneapolis), 186

Mississippi, antidueling statute, 60, 61,
284*n*85

Missouri: adultery laws, 78, 79, 287*n*51;
brothel-licensing experiment
(St. Louis), 136; libel case against
newspaper, 44, 280*n*17; movie
censorship (St. Louis), 159

Mitchell, Gwen Davis, 325*n*39

Mobility: computerized records as threat
to, 264–265; and fragility of American
democracy, 37–40; geographic, in
nineteenth century, 23–24, 98; and
"passing," 73, 76–77; and reputation,
7; second chances, 28–29; social, in
nineteenth century, 24–26, 30–31, 98,
276*nn*14–15, 291*n*69. *See also* Crimes
of mobility

Moderation: as nineteenth-century ideal,
36–37, 63–64, 161, 257; in sexual
behavior, 11, 64–65; as societal value,
123, 156

Montana, defamation statute, 236

The Moonstone (Collins), 33

Moore, Leonard, 193–194

Moore, William, 154

Moral code: contemporary, 20;
nineteenth century, 17, 63, 272; and
status quo, 3, 12–13

Morality, movies as threat to, 156–157, 158, 159, 160–162. *See also* Prudery; Values

Mormons, and issues of polygamy, 13, 121–124, 275*n*26, 296*n*76

Morrill Act, 122, 123

Morrow, Kate, 107

Motion Pictures Producers and Distributors Association, 161–162

Movies: censorship of, 156–164, 249, 304*nn*82,84–85; defamation in, as libel, 42; self-regulation of, 161–162, 305*n*96

Mrs. Warren's Profession (Shaw), 156

Murder, and the "unwritten law," 107–109

"The Murders in the Rue Morgue" (Poe), 33

National Board of Censorship of Motion Pictures, 157

Nazeri, Janet, 238

Neal, Mary, 211

Neal, Thomas, 211

Nebraska: obscenity law, 301*n*28; slander, 51

Neff, John, 243, 324*n*36

Neiman-Marcus, 238

Nelson, George, 102

Nevada, punishment for wife beating, 71

Nevilles, W. A., 95

New Hampshire, defamation statute, 322*n*6

New Jersey: alienation of affections case, 119; libel laws, 58, 283*n*73; prostitution (Newark), 126; war against vice, 187

Newman, Mitchel, 85

New Orleans, prostitution, 126, 131, 132, 133

Newspapers: American, irresponsible behavior by, 44–45; and blackmail, 93, 94, 291*n*61; censorship of, 149–150; defamation actions against, 244–245; libel cases against, in nineteenth century, 43–46, 51–52, 280*nn*17,23,25, 281*n*44; yellow journalism by, 214, 318*n*2. *See also* Mass media

New York: abortion, 180, 181; adultery, 95–96, 182, 310*n*34; breach of promise, 113, 208–209, 294*n*43; disreputable pres (New York City), 43; movie censorship, 157, 158–159, 304*nn*84–85; obscenity law, 179, 309*n*17; pornography, 146, 147; privacy law, 215–216, 318*n*7; prostitution, 125–126, 128, 129–130, 131, 136, 296*n*81, 298*n*103; seduction law, 101, 102, 292*n*15; slander case, 50; unwritten law, 109; white slavery, 184–185, 310*n*42, 311*n*45; women at prizefights, 163, 306*n*105; Zbyszko libel case, 45–46

New York Times, words avoided in, 306*n*116

New York Times v. Sullivan, 239–241, 242, 245, 246, 248

Nicholson, Roberta West, 208

Night Riders, 158

Night-walkers, 127–128, 297*nn*89,93–5

Nineteenth century, 19–40; bankruptcy laws, 27–28, 276*n*21; determinants of social status in, 26–27; economy, 22–23, 27, 277*n*23; geographic mobility in, 23–24; social mobility in, 24–26, 276*nn*14–15; standards and norms, 257

Nisbett, Willie, 107

Norms: 1, 5; against snitching, 99–100; and etiquette books, 35–37; reputation determined by, 1–2; of respectability in nineteenth century, 36–37; sexual, and polygamy, 123–124

North Carolina: alienation of affections, 211, 317*n*150; cohabitation statute, 287*n*47; "services" doctrine in seduction case, 103; wife-beating case, 70–71

Nudity: and prudery, 167–168, 306*nn*120–121, 307*n*122; taboo against, 68

Nunez, James, 75–76

Nunez, Joseph, 75–76

O'Brien, Honora, 206–207

Obscene libel, 144, 283*n*81, 303*n*63

Obscenity: censorship of alleged, 144–156; discussion of sex as, 146; early prosecutions for, 144–145; English laws against, 144, 154–156, 303*n*65; and freedom of speech, 194–196; laws against, 145–146, 147–148, 150, 179, 301*nn*20,28, 302*n*40, 309*nn*15,17; Supreme Court decisions on, 249–251; twentieth-century cases and laws, 192–196, 313*nn*79,82,84,87; youth protected from, 150–151, 179

Oelkers, Louise, 95

O'Harrow, Robert, 265

Ohio: model red-light districts (Toledo, Cleveland), 138; movie censorship, 158; seduction statute, 292*n*2; slander statute, 51, 281*n*42

Oklahoma, blackmail statute, 85, 288*n*19

Olmstead v. United States, 262–263, 328*n*12

Olson, Arthur P., 112

Olson v. Saxton, 112

Opium Exclusion Act, 190

Oregon: breach of promise and seduction, 114; seduction case, 104; Tin Plate Ordinance (Portland), 188

The Origin of Life (Hollick), 146

Oxford Dictionary, words omitted from, 165, 306*n*113

Page, William, *Cupid and Psyche,* 167

Paparazzi, 229, 321*n*45

Parke, J. Richardson, 64, 309*n*30

Parker, Gilbert, 90–91

Passing, racial, 73–77, 286*nn*35,41

Patton, Mollie, 112

Pavesich, Paolo, 216

Pavesich v. New England Life Insurance Co., 216

Peck, John Weld, 152–153

"Peeping Tom society," 259, 269

Penal code: double standard in, 65–66; purposes of, 12–13, 79–80; unenforced, on sexual misbehavior, 68–69, 285*n*4

Pencille, William D., 95

Penguin Books, 152

Penitentiary system, nineteenth-century American, 38–39

Pennsylvania: bestiality definition, 275*n*25; breach of promise, 115, 316*n*130; criminal libel, 246, 325*n*46; movie censorship, 158; prostitution (Philadelphia), 126; prostitution regulation (Pittsburgh), 136; seditious libel, 53, 54

Pennsylvania Chautauqua Circle, 150

People v. Williams, 95

Perkins, Louise C., 115

Pickwick Papers (Dickens), 116

Pinkerton, Allan, 92–93, 94

Plumley, George, 323*n*19

Poe, Edgar Allan, "The Murders in the Rue Morgue," 33

Politics: celebrity culture in, 228; censorship in, 143–144; respectability redefined in, 327*n*2

Pollard, Madeleine, 205

Pollock, Alexander, 117–118

Pollock, Ellen, 117–118

Polygamy, 13, 121–124, 275*n*26, 296*n*76

Pornography: availability of, 69, 146, 149; in contemporary times, 251–252; and freedom of speech, 202, 315*n*110; prosecutions for, 146; in twentieth century, 192–196. *See also* Obscenity

Post, Robert, 6, 48–49

Poverty, nineteenth-century American view of, 39

Pregnancy, and censorship, 171–172, 173, 307*nn*133–134, 308*n*138

Press. *See* Mass media; Newspapers

Price, James, 44

Privacy, 213–234; in contemporary times, 4–5, 20, 272; invasions of, by media, 214, 229–230; and male supremacy, 233–234; and mass media, 258–259, 260–261, 328*nn*4–5,7; and reputation, 4; and social stability, 214–215; and space, 233, 258; and technology, 5, 267–271, 330*nn*37,44; tort of invasion of, 213–214; and Victorian compromise, 213, 271. *See also* Secrecy

Privacy, right of: and common law, 214, 215; and contraception, 197–198; current concern about, 231; early cases, 215–216, 318*n*6; in Europe, 225, 230–231, 325*n*43; of private citizens, 216–220, 319*nn*15–17,19; of public figures, 220–225, 248–249, 320*nn*28,30; Warren and Brandeis article on, 214, 215, 220, 243–244, 318*n*4

Prohibition, 15, 19, 170, 190, 192, 262

Property rights, of women, 23, 276*n*4

Prostitution, 124–139; arrests and prosecutions for, 127–130, 132–133, 137–138, 297*n*95; servant women and charity girls, 135–136; men's immunity from prosecution for, 10–11, 132, 139, 298*n*117, 300*n*143; and men's sexual

desire, 132, 134–135; nineteenth-century laws on, 11–12, 127–128, 136, 297*n*89; pervasiveness of, 125–126, 296*nn*81,83; and red-light districts, 130–133, 298*nn*108,116; regulation and licensing of, 136–137, 168–170, 307*nn*128–129; and war against vice, 183–190, 312*n*60; as white slavery, 184–186, 310*n*42, 311*nn*43,45. *See also* War on vice

Protection of reputation: common law marriage doctrine and, 110–111; laws against blackmail and, 97–100; collapse of old system of, 204–205; reasons for, 6–7; role of law of defamation and, 3, 6, 43, 46, 49, 273*n*2; and stability of society, 2; truth and, 9–11; in twenty-first century, 20–21

Protection of society: and criminal law/penal code, 12–13; as function of Victorian compromise, 67–68; and law of defamation, 48–49, 56; and privacy, 214–215; and protection of reputation, 6–7; role of censorship and, 149–150, 164–165;

Protestant ethic, 17, 37, 40, 161, 254

Proxmire, William, 243

Prudery: in language, 165–166, 306*nn*113,116; and sex and nudity, 166–168, 306*nn*118,120–121, 307*n*122; of U.S. vs. other Western nations, 165–166, 168–171

Public figures: and defamation, 239–244, 242*nn*30–32,35,38; limited, 280*n*25; right of privacy of, 220–225, 248–249, 320*nn*28,30

Pudd'nhead Wilson (Twain), 74

Quincy Wilson v. Daily Gazette Company, 243

Racism, and movies, 160

Ramsey, Carolyn, 71, 293*n*26

Rape: statutory, 111, 183; and virginity, 293*n*21

Reade, Charles, 155

The Red Kimono, 217, 319*n*14

Red-light districts: and prostitution, 130–132, 298*nn*108,116; and Victorian compromise, 66–67, 132–133, 137–138; and war against vice, 186–188, 311*nn*53,56, 312*n*60

Reeve, Tapping, 54

Reid, Dorothy, 217

Religion, in U.S., 170, 255–256

Rembar, Charles, *The End of Obscenity*, 251–252

Reputation: character vs., 20, 46; defined, 1, 3; economic value of, 3, 6, 7, 27, 277*n*23; honor vs., 8–9; as intangible property, 6; and law of evidence, 273*n*1; norms as determining, 1–2; and privacy and secrecy, 4; and progress of American democracy, 140–143; and secrecy, 4; social value of, 6–8. *See also* Protection of reputation

Respectability: defined, 26; and moral code, 12–13; norms of, 36–37; redefined, 259–260, 327*n*1–2; and social status, 26–27

Reynolds, George, 122–123

Rhinelander, Leonard, 76, 306*n*104

Rhodes, A. B., 70–71

Rhodes, Elizabeth, 70

Rice, Edmund, 132

Right of privacy. *See* Privacy, right of

Ringley, Jennifer, 261

Ripley, J. B., 36

Rips, Michael D., 82

Robery, John C., 291*n*67

Robinson, Richard, 298*n*117

Roe v. Wade, 198, 314*n*95

Rogers, Earl, 216–217

Rolland, Cora, 60–61

Roosevelt, Franklin D., 222, 319*n*22

Rosenberg, Norman, 48, 57, 273*n*2

Roth v. United States, 195–196

Russell, Edward J., 94

St. John, Adela Rogers, 217

Sanger, William, 105, 125–126, 134–135, 296*n*83

Saxton, John, 112

Scheppele, Kim, 83

Schinnerer, Mark, 307*n*134

Schnitzler, Arthur, 151

Schofield, Amelia Jane, 123

Second chances: bankruptcy laws as providing, 27–28, 276*n*21; blackmail as endangering, 99; and criminal conversation and alienation of affection, 120; and divorce, 28; mobility and, 28–29, 34; and seduction laws, 104, 109; technology threatening, 264–265

Secrecy: and adultery and fornication laws, 77–79, 287*nn*44,47,51; as necessary for social order, 215; reputation dependent upon, 4; and Victorian compromise, 11, 69. *See also* Privacy

Secrets, defined, 273*n*3

Sedition Act (1918), 144, 323*n*24. *See also* Alien and Sedition Acts (1798–1801)

Seditious libel: as defamation, 53–54, 282*nn*50–51; shift away from, 61; and social control, 66; truth as defense for, 53, 54, 56–57

Seduction, and breach of promise, 113–115, 294*n*44

Seduction laws, 101–109; and black women, 106, 293*n*19; enforcement of, 107; and marriage, 101, 105, 107;

second chance offered by, 104, 109; and
services doctrine, 102–104; state and
Canadian statutes, 101–102, 292*nn*2–3;
and Victorian image of women, 104–
105; and virginity, 102, 106

Seltzer, Thomas, 150–151

Services doctrine, and seduction laws,
102–104

Sex: attitudes toward, in twentieth
century, 201–203; discussion of, as
obscene, 146; education about, 202,
260; gender differences in desire
for, 73, 134–135, 299*nn*124,126; lack
of enforcement of laws on, 68–69,
285*n*14; moderation in, 64–65; and
nudity, 167–168, 306*nn*120–121,
307*n*122; protecting students from,
171–173, 307*nn*133–134; Victorian
compromise and, 4, 273*n*4

Sexual Offences Act (England), 200,
314*n*101

Sexual revolution, 196, 202–203, 212,
258, 272

Shakespeare, William, 1, 6, 156

Sharpless, Jesse, 145

Shaw, George Bernard: *The Doctor's
Dilemma,* 163; *Mrs. Warren's
Profession,* 156

Shaw, Lemuel, 59–60

Sickles, Daniel, 108

Sickles, Teresa, 108

Sidis, William James, 223

Sidis v. F-R Publishing Company, 223

Sillars, Malcolm, 240

Sinclair, M. B. W., 316*n*135

Sipple v. Chronicle Publishing Co., 320*n*30

Slander: in colonial period, 47–48;
defined, 41; lawsuits for, 42, 280*n*15.
See also Defamation

Slander per se: accusations of
homosexuality as, 323*n*20; accusations

of unchastity as, 49–51, 52–53;
defined, 42

Slaves: racial composition of, 74;
prosecutions for abuse of, 286*n*23.

Smith, Joseph, 121

Smith, Matthew Hale, 93

Smith, William Corbett, 88

Smolla, Rodney A., 325*n*39

Social change: and death of Victorian
compromise, 190–191; forces behind,
17; resistance to, 19

Social class: and age of consent laws, 183,
310*n*39; and American contemporary
culture, 232; and breach of promise,
115–116, 206–207, 316*n*123; and
censorship, 164–165; and concern
about reputation, 8; and confidence
men, 30, 277*n*36; in Europe vs.
America, 24–26, 170–171, 276*nn*14–15;
hidden system of, 40, 279*n*58; and
honor, 8–9, 274*n*14; and libel, 62; and
wealth, 26, 27

Social control, 40, 66, 67, 69

Social hygiene movement, 188–190,
312*nn*63,68,70

Socialization, and education, 14

Social norms. *See* Norms

Social status. *See* Social class

Society: consumer, 253–255; "deference"
vs. "market," 48–49; and legal system,
5; and market, 7, 48; Peeping Tom,
259, 269; stability of, 2–3, 66, 214–215;
Victorian compromise as theory of,
14. *See also* Protection of society

Sodomy: blackmail alleging, 88–89,
90–91; laws against, 89, 200, 238,
314*n*103; as victimless crime, 77. *See
also* Homosexuality

Spain: blackmail statute, 87, 289*n*33;
breach of promise, 318*n*154; criminal
libel, 247; right to personal honor, 42

Speeding laws, 12, 67, 138–139

Spencer, J. R., 245

Stalking, 229, 321*n*55

State v. Coleman, 95

Status quo: legal system as guarding, 2–3; sedition laws as protecting, 54

Stenhouse, Mrs. T. B. H., 121

Sterilization, eugenic, 177–178, 308*n*12

Stokes, Mrs. G. W., 216

Stratton, Charles, 105

A Study in Scarlet (Doyle), 33

Sullivan, Arthur, *Trial by Jury*, 116, 295*n*54

Die Sünderin, 164

Tappan, Lewis, 277*n*23

Technology: and computerized records, 264–265; and privacy, 5, 267–271, 330*nn*37,44; surveillance, 262–264, 266–267, 328*n*12, 329*nn*16,18

Temperance movement, 36, 71, 170

Temple, Abraham, 47

Tennessee, seduction law, 105

Texas: fornication laws, 78; privacy invasion by videotape, 269–270, 330*n*37; seduction case, 107; sodomy statute, 200

Thaw, Evelyn Nesbit, 109

Thaw, Harry K., 109

Theft Act (England), 87, 289*n*32

Thomason, Paulette, 238

Tilton, Elizabeth, 7

Tocqueville, Alexis de, 38

Torregano, Ernest J., 74–75, 286*n*37

Trademark law, 3

Traps for the Young (Comstock), 149

Trial by Jury (Gilbert and Sullivan), 116, 295*n*54

Trollope, Anthony, 25, 45, 278*n*40; *John Caldigate*, 278*nn*40,42

Trollope, Frances, 25–26, 28, 31, 276*nn*14–15

Tropic of Cancer (Miller), 194

Tropic of Capricorn (Miller), 194

Tropp, Leonard, 216, 217

The Truman Show, 328*n*5

Truth: and blackmail, 10, 91; protection of reputation of victims of, 9–11

Truth as defense: and antidueling statutes, 60–61, 284*nn*85,89; in contemporary defamation cases, 236; in libel cases, 54–60, 61–62

Turnbull, Annie, 111–112

Turner, Graeme, 320*n*35

Twain, Mark, *Pudd'nhead Wilson*, 74

Ulysses (Joyce), 153–154, 156, 193, 303*nn*59–60

United States v. Rebhuhn, 251

Unlawful Internet Gambling Enforcement Act, 315*n*107

The Unwritten Law, 157

"Unwritten laws," 107–109

USA PATRIOT Act, 266

Utah, Mormon polygamy, 13, 121–124, 275*n*26, 296*n*76

Values: immigration as threat to, 182, 191; and legal system, 2, 5; and movies, 157, 160; technology as threat to, 264, 265; traditional, 12–13, 19, 179, 182, 191, 201, 254, 255. *See also* Moderation; Social norms

Vanderbilt, Jacob, 117

Venereal disease: advertising treatments for, 301*n*28; campaign against, 188–190, 312*nn*68,70; and prostitution, 136, 169, 184, 186–187

Venezuela, breach of promise equivalent, 117

Vice. *See* War on vice

Vice districts. *See* red-light districts

Victimless crimes: and Victorian
   compromise, 77–80. *See also specific
   crimes*

Victorian compromise: and censorship,
   148–149; defined, 4; double standard
   of, 11–12, 66–67, 72–73, 79; and
   privacy, 213, 271; and prudery, 165–
   171; and red-light districts, 66–67,
   132–134, 137–138; respectability
   protected by, 13; social function of,
   67–68; speeding law analogy, 67,
   138–139; as theory of society, 14; and
   victimless crimes, 77–80; violations
   of, in secrecy, 69

Victorian compromise, death of:
   and abortion laws, 179–181, 182,
   309nn25,30; and adultery laws, 182;
   and age of consent laws, 182–183,
   310n35; and changed sexual attitudes
   and mores, 192–203; and decline
   of breach of promise and related
   doctrines, 205–212; and eugenics
   movement, 176–178, 308nn4–5,12;
   moral policies following, 178–179;
   overview of, 4, 15–19, 272; and
   prostitution, 183–190; social change
   contributing to, 190–191; and war on
   vice, 15, 175–176

Video Privacy Protection Act, 270

"Video Voyeurism" law, 270

Virgil, Mike, 223–224

Virginia: antidueling statute, 60–61;
   indictments for fornication or
   adultery, 285n14; miscegenation law,
   286n35; prostitution (Norfolk), 126

Virginity: and breach of promise cases,
   113, 294n41; and rape, 293n21; and
   seduction, 102, 106

Virtue, of women, 8, 49, 73, 237

Walker, Edwin, 241

Ward, Angelina, 51

Ward, Violet, 117

Warren, Samuel D., 214, 215, 220, 243–
   244

War on terror, 266

War on vice: and destruction of Victorian
   compromise, 15, 175–176; end of, 15–
   16, 192; and Prohibition, 19, 190, 192;
   and prostitution, 183–190, 312n60;
   and red-light districts, 186–188,
   311nn53,56, 312n60; and social hygiene
   movement, 188–190, 312nn63,68,70

Washington, D.C.: murder trial of Daneil
   Sickles, 108; prostitution, 129

Washington state: defamation statute,
   237; red-light district (Bellingham),
   133

Waterman, Willoughby, 130, 188

Wealth, and social class, 26, 27

Weber, Max, 37

Wells, H. G., *Ana Veronica*, 153

Welsh, Alexander, *George Eliot and
   Blackmail*, 289n36

Whitely, Abner, 44

White slavery, 184–186, 310n42,
   311nn43,45; campaign against, 184–
   186, 190, 191, 197, 310n42, 311n45; and
   Mann Act, 89–90, 184–185, 311n43;
   and movies, 160, 162

White Slavery Traffic Act, 89–90, 184–
   185, 196–197, 311n43

White, Stanford, 109

Whitney, Cornelius Vanderbilt, 205–206

Wife beating, 69–71, 285n18

Wilde, Oscar, 88

Wilgen, John, 29

Wilkerson, Sarah, 106–107

Wilkins, Samuel, 92–93, 94

Williams, Elsie, 95

Williams v. Ohio, 90

Wilson, Edmund, *Memoirs of Hecate County,* 195
Wilson, Sarah, 289*n*24
Wiretapping, 262–264, 328*n*12, 329*n*18
Wisconsin: alienation of affections case, 118; breach of promise case, 112; libel cases against newspapers, 43–44; prostitution arrests (Madison), 300*n*43
Wolfenden, John, 314*n*101
Women: accusations of unchastity of, as defamation, 49–52; age of consent for, 111, 182–183, 310*n*35; as blackmailers, 91–96, 290*nn*55,57; ideal roles of, 37, 108; property rights of, 23, 276*n*4; protection from

corruption and vulgarity, 162–163, 305*n*102, 306*nn*104–105. *See also* Gender differences; Virtue, of women
Woolsey, John, 153–154
Wormington, Henry, 209
Worthington Co., In re, 151–152
Wright, W. C., 107

Yellow journalism, 214, 318*n*2
Yelverton, William Charles, 32

Zaffere, Frank D. III, 316*n*32
Zbyszko, Stanislaus, 45–46
Zbyszko v. New York American, 45–46
Zenger trial, 53–54